A HISTORY OF SCOTLAND

A HISTORY OF SCOTLAND

NEIL OLIVER

Weidenfeld & Nicolson

LONDON

First published in Great Britain in 2009
by Weidenfeld & Nicolson

1 3 5 7 9 10 8 6 4 2

Text © Neil Oliver 2009

A CIP catalogue record for this books
is available from the British Library.

ISBN: 978 0 297 85663 4

Editorial by Linden Lawson

Typeset by Input Data Services Ltd,
Bridgwater, Somerset

Printed and bound in the UK by
CPI Mackays, Chatham ME5 8TD

FSC Mixed Sources
Product group from well-managed
forests and other controlled sources
www.fsc.org Cert no. SGS-COC-005628
© 1996 Forest Stewardship Council

Weidenfeld & Nicolson
The Orion Publishing Group Ltd
Orion House
5 Upper St Martin's Lane
London WC2H 9EA

An Hachette UK Company

www.orionbooks.co.uk

For Trudi and Evie

CONTENTS

LIST OF ILLUSTRATIONS

ACKNOWLEDGEMENTS

The best bit about writing a book is gathering together the names you want to remember when all is said and done. With a book called *A History of Scotland* it is especially satisfying – counting all the people who helped, into something that sounds rather grand.

Michael Dover at Weidenfeld and Nicolson was patient, encouraging and wise throughout the process just his tone of voice on the phone was enough to instil calm when deadlines loomed large. Huge thanks also to Linden Lawson: her careful and constructive copy-editing made all the difference. I am grateful to Rosie Anderson, my proof-reader, Kate Inskip, my indexer, and Caroline Hotblack and John Morrice for picture research. To the whole team at Weidenfeld and Nicolson, in fact, many thanks.

Neil MacDonald and Richard Downes at BBC Scotland deserve a special delivery of gratitude for the idea of the 'Scotland's History' project – along with Audrey Baird, Fiona Crawford, Sandra Breslin and the rest of the dedicated production team. To all, my sincere thanks, especially to Jon Morrice, Stevie Whiteford, Katie Holman, Julia Jamieson and Careen Murray.

This book would have been well nigh impossible without the help and advice of the directors behind the various episodes: Sarah Barclay, Clara Glynn, Bill MacLeod, Jane McWilliams, Colin Murray, Tim Niel and Andrew Thompson. Without them I would hardly have known where to start and my heartfelt thanks are owed to all.

Neville Kidd directed the photography on every programme in the series, with the help of Francis MacNeil. Douglas Kerr looked after all of the sound with the utmost care. I can only speak for myself, of course, but for me the filming of the series was just a pleasure.

Lovely Eugenie Furniss at William Morris Endeavour Entertainment takes scrupulous care of me, as does the equally special Sophie Laurimore. Love to both as always.

But, for all that, no one is more deserving of my gratitude than Trudi, who takes care of *absolutely everything that matters* while I either swan about the countryside being well looked after or hide in the study at home moaning about supposedly impossible deadlines. Really, it is all down to her and I could never thank her enough.

As always, any and all mistakes in this work are mine and mine alone.

INTRODUCTION

How do you do justice to a history of Scotland? The scale of the subject, coupled with the sheer volume of books already available, makes the task daunting enough. By pitching my best efforts in amongst the rest, I am making of myself a minnow in an ocean heavily populated by leviathans – not to mention several sharks and the occasional venomous jellyfish. But Scotland is a place I have loved all my life. For me, therefore, writing about Scotland is like writing about a loved one and the fear of not doing right by her is almost overwhelming.

I found the only way to get started in the first place was to accept, even to celebrate, the fact that Scotland's history belongs to every one of us: to all who live there now as well as to any whose family trees stretch a root all the way back to the old country from wherever they find themselves today. The biggest mistake is to imagine that only academics have a say in recording and commenting upon the story of this land and this people. On the contrary, I believe it is the responsibility of every one of us to understand how and why our nation turned out the way it has. Failure to do so is to live for ever on one, randomly selected page of a novel. History is the collective memory we can use to start the book at the beginning – to understand the emergence of the characters and plots we share our own few lines with. How can we fail to be fascinated by history when we are, all of us, its survivors? 'To live at all is miracle enough', said Mervyn Peake, and it is history that explains the mystery of how any of us are even walking the earth. Without that understanding we are adrift like goldfish in a bowl, condemned to greet every moment of the present with wide-eyed surprise.

Scotland's history is also a crucial component of the history of Britain, of Europe and of the world. The unfolding story north of the Border has inevitably shaped the stories of the neighbouring countries of this (for now at least) United Kingdom. Scotland, England, Ireland and Wales are like tenants of a shared house. We each have our own room but we meet the others in the hall, the kitchen and the living room all the time. Scotland has also shaped the story of the wider world. Scots have long been the world's vagabonds, 'the tattered outcasts of the earth', and our very natures have dictated at least a few lines of the story of every other country on the planet.

Apart from anything else, history is always family business – the good, the bad and the ugly as well as the downright shameful and embarrassing – and discussing it in public always leads to arguments. Scotland's history, like every other, is an amalgam of fact and opinion – and there are at least as many of the latter as the former. And that is why it is the most fascinating and engaging stuff of all. There is nothing like a good old row.

I was curious about my own family from the very beginning. I wanted to know where we had come from and why. Why we lived in the house we did, in the town we did. Who were our relatives and where did they live, and what did they do, and why? Eventually I realised this was the beginning of an interest in history: I simply needed to understand how the people I knew fitted into the bigger story. Having done that, the bigger story became just as fascinating and compelling as anything happening at home.

So when I was given the chance to get involved with BBC Scotland's 'Scotland's History' project I recognised it as a once-in-a-lifetime opportunity. All-singing, all-dancing productions like this, with television and radio programmes, books, websites, music and concerts do not come along very often – perhaps once a generation – and to have the chance to be identified with my own generation's telling of my nation's story was completely intoxicating.

I started my working life as a field archaeologist, helping to excavate and record sites from all periods of Scotland's past, from the Stone Ages to the Industrial Revolution. My first 'dig' was at Loch Doon, near the village of Dalmellington, in Ayrshire. It was directed by a dear man called Tom Affleck who had made a second career for himself, relatively late in life, out of his lifelong fascination with archaeology. Tom's first degree, completed just after World War II, had been in botany and for years he had been a market gardener. But, happily for many of us, he went back to university in the 1970s to pursue his second academic love. By the time I met him, in the mid 1980s, he was working towards his doctorate in the subject.

We were investigating what proved to be a campsite used by hunter-gatherers thousands of years ago and for the most part we were finding little more than tiny chips of flint and chert, the debris of stone tool-making long ago. Tom had a genius for passing on his enthusiasm, however, and to make the whole exercise more worthwhile he took the time to show us an astonishing product of his painstaking efforts at the site in previous years. He walked a group of us to an unprepossessing patch of ground, on a natural terrace overlooking the gunmetal grey waters of the loch, with a roll of white paper under his arm. This he opened out to reveal a carefully drawn plan of the little plot of stony earth we now stood beside. It showed the precise locations of hundreds of fragments of flint that had been recovered from an area measuring just a few feet square. At first sight it appeared to be – and essentially was – a random scatter. But, after a few moments, Tom pointed out four little sub-circular patches within the plan that were entirely blank. Each was no larger than a beer mat and together they formed a fairly neat rectangle. So what? 'The two larger ones are where his knees were,' said Tom, pointing at the larger pair of side-by-side blanks. 'The smaller ones were left by his toes.'

All at once the pattern made sense. There on that patch of ground someone had knelt down for a few minutes to knap and shape a few stone tools. The tiny fragments were the debris left behind and, of course, none had landed on the four spots occupied by knees and feet. But that ancestor had knelt on that spot *several thousand years* ago. We had precious little information about this long-lost individual – even whether it was a man or a woman – but we knew with absolute certainty where he or she had spent some moments of their life, and what they had been doing while they were there.

I was stunned then and I am still stunned now, more than twenty years later. Here was a near-physical connection to an ancient, otherwise anonymous life. With reference to the plan it was even possible to place a hand where those knees and toes had once been. To be able to find a spot where someone had knelt down; to realise that even a few, seemingly inconsequential minutes of a life leave a trace that can be found thousands of years later is profoundly moving for me.

That moment on that hillside with Tom, who died prematurely just a few years later, changed my life for ever. From then on I realised history – even the ancient past – was close by and all around us. History is right here and we can touch it. (I am well aware that archaeology and history are to be regarded as largely separate disciplines – the latter made of documents, the former of material remains – but for me the two have more to connect them than to keep them apart.)

I believe that we are made of the land we live on. We breathe the air and drink the water. Sometimes, some of the food we eat is local too, and not flown in from thousands of miles away. The landscape – our awareness and appreciation of it – surely shapes us as well. In this way, then, we gradually assimilate the very stuff of the little patch of the earth we call home. Atoms of it are briefly made part of us and so those of us who live in Scotland are therefore made, at least in part, *of* Scotland.

So for me a history of Scotland is personal and the completion of the project has been a transforming one. I saw up close, in the Bibliothèque Nationale in Paris, the 'Chronicle of the Kings of Alba' – the so-called 'birth certificate' of Scotland – and in Lincoln Castle one of the four original copies of Magna Carta. I walked the streets and lanes of the medieval hill town of Anagni, south of Rome – some of the same that were walked by Scots churchmen 700 years ago as they strove to persuade the Pope to recognise Robert the Bruce as King of Scots – and visited the château in Amboise, on the bank of the River Loire, where Mary Queen of Scots spent much of her early life.

The filming took us all over Scotland and the rest of the UK as well, of course, from the Up Helly Aa Viking festival on Shetland in the north, to Dover Castle, where a teenage Alexander II, King of Scots marched an army to pursue his claims on English soil in the early thirteenth century; from the Holy Island of Iona in the west, first home of Christianity in Scotland, to St Andrews Cathedral in the east, the shrine that eventually over-shadowed its predecessor. For me the most poignant of all was Finlaggan, on Islay, once the centre of the Lordship of the Isles. Little remains to be seen and yet it was once the beating heart of an empire that rivalled the demesne of the kings of Scots themselves. There is a reminder among those few ruins about the transient nature of power, and of importance.

If I loved Scotland before this project, I love the place even more now. I thought I knew her well enough, but the discoveries and rediscoveries of the past two years have been a revelation. Some of the story is stuff to make any Scot proud; plenty of it should make us hang our heads in shame. But when you love someone, you love them completely or not at all, the good and the bad.

Scotland's story is one of the oldest on the face of the earth. Some tiny part of it is my story and my family's story. It is enough just to belong.

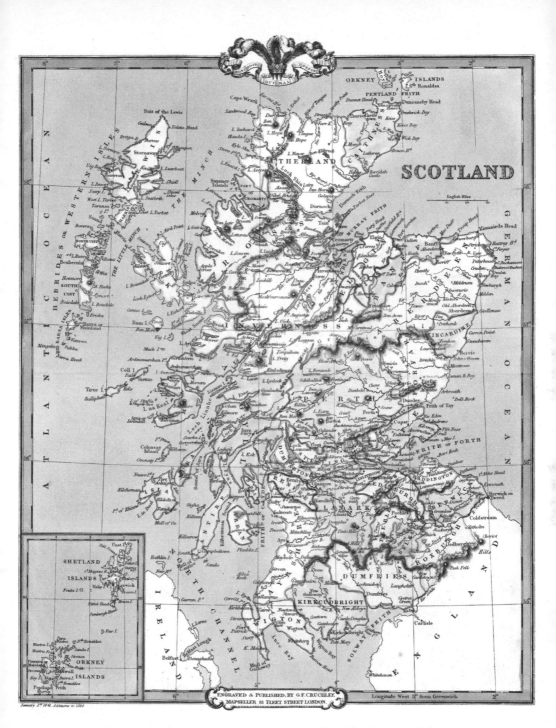

A mid-nineteenth-century map showing Scotland firmly part of the Union

CHAPTER ONE

FROM THE
BASEMENT OF TIME

'I was born on a storm-swept rock and hate the soft growth of sun-baked lands where there is no frost in men's bones.'

Liam O Flaithearta

So, where to begin?

The first words of this history of Scotland go to an Irishman and his thoughts of Inis Mór, largest of the Aran Islands off Ireland's west coast. But there is a way of feeling about a place, about home, that transcends nationality and geography. Sometimes the right words are found in the wrong place and remembrance – the reach of memory – matters as much as history.

Before memory or history – beneath everything – is the rock. We are shaped and tested by it. Just as we are of the people we call family, so we are of the land we walk on every day. Magic is elusive stuff, but in the ancient landscapes of Scotland there is the genuine shimmer. It's also a tough and demanding place – much of it made more of storm-swept rock than anything sun-baked. This is important. It is the landscape that has authored the story of this place, and this people, far longer and more indelibly than any work of our own hands.

The most enduring reminders of the first people are made of the stone – freed from the bedrock and raised towards the sky; used as canvases for works of art; piled high as houses of the living and of the dead; scorched and cracked by home fires of long ago; chipped and polished as tools. But it is not enough to start with the people who *used* the stone; the correct place to begin is with the stone itself. In the very creation of the bedrock – and the coming-together of a few battered, well-travelled fragments of it to form a patch of dry land that would one day be called Scotland – is a message, a premonition maybe, about the making of the nation, and its future.

It does not matter what moment you choose to begin a story like this: there will always be someone who says you have come in too late. So, to counter that particular criticism, this history of Scotland begins four and a half billion years ago when the planet was formed. Half a billion years before that a dying star had exploded, filling a corner of the universe with super-heated gas and vapour. Amid the chaos a new sun sparked into life and around it swirled the steadily cooling wreckage of its predecessor, the stuff of worlds and Scotland and us. Hot clouds cooled, condensing into clumps and clots. Some came together to make this earth, an object with sufficient gravity to hold, eventually, a thin silk of life-supporting atmosphere around itself.

Long before the advent of anything like atmosphere and life, an object not much smaller than earth smashed into the young world, pulling away a great dollop of it. The mystery assailant continued on its way, hurtling onwards in its orbit of the sun, or elsewhere into infinity, but the gobbet was held in place by earth's gravity. The force of the collision had raised the temperature of the debris to boiling point and at first it was a glob of liquid that was trapped in our orbit. In time it cooled and solidified as the moon. Aeons later men and women living in the land before Scotland would count the phases of that silvered travelling companion and track its passage across the sky. They would raise huge stones, in circles and avenues, to help them remember and predict its comings and goings. But all of that would have to wait. For now there were billions of years to pass and thousands of miles for the rocks to travel before they could come together as a land for Scots to walk upon.

Earth had reeled drunkenly back from the blow that made the moon. The axis around which our planet spun was now askew for all time – leaning at a jaunty angle – but it kept on spinning like a wonky top. The ceaseless rotation makes of earth a giant dynamo, generating an electrical-magnetic force field that protects all life against the deadliest of the sun's radiation. The Aurora Borealis – the Northern Lights that can be glimpsed in Scotland when the conditions are right – are an effect of the relationship between that crackling cloak and particles from the sun.

The same magnetism dictates where on earth the North and South Poles are positioned. These are not constant and have moved around the planet many times, causing chaos on each occasion. But individual rocks remember where north was located at the moment they were made and carry a permanent echo of it within themselves. Geologists listen to the echoes and tell where on the surface of the globe the various bits and pieces of Scotland were at the moment when each different type of rock came into being. If geology is the birth certificate of a rock then it is the restless magnetic field that has carefully filled in the box marked 'place and time'.

Earth's orbit of the young star had been altered too by the moon-making collision, reshaped into a regular oval called an ellipse. The warmth of the sun would no longer be constant on this planet for the duration of each of our yearly circumnavigations; we would be further from the fireside at some times than at others. In that moment the cycle of seasons was ordained.

The monstrous temperatures caused by the collision had made earth mostly liquid again as well. As it cooled, concentric layers formed and, on the outside of the ball, a thin crust hardened. The material beneath remained liquid and as the heat circulated, rising to the surface and then sinking back down towards the interior, the currents and flows contrived to keep the outer shell in perpetual motion. Composed of continent-sized scales, the crust proved to be a violently unstable casing. These thin scales, or 'tectonic plates', ground together at their edges like pieces on a constantly moving jigsaw; or were pulled apart to create fissures from which the molten interior could ooze like albumen out of a cracked egg. The plates slid on top and underneath one another, allowing the uppermost to harden in the cold universe outside while the lower was pushed back into the Hadean furnace below.

But while the complete history of the country and nation of Scotland would chart the shaping of the rocks from the time of earth's messy birth, the fact is there is no physical evidence at all of the place – of the rocks it is made of – for a whole third of the planet's existence. Only after a billion and a half years does the geology of the northern third of the land now known as the British Isles begin to reveal how it got where it is today and, more interestingly, where it had been all the while.

The oldest of the rocks beneath the feet of Scots are the Lewisian gneisses. These form the basement bedrock of Lewis, the rest of the Western Isles, the Inner Hebrides and some parts of the seaboard of the north-west. They were formed deep beneath earth's crust three billion or more years ago. Calanais stone circle on Lewis was built of monoliths of Lewisian gneiss nearly 5,000 years ago. But the rock of which it is made – the rock of which

Lewis is made – began its journey towards that time and that place at least three thousand million years before that.

As the endless years ground past, so more of what would be Scotland's bedrock formed – the ancient Torridonian sandstone, some of it a memory of times when desert blanketed the land; limestone laid down first as sediments by long-lost rivers and vanished oceans; great sheets of basalt and granite that spewed, as magma, through tears rent in the gneiss to form the heart of the Harris mountains; yet more granite took shape as the Cairngorms, and parts of the Southern Uplands. Hellish temperatures would, in time, cook some of the limestone to marble and some of the sandstone to quartz.

The various fragments of landforms that would eventually join up to make Scotland are on an endless journey across the globe. As the plates moved across the face of the earth – great rafts of stone afloat upon a molten sea – so the parts that would become Scotland moved with them. For most of the time they were located south rather than north of the Equator. Yet more aeons passed while the disparate building-blocks of this country moved around the South Pole or floated north towards the Equator and beyond. The rock that would be Scotland has been home to tropical forests, deserts and swamps as well as to verdant grasslands and uncounted acres of temperate woodland; it has borne upon its decks lizards and dinosaurs, lions and wolves, hippos and elephants; bears and giant elk, as well as human beings of ancient vintage – the passengers boarding when the climate suited them and getting off again when it did not. The land has frozen beneath ice miles thick, been set free and then frozen again.

The unimaginably powerful forces driving its passage across the face of the globe also twisted, buckled and folded the rock of Scotland like so much toffee. For a hundred million years most of it was submerged beneath a tropical sea. Tiny animals lived and died in the soupy water and when the countless trillions of their bodies sank to the bottom they formed layers of chalk hundreds of metres thick. Millions of years later that same chalk would be scoured away by glaciers, leaving scarcely a trace.

Five or six hundred million years ago some of the rocks of Scotland were on the edge of a continent known by geologists as Laurentia. On the other side of the so-called Iapetus Ocean – a body of water at least as wide as the modern Atlantic – lay the continent of Avalonia and the rocks that would, one day, form England and Wales. For the next two hundred million years the movement of the plates caused that ocean to close up, its waters consumed or pushed elsewhere by the process.

By four hundred million years or so ago, Laurentia and Avalonia had drawn close together. One plate slid beneath the other as they came on and the violence of their advances forced above the surface of that ocean an offshore arc of islands. These in turn were sandwiched and enveloped by the final coming-together of the two continents, their peaks and valleys forming what would eventually be the Highlands of Scotland. For the first time the lands that would be chiselled out as Scotland and England were joined together as one. Long since torn asunder, geologists refer to this huge continent as the Old Red Sandstone Continent and it sat somewhere south of the Equator. As well as the future parts of the British Isles, it also contained Greenland and America.

Scotland still had thousands of miles of lazy meandering to go. By three hundred million years ago all the continents of earth were fused together – a vast landform called Pangaea, or 'all-earth'. The whole huge lot of it drifted northwards, with the building-blocks of the British Isles land-locked deep in its interior. For part of this time the rocks of our land were covered in a desert that was home to early dinosaurs. The footprints they left long ago in sediments are still being uncovered in Scotland today.

The world kept turning and the plates kept slipping and sliding. Pangaea split along its several seams and, as a new rupture got under way, the salt water that would one day be the Atlantic Ocean began to collect in one great abyss. Something like sixty million years ago, as the Atlantic continued to widen, the rocks of Scotland parted company with the landmass that would become North America. Left behind on the eastern side of the ocean, they were from now on parts of the future British Isles and Europe. Sea levels fell and for the first time the outline of the British Isles was revealed, although just a rough sketch.

It had been no amicable divorce; the rending-apart of continents had put earth's crust under unbearable stress. Temperatures rose beneath the tortured skin and a great chain of volcanoes burst into life. Among others these would come down to us as Ailsa Craig, Ardnamurchan, Arran, Mull, Rum, Skye and St Kilda. By the time the rocks arrived where they are today – a position no more permanent than any other they have held – they amounted to the most battered and ragged parcel of flotsam imaginable, unrecognisable even to its sender.

All in all, it is a tale almost impossible to be believed but it bears a

message and a reminder: just as the emergence of a nation, a political entity
called Scotland, was never inevitable, so the cohesion of its rocks – four or
five shards of four or five different landmasses – was anything but pre-
ordained.

The places we know as the Western Highlands; the Northern Highlands;
the Central Highlands; the Central Lowlands and the Southern Uplands
are just leftovers from other times and other places: parts of a work still in
progress. The shards came together by chance, a whim of pressure and
time. It could all have been so different and in a hundred million years or
so it will likely all be different again. Nothing is or ever has been permanent;
everything is on the move and the only constant is change.

From about thirty million years ago the forces of glaciation were at work
around the world. During the past three million years they have sculpted
the whole of our land with an energy and violence akin to the wrath of
God. The ice has formed and thawed, again and again: long cold periods
called glacials followed by shorter warm periods called interglacials. We
still live in the Ice Age and during the last three-quarters of a million years
the cold periods have been more intense and longer in their duration than
before – around 100,000 years each. It has been the advance and retreat of
the ice that has ground Scotland's mountains down to broken teeth – mere
stumps of what they once were – and bulldozed millions of tonnes of rock
out of the valleys into the lowlands and sea beyond. The last signature to
be written upon this land before ours has been that of the ice.

Modern humans, people indistinguishable from us, lived first in the
southern-eastern parts of Africa. A suitcase-full of bones is all that remains
to testify to the emergence there of *Homo sapiens sapiens* something like
100,000 years ago. From that warm cradle they spread northwards and then
east and west, gradually moving out in all directions until every part of the
old world felt their feet upon it.

The earliest evidence of the presence of modern humans in the British
Isles is from Kents Cavern, in Devon. The jawbone of a woman was recovered from the limestone cave and radiocarbon-dated to around 30,000
years ago. She is the sole survivor of her time – of the world of the British
Isles before the last glacial – and despite the millennia between her and us,
we are one and the same. Bones from other sites in England – at Swans-
combe in Kent and Boxgrove in West Sussex – reveal the presence of
ancestors that are hundreds of thousands of years older. These were early
humans of the type that predated even *Homo sapiens neanderthalensis* –

Neanderthal Man – and recall a time when the people who came before us hunted giant deer and rhino in a climate much kinder than our own.

But of Scotland's first humans – those who lived in the northern third of Britain in the time before the onset of the last glacial – not a trace has been found. It's safe to assume they were here but every hint of their physical presence – be it tools, shelters, butchered animal bones, artworks or their mortal remains – all of it has seemingly been erased by the ice.

The last glacial began around 25,000 years ago. Perhaps the planet wobbled on its axis, tilting the northern hemisphere even further from the warmth of the sun; maybe its orbit was altered again, becoming more elliptical and straying further from the life-sustaining rays at both extremes of its journey. Whatever the trigger, the deterioration in the weather would have been rapid enough for any humans living in the land before Scotland to notice the change.

Over the course of a few generations the temperature dropped markedly. There was seldom rain any more – especially on the high ground – just snow that grew deeper and deeper until its own weight compacted the lower layers into ice. Huge domes of snow and ice formed and grew within the mountain ranges of the north, rising and enveloping the tallest peaks. As the ice sheet spread, a vicious cycle was established. More and more of the northern hemisphere turned white and reflected the heat radiating from the sun, accelerating the cooling process. Less and less water fell upon the land as the ice claimed and drew towards itself whatever precipitation was forming in the atmosphere. Sea levels began to drop for the same reason and all the while the great domes of ice grew thicker and heavier.

Too great to be contained within the mountains, the ice spread out into the landscape around and below. Where it touched the land a scum of watery sludge became a lubricant that enabled the frozen mass – several miles thick – to nudge and grind southwards. Rock trapped in the lowest layers and in contact with the land surface acted like the coarsest-grade sandpaper imaginable. On Skye's Cuillin the smoothed and polished scars etched deep into the rock reveal the direction the ice sheet took across the bedrock. The weight of the ice pushed the very land itself down into the crust below. At the height of the glacial, parts of northern Europe would be many hundreds of metres lower than they are today, depressed like one end of a couch beneath a fat lady's bottom.

The ice drove all before it. Humans and animals alike migrated ever southwards, beyond its reach. Great glaciers grew out from the mountains of snow and ice and pushed through valleys, making them deeper and wider. Uncountable tonnes of rock were quarried out of the mountains and bulldozed into the valleys below. Beyond the Highlands and towards the south the glaciers left a gentler, less spectacular landscape of rolling hills and river valleys. As well as scouring and quarrying, the ice sheets deposited new material. Silts and gravels in vast quantities were spread out across the low-lying terrain – deposits that would develop into some of the most fertile farmland in the British Isles.

Around 16,000 years ago the last glacial was at its peak. The ice sheet had reached as far south as Wales and the midlands of England and all traces of human habitation had been wiped from the land as completely as chalk dust from a blackboard. From that time onwards, however, temperatures began to rise. Maybe the planet tipped back up on its axis, increasing the effect of the sun's warmth; or maybe our orbit took on a more circular path. In any case earth began to warm up and so the ice melted and receded.

Valleys cut by ice, rock and time filled with melt water. As vast volumes of water returned to the sea, so the waves lapped higher. Over centuries and then millennia the coastline we recognise took shape. The unmistakable outline of Scotland's western seaboard is what happens when the sea floods troughs excavated by glaciers. The fjords of Lochs Alsh, Broom, Duich, Eriboll, Fyne, Hourn, Laxford, Linnhe, Long and Torridon and more were all cut and sculpted by the ice before being drowned in the rising sea.

Inland, beyond the reach of the tide, other huge, ice-cut scars filled with melt water to create lochs like Affric and Arkaig; Luichart and Lochy; Monar and Mullardoch; Morar and Ness. Great rivers flowed out of the Southern Uplands to water the fertile plains below. The Firths of Clyde, Forth and Tay offered easy access deep into the interior.

Seawater and melt water alike revealed, in the manner of a highlighter pen, ancient fault lines and geological schisms. Loch Maree and Loch Broom, Loch Shin and Loch Laxford were cut by glaciers that exploited the north-west to south-east grain of the Lewisian gneiss. The Great Glen – running contrariwise from north-east to south-west – follows the path a glacier took along the massive geological fault line between two tectonic plates that cuts across Scotland like a sword wound. These landforms, shaped first by geological forces and then modified by ice, are marks deeper and more profound than any yet made by humankind.

Long before any human foot made its imprint, geology and ice conspired to ensure the land of Scotland would be split in two. The thin, acid soils that gradually formed in the valleys and rugged slopes of the north and west would only ever be suitable for the least demanding of domesticated animals, the toughest crops. South and east of the Great Glen would form the much richer soils that, in time, were turned into a 'bread-basket' of arable farming. The destinies of the peoples who would eventually reach and settle these two quite distinct terrains were pre-determined, at least in part, by the nature of the land itself.

All of that lay in the future. As the climate improved and the ice receded – from around 12500 BC onwards – tundra gained a toehold. The sub-soils remained frozen all year round but during short summers a thawing of the topsoil allowed a greening of the landscape for the first time in thousands of years. Grazing herd animals came then, lured north by the promise of food. Mammoth, woolly rhinoceros, bison, giant fallow deer and reindeer – all of them walked the land during a time when Scotland was embraced by a sub-Arctic climate. It was a tough life but one that suited hardy animals that thrived in the chill and enjoyed wide open spaces where predators could be seen from afar.

The land continued to warm up and the seeds of other species arrived from the south, borne on the winds. More came in the guts of the herd animals themselves until, in time, woodland replaced the open plains. Animals that had felt secure in the open – like the reindeer and the bison – left for green pastures elsewhere or fell to extinction. In their place came beasts that preferred the cover of trees and browsed among the shadows of the forest floor.

Scotland drew across herself a cloak of aspen, birch, elm, hazel, lime, oak and pine and through the dappled gloom moved all the creatures of the woods – wild cattle, boar, deer both red and roe, elk. Through the canopy above moved polecats, martens and birds. The rivers and streams wending their way towards the coasts harboured beaver, otter and wildfowl as well as all manner of fish – and where there were prey animals there were hunters like fox, bear, wildcat and wolf.

If there ever was a time when animals had the place to themselves, it could not and did not last. Beasts to hunt and wild foods to gather – these were lures that drew another opportunistic predator into the northern lands, the deadliest and most implacable of all. The ice retreated, life returned to the land and so came man.

It is impossible to be certain when the first people reached Scotland after the ice – but they found an environment still in flux. The thaw had caused a rise in sea levels at first, but as the weight of the glaciers diminished, the land began to rise faster than the water. Freed from the pressure of the fat lady's bottom, the couch started to regain its shape. The land slowly reared up out of the sea in a process that continues to this day – indeed Scotland is still on the rise while England, at the other end of the couch, dips steadily into the Channel.

Just to complicate matters, after the first few centuries of warming, the ice returned to northern Britain. The so-called 'Cold Snap' set in some time after 10000 BC, recklessly undoing all the good work. From a central point somewhere between Loch Lomond and Rannoch Moor, the glaciers established themselves once more and advanced through the valleys all over again. All life – plants, animals and perhaps humanity too – was driven out for yet more centuries until a final thaw set in.

By around 8000 BC the Cold Snap was over and the last of the ice had melted. The water returned to the oceans. Sea levels rose once more and a complicated dance began between the rebound of the land and the rising of the sea – sometimes the one gained most ground, sometimes the other. All around Scotland there are 'raised beaches', cliffs that once edged the sea but are now far inland. Elsewhere divers have found undersea shelves that once were dry land before the waters rose and swallowed them.

In any event, for the first settlers this was a land made more usefully of water than solid, open ground. For thousands of years much of the land was covered by trackless forest and they would have travelled by river and sea. If the first traces of human habitation were on the coasts and riverbanks, then the rivalry between the rising sea and the rebounding land – until around 4000 BC – will have obliterated many of the first footfalls.

Geologists and geographers say the islands of Islay and Jura, off Scotland's west coast, may have been at the centre of an area that became – and remained – ice-free comparatively early. In 1993 an archaeology student taking part in a field-walking project at Bridgend near the Bowmore Distillery on Islay found a stone arrowhead. It was made and lost around 11,000 years ago and proves people were keen to exploit the northern territories of the British Isles as soon as the retreat of the ice made that possible – perhaps during or just before the time of the Cold Snap. Finds from the earliest periods are rare indeed but the absence of evidence is hardly evidence of absence and no doubt other traces await discovery.

The island of Rum sits like a dumpy diamond 15 miles or so offshore from the north-west coast port of Mallaig. It measures 8 miles north to south and roughly the same east to west, amounting to around 10,000 hectares of land that is almost entirely mountainous and barren. In the whole of the 28-mile coastline there is only one inlet – Kinloch, at the head of Loch Scresort, on the eastern side – and it is here that pioneers would have made landfall, just as visitors to the island do today.

At least as early as 9,000 years ago, people found their way to the place – perhaps from Islay and Jura, off to the south. Anyone who has spent time in a little boat in the waters off Scotland's western seaboard will know the way land and water combine in a confusing muddle. Sea lochs merge with the sea itself; islands and islets appear on all sides, or is that the coast? Unless you are looking at charts all the while, it is easy to lose track of whether it is mainland or island ahead.

The modern obsession with cars gives a view of the landscape that is utterly at odds with that of our ancestors. Where we see a river, firth or channel as an obstacle to be crossed by bridge or ferry, people who travel mostly by boat see highways, even short-cuts. For pioneers travelling in boats the concept of an *island* would be meaningless a lot of the time. Who cared if the destination was on the 'mainland' or not, when the best way to travel was, anyway, via the water?

That said, there is something about Rum, something at once compelling and forbidding. It is a gloomy, looming presence that casts a spell now and surely did all those thousands of years ago. Gavin Maxwell got it right in *Harpoon at a Venture*:

> Rhum is a strange place, eerie and haunted if ever a Hebridean island was. It is all mountain – hills as dark and savage as the Cuillins themselves, and falling for the most part steeply to the sea. The hills even carry the name, the Cuillin of Rhum, but they seem to have a different soul, something older and more brooding . . . If there is a place where I could believe every Gaelic folktale and wild superstition, it is in their shadow.

I quoted that passage in my undergraduate dissertation, written over twenty years ago now, when Rum was still spelled the way prudish teetotal Victorians preferred – with an 'h'. I had taken part in an excavation of the so-called 'Farm Fields' overlooking Loch Scresort in the summer of 1986 and I wanted to be part of the excitement the finds had generated – at least among archaeologists. Forestry workers employed by the Nature

Conservancy Council had noticed large quantities of chipped stone, as well as a beautiful barbed and tanged arrowhead, during ploughing – and archaeologists had come to investigate. What the foresters had stumbled upon was, at the time, the earliest known prehistoric settlement site in Scotland.

The stone chips and tools – over 150,000 of them were found in the end – were the work of people who lived in a time classified by archaeologists as the Mesolithic. Labels like Palaeolithic, Mesolithic and Neolithic – Old, Middle and New Stone respectively – are often as much of a hindrance as a help but they give some sense of order within what would otherwise be an even more confusing chaos of artefacts of different ages and styles. But people do not go to bed Mesolithic on Friday only to get up on Monday Neolithic, having decided over the weekend their lives would be better if they embraced a new technology. Changes and advances of such importance do not happen uniformly, far less overnight, and people with different approaches to life and work would have existed side by side for centuries or longer.

The importance of the site at Kinloch was confirmed by radiocarbon dates that revealed just how long ago those pioneers had begun spending time on the island – over 7000 years BC. Other evidence from the dig – shadowy traces of shelters and fires – revealed they had not just been day-trippers either. On the north-west coast of the island is a mountain called Creag nan Stearnan, 'Bloodstone Hill', and it was this that made Rum a particularly useful destination for the bands of hunter-gatherers who pulled their boats ashore at Kinloch all those millennia ago. Bloodstone is a chalcedonic silica that can be flaked and worked into sharp tools, much like flint, and the chalcedony of Creag nan Stearnan is particularly good-quality. It was ideal for making small blades – microliths – that could be mounted in shafts of wood, horn or bone to create a serrated edge. (Archaeologists identify these microliths as the defining characteristic of the tool-making practices of the Mesolithic – hundreds of generations of people, classified just by tiny chips of stone.)

As well as coming to the island to collect supplies of the raw material and to work some of it into tools, the bands of hunter-gatherers stayed on Rum – perhaps for weeks or months at a time. Nodules of bloodstone were collected at Guirdil Bay, below the mountain, and finds there showed the stone was quality-checked in situ before 'blanks' were worked up for completion back at a well-established and well-organised campsite at Kinloch.

To make their stay more comfortable the travellers erected substantial shelters similar to tipis – frameworks of branches harvested from the hazel, birch and willow trees known to have grown on the island at the time, and covered with brushwood or animal hides. The people who lived upon and exploited the land before Scotland, 10,000 and more years ago, were the same as us in every way. In terms of their potential, their physical and mental abilities and their appearance they were fully modern human beings indistinguishable from any person alive today. Their circumstances differed from ours enormously, their achievements limited by their technology. They are separated from us only by time.

If they arrived early enough in the story to hunt the reindeer and caribou of the Scottish tundra then it is worth comparing those first forays, into the wild lands of the north, to lives lived just beyond the reach of memory.

> Their bodies were covered with fur and soft tanned leather. Eyelashes and cheeks and lips were so coated with the crystals from their frozen breath that their faces were not discernible ... But under it all they were men, penetrating the land of desolation and mockery and silence, puny adventurers bent on colossal adventure, pitting themselves against the might of a world as remote and alien and pulseless as the abysses of space.

These are Jack London's words in *White Fang*, as he imagines the hardships of prospectors in Canada's Yukon in the late nineteenth century; men in search of gold.

'But under it all they were men': this is the certainty we should have in mind when we picture Scotland's first adventurers – people made small by the enormity of a land newly forged, yet undaunted and ruthlessly determined in the face of it. Judging by human bones found elsewhere in northern Europe, the first people to arrive here after the ice were probably slightly smaller in stature than today's average. The men would have stood between five feet six and five feet nine inches tall, the women no more than five feet five. People learn over time to make the best use of available resources and those ancestors would have been equipped with skills acquired and passed down through thousands of years.

They might have been new to Scotland, but modern humans had been at large on the planet for at least 90,000 years before any of them went there after the last glacial. Their material culture – the things they made and used to exploit their environment – would have been the products of ancient experience and experiment. They may well have been more skilful, and better equipped to take on The Wild, than any nineteenth-century prospector.

Since they would have wanted warmth and protection from the elements they would have worn well-made, neatly fitting clothes and footwear of animal skin and fur, fastened by buttons and toggles of bone, horn, wood or stone. Stone survives best, after millennia buried in the earth, and so archaeologists tend to recover more things made of that material than any other. But stone would have been no more important to the early settlers than any other material, perhaps less. Their tool kit would have included spears and knives for hunting; cords and ties for fashioning snares and traps; equipment for cutting, for preparing skins and hides, for maintaining their clothes – needles for stitching and mending – as well as bags and baskets for collecting wild foodstuffs. They would have carried the means to make fire. They wore jewellery and other symbolic items – totems declaring who they were, how they related to each other, how they mattered to each other. Most important of all, they would have carried in their heads the practical wisdom of countless generations of their forebears.

On arrival in Scotland, after 8000 BC at least, they would have found themselves surrounded by natural riches beyond the dreams of avarice: animal prey of all kinds; wild foods of every sort. The rivers – and the seas around the coastline – teemed with fish and shellfish. It was a cornucopia and would have provided a diet and lifestyle healthier in many ways than any we know today. Disease and injury would have posed ever-present threats to life and limb, but what those people lacked in drugs and treatments we take for granted would have been compensated for by the fruits of a wholly different understanding of the natural world.

The bands of hunter-gatherers would have touched every inch of the coastline during the thousands of years when their way of life was the only way of life. The ghostly traces of lives lived suggest those first people were nomads – wanderers rather than settlers. They kept no animals – except dogs perhaps, for security, for company and for the hunt – and farmed no crops. Instead they moved from place to place, on a seasonal round dictated by needs and appetites, probably along routes established long ago and handed down through the generations. They penetrated the interior of the land as well, taking advantage of rivers and streams that were navigable by their small boats. But the islands off the west coast would have been particularly attractive, so accessible are they even by the smallest craft in the hands of able mariners.

It is the modern concept of remoteness that has made those islands so interesting and so rewarding for archaeologists. While much of mainland Scotland has been developed by farming and forestry, as well as by urbanisation, industry, road-building and the like, the Inner and Outer Hebrides as well as the islands of Orkney and Shetland have seen much less in the way of destructive interference with the landscape. It is for these reasons that so many more ephemeral traces of early habitation have been found offshore, often sealed beneath peat that has grown undisturbed for thousands of years. Artefacts and other traces recovered from sites on islands like Colonsay and Oronsay, Islay and Jura, as well as Rum, give just a glimpse of the whole picture.

While the island fastnesses have kept safe a great deal of material from the earliest periods of human settlement in Scotland, many sites of Mesolithic activity have been found on the mainland too. At East Barns, near Dunbar on the coast of East Lothian, archaeologists were called in to examine fields soon to be consumed by a limestone quarry. They found traces of a large, oval-shaped house built of stout posts. Organic material was radiocarbon-dated and showed the 'house' – a large tipi-like structure – had been built and occupied around 8000 years BC. Further west, at Cramond on the southern coastline of the Firth of Forth just outside Edinburgh, stone tools, made of chert, were found alongside burned hazelnut shells, an abundant food source. Dated to around 8500 BC, these slight remains are the earliest proof of human habitation found in Scotland so far, older even than the campsite on Rum. The hunter-gatherers at Cramond had chosen well. They made their tools and gathered food where the River Almond meets the Forth, giving them access to both marine and freshwater foodstuffs.

Something like a thousand years later, around 7500 BC, a family used a natural rock shelter at Sand, near Applecross in Wester Ross. They made tools of stone, animal bone and antler and used them to hunt red deer and birds. They collected shellfish and piled the empties into a large rubbish dump, or midden. More intriguingly, they fashioned jewellery from cowrie shells and the tusks of wild boar, and collected red ochre and a kind of dog whelk shell that produces a purple dye. Abundance of food clearly left plenty of time for the finer things in life.

It will never be known how large – or how small – was the population of hunter-gatherers who lived out parts of their lives in Scotland in the first thousands of years after the ice. None of the higher estimates go beyond the figure of a few thousand and the lower guesses dwindle into the hundreds – but we have learned enough to say Scotland was a familiar and well-used environment soon after the final thaw set in, ending the Cold Snap of 8,000 years or more ago.

Regardless of fluctuations in the weather, the restless readjustments of the sea level, Britain would have been viewed as a worthwhile destination. People would have moved in both directions – both towards as well as away from the rest of Continental Europe – and word would have gone back to similar populations in other parts, of rich hunting and easy fishing, of a dizzying range of wild foods ready for the collecting, of a tolerable, even pleasant climate. Over generations and then centuries, people would keep coming.

The hunter-gatherer lifestyle is one that demands large amounts of territory for each comparatively small group of people. New arrivals from the south and east would be greeted cautiously – and likely invited to keep heading north and west. Each successive band of travellers would have seen the wisdom, even the necessity, of moving on in search of empty land. This is not population pressure – it is what has been best described as like day-trippers armed with picnic hampers and rugs walking further along a beach to get to a clear spot where they can spread out their things.

The greatest frustration is that while we have been able to build up a fairly detailed picture of the practicalities of hunter-gatherer life, we know nothing about what those ancestors thought about the world. But if the spiritual lives of Scotland's first inhabitants are lost to us, we can at least wonder at evidence found elsewhere. At Vedbaek, in the north-east of modern Denmark, archaeologists found a settlement used by Mesolithic people around the time of the earliest expeditions into Scotland. Traces unearthed there suggested the site had been visited again and again, perhaps for centuries. Most beguiling of all, however, was the find of a cemetery. The handful of burials confirms, as nothing else found from that period either before or since, that people have always looked with bewildered awe into the abyss.

In one grave painstaking excavation recovered not just the mortal remains of a woman, but also a keepsake that spoke of someone who knew and loved her. Around her neck had been a string of stags' teeth collected from more than forty different animals. Did she have a son or a husband or a father who was a great hunter? Was it thought that by wearing such a thing she would be recognised elsewhere as a person of status, a woman who had known the protection of a hero? And if the burial party acknowledged and honoured that relationship in death, surely they felt the same way about such unions in life.

Beside her was the skeleton of a baby – perhaps her baby – laid on a swan's wing. A little stone knife, a token, was beside the baby's waist. Other occupants of the graveyard had been buried with their heads or feet cradled in the crowns of deer antlers. How and why had these people died? Were they the victims of a tragedy that devastated a community, taking several of its members at once; or had they died singly, over a long time? Was there a battle, a murderous raid by rivals, an outbreak of disease? And what of the mother and baby placed in the ground with so much care and imagination? Was the bird's wing there just for comfort's sake, a lining placed in the grave by someone left behind who couldn't bear the thought of his baby being cold? Or is it about a tiny soul taking flight, following the flocks of migratory birds towards a warmer place half remembered and far away?

It is not much of a stretch to allow for ideas like those of the people of Vedbaek having been shared by Scotland's first inhabitants. Until the fourth millennium BC, the British Isles were connected to Europe – indeed, they were not 'isles' at all but part of the main. As well as making for the coastlines of Britain in their boats, early would-be settlers could also have walked dry-shod. It is hardly controversial to imagine people living in the territory that would one day be Denmark, having had connections with people who journeyed either by land or by sea to Britain, taking their spiritual ideas with them.

The rich fishing grounds of Dogger Bank, in the North Sea, have as their bed the submerged landmass of Doggerland. In places the water there is only 10 metres deep and from time to time trawlermen have pulled up in their nets ancient man-made tools and animal bones. Not so very long ago this was another country – not just a bridge between Britain and Europe, but also a destination in its own right. 'Dogger' is a Dutch word for a kind of fishing trawler and it is salutary, in times of global warming and predicted sea-level rises, to note that what was so recently a huge, rich territory populated by people and animals is now 10 metres beneath the hulls of fishing boats and car ferries.

The weather was improving all the while. By about 4000 BC, around the time when Doggerland and the rest of the bridge to Europe was finally inundated and overwhelmed by the deepening North Sea, the temperatures were a good deal higher than today. The climate was warmer and drier and sea levels were so high that Scotland was all but cut in two. The Firths of

Clyde and Forth were at their deepest, penetrating the interior from west and east until only 10 miles or so of dry land united north and south.

The way of life of the hunter-gatherers was pursued for thousands of years – longer than any other that has evolved since. In the right environment it provided plenty to eat, comfortable shelter and warmth while demanding relatively little work. There would have been plenty of time for leisure and family life, conversation, playing with the kids – as well as thoughts about the mysteries of life itself. It is hard to imagine why people would ever swap such a lifestyle for a regime of daily toil. But that was exactly what some would have been advocating in Scotland from around 4000 BC onwards, the time described as being 'of the New Stone' – the Neolithic.

No one imagines any more that the switch to farming – crops or animals – happened rapidly or as part of a uniform process. Archaeological evidence from the so-called 'fertile crescent' of the Near East – in the Levant and Mesopotamia around modern-day Iraq – shows farming was established there by around 9000 BC. It then took all of 3,500 years to reach the Mediterranean and at least 2,000 more to make the crossing to Scotland and the rest of the British Isles. Farming may not have been the majority occupation in Scotland until as recently as 2000 BC. Conversion was no overnight sensation and it was not foisted upon work-shy hunter-gatherers at the point of a pitchfork either. Instead the benefits of the alternative lifestyle – food stores for lean times, animals ready to hand without the need to hunt them down, a permanent home – gradually won people over.

Both ways of life existed side by side for hundreds or thousands of years. Some hunters may have tried the new way only to revert to old habits out of simple preference; likewise, some farmers may have seen the virtues of nomadic hunting and gathering and thrown down their ploughs in favour of the easy life being lived by the wanderers they saw passing through the fringes of their territory every once in a while.

Inundation by rising sea levels may have provoked a change in the way people viewed the land. The loss of territory in some areas – the final drowning of Doggerland, for example – was rapid enough for people living nearby to realise what was happening. Perhaps they began to wonder whether or not a day would come when there was no dry land left at all. Under such circumstances it may have seemed wise to start caring for the land, tending it rather than taking it for granted. Spokesmen evangelising about the benefits of farming could easily work in a few lines about the need to stay put, to take possession of the land, to grow crops and keep animals on it – or risk losing it for ever beneath the next tide.

The notion of immigration by farmers – of large-scale movement of people from a steadily over-populating east towards the empty west – has been in and out of fashion over the years. It was an early explanation by archaeologists for what they interpreted as the abandonment of nomadic hunting and gathering in favour of permanent settlement among cultivated fields. Then others began to argue that farming is knowledge, a set of skills that might simply have been passed across Europe by word of mouth without the need for any great movement or invasion by the farmers themselves. Most recently, in light of the study of human DNA, it has become apparent that if there *was* a spread of new people into the west, out of the east, it involved relatively few incomers.

Scientists led by Professor Clive Gamble of Royal Holloway, University of London and Professor Martin Richards of Leeds University studied the DNA of ancient human remains from sites across western Europe. Oxford University's Professor Bryan Sykes, a member of the team, examined DNA collected from a tooth belonging to the skull of so-called 'Cheddar Man', a modern human skeleton found in Gough's Cave in Cheddar Gorge in Somerset in 1903 and later radiocarbon-dated to 7000 years BC. The DNA sequence he recovered was compared to the DNA of pupils and teachers at the nearby Kings of Wessex Community School – and found to match that of two children and one man. History teacher Adrian Targett and Cheddar Man were connected, across 9,000 years, by an unbroken strand of DNA. What this meant in simple terms was that the people living around Cheddar Gorge now are of the same stock as those hunter-gatherers who came to Britain after the ice melted.

Despite the passing of millennia, the arrival of one foreign culture after another, no real watering-down of British DNA has taken place in the last 10,000 years. Tests across the wider population of these isles have returned the same result: something like 80 per cent of us have the DNA of the hunter-gatherers. Whoever arrived after the hunters – the first farmers, Romans, Anglo-Saxon colonists, Viking raiders, Norman conquerors or anybody else – they never came in numbers sufficient to alter fundamentally the bloodstock of the resident population. We are mostly the same people we have always been.

In some parts of Scotland – the mountainous north and west for example, with its thin, acid soils – farming must have been tough. The climate was continuing to change too and not for the better. By around 3000 BC cooler, wetter conditions were developing. These were circumstances less suitable for the forests, and trees would have begun to find it hard to grow, particularly in the Highlands. If the trees were failing, what hope for crops, or for animals that needed *something* to live on. Tough or not, farming took root throughout the land. If the forests were being thinned out by changes in the weather, farming would shortly diminish them further still. Arable crops require cleared fields and from 4000 BC onwards the sound of stone axe upon green wood became increasingly familiar.

If those farmers understood the value of fertilising the fields – with seaweed and with animal manure – then they would have been able to take several harvests from the same ground before having to clear more. If they learned the benefits of rotating their crops, that too would have prolonged the fertility of any patch of land. But eventually – and as more and more of their neighbours abandoned the hunt in favour of the farm – more and more fields would have been required, more trees felled. Once farming took hold, deforestation became an irreversible process and humankind had begun to make its first significant impact upon the landscape.

On the kind of diet provided by simple farming – cereals for porridge and bread, milk and cheese, occasional meat – the population of Scotland began to increase. People depended upon specific patches of land in ways that had been unknown during the millennia of hunting and gathering – and with that dependence came a sense of ownership. For the first time, families and clans felt the need to stake a permanent claim on the fields they worked and therefore controlled; boundaries appeared, marked by hurdle fences perhaps, or lines of boulders. Group identities became increasingly important, along with an awareness of home turf – what land do you belong to? And then ... what land belongs to you?

During the fourth millennium BC, the Early Neolithic, people began building houses for their dead. The first tombs were of timber, the later ones of stone, but the function was always the same – the storage of bones. The custom was to leave the corpses of the dead exposed in the open long enough for the flesh to be picked off by scavengers or lost to decay. Once the remains had been reduced to mere bones, the skeleton was gathered up and placed within a purpose-built structure. Although the bones of men, women and children – people of all ages and both sexes – were placed inside the tombs, there are never enough to account for all of the community's dead. They hint at an egalitarian approach to dealing with the dead, but only a small percentage was ever selected for that particular burial rite – everyone else, the vast majority, must have been disposed of elsewhere.

Although the bones were stored in the tombs this was not the end of the matter. The tombs stayed open, accessible to the living. Over long periods of time, even centuries, the bones of more members of the group were placed inside. From time to time the ancestors were returned to the light of day for rituals that reminded the living just how long their people had been laying claim to the territory. Our ancestors were comfortable with – comforted *by* – the physical remains of their dead relatives.

It is ironic that the most noticeable relic of the culture of the earliest farmers is houses built not for the living but for the dead. That said, there have been some famous finds of homes of a handful of those first farming communities. Just as tools of stone are more likely to survive the ages, so too are *homes* of stone. Timber would have been a common building material in the past but is unlikely to last anything like as well as stone in the archaeological record. Homes built of posts and stakes, of wattle and daub are largely absent, appearing just now and again as shadows and stains that only the most diligent digger will spot or 'feel' with a trowel while excavating. It is therefore the structures of the infinitely more durable stone that have survived – and these can easily colour and distort our image of the homes of the majority of our ancestors.

At Knap of Howar on the island of Papa Westray on Orkney, archaeologists excavated two well-built houses that were occupied for half a millennium either side of 3600 BC. They are built close together – roughly rectangular in shape, though with rounded corners – and are of dry-stone construction. The entrances are low down, probably for protection from the wind and weather, and a further passage connects the two buildings. Animal bones recovered from the site suggest the farmers kept cattle, pigs and sheep and also grew a small amount of cereal crops.

By 3100 BC a farming community was up and running at Skara Brae, close to the Bay of Skaill on the west coast of Mainland Orkney. The site came to light in 1850 when a storm took a great bite out of a bank of sand dunes close to the sea. Revealed beneath the sand and grasses was a cluster of houses that had been enveloped by the dunes unknown centuries or millennia before (it is possible that a severe storm and consequent inundation by sand may even have been the reason the village was abandoned in the first place). Seven self-contained buildings survive, along with an eighth structure that was probably a workshop. In its original form the village may have had more homes – houses lost to earlier erosion by sand and sea centuries ago – and it was occupied continuously for at least 500 years before it was abandoned.

Visitors view the houses from above, by walking on carefully tended turf that has been allowed to grow along the tops of the walls. It is impossible not to marvel at the skill of the builders. Into an enormous midden of their own rubbish, they burrowed passageways and excavated house-sized chambers. These tunnels and spaces they lined with elegantly constructed dry-stone walls built of the naturally occurring Orkney flagstones. As the walls passed above head height, the builders stepped the successive layers of stonework inwards so that they began to close over. The passageways and houses could then be topped either with capstones or with roofs of timber accordingly.

The passageways linked the houses, one to another, to create a veritable warren, snugly insulated against the weather. The midden would have smelled a bit rich in warm weather – especially from the point of view of our modern, deodorised sensibilities – but the protection it afforded from the elements would have made it indispensable. The atmosphere may have been ripe but for folk gathered by roaring fires while storms raged all round, they would have been the cosiest homes imaginable. Inside each was a stone 'dresser' upon which valuables could be displayed. Sleeping spaces were marked out with stones and a large hearth occupied the centre of each home. There is even evidence for a running water channel passing by each of the houses to create what may effectively have been flushing indoor toilets.

Looking down on Skara Brae is a surreal experience, like a glimpse of something more than just the work of people – something grown in the earth rather than built; or like a giant wasps' nest cut in two to reveal cells and passageways within. The preservation – and ongoing conservation – gives a look of manicured perfection that suggests the whole place might have been built just a year or two ago as a film set.

Sometimes it feels like its inhabitants have just this minute walked away. On a day when it is busy with tourists the murmur of many voices serves to remind you the village would have teemed with life and industry. It is at such moments too that you cannot help but wonder what the inhabitants would have sounded like. It is supposed their language would have been something akin to Gaelic or Welsh – an ancient tongue that had travelled across Europe from east to west before arriving in these lands along with the first hunter-gatherers. Whatever it was, they left no written trace of it. We do not know what they thought of the world around them. We do not even know what they called themselves. So the village of Skara Brae is a silent, voiceless place, fossilised within a silent, voiceless world.

As farming became the norm the increasing population – made possible, even inevitable by such a lifestyle – put pressure on the land for the first time. All the ground that could be exploited for crops or animals was steadily claimed, cleared and occupied, not just the fertile lowlands and valleys, but the higher terrain as well – all of it was eventually put to use. As the third millennium BC wore on, tensions between families, clans and tribes reared their heads for the first time. After centuries and millennia when there had been room enough for people to keep out of each other's way, from now on the farmers were forced to find means of coping with one another.

Whatever tension the increasing population generated was undoubtedly exacerbated by a deteriorating climate. From around 3000 BC onwards Scotland became ever cooler and wetter. Blankets of peat had been forming in the dampest areas since the middle of the eighth millennium and now they advanced more rapidly, reducing the amount of land suitable for crops. The advance of peat is still not fully understood but seems to be triggered by an excessively wet climate. When dead vegetation and fallen leaves become waterlogged on the ground surface rather than decaying and fertilising the soil, a steadily thickening organic mat starts to form. If this pattern continues for years, peat is the result. The whole process may also be triggered, or at least made worse, by large-scale clearance of woodland – either by climate change, disease or the hand of man. No one really knows.

If there ever had been a time of Utopian peace – balmy weather, plentiful resources, and a near-empty land basking beneath endless skies – then it was over for ever by around 2500 BC. By then the landscape was dotted with a new kind of monument – places of religious and magical importance that were, for the first time, off-limits to the hoi polloi. These were the henge monuments – tall, usually circular banks and deep ditches built to enclose areas and conceal rituals from prying eyes. Sometimes an earlier, communal tomb is enclosed inside the prohibited area – but hidden now, its entrance obscured and visited only by those qualified or entitled to do so.

Some of the dead were being treated in a different way as well. Where before the tombs had acted as communal storerooms for the bones of many people, now certain individuals were granted burial in tombs and graves made just for one. For the first time there is the suggestion of hierarchies and elites. Some people and their families were deemed special – deserving of special treatment in death as in life. The great tomb of Maes Howe, near Tormiston Mill on Mainland Orkney, was built on a site that had earlier been marked off and enclosed by a henge. The tomb is an architectural marvel constructed of enormous stones, some weighing as much as 30 tonnes but fitted together without the need for mortar. This was a last resting place not for representatives of all of the society's dead, but for a special few. It is the advent of *them and us.*

Close by Maes Howe, and related to it, are the stone circles of Stenness and Brodgar. More sites – fragments of a long-lost religion or science – are all around. What a place Orkney must have been when that whole landscape of ritual and ceremony was complete and in use. For people tending their fields, herding their animals, the ritual and ceremonial places would have been a constant and unavoidable presence. Throughout the day, as they went about their business, they would find themselves near one or other of the monuments. Carefully sited to be visible from miles around, those circles of stone, tombs and processional ways between them would catch the eye and hold the attention again and again. Here was a world where daily life and spiritual life existed side by side. There can be no doubting, either, that a ruling class had emerged with the clout to demand and organise the building of such places.

Stenness and Brodgar were half a millennium old by the time the henges and circles of Avebury were built in Wessex. The rest of the henges there-abouts are similarly young, by comparison to those in Orkney. Whatever the new religion was, it emerged first in the far north. Only the earliest phases of Stonehenge are as old, suggesting that the idea for circles made of ditches, banks and stones may have been passed from north to south. Calanais on Lewis suggests the same presence – of an elite inspired by a new way of interpreting the mysteries of the world; so too the awe-inspiring ritual landscape of Kilmartin Valley, in Argyll.

By the middle of the third millennium BC a new alchemy was abroad in the land – the ability to make jewellery, tools and weapons of metal. Bronze, the metal in question and the one that gives the age its name, is an alloy of copper and tin. This posed a very specific problem for those people in the northern third of Britain who were keen to wear and bear things made of it: copper occurs naturally in Scotland but tin – the metal that hardens soft copper enough to hold a sharpened edge – does not. Since tin had to be acquired from many hundreds of miles away, on the south-west tip of the British Isles, those wanting it had to be able to obtain some sort of surplus for trading purposes. They also had to be in the business of making and maintaining trading links over large distances.

Elites that had emerged to control the building of – and access to – the magical places in the landscape – the tombs and henges – now found ways to control both the jewellery that displayed their status and the weapons required to enforce and perpetuate it. Bronze items began to appear in individual graves, adding to the impression that here was a special person. Not only could he or she afford the jewellery or the weaponry in life, they could also take it with them into eternity.

As the Bronze Age continued, so the population increased. In some areas, farmers were laying claim to the uplands – territory that had previously been overlooked in preference to the more easily accessible and more fertile lowlands. But the move into the harder terrain was undertaken while the climate was continuing to worsen. Those forced to live on the fringes – on the thin soils of the uplands – would be the first to feel any pressures. Lives already made difficult and tenuous by less productive land were especially vulnerable to the vagaries of the weather.

Metal-working technology continued to develop and by the advent of the first millennium BC it was tools and weapons of iron that commanded most respect and required greatest control of surplus and trade. As some parts of the uplands became impossible for farming, the dispossessed descended into the lowlands to face land squabbles that would be settled by warriors armed with iron swords and shields. The wheel, too, had trundled into the north by 1000 BC, making possible wagons for work but also chariots for warfare.

Precious metalwork was being thrown into lochs, rivers and mires as well – sometimes in startling quantities. These were no accidental losses, but deliberate offerings. It seems that from the moment people mastered the making of metal objects, they found a need to give some of them up – to nature, to God, to someone unseen but whose presence was unmistakable and undoubted. In Duddingston Loch in Edinburgh a cache of fifty-three bronze knives, spearheads and swords was recovered in 1780. The whole lot of it – a collection of inestimable material value to those who sacrificed it – had been thrown in at one time and one place. Many more of the same events would occur once iron was available too.

Offering up valuables to the invisible was a practice that endured for centuries, or longer. Perhaps it was about 're-seeding' the land with what had been taken from it. Ore was harvested like any other natural crop and so it might have made sense to give some of it back to ensure supplies did not run out. Watery locations may have been chosen in an attempt to appease or appeal to the weather. Perhaps a gift of powerful weapons and valuable jewellery might persuade the rain gods to do the bidding of the priests.

While the hills were emptying in the north and west of Scotland, the ruling elites in the south and east began enforcing control of their own uplands by building grand hill forts on top of the most prominent summits. The effects of climate change were not uniform throughout the land, and the uplands of southern Scotland may have remained attractive for longer than those in the north. Eildon Hill in the Borders had space for as many as 6,000 people but its severely exposed location, coupled with the absence of a water supply, make it obvious the place could never have been permanently occupied on such a scale. It is more likely Eildon and other similar forts were places for gatherings and festivals – and where people from the surrounding area, together with their livestock and other valuables, might retreat to in times of acute strife. Partly defensive and partly for show, these lofty residences speak loudly and clearly of control – control of a population large enough first of all to tackle the building jobs and then to maintain and occasionally defend the places.

As the first millennium BC drew towards its conclusion a unique type of building emerged in the north and west. For a few centuries either side of the time of the birth of Christ, the individuals and families that mattered were using brochs as homes and as symbols of power. These great cooling-tower-shaped structures appeared on the coast at places like Gurness and Mousa – and at hundreds of other locations besides – and suggest the lives and ambitions of powerful landowners, even petty kings. They also suggest specialist builders, called in and then moving on when the job was completed. With thick circular walls rising many metres in height and enclosing a fairly small internal space that was easily defended, the brochs were a way of underlining and displaying power, even if only on a local scale. Consider too the impact on the locals – farmers used to building and living in simple homes of wood, turf and stone – of seeing these alien towers grow up on headlands and other prominent positions around their coastlines.

By the time of Christ, those living in the northern third of Britain were under a fair amount of pressure – pressure that was at least in part of their own making. The land could not comfortably support many more people than were already living on it and yet the population was continuing to grow. The climate had been on a steady downward spiral for longer than anyone could remember – colder and wetter – and land that had once been fertile was barren or inhospitable now. With living space at a premium, control of it had become the major preoccupation for those able to demonstrate power and authority.

Dominant individuals and families had emerged long ago – able to exercise their will over the masses, to lay claim to surplus crops and animals, to cajole or coerce large numbers of people into building great monuments, ostentatious defences. They bore jewellery and arms in life and took them to their graves with them when they died. In this way, men and women of ambition had consolidated their control over their own patches of territory, their own turfs, their own tribes and clans.

Networks of commerce and trade had made possible the import not just of goods and weaponry, but also of new ideas from far and wide. Soon it would not be a matter just of new ideas, but also of new people. Internal pressures would have been building for some time; no doubt different groups vied with one another, testing the limits of power. Scattered across the land was a patchwork of disparate tribes and clans, each with their own separate identities. There would have been local allegiances and loyalties as well as petty squabbles about territory; but each was an entity in its own right, largely independent of its neighbours.

Underneath it all was the rock, the land itself, forged and proved by billions of years of fire and water and ice. Only very recently – in the last few moments really – had people made their presence felt upon it. But in those few thousands years – no time at all in the lifetime of the rock – they had pushed the place towards a natural limit. For now it was a tolerable limit, but a limit just the same.

At the end of the first millennium BC, the people of the land before Scotland existed within a status quo that had evolved to fill the space allotted to it. It was a sophisticated world of inter-related yet largely autonomous tribes and clans. Local chiefs might command local respect – but none had yet found the clout to reach further afield.

For most people the daily concerns were what they had been since time out of mind and would be for centuries to come – making sure there was food for the table, that the fields and animals were tended, the boundaries maintained. There were loyalties to be kept, relationships to nurture, rivals and foes to be borne in mind at all times. There were also attempts to understand and tame the fickle forces of the world. Religions – or something like them – had been evolving for thousands of years to help people control the uncontrollable.

Here in the northern third of the British Isles was a society and a civi-lisation that was a going concern – that had been so for thousands of years. No one up here was sitting around waiting for outsiders to arrive and tell them how to live, how to think, how to be. There was no centre, no dominant identity and no *nation*. But that was because no such concept had yet been required.

The land before Scotland functioned perfectly well. It was complex, it was sophisticated and it was whole – a busy world in its own right. In the end it was a pressure from without, from beyond the familiar horizons, that would change everything.

***

The boats set sail from the Orkney mainland in the spring of AD 43. The trip in prospect could hardly have been completed in one go – the distance was too great, the boats designed for coasting from one safe harbour to the next – but it was a routine undertaking just the same. In the end it would have taken several weeks to cover the distance, but posed no unfamiliar risks or problems.

Boats had been plying up and down the length of the long island for thousands of years carrying people, livestock, surplus crops and other trade goods, as well as the news and gossip from elsewhere that is the stock in trade of people on the move. In 325 BC the geographer Pytheas had been sent out by the leaders of the city of Massilia – Marseilles in modern France – to explore the origins and destinations of their various trading goods. When he wrote up his travels a few years later, in a work he called *On the Ocean*, he described a journey round the coastline of Britain that took in, among other near-mystical places, the Orcas, or Orkney Islands.

It was via journeys such as these that the science and magic of the henges and stone circles had been passed from north to south three millennia before. If that religion had depended upon travel overland it would likely still have been on its way south in the first century AD, lost in a wood somewhere or bogged down in some trackless mire. Stonehenge, Avebury and the rest might never have been built.

If there was anything out of the ordinary about the trip south from Orkney during the April and May of AD 43, it was the importance of its principal passenger. Any loss of life at sea was to be regretted but the consequences of losing a king did not bear thinking about. It was also vital the trip be completed in good time because the man the king needed to see would not be in Britain for long. He had considerable interests elsewhere, to put it mildly. It would not do at all to be late for such a man – in fact the possible repercussions of that breach of etiquette might be dire.

Thanks to the skill and experience of the seamen in charge of the little flotilla, the journey was completed in good time. So it was that the King of Orkney arrived in Camulodunum, the place we know today as Colchester but for long the capital of the Trinovantes tribe of southern Britain. Along with ten other British kings he bowed his head to Tiberius Claudius Caesar Augustus Germanicus, Emperor of Rome and conqueror of Britannia. Such a rendezvous, dependent upon keeping up with the news in distant places and being able to stick to a complicated and demanding schedule, might sound remarkable for a man living in Orkney in AD 43. But Claudius only stayed in Britain for sixteen days, so the king's knowledge of the itinerary had to be detailed and precise – to enable him to leave home long before the emperor even arrived in Colchester.

It is tempting to imagine the first-century inhabitants of the far north of Britain as somehow cut off and existing in a vacuum, a primitive space in which they knew and cared little about the world beyond their horizon. Nothing could be further from the truth. Whatever else they might have been, the people of the land before Scotland were not primitive, neither were they cut off. While people, goods and information travelled more slowly than today, they moved with just as much urgency and determination.

The existence of Rome and her empire – ceaselessly on the move and covering more and more of the world with the shadow of her hand – would have been common knowledge among the tribes living the length and breadth of the British Isles. No doubt even in Orkney – and certainly around the hearths of the royal palace of Gurness, where the king made his home – people would have remembered the stories of the last time the Romans had made landfall on the British side of the English Channel.

Emperor Julius Caesar had tried invading Britannia on two occasions, in 55 and 54 BC, determined to place this northern land under his thrall –

but to no avail. He was forced to pull his forces out on both occasions. In 44 BC he was murdered by his fellows – at least in part because they feared he was about to make a foreigner, an Egyptian named Cleopatra, Empress of Rome. Did word of that legendary beauty, even just her name, make it to the cooking fires of Gurness in the last years of the first millennium BC?

The Romans of 54 BC had observed, among other things, how the locals in Britannia painted their bodies with blue woad so that their very skins declared their identity and their place in the world. It was a practice the Roman soldiers had noticed again and again among the so-called bar-barians, people of many different names who had sought to defy them all across northern Europe. It is yet another sign of the long-distance connections and relationships carefully cultivated and tended by Iron Age Britons. It was also an observation of local custom that would prove telling more than a century later when another Roman emperor sent his soldiers across the water.

So the decision by a King of Orkney to travel hundreds of miles in order to bend the knee before Emperor Claudius of Rome comes as no surprise. All kings, or at least those who want to survive longer than the ceremonies that name them as such, are politicians. It made sense for that local ruler to put himself in front of the most powerful man in the world. If he had differences of opinion with tribes on the British mainland, it might have suited him perfectly to try to ally himself with the man who might well prove to be the new leader.

Until recently the only evidence for the meeting was revealed in relief on a fragment of a triumphal arch in Rome. Even so, many historians were convinced the mention of a King of Orkney was no more than a mis-translation, a misunderstanding. More recently archaeologists working at Gurness unearthed fragments of Roman pottery. To be more specific, they found shards from a style of amphora, clay bottles used for transporting wine and olive oil, which had gone out of use completely by AD 60. If the trading connections were moving fine Roman wine and oil to a powerful man living in Gurness before AD 60, then it is possible that news of a visit to the southernmost territories by the Emperor of Rome himself reached that man as well.

So when the time comes to imagine the first forays by Roman soldiers into Scotland, it is important to remember it was not a case of wide-eyed local primitives suddenly coming face to face with an alien culture of which they knew nothing. This was not the arrival of Martians for a one-sided war of worlds but a clash of two civilisations, each of which believed they were morally superior to the other. By the time the Romans arrived here in about AD 82, the people of the north knew those would-be invaders very well.

Julius Agricola had been appointed Governor of Britannia in 78 AD. As soon as he landed he embarked on an ultimately successful campaign to crush the tribes of Wales. By the following year he had the north of England firmly under control as well. Roman domination of the British Isles was travelling north like a rising tide. In AD 80 the legions moved northwards again for a campaign Agricola believed would complete the empire's conquest of Britannia. Within two years Roman rule was established as far north as the line across the country marked by the Clyde and Forth rivers.

As a Scot, it is hard to think about what happened next without feeling some spark of ancient defiance light up in the brain. You know it is wrong, something left over from the honour rituals of the playground, but it is there just the same. The fact is that north of the Forth and Clyde line, the Romans encountered a stubbornness on the part of the locals that they never managed to overcome.

Among the southern tribes of Scotland – the Damnonii; the Novantae; the Selgovae; the Votadini – were peoples that became fully Romanised before the end, accepting of and grateful for the lifestyle afforded by being clients of the empire. In the weeks and months after those initial conquests of the more co operative tribes, the Roman soldiers took care to build the usual forts and fortlets that would let them sleep easy in their beds. They knew enough about the ways of barbarians to understand the importance of covering their own backs, even in settled territory.

But north of the two great rivers that narrowed the land to a mere strip of solid flatland between mountain and mire were tribes of a different sort. These were people the legionaries often lumped together under one name – Caledonians. Right at the start there was a taste of things to come when the Legio IX Hispana was attacked at night by tribesmen who came howling down upon them out of the darkness. Only the last-minute intervention of large numbers of Roman cavalry avoided a wholesale rout.

The Caledonians favoured tactics that would work well down through the millennia for soldiers from these parts faced with overwhelming numbers – hit and run. Agricola, determined to draw towards him a combined enemy force that he could tackle and annihilate in one go, set about harrying the population. Winter was approaching and the Romans busied themselves capturing every food store they could find.

CHAPTER TWO

THE LAST
OF THE FREE

'And some there be ... who are perished, as though they had never
been; and become as though they had never been born ...'

Ecclesiasticus

Starvation snapped closer at Caledonian heels than any Roman dog of war
when the first named 'Scot' stepped out of the dark to make his stand.

We know his name because Agricola's own son-in-law wrote it down.
More than twenty years later, Gaius Cornelius Tacitus wrote *De vita et
moribus Iulii Agricolae* – 'About the life and character of Julius Agricola'.
Better known today as the *Agricola*, it was a book designed to heap praise
on the general and to demonstrate how it was possible for a good man to
rule effectively and courageously without becoming a despot. It also gives
some insights into not just what the Romans encountered in Britannia in
the latter part of the first century AD, but also what some Romans thought
about the behaviour of the Roman Empire itself.

With the great general heading north – into the lethally dangerous
territory of the Caledonians – Tacitus wanted to underline his father-in-
law's bravery by finding him a worthy foe. It is in this context – that of
useful literary device as much as anything made of blood and bone – that
Scotland's first hero strides to centre-stage.

In the autumn of AD 84 a massed force of Caledonians – according to
Tacitus, 30,000-strong – gathered in the shadow of a great glen to try and
turn back the tide:

> ... and still they came, flocking to the colours – all the young men and those
> whose old age was fresh and green, famous warriors with their battle honours
> thick upon them. At that point one of the many leaders, named Calgacus, a

man of outstanding valour and nobility, summoned the masses who were already thirsting for battle and addressed them ...

Battles against Rome have been lost and won before, [said Calgacus] but never without hope; we were always there in reserve. We, the choicest flower of Britain's manhood, were treasured in her most secret places ... We, the last men on earth, the last of the free, have been shielded before today by the very remoteness and the seclusion for which we are famed ... Romans ... Brigands of the world ... the wealth of an enemy excites their greed, his poverty their lust for power ... Robbery, butchery, rapine ... they create a devastation and call it peace [*ubi solitudinem faciunt, pacem appellant*].

Archaeologists and historians still argue about the location of the battle. Tacitus called the place '*Mons Graupius*' – the Grampian mountain – and a popular interpretation puts the fighting on and around the slopes of Bennachie, in Aberdeenshire.

Content that he had said all that was required, Calgacus – a name that means 'the swordsman' – signalled the launch of countless spears towards the massed ranks of 20,000 Roman soldiers lined up on the slopes below them. 'The fighting began with exchanges of missiles, and the Britons showed both steadiness and skill in parrying our spears with their huge swords or catching them on their little shields, while they themselves rained volleys on us,' wrote Tacitus. It was the 8,000 or so auxiliaries in the front line that bore the brunt of the aerial bombardment – but still a mighty reply was made in the form of Roman missiles hurled back towards the bellowing faces of the Caledonians. Then it was time for sword work, face to face. 'At last Agricola called upon four cohorts of Batavians and two of Tungrians to close and fight it out at the sword's point. These old soldiers had been well drilled in sword-fighting, while the enemy were awkward at it, with their small shields and unwieldy swords, especially as the latter, having no points, were quite unsuitable for a cut-and-thrust struggle at close quarters.'

Then the Roman cavalry, 3,000-strong, was dispatched around the flanks of the tribesmen. According to Tacitus the Caledonians lost 10,000 men dead before the remainder broke and fled back into the trackless hills. Calgacus, along with the bulk of his forces, disappeared then too, never again to be heard of by history. 'The next day revealed the effects of our victory more fully,' wrote Tacitus. 'An awful silence reigned on every hand; the hills were deserted, houses smoking in the distance, and our scouts did not meet a soul.'

As well as the location of Mons Graupius, as well as the fact or fiction of the man called Calgacus, historians debate whether there ever was a climactic battle between Caledonians and Romans. To be 'climactic', some of them say, many more than a third of the tribesmen would have to have been slain or taken prisoner. To let 20,000 armed and defiant men – their great and valorous leader among them – escape back into their Highland fastnesses could hardly be counted as securing the conquest of Scotland.

But what cannot be denied is that Agricola was shortly summoned back to Rome (allegedly because Emperor Domitian had grown jealous that his bold general's achievements were eclipsing his own) and that he was treated there to a 'triumph'. These were celebrations enjoyed only by Roman war leaders who had notched up unparalleled victories. If Agricola had topped off his proven conquests of the rest of Britannia by trouncing the massed forces of the troublesome Caledonians, then he would indeed have been granted his triumph.

Regardless of what actually happened, it is worth being aware that both the descriptions of the 'first Scot' and the details of the Roman 'conquest' of Scotland have been handed down to us by foreigners, by *others*.

The words of Calgacus have exerted a powerful influence on the national imagination since they were first committed to parchment nearly 2,000 years ago; they might just as easily have been spoken by William Wallace himself – indeed the sentiments can be heard tolling like distant bells in the background of Churchill's speeches. There is one obvious problem, however: they are not and could never have been the words of Calgacus or any other 'Scot' of the first century AD. They are instead the words of Gaius Cornelius Tacitus himself, writing twenty years later in hope of delivering a timeless message about the morality of Rome. If a man like Calgacus ever strode across the heather-covered slopes of a Grampian mountain to preach fire and war to his fellows, he would have spoken not in the measured Latin phrases of a Roman historian but in the tongue of the natives living the length and breadth of Britain in those days – the language that survives in the ancient roots of modern Welsh.

Right here, in this moment, is where the mythologising of Scottish history began. Be warned – almost everything we know, or think we know about Scotland during the centuries after the first contact with Rome, was written down not by our ancestors, but by those who encountered, sometimes lived among and often clashed violently with them.

Any wayward patriotism – the sense that Scots, 'the last of the free', somehow defied the Romans while all others fell before her – has to be tempered by a couple of facts. Firstly, it was the case in the first centuries A D (and was to remain so for centuries to come) that the northern territories required more money to subdue them than they were ever going to be worth in terms of material gain. Why keep sending expensive armies north in hope of securing ownership of thin soils that could barely sustain a crop and barren mountains devoid of minerals? Secondly, Rome had always to sacrifice any hopes of controlling the north in favour of pulling men and resources back out of Britannia whenever imperial borders elsewhere came under pressure.

However effective their efforts really were is not clear, but the individual tribes among the Caledonians never did let up their attempts to harass and punish the Roman squatters at every opportunity. By A D 122 the invaders had acknowledged the scale of the problem by building the most extravagant and impressive boundary anywhere in the empire.

Hadrian's Wall drew an unbroken line from one side of the country to the other, between the Tyne in the east and the Solway in the west. So that none could doubt the might of those who had built it (in just six short years, the work of three legions) it bristled with forts and watch-towers. It was painted brilliant white with lime mortar to make it visible for miles around. On the one hand it was a means of controlling trade moving north and south – passage through heavily guarded checkpoints along its length providing welcome opportunities to collect taxes. More than that, the wall was a line in the sand: where civilisation ended and barbarism began.

Twenty years later the Romans made yet another attempt to push north and finish the job of subduing the tribes. As a demonstration of their commitment they built another barrier – the Antonine Wall – stretching nearly 40 miles from Old Kilpatrick on the Firth of Clyde in the west to Bo'ness on the Firth of Forth in the east. It was not to be, this dream of total conquest. Within twenty years of drawing the new line in the sand they were forced back behind Hadrian's Wall – where they would remain for the rest of their stay in these islands.

The tribes of Caledonia made life intermittently unpleasant for the Romans during the four centuries or so they spent here. Even the wall itself was the target for attacks of varying degrees of seriousness. For their own part the invaders kept trying to score the final success that would bring the remainder of the country to heel – but always they were undone, usually by events elsewhere. Long before the end of the Roman occupation, Britain was attempting to claim independence from the empire. Finally, in A D 410, Alaric the Goth captured the city of Rome itself. The time of the Roman

Empire had passed and, back in the stubbornly defiant lands of northern Scotland, the Caledonian tribes were on hand to speed the final expulsion of the enemies at the gate.

It had been the Romans themselves who referred to the northern peoples, those living north of the Forth/Clyde line, as Caledonians. This was a name they applied not just to the people of one specific tribe – the Caledonii who inspired the label – but one that was used as a catchall to describe the whole rebellious lot of them. The Romans even blamed their inability to bring the place under control, in part at least, to the great and impenetrable Forest of Caledon. It seems this was an exaggeration at best and a fiction at worst. By the time of the Romans, clearance of the trees had been going on for thousands of years. The Forest of Caledon probably found its way into progress reports as the kind of excuse a struggling commander might need to appease impatient superiors back in Rome.

Among the Caledonians, and a powerful constituent part of the whole, were tribes like the Maeatae – a name lost to all except students of Roman history. But in AD 297 a word was written down for the first time that was to reverberate through Scottish history until the present day.

When the Romans first reached Scotland they noticed the locals still painted and tattooed their bodies with elaborate, evocative designs. Once upon a time this had been common, not just for the peoples of the British Isles but among all the Celtic tribes of Europe. By the end of the first century, though, it was a practice that had begun to die out. For the legionaries making their first forays north of the Clyde and Forth rivers, the sight of people still adorning their faces and bodies with paint and dye must have been proof, at least in Roman eyes, of the primitive nature of the foe. So it may have been as a soldiers' nickname that the word *Picti* was first used and heard – something vaguely abusive or dismissive like 'Raghead' for an Iraqi or 'Wop' for an Italian. It is also possible it was a Latinised form of what the tribesmen called themselves, but in any case it meant 'the painted ones' or perhaps 'the people of the designs'.

If ever there was a case of east meeting west in a welter of mutual confusion, it was the relationship between the citizens of empire and the painted ones. In AD 211 an extraordinary encounter took place. Two women – a Caledonian princess known only as the wife of a Maeatae chieftain called Argentocoxus and the Roman empress Julia Domna, wife of Emperor Septimius Severus – met during treaty negotiations and each must have seemed fantastically exotic and foreign to the other.

The empress had heard the barbarian women gave their love freely to many men. When she put this to her counterpart, the princess replied with all the haughty majesty of a woman of the highest rank: 'We fulfil the demands of nature in a much better way than do you Roman women; for we consort openly with the best men, whereas you let yourselves be debauched in secret by the vilest.' This exchange speaks volumes about different worlds. The Romans never understood the people of the north – and were themselves treated with hostility and misunderstanding in return. To the people of the designs, the Romans were would-be conquerors, wishing to put the whole earth beneath the yoke of tyranny. To the sons and daughters of Rome these painted tribesmen and women were only a curiosity, to be kept at arm's length.

Whatever else they might have been, the Picts were the direct descendants of the first bands of hunter-gatherers to colonise these lands after the retreat of the ice 12,000 years ago. If the name started out as soldier slang, it has survived into the present as something else. That one syllable comes down to us from the past hushed by mystery, but synonymous with pride.

Part of the explanation for the aura of other-worldliness that has surrounded the Picts lies entwined within their enigmatic designs and symbols – not just tattooed on their bodies but also carved into standing stones and worked into exquisite jewellery. It is a lost language, a world of meaning that feels almost within our grasp and yet defies all attempts at decoding. But those symbols – eternal and eternally mysterious – are just part of the reason these ancestors have exerted such power over the imagination. The stuff of magic is upon them because they themselves have seemed lost, disappeared.

We know the Picts were here for centuries – long before and long after the Romans; we know they had a rich and complex culture. This was a quintessential warrior society and their need to express themselves was so strong it had to show on their flesh. For all that, they managed somehow to vanish entirely from history; indeed they seem to have perished, in the words of Ecclesiasticus, as though they had never been. Most enigmatically of all, in the end they contrived to leave the stage at the very moment when the kingdom of Scotland was created. But it is only by finding a way through the fog surrounding the fate of the Picts, finding the explanation for their disappearance, that we can understand the true nature of the birth of the Scots nation.

Evidence of Pictish culture – more straightforward and revealing evidence – has come from the peaty waters of Loch Tay. Here, 3 metres down, archaeologists came across the remains of an ancient stronghold – fragments of a thatched roof and stumps that were once the stilts of a dwelling that stood above the water; a dwelling in which Pictish people would have lived.

Crannogs were built in Scotland for thousands of years – in some cases they were still in use in the seventeenth century – and were certainly part of the Pictish way of life. It took a great deal of effort as well as sophisticated technology to build out into water. Explanations for such labour-intensive effort range from defence and security – the only access to such dwellings was over a narrow bridge or causeway, either of which was easily defended – to the suggestion that the residents were maximising their farmland by moving the clutter of their homes out onto the surfaces of the convenient and plentiful lochs. Whatever the reason for balancing a home over water, a crannog is a substantial dwelling and Pictish society had to be well organised to construct such things. In the village of Kenmore, on the shore of Loch Tay, members of the Scottish Trust for Underwater Archaeology have built a full-size replica of the kind of crannog that would once have been commonplace.

It has stood for more than ten years now and if you come across it unexpectedly, you could be forgiven for thinking it has been there centuries longer. The walk across the narrow, high-sided bridge that links the house to the mainland is a journey through time. Inside, the crannog is spacious and surprisingly comfortable. A thick carpet of dry bracken and straw covers the floor of woven branches, so it is soft and silent underfoot. It is instantly easy to imagine how small items must have got lost in the tangle every day, only to discover their way eventually into the water beneath, for archaeologists to find in centuries to come.

A central hearth dominates the circular interior and supplies the majority of the light. Around the walls, partitions mark out private sleeping places on two levels. There is also plentiful room for storage and every inch of every horizontal beam and branch seems draped with something useful – drying foodstuffs or raw materials for making clothes, tools and the rest of the paraphernalia of daily life. The gentle lapping of the waters of the loch against the upright posts that support the whole structure provides a constant, soothing music. It has to be said, though, that the fire blazing in the midst of all this tinder is a constant worry to modern eyes. Surely these dwellings fell victim to fire on a regular basis.

The construction process convinced the archaeologists that whoever lived in such places was in control of people and resources in large quantities. Remains recovered from the loch revealed the Iron Age inhabitants enjoyed a rich and varied diet and that they were sitting within trading networks that reached far and wide. Some of the small objects recovered from the water and silt were made of jet – the fossilised remains of ancient monkey puzzle trees – and must have come from at least as far away as Whitby in Yorkshire.

The Kenmore reconstruction, based on the excavated remains of the Oakbank Crannog which was found on the north-east shore of the loch, could accommodate at least twenty and perhaps as many as forty people. It seems likely that while a high-ranking family may have lived in it full-time, dependants living onshore in less secure housing might have retreated to the crannog, effectively a water castle, for protection in times of strife.

By the time the Romans abandoned Britannia, the people they had called Picts were a long-established and distinctive presence occupying the north and east of the country. The most powerful of their men styled themselves as kings – of the sort that had made the trip from Orkney to Colchester to meet an emperor four centuries before. They controlled enough of the surplus from fertile farmland in the eastern part of their domains to enable them to commission jewellery, weapons and artworks from specialised craftsmen. The standing stones that bear the unmistakable designs they demanded of their sculptors have been interpreted as marking out a territory that was supposedly divided, at one stage, into seven provinces: Cat (Caithness); Ce (Marr and Buchan); Circin (Angus and Mearns); Fib (Fife); Fidaid (Moray and Easter Ross); Fortriu (Strathearn and Mentieth) and Fotla (Atholl and Gowrie). More recently, historian Dauvit Brown has dismissed these as a fiction that fails to represent the true territorial divisions within Pictland.

Powerful men and their families had emerged as a nobility whose pastimes included the hunt and who had personal and trading links that connected them to powerful men elsewhere. Some of these links were friendly, about the exchange of artistic and spiritual ideas as well as commerce; some points of contact were less cordial.

To the south of the Pictish territory were lands dominated by the Britons – people who spoke a language similar to that of their northern neighbours but who were different nonetheless. These were the descendants of tribes that had lived directly under Roman rule. Among them were the Gododdin, descendants of the Votadini, with their stronghold around the volcanic rock of Din Eidyn (Edinburgh). A separate group clung to Alt Clut, mighty Dumbarton Rock, in Strathclyde.

To the west of the territories of the Picts and the Britons were the Gaels. If this is not confusing enough already, it is about to get much worse.

Depending on what other books you read, the Gaels are sometimes referred to as the original Scots. The origin of the name lies in *Scoti*, the translation into Latin of Gael, or Gaedil. As well as being a translation, Scoti also had unfavourable connotations. For some users of the word it meant something like 'pirates' – and it holds within it an echo of a time when these people were viewed, at least by someone else, as marauders who came from the sea.

Historians cannot agree on whether or not the Gaels – the Scots – came originally from Ireland. There is a tenth-century Irish document called *Senchus fer nAlban* – 'The History of the People of Scotland' – that says the Gaelic-speaking Scots had no doubts they were relatives of the Gaels of Ireland. Maybe it is easier to accept that people living on the west coast of Scotland and on the eastern coast of Ireland would have felt connected, rather than separated, by the seawater between them. A relationship that may have started thousands of years before could easily have given rise to peoples on both sides of the Irish Sea who had more to connect than to divide them. An ancient tale, which is supposed to explain the origins of the Gaels, has a chieftain of the Dal Riata tribe of Antrim – one Fergus Mor mac Eirc – arrive in Argyll around AD 500 to establish his own kingdom. The legend goes that he brought his followers across the sea to find more room for himself and his heirs.

Whatever their origins, the Gaels had put down deep roots on and around the western seaboard by the start of the sixth century. Right at the heart of their kingdom was the hill fort of Dunadd, rising like a clenched fist out of the flatlands that surround it. Brooding, menacing Dunadd glowers over the southern end of Kilmartin Glen above Lochgilphead, in Mid-Argyll. Its height, around 54 metres, is made more impressive by the flatness of the valley floor – a mire known then and now as Moine Mor, the Great Bog. Sea levels were higher in AD 500 than today and the rocky citadel of Dunadd would have provided the perfect location for a people who needed to oversee and defend the comings and goings of their ships.

Four massive circular embankments defended the fortress. Much of the hard work had already been done by nature and gaps between cliffs of natural bedrock were plugged with dry-stone walls 10 metres thick. A narrow natural defile was left as an easily defended entrance that could be barred by gates in times of trouble. The whole thing is shaped much like a lopsided wedding cake, and on each successive tier there would have been plenty of room for houses, stores and workshops built of timber and stone. The Gaels who lived here had much in common with their Pictish neighbours in the east as well as with the Britons to the south – not least an appetite for war. But there were enough differences – subtle, cultural quirks – to mark them out as separate. While they sometimes formed alliances, they were just as often at each other's throats.

Archaeological evidence from Dunadd reveals a gentler, reflective side of the Gaels: an artistic tradition with a delicate beauty all of its own. Crucibles for melting gold, silver and bronze were found, along with moulds for casting brooches. Such a demand for and abundance of fine jewellery of the most expensive kind could mean just one thing: this fortress was home to the kingdom's elite. The Gaelic kingdom was run from here; the kings them-selves made upon its bedrock. Just below the summit of Dunadd, on a smooth and level shelf, a footprint has been carved (the original was being worn away by many Cinderella visitors and what you see when you visit now is a convincing replica put in place by a helicopter). The ceremonies that were once held here married the kings to the land they sought to rule. For the crowds gathered below, the heir apparent would have appeared in silhouette against the sky as he stepped out onto the rock. At the appointed time he would have placed one naked foot into the footprint, demonstrating to his subjects that this land was both his servant and his master.

There was evidence too for the sophistication of the trading links of the Gaels. A piece of yellow orpiment, used to make ink for illuminating manuscripts, was recovered from Dunadd. This valuable mineral had been imported from one of the Mediterranean countries and is a tantalising hint about a change that had come over the Gaels by the end of the sixth century – a change that drove an unbreakable spiritual wedge between them and their Pictish neighbours. Illuminated manuscripts – and the very skill of writing, the *literacy* that creates them in the first place – came to the Gaels in the hand baggage of Christianity. While the Picts would hold onto their ancient pagan beliefs for many years to come, the Gaels had accepted conversion by one or other of the missionaries who were there in the years after Emperor Constantine turned Rome herself towards Christ.

While much of the hard work of converting the Gaels was undertaken by unnamed men of God, lost to history, one figure has had the lion's share of the glory. Columba – *Colum Cille*, 'Dove of the Church' – had either left or been driven out of Ireland in AD 563. He was a son of the O'Neill clan, the most powerful in Ireland, but his warlike approach to conversion in his homeland had culminated in a bloodbath that could not go unpunished. Exiled from all he had known, he used his family name to ingratiate himself with the Gaelic warlords of western Scotland. He was present at the inauguration of King Aedan mac Gabhrain in 574, and for his efforts he was rewarded with the gift of an island. Iona, to the west of Mull, would be Columba's home for the rest of his life. The monastery he established as a humble collection of huts would become one of the brightest Christian lights in all of Dark Age Europe.

Tradition credits Columba with the single-handed conversion of the tribes to Christianity. But almost all we know about him comes from a single source: 'The Life of Saint Columba' written around a century after his death by one of his own successors. Adomnán, a later abbot of Iona, was one of the great spin-doctors. Columba had founded Adomnán's monastery and it would have made perfect sense for the latest man in the post to make his predecessor the father of Christianity in Scotland.

There is no denying that Columba's work brought stability to the region around Iona and much further afield. As a noble man and a man of God he was able to open doors that would have remained resolutely closed to preachers of more humble birth. As well as the new faith – a creed that offered answers to the eternal questions – Columba brought literacy to the kings. Here was magic every bit as powerful as the ability to make metal. This holy man wielded the pen as well as he had ever wielded a sword and persuaded the rulers that he could take the very words from their mouths and make them permanent. Once a king's wishes and demands were written down, copied and circulated, there was the basis of a legal system, of contracts and treaties. People, families and tribes could be bound one to another under terms that could be seen and understood by anyone who could read. The written word, like the soul of a man it seemed, could be raised up into the light by the hand of Christ. The monks of Iona, working in their sparse scriptorium near the beating heart of the monastery, eventually produced The Book of Kells.

Kells, 40 miles north of Dublin in County Meath, was home to the book for centuries, but it was on the hauntingly beautiful island of Iona, a stone's throw from Mull, that it was created. By any standards it is a masterpiece. It comprises the gospels, together with a handful of other texts, but it is the artwork that marks it out for greatness. People, animals and mythical beasts; knotwork and swirling patterns of the most intense intricacy; 10,000 dots of red ink around a single capital letter; livid, living colours like the yellow orpiment from the Mediterranean, found at Dunadd; blue lapis lazuli from Afghanistan. The peak of artistic achievement reached by the creator or creators of The Book of Kells is unsurpassed.

Iona today feels remote: a tiny island to the west of a small island, to the west of Argyll in western Scotland. But in the time of Columba and for centuries to come it was a central point on the map of faith. That men living and working there could produce such a masterpiece is testament to what the place once meant. A thirteenth-century scholar praised the artistry of The Book of Kells: 'You might believe it was the work of an angel rather than a human being,' he wrote. Not everyone was so impressed by the work of the Christians' God. While the Gaels had embraced Christianity long before the coming of Columba, their Pictish neighbours remained resolutely committed to their old religion. They put their faith in druids rather than monks and relied on memory, the oral tradition, rather than the written word.

The gods, old and new, could hardly have been expected to live side by side. According to Adomnán it was Columba who took it upon himself to face down the old ways. Into the heart of darkness he travelled, to confront the witchcraft of the Picts, and after many hardships he reached the head of Loch Ness and the fortress of King Bridei, possibly at Craig Phadraig, near modern Inverness. Finding the gates barred against him he made the sign of the cross, at which point they opened of their own accord. A battle of supernatural wills followed, with Columba and his cross on one side and Bridei's druid on the other. Columba's voice was said to sound like thunder and he brought the druid close to death before, in the finest Christian tradition, relenting and sparing his life. Columba had won the battle but the king remained a pagan.

The religious wedge separating Pict and Gael remained in place for decades, long after the dove of the Church had come and gone. But the journey of the painted ones towards Christianity left its trail upon their stones. For centuries they had favoured mysterious symbols – Z-rods and V-rods, discs, combs, mirrors and other strangeness – as well as all kinds of beasts, both real and imagined. But the eventual conversion of the people – or at least of those with the wealth to commission works of art – shows itself in the later stones.

A collection of thirty-eight Pictish stones from the site of a royal centre near Arbroath reveals the time, fossilised in stone, when both pagan and Christian traditions could feature on the same slab. The Drosten Stone has on its reverse some of the classic images so beloved of the Picts – discs, a crescent, a comb, as well as unsuspecting animals being targeted by a huntsman armed with a bow. All of the images appear in relief, with the stone carefully chipped and pecked away until the symbol or animals stands proud of the background. A hind is lovingly depicted, her suckling fawn entwined with her legs – just one element of a masterpiece that makes plain the skill of the artist. On the front of the stone, in the prime location, is a cross – the empty Celtic cross that represents the risen Christ. A pagan past and the promise of salvation, each philosophy backed by the other.

This policy of inclusion – bringing the central messages of the new faith to the fore while respecting the images and sacred places that had comforted people for centuries – was part of Christianity's success. As an invader, it not only succeeded in gaining a hold but also out-stayed all the others. The Gaelic religion spanned northern Britain and acted as glue, bringing together and holding together disparate peoples beneath the overarching roof of the Christian faith.

If Columba had been part opportunist – using his rank and literacy to persuade the kings of his generation that there were practical as well as spiritual advances to be had from embracing Christ – then his successor Adomnán was cut from the same cloth. Seizing his own moment, he won agreement from more than fifty kings for a new law. Dubbed 'The Law of the Innocents' it was a Geneva Convention for the Dark Ages. It protected women, children and monks in times of war: 'Women may not be killed by a man in any way, neither by slaughter or by any other death, not by poison, nor in water, nor fire, nor by any beast, nor in a pit, nor by dogs, but shall die in their own lawful bed.' Life for most remained nasty, brutish and short but Adomnán's Law was powerful proof of the civilising influence of Christianity. Like the Gaels, the Picts had learned the wisdom of accepting written rules.

They seem to have had it all, these folk who had now added the Latin alphabet to their already ample collection of meaningful signs and symbols. Their culture, rich and sophisticated, was developing new touches all the while. Trade connected the Picts to the wide world, bringing ideas as well as goods to buy and sell. Their low-lying farmland was among the most fertile in Britain and certainly the most productive in the north. Control of the bread-basket of northern Britain provided the fodder for yet more fighting men; power begets power. But as Calgacus had observed all those centuries before, an abundant land excites the greed of others and the territory of his descendants was not to be left in peace.

For part of the seventh century it was the Britons, reaching out with grasping hands from strongholds like Alt Clut, in Strathclyde, who caused the Picts most grief. Between AD 631 and 653 the annals suggest the Picts had several kings descended from the British house. For most of that time it was another people who focused their envious eyes on the north. The Angles were a Germanic people that had come to these shores during the chaos that followed the Roman withdrawal in the early 400s. They had come first as guests but stayed to dominate, establishing the mini-kingdoms of Bernicia and Deira across the middle of northern England.

Early in the seventh century those two joined as one in the kingdom of Northumbria and wasted no time in expanding the territory even further. At first it was to the south of Scotland that they turned their attention, claiming first of all the land of the Gododdin around the volcanic rock fortress of Din Eidyn. Then it was the turn of the Picts, and a succession of Anglian kings tried to add the rich lands north of the Forth to their demesne. At first they settled for installing puppet kings in the land of the Picts and by the second half of the century they were demanding tribute from the kings of the Gaels as well.

In 671 or 672 the Picts drove out one of the puppets – a so-called King Drest – and in so doing attracted the fury of the Anglian King Ecgfrith, who had put him on the throne in the first place. In his vengeful wrath Ecgfrith slaughtered an entire Pictish army that dared stand against him – and much of the Pictish nobility along with it.

Out of the carnage stepped another King Bridei. For years he had made war among his own people, attacking fortresses and strongholds like Dunottar, near Aberdeen, and the hill fort of Dundurn in Perthshire. He was a man who would be king and sought nothing less than to bring together all the Picts into a single entity. Enraged by the continued defiance, Ecgfrith marched an Anglian force north in 685. Bridei and his Picts drew away, luring their foe ever onwards, deep into land that suited Pictish purposes. On boggy, treacherous ground at a place called Dunnichen, near Aviemore, Ecgfrith and his Anglians were rounded up and slaughtered.

Dunnichen – also called Dun Nechtain, or Nechtansmere in some of the books – may well be the battle commemorated on the nearby Aberlemno Stone, a Pictish monument made a hundred years later. It depicts a blood-bath in graphic detail, in much the same way that the Bayeux Tapestry remembers the Norman victory at Hastings in 1066. In one corner of the fight are bare-headed, long-haired Pictish warriors, on the other the Angles wearing distinctive metal helmets. By all accounts it was a one-sided encounter. The massed and disciplined ranks of Pictish spearmen drove their enemy into the cold, dark waters of a loch and butchered them there. The final relief, in the lower right-hand corner of the stone, shows a raven pecking at the dead face of a fallen prince of the Angles. Bridei had done much more than win a battle. By the power of his own will he had forced the Picts to unite under the leadership of one king. The new confederation had a new name as well – it was *Pictland*.

There are over 200 Pictish stones still standing in the modern landscape. By mapping their locations, it is possible to trace the extent of the kingdom. Following the defeat at Dunnichen the Angles were driven back down south – and in the years to come the Picts gained the upper hand with the rest of their neighbours as well. In the west, both the Gaels and the Britons were overwhelmed and, while each was able to retain some vestiges of its identity, both were forced to pay homage to the Pictish kings. By the middle of the eighth century, the confident young kingdom of Pictland was unquestionably the dominant presence in northern Britain.

But if they seemed invincible, it was just an illusion. As before with the Angles, the wealth and prominence of Pictland drew the attention of those with a hunger for the wealth of others. The new wave of aggressors was in a league apart, warriors with no time for Christian niceties – not for Adomnán's Law or anyone else's. Instead they worshipped the old gods of war, Odin and Thor.

The first flood of Vikings to land on British shores hailed from Norway. Large country though it is, comparatively little of it is suitable for farming. Geologists and geographers point to climate as an influence as well: during a time classified as the Medieval Warm Period, temperatures rose in much of northern Europe. Land that was suitable for farming, in a country like Norway, would have become more productive, possibly allowing for popu-lation growth. But the new people would simply have increased pressure on the available land and the need to look elsewhere would have intensified.

During the eighth century Norway, like the rest of Scandinavia, was also in the early stages of state formation. Warlords were on the rise; local kings were on the make. Men seeking to attract and maintain supporters would have needed weapons for fighting as well as gold and silver for paying wages. Those in the western parts of the country suffered most for want of land, and would-be kings there were under pressure to keep up with the activities and ambitions of rivals further east. All of this combined to force the most adven-turous, the most ambitious and the most ruthless to look across the sea in hope of finding a new path to wealth and power. So it was that towards the end of the eighth century, war bands of Norwegian Vikings took to their lethally efficient longboats and headed west in search of plunder.

For several years there has been a trend among some archaeologists and historians to portray the Vikings as a misunderstood people. Instead of bloodthirsty killers, think peaceful traders and farmers in search of new lands to colonise. They certainly turned coloniser in later centuries – and used plundered gold and silver to buy lands and estates outright – but the first contacts were anything but peaceable.

Their reputation also has been especially bad because of the kind of people they were targeting in those early years: monks and nuns. If you are pagan, you are going to attract criticism if you start attacking communities that are in the habit of writing things down – Christian communities, at that. It had not taken the pagan Vikings long to work out that churches and monasteries tended to be places where fine gold and silver, as well as other portable valuables, were likely to be kept. To make such places even more tempting, they were home not to warriors but to men and women armed with nothing more than faith and prayer.

The Anglo-Saxon Chronicle noted in the year AD 793: 'On 8 June the ravages of the heathen men miserably destroyed God's church on Lindisfarne with plunder and slaughter.' None was spared during such attacks and while the monks of the monastery on the Holy Island of Lindisfarne were the first recorded victims, their experience would be endured again and again by communities the length of the country. 'Everywhere Christ's peoples are the victims of massacre, burning and plunder,' wrote one monk seventy years later. 'The Vikings overrun all that lies before them and no one can withstand them.'

It seemed nowhere on the coastline was safe – and certainly not on the coastline of Scotland. The Vikings were not choosy and took what they wanted wherever their longships could reach. The monastery on Iona was looted for the first time in 795 but would suffer two more assaults of even greater violence. It was the constant threat posed by those Northmen that prompted the eventual abandonment of Iona and the removal of treasures, including The Book of Kells, to the monastery of that name in Ireland.

It was the Northern Isles of Scotland, however, that bore the brunt of the Vikings' unwanted attentions. In 1958 an archaeological excavation was searching for the remains of an early Christian church on St Ninian's Isle, in Shetland. The place had fallen into disrepair after the Reformation and the steady advance of sand dunes had long since swallowed any trace of it. A schoolboy, Douglas Coutts, was helping the archaeologists when he found a sandstone slab lightly incised with a cross. The slab had been broken and beneath it he found a collection of Pictish silver bowls, cups and jewellery, dating from before AD 800. The hoard has become known as the St Ninian's Isle Treasure. There were traces of a wooden box that had been used to contain the treasure, but the bowls were overturned and all the other items in a tangle around them. It seemed the box had been buried upside down – and in a hurry. All the evidence suggested the monks had quickly hidden their most precious belongings under the church floor, desperate to protect them from a Viking raid. That no one ever came back to retrieve the hoard is a sobering clue as to what befell the monks.

The Vikings who roamed Britain's shoreline were not only interested in gold and silver. They came in search of people as well. Captured men, women and children were shipped back to Scandinavia and then on to Constantinople, where they were traded for Middle Eastern gold and silver. It was a ninth-century international slave trade that swept thousands of natives of these islands halfway around the known world.

Over the next hundred years the Vikings did indeed turn colonisers, claiming and settling vast swathes of Northumbria, Ireland, the Hebrides and the area of the Gaels. Danish Vikings began to get in on the act as well, though they concentrated on England. The reach of the Vikings was astounding by any measure. Eventually they had control of territory in regions as diverse as Normandy – the land of the Northmen – France, Greenland, Sicily and parts of Russia. It is also beyond doubt that they were the first Europeans to reach North America, centuries before Columbus.

The north and east of Scotland was comprehensively invaded and settled: like a silent witness coiled within the cells of the living, the DNA of people living in Orkney today makes it plain the Vikings either slaughtered the Pictish men or forced them to leave the islands for ever. The vast majority of the men have Scandinavian DNA – grim evidence of slaughter or eviction. The women are mostly descended from the islands' original inhabitants, ultimately from the hunter-gatherers who settled Scotland after the retreat of the ice. It seems that while the Vikings got rid of the local men, they took the local Pictish women as wives. Some form of ethnic cleansing is also suggested by the fact that almost no Pictish place names survive on Orkney or Shetland. Everywhere the hills, bays, villages and towns bear names with Scandinavian roots.

At Brough of Birsay, on a tidal island just off the north-east tip of the West Mainland of Orkney, is stark evidence of the way in which one culture was completely consumed by another. Roundhouses of the style preferred by Picts for hundreds of years are abruptly overlain by the rectangular longhouses of the Vikings, cuckoos in the nest. In some of the Viking houses, Pictish artefacts were found, suggesting the new landowners had even kept the personal belongings of those they had dispossessed.

Every year on the last Tuesday in January the modern people of Shetland celebrate their Viking history with an all-night celebration they call *Up-Helly-Aa*. Squads of men dress in extravagant costumes – not all of them Viking – and parade through the streets of the Shetland capital, Lerwick. Every one of them bears a huge burning torch and at the climax, hundreds upon hundreds of torches are flung into a replica longship that is the focus of the night. The flames swiftly consume the vessel and the crowds remember how their forebears chose to burn their boats and stay on the islands, rather than return home to Norway.

It is no ancient festival. It was invented at the end of the nineteenth century as a way of bringing a sense of purpose and excitement to a time of year that is, otherwise, staggeringly bleak. It is a thrilling spectacle nonetheless. But if you forget the air of celebration and pageantry and imagine instead the horror of waking up one morning to find a howling horde of murderous warriors leaping from their longships onto the beach below your home, then it is easy to understand how such a sight would have been a glimpse of how the world ends. It would have meant the end of everything you understood and everything you had ever held dear – unless of course somebody somewhere could find a way to stop it.

The Vikings had made their bloody, pagan entrance into a land of four peoples, four kingdoms – Picts, Gaels, Britons and Angles. Christianity was a common denominator, uniting them in theory but not in practice. Dominance by any one of them over the other three depended, at any given moment, upon the ambition, ability and military might of individual kings or warlords.

Trying to understand who was who in eighth- and ninth-century Scotland (remembering all the time that there was no such place as Scotland yet) is like trying to read Tolkien's *Silmarillion*. For much of the time the history of Dark Age, or if you prefer, Early Medieval, Scotland is a dizzying list of unfamiliar, unpronounceable names that seem more likely to have come from Middle Earth than anywhere in the real world. One shadowy figure – sometimes a Gael, sometimes a Pict, sometimes a Briton or an Angle and as often as not a half-breed product of a marriage alliance between any two of the above – follows another through brief ascendancy to power, unlamented death and eternity in an unmarked grave.

Look at this passage from Alex Woolf's masterly but undoubtedly challenging account of it all in *From Pictland to Alba*:

> In Pictavia, the deaths of the great Onuist son of Wrguist and his brother Bridei and their immediate successor Ciniod son of Wrad and his brother Elphin, were followed by a period of instability in which four kings (three apparently from Onuist's family) ruled in quick succession. From 789, however, Pictavia gained another strong ruler, Constantin son of Wrguist, who was to reign until his death in 820. The instability in Pictavia seems to have allowed the Dal Riata to reassert its independence, first under Aed Find son of Eochaid and his brother Fergus and subsequently under Donncoirce. Donncoirce seems to have been succeeded by Conall son of Tadg who had apparently challenged Constantin's succession to the kingship of Fortriu in 789.

I read all this and expect Orcs to put in an appearance at any moment. This is a difficult and confusing period – all of the details are gleaned painstakingly from what few written sources actually survive from anything like the time in question. The simplest way of looking at it all seems to me a matter of accepting that by the time the Vikings were making their presence felt in the 790s, there was still everything to play for in the big game of fighting for control of the territory and the peoples that would one day come together as one nation.

After Bridei's success at Dunnichen he was followed onto the throne of Pictland by several kings who managed to hold the fledgeling state together. For part of the middle of the eighth century the Gaels of Dunadd freed themselves from Pictish overlordship and emerged once again as an independent presence. One of the Gaelic kings, a man named Cenel mac Gabhrain, may even have had control of Pictland as well. The balance swung back then, in the direction of the Picts, with the eastern kingdom having some sort of domination over its western rival, at least for a while.

In 839 something dreadful befell the ruling Pictish dynasty. An entry in one medieval Irish chronicle – The Annals of Ulster – records that 'The heathens [Vikings] won a battle over the men of Fortriu [Pictland] and Wen son of Onuist and Bran son of Onuist and Aed son of Boanta and others almost innumerable fell there.' These last six words, committed to parchment by an unknown Irish scribe, speak volumes. In AD 839 the dominant native aristocracy – a ruling group with, no doubt, Pictish, Gaelic, British and Angle blood flowing in its veins after centuries of war and marriage – was brought to a final, climactic battle by a massed Viking army. The result was catastrophic defeat for the Picts and that native blood – of kings and kings-in-waiting – stained red the grass of some unknown and unmarked field. The scene of the battle is lost to history but it created a power vacuum at the very top. Into that newly empty space strode a man whose name is familiar to every Scot: Kenneth MacAlpin.

Often styled Kenneth I, he is one of the great heroes of Scottish history. Whatever else, he was certainly a warlord but he appears almost from nowhere: maybe a Gael, maybe a Pict, maybe a bit of both. According to the version of events taught to countless generations of Scottish school-children he steps into the apocalyptic aftermath of that forgotten battle and unites the survivors. Now fighting together as one, Picts and Gaels defy the Vikings and drive them off. For his efforts – and his success in uniting the peoples – Kenneth MacAlpin is crowned the first King of Scotland.

If only history was that simple. The idea that Kenneth MacAlpin was ever King of *Scotland* is a myth. It has persisted for centuries and is certainly the story I learned at school. But the simple, if inconvenient, fact is that Kenneth MacAlpin and his immediate successors were recorded by the scribes as Kings of *Pictland*. The Vikings had retreated to the north and west, and to the islands, but were still active and possessed of their own distinct culture and identity. The same was true of the Gaels and the Britons, and of the Angles to the south. It is not until forty years after Kenneth died that we get the first mention of kings of Scotland.

The birth of that new kingdom lies not among the achievements of Kenneth of Pictland, but is to be found instead in the pages of a book now held in the collections of the Bibliothèque Nationale in Paris. The so-called 'Poppleton Manuscript' was put together around the middle of the fourteenth century. It was commissioned by a monk called Robert of Poppleton, hence the name, during his time at a monastery in York. It is a collection of writings of various ages and on various subjects and nothing new was composed for it. Instead it is a compilation, its authors tasked with copying the much older work of others onto the pages of a single volume. It sits in Paris because it was bought by a French courtier at the end of the seventeenth century along with other, similarly obscure historical papers. It is as though Scotland's birth certificate ended up at a car boot sale and was spotted by a French passer-by with an eye for a bargain.

One of the documents within the book is called the 'Chronicle of the Kings of Alba'. It is not known exactly when the original was composed but it is a list of twelve kings of the House of Alpin, of Kenneth Mac*Alpin*, during the period from the ninth to the eleventh centuries. It is a witheringly complicated document. By the time Poppleton's scribe set to work, the original had been copied and added to for centuries, and by several unknown hands. But it is of crucial importance because it covers a moment of transition – the ten years or so between AD 878 and 889 when all references to Pictland disappear and the kingdom we might recognise as a newborn Scotland emerges for the very first time.

Hanging from a handful of the names on the list is the story of Scotland's lost decade. The first of the characters with a key role in those crucial, mysterious years is Aed (pronounced ay-ETH), youngest son of Kenneth Mac-Alpin. He had the misfortune to ascend the throne of a kingdom in crisis, just as newly resurgent Viking forces returned to plunder Pictland once more. For two years they helped themselves to cattle, slaves and tribute. Pictland was conquered anew and the Northmen took their leave of the place only when there was nothing left to take. Aed's kingdom was a ruin and, as far as his people were concerned, he had done nothing to stop the devastation.

Of Aed's time upon the throne, just a year, the Chronicle of the Kings of Alba says the shortness of his reign 'bequeathed nothing memorable to history' – a damning indictment indeed. The Annals of Ulster add that he was killed in AD 878 'by his own companions'. The belief that the King of the Picts was put to death by his own followers hints at desperate times and desperate men. The scene of the murder is identified as *civitas Nrurim*. It seems likely Nrurim was in Perthshire, but there is no agreement on quite where. The word *civitas*, though, means it was the site of an important church. So it was on or close to hallowed ground that Aed met his fate, done to death by men he thought were his friends.

According to the twelfth-century king-lists it was one Giric, son of Dungal, who committed the crime. Giric also appears in the Chronicle – as a King of Pictland. Giric was no Pict; he was a Gael. The kingdom of the Gaels had suffered too at the hands of the Vikings and many refugees, Giric among them, had fled east into Pictland in the hope of making a better life for themselves amongst the erstwhile enemies of their blood. Giric was no Pict and he was no aristocrat either. Rather he was some kind of nobleman – and a man on the make, who used guile and wit to win a place at the side of the king. He had already fled one homeland to escape the thralldom of the Vikings and when Aed proved himself impotent in the face of them, the Gael took matters into his own hands.

After murdering Aed, Giric instigated a regime change. He rid the court of his Pictish rivals and replaced them with his own men. He took control of the Pictish Church as well, appointing a Gaelic bishop to reform it. It had been nothing less than a palace coup. Giric was remaking the kingdom of the Picts in his own image – as a land fit for Gaels. To complete his takeover – and to make his position secure at the top – he seized Pictish estates and handed them over to his Gaelic followers.

Despite all his efforts, Giric could not sleep easy in his bed. Aed was dead but his young son Constantine was not. Neither was Constantine's cousin Donald, slightly older and a grandson of Kenneth MacAlpin. In the eyes of the Picts – who had seen their king murdered, their homes handed over to Gaelic interlopers, their Church corrupted by a foreign bishop – those boys were the rightful heirs to the Pictish throne. While they breathed, Giric the usurper would never be secure.

Before Giric had a chance to snuff out the threat, men loyal to the House of Alpin spirited the youngsters away to Ireland. It might have seemed a strange move – to send two Pictish princes to a Gaelic country – but there was a warm welcome awaiting them. At the fortress of Ailech, in the north of the country, Constantine and Donald were taken in by their aunt, Mael Muire, daughter of Kenneth MacAlpin and wife of the most powerful king in the land, Aed of Tara. Over and above the considerations of politics, the Irish exile of the princes was about family – and yet it would also have had profound effects on the pair. Constantine was just a little boy when he arrived at Ailech, perhaps no more than five years old and wholly unmade, unshaped. Donald was older, in his early teens, but still young enough to be susceptible to the ways of the new world in which he would spend his adolescence.

Picts or not, family or not, it was a Gaelic court they found themselves within and they grew up steeped in a culture that would otherwise have been foreign to them. There was also the matter of faith and Donald and Constantine would have at least become acquainted with the Gaelic style of worship. It seems ironic – they were saved from a Gaelic takeover of their homeland and yet their salvation was as transforming as anything happening in the land of their fathers.

After a decade or more in Ireland, the exiles were ready to return home and claim their birthright. With righteous revenge in their hearts they sailed back across the Irish Sea and raised a rebellion against the usurper. Giric must have known the day would come – and it seems likely he chose the mighty fortress of Dundurn in Perthshire for the showdown. Behind its massive walls Giric might have felt he would prevail but in the end age and guile were not enough to counter the youth and innocence of those he had wronged.

One of the chronicles has it simply that 'in Dundurn the upright man was taken by death'. The wistful, almost elegiac tone suggests there were those who lamented the fall of Giric; but archaeological remains at Dundurn paint a darker picture. Burned timbers and arrowheads were recovered during excavations and these at least bear witness to some kind of violence. Given the ire of Donald, Constantine and those loyal to the House of Alpin, it is tempting to imagine Giric met his death in that moment, among those flames.

In any event, Donald reclaimed the Pictish throne. If his supporters had expected Giric's Gaelic reforms to be swept away, replaced by the old ways, they were disappointed. Donald and Constantine had left as Pictish children, but they returned as Gaelic princes. The same transformation Giric had visited upon the land had been wrought upon the heirs of Mac-Alpin as well. They viewed their homeland now with different eyes. Far from being rolled back, under King Donald the Gaelic takeover continued and was made permanent. When he died in AD 900 chroniclers in Ireland recorded his passing, not as the death of a King of Pictland, but of *Alba*.

Here then is the advent of something quite new. Alba – the name Gaelic-speakers had always given to their territory – now meant the kingdom born of the union of Picts and Gaels into a single entity. The Chronicle of the Kings of Alba contains the earliest known use of the word *Albaniam* – the Latin translation of Alba. This is the moment when a single kingdom was created: where before there had been Picts and Gaels, two separate peoples, kingdoms, cultures and identities, now there was one – the people of Alba. The Gaels, however, had long borne the nickname *Scoti*, 'marauders from the sea', making Alba the land of the Scots. This single page of the Chronicle of the Kings of Alba, bound in a book that sits at the heart of the capital of France, may be regarded as the birth certificate of Scotland.

Donald was followed onto the throne by his cousin Constantine and by then Scotland was a Gaelic kingdom. They say the world ends not with a bang but with a whimper, and so it had been for the world of the Picts. But while their separate identity went into history, there was no apocalypse, no genocide. Instead, they slowly put aside their culture in the manner of clothes that were out of fashion, that no longer quite fitted. Those who had been Picts sloughed off their old identity and put on instead the garb of the re-branded Gaels: the Scots. In a masterstroke of genius, the Gaels called the new world Alba – a name that marked a fresh start for them as well. But it was a Gaelic rose by another name.

Over the next few generations the Pictish way of life, their *otherness*, disappeared. Everything about them – the way they worshipped God, the way they carved their stones and shaped their finery – fell from favour. Crucially the very language they had spoken – the way they understood and expressed themselves – was replaced with Gaelic. Gaelic had become the language of power. But these were not sad days – not for the Gaels or for the Picts. Fashions change and in being part of the new, by turning away from the past, the Picts secured for themselves a place in the present and the future.

In AD 906 Constantine travelled to Scone for a ceremony to celebrate his accession. Like the creation of Alba it was about the making of something quite new – but something that had ancient ingredients mixed within it. This is the first mention of Scone in the historical record and so it too appears to have been part of the new, established as a political centre not long before AD 906. From now on it was to be the place where kings of Scotland were made.

Seated upon a block of old red sandstone that had been quarried nearby, Constantine received the blessing of a Gaelic bishop called Cellach. It may be that Bishop Cellach had been a supporter of Giric and that the ceremony was in part a public demonstration of continuing spiritual backing for the new king. Cellach and Constantine also declared together that the rights of the Church would be upheld. Perhaps the ceremony had elements too of a coronation, with the king sat upon and wedded to the bedrock in a self-conscious nod to the footprint ceremony of Dunadd.

The stone used as a seat that day was the same we know now as the Stone of Destiny. For centuries after and up to the present day it has been used in the inauguration of kings and queens. It is on display now in Edinburgh Castle – nothing more or less than a block of the land itself. It is the legacy of the rivers, seas and deserts that worked unwittingly and long ago to make this place. It is a memory of the sand and water of other places and other times. But for all of the time of man it has been rock. The chip of it that is the Stone of Destiny has, like the rest of Scotland, been fought over time and again. It has become the stuff of myth, fantasy and romance – the very symbol of a nation. It is the rock and the rock has always been at the root of it all.

Call it coincidence, call it fate, but around the time Alba came together as a power in the north, another unified entity had crystallised in the south of the British Isles. Constantine was King of Scotland, but a king called Aethelstan ruled in the territory of the Angles, *Angleland*, England. Aethelstan had advanced into Northumbria, driving off the Vikings, and now dominated a huge swathe of what would be known in time as England.

Enough was not enough, however, for the King of the Angles. An admirer of the Romans, he considered himself their natural successor. As such, nothing less than conquest of the whole of Britain would satisfy his hunger. Like the commander of the imperial legions centuries before him, Aethelstan pushed northwards, driving Constantine and his warriors back. Finally the King of Scots was brought to bay behind the walls and natural defences of mighty Dunottar, an awesome promontory fort near Aberdeen. Only a narrow, steep-sided sliver of land connected it to the main. Sheer cliffs into the sea made any other approach impossible. Constantine was secure as long he stayed on the rock, but his kingdom had effectively been reduced to the few acres within the fortress.

Like Calgacus he faced a stark choice between surrender and final pitched battle with a superior army. But Constantine was a man of imagination, who refused to have his hand forced by circumstances that most would have seen as overwhelming. Instead of fighting or giving up his kingdom he struck a deal. In return for acknowledging Aethelstan as his overlord, Constantine retained his status as king. His deal-making worked in the short term. The Angles withdrew and Constantine was left alone. But for the young men gathered around him in the febrile atmosphere of state-building, he was seen to have sold out. The future was non-existent for kings who bowed to enemies – Aed's fate at the hands of Giric had made that clear – and Constantine understood that to survive he had to turn the tables on the overlord. What he did next would have been unthinkable even in the recent past: he made peace with the Vikings. Just as the tribes had come together to face Rome – a foe that threatened all of them, enabling differences to be set aside – so a rainbow alliance of disparate peoples united to defy Angle-land.

In AD 937 the very fate of Britain was at stake and all of her peoples took up the cudgels to settle the matter. Out of the south came Aethelstan at the head of an army tens of thousands strong. From the north came another huge force: Constantine and the Scots of Alba, Britons from Strathclyde, the King of the Vikings from across the Irish Sea. After weeks on the move, the huge armies finally met near the mouth of the Mersey River, at a place called Brunnanburh.

For lifetimes to come it was remembered simply as the 'Great Battle'. It was the ultimate Dark Age bloodbath and defined the shape of Britain into the modern era. An Anglo-Saxon account of the fighting describes how: 'They clove the shield wall, hewed the war lindens with hammered blades; the foe gave way; the folk of the Scots and the ship fleet fell death doomed. The field was slippery with the blood of warriors ... The West Saxons in companies hewed the fugitives from behind cruelly with swords mill-sharpened.' All day they fought, face to face in a butcher's yard the like of which none had seen before. Only the coming of night brought an end to it and by then the fields and beaches were strewn with the dead and dying. Animals moved among the cooling remains, wolves and carrion crows. It was an unlikely fellowship of death: Scots, Angles, Vikings, Saxons, Britons, men of Wales, Gaels from Ireland, Northumbrians, Icelanders.

From the greatest to the lowliest of men, anyone with a mind to lay claim on the future of Britain had come to Brunnanburh. Constantine's eldest boy was among the slain. Like thousands of others he lay dead upon a sward and a day forgotten now by all save the poets and the chroniclers. The Angles held the field. On paper it was their victory. But in truth, both sides had been so grievously hurt there was no triumph to be celebrated. Aethelstan, heir to Roman ambitions, had been forced to accept there would be no conquest of Scotland. Any attempt to subdue the men of the north would cost more than he had to give. Constantine and the survivors of the northern alliance dragged themselves away from that awful place, back to their homelands.

Everyone has heard of Hastings, of 1066. But who has heard of Brunnanburh? Even the site of the battle has been lost. The best bets place it on the Mersey but there is no consensus. Others place the fighting in the Midlands or the east of England; others say it was somewhere in south-west Scotland. And yet this more than anything that happened in Kent a century and more later was what determined the shape of the Britain we live in today. In 1066 the Normans took over an England that was already made. In 937 the fighting was a battle for *Britain*, when everything was still to play for.

Brunnanburh was a showdown between two very different ethnic identities: a Norse/Celtic alliance versus an Anglo-Saxon one. It aimed to settle, once and for all, whether Britain would be controlled by a single 'imperial' power, or remain several, separate independent kingdoms. Brunnanburh represented a split in perceptions which, like it or not, is still with us today.

Kenneth MacAlpin has gone down in history as the first King of Scotland. He certainly founded the Scottish royal line but he lived and died as an opportunistic *Pictish* warlord. The job of securing the kingdom of the Scots was the work of Kenneth's grandson Constantine. He ruled for forty-three years – an extraordinarily long time for a tenth-century monarch – and it was his ability to stay on top, to stay alive, that ensured Scotland's survival as an independent entity. Scotland is a testament to Constantine's personal courage, political astuteness and staying-power. He was capable of the unexpected right to the end. After those forty-three years of rule, Constantine relinquished his kingship. Just six years after the greatest battle of his life, he stepped down from the throne, of his own accord, and walked away. There was so much for him to think about; perhaps he wanted the time and the peace to make sense of it all ... from exile to Ireland as a little boy, the return with Donald to overthrow Giric, accession to the kingship of his homeland, brief subservience to Aethelstan and the climactic horror of Brunnanburh. By the end he had saved his kingdom and lost his own son.

He took his memories and his sadness to St Andrews. Years of Viking violence and the fusion of the land of the Picts and the Gaels into Alba had shifted power – both secular and spiritual – from west to east. Iona was still a working monastery, kings were still buried there, but its day at the centre of things had passed. Now, fittingly, the Church of the risen son favoured the coast of the rising sun. The two bright lights at the heart of the new kingdom's religious life were Dunkeld and St Andrews. Columba had been the predominant Scottish saint but more recently the bones of a new man, an apostle of Christ himself, no less, had arrived in the land. The primacy of St Andrews was underlined during Constantine's reign and it was at the religious heart of his kingdom that he lived out the rest of his days, in a cave near the sea.

In 1140 an English historian, the Archdeacon of Huntingdon, felt able to consign the Picts, the last of the free, to history. He wrote: 'We see that the Picts have now been wiped out and their language also is totally destroyed so that they seem to be a fable we find mentioned in old writings.' But while Constantine had withdrawn from the world, content to disappear into the shadows, the Picts had remained in the midst of it all. They had given up the designs that gave them their name, even surrendered the name itself – but in so doing they had fused together with another people to make the world anew. Two peoples, Picts and Gaels, had been thrust into the fires of adversity and had emerged forged as one.

Now the story of the kingdom of Alba – of Scotland – had begun.

***

After Constantine, the kings of Scots shuffled back into the mist of ano-
nymity and obscurity, characters familiar only to specialists. For most of
us, the names of the first few of his successors conjure nothing to mind –
first his nephew Malcolm ... then his youngest son Indulph ... then Dubh
... then Cuilen ... even the spellings of the names are unreliable, changing
from book to book.

To the vast majority of people living in Scotland (and they would hardly
have recognised the name) the rise and fall of those kings mattered not a jot.
The mass of them had depended on subsistence farming from the beginning
and depended upon it still. From day to day, life was about making sure there
was something to eat and a roof overhead – regardless of which warlord
might be about to put his foot in a hole in a rock and be named ruler.

During the 800s, the mouldboard plough made a greater impact on
people's lives than any machinations of the ruling classes. This new piece
of farming equipment was a revelation, enabling much quicker preparation
of ground for sowing. It also turned over more of the sod, creating deep
furrows that encouraged better drainage in wet areas. In this way, soils that
had previously been too heavy to work were now opened up to agriculture.

The people of the tenth century were Scots, but if they were living in a
new world it must have seemed to most that the old world's cares were all
around. Serfs worked the land and were owned by its owners, like the beasts
that grazed upon it. This was an unhappy hereditary status, passed by
parents to children, but at least it carried with it some securities and
certainties. They would always have work; always have food. The most
vulnerable members of society were those who, though legally free, owned
no land. In times when the population was small the strength of their backs
might be in demand and relatively costly to those that needed it to buy it.
During times of population increase, however, when labour was cheap and
plentiful, landless farmers and their families suffered terribly.

Long before the 'feudalism' of the Normans defined the relationship
between people and land, and between landed and landless, the people of
Scotland owed rent of one form or another. Those towards the lower end of
the social scale paid for access to the land they lived upon with the sweat of
their brows. In addition to working their own plots, they owed some of their
labour to whoever controlled the land. This would mostly be in the form of

working a rich man's fields for him – but might mean military service from time to time.

When a landowner was ordered to provide a fighting force for the man above him in the hierarchy, he would tell those who had farms on his land to put down their tools and take up arms on his behalf instead. Further up, rich men owed to richer men the duty of raising whole armies. At the top sat the king – sometimes cajoling and manipulating, sometimes bullying and murdering as he battled to hold onto the throne. He needed the support of at least some of them for all of the time, and would seek their counsel whenever it seemed politically astute to do so. This was how things were done long before the arrival of Norman ways . . . feuing and parliaments and Domesday Books.

On it goes, the infancy of Scotland, until 1034 and a name and a story that does ring bells. In that year died Malcolm II, last of the heirs of Kenneth MacAlpin. He was followed onto the throne by his grandson Duncan – the same described by Shakespeare as much revered and gentle. In fact he was a young man who had been promoted well beyond his level of competence. He blundered into several ill-judged military campaigns including a clumsy raid on the north of England that culminated in a disastrous attack on Durham in 1039. In the summer of the following year he sallied north to try and put the fear of death into a man whose name meant 'son of life'. Macbeth was a mormaer – an earl, of Moray. He had the blood of kings of Dal Riata in his veins and his wife Gruoch was also of royal stock.

When Malcolm II died, Macbeth and Gruoch had reason to expect they might rule in his stead. That Malcolm had nominated his grandson for the job – an unusual act in itself – upset Macbeth. It was for this reason that Duncan invaded the north with a view to cowing his rival. The royal territory of Scotland was much smaller than what we understand by the word today – and the further he travelled from his centre, so his power weakened or evaporated altogether.

Duncan I died in battle with Macbeth, somewhere near modern Elgin, and the victor replaced him on the throne. Macbeth then drove both of Duncan's sons, Malcolm and Donald, into exile and reigned successfully for seventeen years; as rightful a king as many before or after. Only the return of Malcolm the son ended it all for the son of life. Macbeth was defeated in battle and killed in 1057.

Malcolm III is better known to history as Malcolm 'the Great Chief', Malcolm Ceann Mor. He was ruthless, a quality befitting a man who would found a dynasty. Macbeth was dead but his stepson, Gruoch's son Lulach, might find enough support to mount a counter-attack. Malcolm hunted him down and killed him too. But just as it was Kenneth MacAlpin's heirs who truly created and secured Scotland, so it seems to historians that it was Malcolm's heirs who have the stronger claim on the moniker of Great Chief. In any case, for the next 230 years the Ceann Mor – or Canmore – dynasty would rule Scotland.

Malcolm III took Margaret as his second wife. She was a relative of Edward the Confessor, the English king who died fighting King Canute of the Danes in 1016. More importantly, she was sister to Prince Edgar, who had been beaten to the throne of England in 1066 by Harold. After William the Conqueror defeated and killed Harold at Hastings the same year, replacing him on the throne, he was initially friendly towards Edgar and his family. But when Edgar became the focus of a rebellion against the new Norman dynasty in 1068, William's mood turned ugly. Edgar tried to flee to the Continent with his mother and his two sisters, Christina and Margaret. According to legend, God himself intervened and blew their ship north to Scotland instead, where it went ashore in Fife. King Malcolm came to meet the royal arrivals and fell instantly in love with Margaret, marrying her practically on the spot. Now Edgar had an ally in the King of Scots – a possible support for any future rebellion against the usurping William and his Normans – while Malcolm had married into the old royal house of England. He was thumbing his nose at the new, southern dynasty in spectacular style.

Malcolm and Margaret together became a legend – a legend that is in truth much more about her than him. Margaret's biographer has handed down to history an image of a devoutly religious woman. It seems she dedicated her life in Scotland to her Christian faith – faithful that is to the Roman tradition rather than the Celtic. It was a parting of the spiritual ways that did not endear her to all. King Malcolm never learned to read and yet his devotion to his wife was such that he would get down on his knees to plant soft kisses on the bindings of her copies of the Holy Scriptures.

Margaret – St Margaret as she became in time – also saw to the building of a little Romanesque church at Dunfermline. At her request, Benedectine monks were sent from Canterbury to establish a priory there. She encouraged renewed interest in the cult of St Andrew and had ferries installed on both sides of the River Forth to make it easier for pilgrims to reach his church on the Fife coast. The towns of North and South Queensferry are named in her honour. But while Margaret worked hard to affect the spiritual life of Scotland, her most enduring contributions to the destiny of the land in which she lived were the future kings she bore Malcolm – their sons Edgar, Alexander and David.

While Margaret was the epitome of piety, her husband had more earthly ambitions. Married into the old ruling house of England as he was, he used the splicing of the bloodlines as an excuse for aggression against King William. He invaded Northumbria in 1070 but succeeded only in bringing trouble upon his own house. William retaliated two years later, invading Scotland and winning a submission from the King of Scots that would carry down through the centuries. Called the 'Abernethy Submission' after the town on the Tay in which it was signed, it recorded that Malcolm accepted his place as 'the English king's man'. He was also forced to hand over his eldest son Duncan, by his first wife Ingbjorg of Orkney, as a demonstration of his obedience. Forever after, English monarchs would look back to the Abernethy Submission as a basis for their claims of overlordship.

Whether he ever felt subject to the English king, it did not stop Malcolm making war against him. Defiant to the end, he died in November 1093, ambushed and killed during another raid on Northumbria. His queen could not bear the loss. She took to her bed and asked that she be brought her most cherished earthly possession, the 'Black Rood'. This was a cross of gold that held within it a fragment of the True Cross upon which Jesus Christ had died; but not even the presence of such an icon was enough to mend her broken heart. She died in the same month as her husband and her body was taken and laid to rest at her little church in Dunfermline.

Malcolm was succeeded first by his younger brother Donald, who had lived in exile in the Western Isles since the murder of their father by Macbeth. This was seen by many of the mormaers and others as an opportunity to rid the country of the English ways they felt Queen Margaret had foisted upon them. Her children sought sanctuary at the English court and it was there that Edgar, Alexander and David grew up.

William II, his eyes on the northern prize coveted by his father, sent Malcolm's son Duncan to seize the throne. He had been a hostage of England since the Abernethy Submission and as far as the English were concerned he was a tame Scot. True to English designs, he duly ousted his uncle in 1094, but was murdered within the year and Donald III resumed his reign. Not be thwarted, William next dispatched Malcolm and Margaret's son Edgar, another exiled Scot well schooled in Norman ways. This time Donald met his match. Defeated in battle, he was hunted down and, in the ancient punishment of fallen kings, blinded. He was made a prisoner then and kept in a dungeon until his death.

With Edgar on the throne the Canmore grip upon the kingship was secure. Pious, peaceable Edgar died without an heir. The royal will left the title of King of Scots, together with the northern half of the territory, to Alexander, elder of the remaining brothers. Lothian and southern Scotland, however, were made over to the younger brother, David.

Alexander and David were two more Scots boys who had grown to manhood under the English king's protection. William the Conqueror's youngest son, Henry I, was on the throne now and married to Edith, a sister of the Canmore brothers. When Alexander married Henry's daughter Sybil, the Scots and English royal houses could hardly have been more closely entwined. One King of Scots after another was growing up a vassal of the English king. It is easy to see how the English monarchs developed their conviction that Scotland herself should be under their thrall.

Alexander, a stranger in his own homeland, could hardly help feeling the need to draw around himself people and institutions he had become familiar with earlier in life. Norman French knights had been made welcome in Scotland since at least the time of Macbeth and now Alexander did the same. He had grown up in England, and had learned too the wider, western European ways of doing things. He kept Scotland's doors open to Norman knights, and encouraged Augustinian canons to set up home in Scone and on the island of Inchcolm in the River Forth, at Dunkeld and at St Andrews.

There was no Norman 'conquest' of Scotland, as there had been of England. Instead the kings of Scots were sensitive to the ways of the wider world – keen, where it suited them, to become what they had once beheld. 'Scotland', after all, had emerged from the melding of Pictish and Gaelic cultures. Now the fledgeling kingdom was absorbing even more. As a fire draws oxygen towards itself, so Scotland sucked in the ideas of others.

Like his elder brother before him, Alexander died without an heir. David was in his forties by the time he ascended the throne in 1124 and, with vast estates and lands across England, already the grandest nobleman in the south. With David I on the throne, one of their own, England could have been forgiven for thinking there was nothing to fear now from the north. Like Alexander, he wanted familiar faces around him and so invited several knightly families to join him in the north. So it was that during David's reign there arrived in Scotland some of the names that would subsequently resonate through the place. To the Bruce family, who were probably from Normandy originally, he gave the territory of Annandale in the south-west; to the Fitzalans, who hailed from Brittany, he gave lands in the area of modern Renfrewshire (for the first of these, Walter Fitzalan, David created the hereditary title of High Steward of Scotland and in time his descendants became the Stewarts). It was at David's invitation that the Balliol family, originally from Picardy, made a home for themselves in the west of Scotland. Although these families were of French descent, they had long been part of English society. Among other grand titles, David was Earl of Huntingdon, a fantastically valuable territory, and as such commanded the attention, even the affection, of many of England's elite. Also arriving in numbers to take up David's offer were Douglases, Giffards, Lindsays, Morvilles, Murrays, Oliphants and Ridels. These were French-speaking nobles whose language, manners and ways the Scottish elite would seek to ape. The peasants who travelled north with the Norman families spoke another tongue – Scots – probably the purest form of the Anglo-Saxon language. It was by this means, the arrival in Scotland of Anglo-Saxon speakers in the train of a transplanted, French-speaking nobility, that Scots was established in southern Scotland at least.

The new King of Scots, friend of so many southern families, was also keen to promote commercial enterprise by granting royal charters to burghs, from which he could collect revenue. Berwick-upon-Tweed and Roxburgh were the first of them, but there would be many more. Indeed many of Scotland's towns and cities date their origins to the reign of David I. It was also under David's rule that Scotland produced her first coinage, a practice made considerably easier after he took control of the silver mines of the north Pennines. Once people had money, quite literally, in their pockets then the whole business of trade and commerce was changed for ever. Cash flowed in and out of the burghs as goods were bought and sold, rents collected. By the last decades of the twelfth century, even the humblest members of Scottish society were handling money.

There was a pious side to the king as well. The four great abbeys of the Scottish Borders – Kelso, Melrose, Jedburgh and Dryburgh – were all David's work. And a legend has it that while hunting near Drumselch church near Edinburgh, David was unhorsed by a white stag. As he lay on the ground, with the beast poised to gore him, he beheld his mother's 'Black Rood' suspended between its antlers. Rather than kill him the stag suddenly withdrew back into the forest. David's vision had convinced him to found an abbey on the site and Holyrood was the result. In addition he founded St Mary of Cambuskenneth beside the Forth, Newbattle on the

River Esk and upgraded his mother Margaret's Benedectine priory at Dunfermline to abbey status. Godly works were much on his mind.

But so too were the ambitions of his predecessors and when the death of Henry I of England plunged his southern neighbour into near civil war, David saw his opportunity to make inroads on Northumberland. With the English distracted by their internal travails, David marched south in the summer of 1138 with an impressive force. The chroniclers recorded how the Scots plundered and burned the northern English settlements and churches they found in their path.

On 22 August they met the English army, much smaller than their own, outside Northallerton. What followed, the Battle of the Standard, was a military disaster for the Scots. At the Scottish centre were the so-called Gallgaels from Galloway, relics of an older world but lively and out for blood. Without waiting for commands, this lightly armed force charged full-tilt into the shade of countless English arrows. They fell like mown hay, rose as best they could and fell again. David's treasured son Henry led a body of horse into the howling thick of it all and was lucky to escape with his life. Seeing that it was not to be his day, David ordered the withdrawal and the rump of the Scots army retreated.

Despite the reverse, David proved a lucky man. Torn by their internecine squabbles, the English were in no position to follow up their advantage. Those Scots that had survived the fighting made it all the way home – and David even managed to secure territorial advances from the peace. Northumberland was handed over to Prince Henry, the territory of Cumberland to the king himself. Where before Scotland's border had taken its line from the River Tweed, now it was closer to the River Tees. It was not to last. Henry of Anjou ascended to the throne in 1154 as Henry II, bringing to an end nearly two decades of uncertainty in England, and promptly rode roughshod over any deals that had been struck with his northern neighbour before his time.

By then, David had already been in his grave for a year, his son Henry for two. In accordance with David's wishes, the throne had passed to his grandson Malcolm IV, known to history as Malcolm 'the Maiden'. In spite of the connotations of his soubriquet, Malcolm was courageous and determined – one chronicler noted that the young king 'terrorised the wicked and insolent by his royal authority and sternness' – but Henry II was too much for him to cope with. Summoned to Chester in 1157, he was made formally to accept the loss of Northumberland, Westmorland and Cumberland.

Malcolm died aged twenty-four in 1165 without children and was succeeded by his twenty-two-year-old brother William IV, known as William 'the Lion' – a man cut from different cloth. A ginger-headed bear of a man, William 'the Lion' would prove to be Scotland's longest-reigning monarch. Throughout his forty-nine years on the throne, he harboured the age-old Scottish obsession with adding Northumberland to his kingdom, an obsession that brought only grief. First he pestered Henry II for rights to the land, to the point where the mere mention of William's name would send the English king into a rage. Next he went to war for it, only to be captured at Alnwick in 1174 and taken before Henry to answer for his crimes. He was only given back his freedom, five months later, after signing the Treaty of Falaise in which he accepted that he must, forever after, pay homage to the English king, 'for the kingdom of Scotland and his other lands in England'. The castles of Berwick-upon-Tweed, Edinburgh and Roxburgh were all turned over to English garrisons. Falaise was an unprecedented surrender of Scottish independence.

For the remaining fifteen years of his life and reign Henry held his vassal to the terms, underlining at every opportunity the bald truth that he was Scotland's overlord. Only after Henry died and his son and heir Richard I needed funds to join the Third Crusade against Islam in Palestine did William finally manage to overturn the Treaty of Falaise. In return for the huge sum of 10,000 merks, Richard accepted a new agreement, known as the Quitclaim of Canterbury, in 1189, which effectively tore up the earlier, humiliating document.

Undeterred by bitter experience, William immediately began repeating his demands for ownership of Northumberland. When Richard was followed onto the throne by his brother John, William contemplated war once more to settle the matter of the north of England. In the end, having lost his nerve as he stood on the brink of actual fighting, he signed the Treaty of Norham of 1209. More humiliation: among other concessions, William had to pay John 15,000 merks' worth of compensation; surrender for ever any claim on the northern territories and hand over two of his daughters, Margaret and Isabel. He expected one or other to become John's daughter-in-law, but in the end both were married off to mere nobles.

William died aged seventy-one in 1214. His lifelong bid to extend the southern boundary of his kingdom had ended in outright failure. He never saw either of his daughters again. He was buried close to the high altar of Abroath Abbey, which he had founded in 1178, and replaced on the throne by his son, Alexander.

CHAPTER THREE

THE HAMMERS OF
THE SCOTS

'They realized that to be in power you didn't need guns, or money or even numbers, you just needed the will to do what the other guy wouldn't.'

Verbal Kint, *The Usual Suspects*

One king's name after another: an endless procession that blurs before the eyes. It is easy to forget they were ever real people, let alone that the most successful of them were soaked in the blood of innocents. It is tempting to imagine a king – especially a king from the distant past – being somehow removed from everyday concerns, maybe *better* than the men around him. This is a mistake, even a disservice to the sort of men who were capable of building nations.

This chapter is the story of two ruthless men: Alexander II, who forged a kingdom in blood and violence, and William Wallace, whose resistance to the nation-breaking King of England hammered national consciousness into the Scots. The events they shaped – and that shaped them – would scarcely work as fiction. Their lives and deaths seem too much to be believed. This is why historical fact is better than any fiction – because beneath it all, behind it all, is the hard truth. These were remarkable men, but they were men nonetheless.

Alexander II was the latest of the Canmores. He was descended from Malcolm – the same who had defeated and killed Macbeth and Lulach and sat upon the throne in 1058. When Malcolm died, in 1093, his younger brother Donald replaced him. Donald III was challenged – and briefly replaced on the throne – by Duncan, Malcolm's son by his first wife.

Luckless Duncan II. He had been hostage of the English for years after the Abernethy Submission. Eventually sent north as a puppet of the English, he barely had time to warm the throne before he was murdered, and Donald III resumed his place. Duncan's bad luck survived him – and passed down through the blood of his descendants like a faulty gene. One branch of Duncan's line produced the MacWilliams of Moray, and they duly inherited the grievance and the bad luck. They grumbled to their kinsmen and neighbours, and among the peoples of the north they found many who had reason to support rival claims to the throne.

Kings of Scots like Alexander II did not control the landmass we would recognise as 'Scotland'. For one thing, although the Vikings had had to face up to the limitations of their power, they still held a vast territory to the north and west. From Orkney in the north and reaching at times as far south as the Isle of Man, was a territory ruled not by the King of Scots but by men of Viking descent.

In 1098 King Edgar had reached a settlement with King Magnus 'Barelegs' of Norway that limited the Vikings to the islands, but this was no insignificant territory. During the twelfth century it gave rise to a line of powerful men like Somerled, who would trouble the kings of Scots for years to come: *Ri Innse Gall*, 'Lords – kings even – of the Isles'.

The advent into the south and west of the Scottish mainland of families like the Bruces and the Stewarts had long ago caused upset among those sea lords. If they answered to any king at all – and that was usually debatable – then it was the King of Norway. Out of sight as well as out of mind, he was the perfect choice of master for a people with a taste for independence.

The new foreign friends and allies of the kings of Scots had their own dreams – notably to extend their personal territories. Faced with such threats to their lands and power – to their independence – the Isles men were often happy to back anyone who might cause trouble for the neighbouring crown. Others on the fringes of royal rule, those in the far north, were of a similar mind – loyal to powerful local families rather than to any distant king.

Alexander II was in the fourteenth year of his reign when the Mac-Williams found the will and the support for one final uprising, in 1228. Once he had crushed them, Alexander needed to show those men of will what will really was. On a mid-winter market day in 1230, in the settlement of Forfar, one of the king's men marched out into the centre of the town square to a position beside the market cross. In his arms he held the recently born daughter of the leader of the MacWilliams, taken from her mother's arms.

Alexander himself watched from nearby as the infant was held up to the people. Content that he had the attention of the assembled crowd, the henchman took hold of the baby by her ankles and swung her with all his might. Her head smashed like an egg against the column of the cross, her blood and brains stained the stones and splattered into the onlookers' faces. In the words of the Lanercost Chronicle: 'The daughter, who had not long left her mother's womb, innocent as she was, was put to death in the view of the market place. Her head was struck against the column and her brains dashed out.' This was the stuff of which kings were made: the will to do what others would not.

Alexander II had been made King of Scots in a ceremony at Scone on 5 December 1214, when he was sixteen years old. His father had died just the day before, but there had been no time for mourning. In the chill of the dawn he and his entourage had been ferried across the River Tay. They had made their way then to the same grass-covered mound of earth from which King Constantine and Bishop Cellach had pledged their allegiance to the land and to each other 308 years before. The place was known by then as Moot Hill, or the Hill of Belief, and on it had been placed the Stone of Destiny, the rock with the power to make kings.

Alexander took his place, seated upon the stone, and listened while a bard recited his Gaelic patronymic, name by name. Like the baby girl he would one day send to an ugly death, he too was *Mac Uilliem*, after a fashion. He was the son of William – William the Lion. But unlike his distant, luckless relative, daughter of a disinherited line, he could count himself son of all the kings, all the way back to the first Scot himself, *Iber Scot*.

Such a ceremony could only have fanned the flames of self-belief that burned within the boy-king. He was red-haired like all the men of his family and he had the temperament to match. From boyhood he had been groomed for the kingship. William had seen to it that he featured prominently in treaties with England and that he was involved in the business of government. The men of his family had fought for generations to preserve their bloodline, and Alexander was determined to do the same.

In order to make his heirs secure, he had first to set about securing his realm. Just as it had his father, it rankled with Alexander that his Alba – his Scotland – rubbed shoulders in the north and west with a patchwork of other peoples and languages: Caithness and Sutherland in the far north, independent in practice if not in theory; to the west the kingdom of the Isles and to the south another fiercely independent lordship, that of Galloway.

England, though, was bigger, richer and stronger by far than any other of Alexander's neighbours. To make matters worse, for the best part of two centuries the English kings had claimed Scotland as their own. It was all a game, in which what you said you owned mattered every bit as much as what you actually held. The first of the Canmores had played the game and recognised English superiority, but subservience was not Alexander's style. As far as he was concerned, he was every bit the equal of an English king. Maybe it was brash, maybe it was arrogant but Alexander II was on a mission to free his kingdom from English overlordship once and for all.

Along with his red hair, Alexander had inherited his father's sense of humiliation at the hands of King John of England. He it was who had denied William the Lion what many Scots regarded as their ancient right to the territories of Northumberland, Cumberland and Westmorland. William had fought all his days to press his rights in the south. He had spilled blood and spent huge sums of money – even offered up two of his daughters in pursuit of his claim. But to no avail. Now Alexander vowed he would give no less, and that he would win more. This was not just about territorial gain; it was about reclaiming what was rightfully his. It was about birthright.

The King of Scots was not alone in his grudge against John of England; there was a long line of English barons with similar grievances. In particular they resented being bled dry by their king's incessant demands for funds to finance his wars in France. In the end, they wrote it all down in what was to become the most famous legal document in English history. Originally called 'The Charter of Liberties', it is known the world over as 'Magna Carta', the great charter. Alexander's claim to the disputed northern territories was added to the bottom of the list, in clause 59. It was a promise 'To do right by Alexander the King of the Scots'. Here was a move of considerable subtlety by Alexander. A majority of the rebellious barons came from the north of England – the very territories he was determined to reclaim – and these were the men with whom he threw in his lot.

The barons had captured London in May 1215, within six months of Alexander ascending to his throne. The document they presented to King John, in a meadow beside the River Thames at Runnymede, had been in preparation since the winter of the year before. It was to a document called the 'Articles of the Barons' – which outlined the concessions to be made by the king – that the King's Great Seal was actually attached (John did not sign Magna Carta; in fact there is no evidence he could even write). 'The Charter of Liberties' or 'Magna Carta' was a document composed later and based on what had been accepted by the king at Runnymede. It was written on vellum – calf's skin – using a liquid called gall, collected and prepared from the lumps that form on oak trees when gall wasps impregnate the bark with their eggs. Once the scribes had done their work of writing out the sixty-three clauses – sometimes called chapters – the gall was dusted either with soot or iron salts. It was this treatment that gave the words the soft golden colour that survives in the four copies known to exist.

For all the high regard in which the words of 'Magna Carta' are held today ('the cornerstone of liberty in the English-speaking world', as it was described in a speech by Lord Woolf in 2005), King John treated it with no such reverence. No sooner had his seal been added to it than he was loudly dismissing it, to anyone who would listen, as 'mere foolishness'. Enough was enough and the barons quickly decided to rid themselves of their troublesome king once and for all.

England plunged into civil war and Alexander seized his moment. With King John preoccupied elsewhere, a Scottish army invaded northern England and laid siege to Norham Castle, in October 1215. Alexander ordered Newcastle to be burned to the ground and took Carlisle as well, for good measure. He was, anyway, no stranger to the battlefield. Despite his tender years he had begun serving his military apprenticeship aged only fourteen when he led his father's army against another MacWilliam – Guthred – in fierce fighting in Moray and Ross. After crushing rebels in his father's lands, he earned the respect of his men; now he would earn that of the English barons by going to war against their king.

By November 1215 English royal forces had retaken the strategically vital castle of Rochester. It had looked likely then that John would turn his attentions towards London, but instead he moved north, towards the heartlands of his rebellious barons. North of the River Humber no less than twenty-five English castles were defying King John. He marched his army into the thick of it and made bloody inroads on the rebellion as he went, taking castles (including Carlisle and Richmond) and forcing many of the barons to flee towards Scotland.

On 11 January the following year the northern barons gathered in Melrose

Abbey to swear fealty to the king for their lands. That king was the King of Scots (it was also almost a family affair for Alexander, since the two leaders of the northern barons – Robert de Ros and Eustace de Vescy – were married to two of his father's illegitimate daughters). As far as Alexander was concerned, now that the barons had sworn allegiance to him the disputed borderlands were his. Riled beyond endurance at the audacity of the King of Scots, John vowed to hunt down the 'fox-cub'. He captured the town of Berwick-upon-Tweed and laid waste to Lothian. But like foxes do, the redhead made good his escape.

With John out of London, the barons then did the unthinkable, the unforgivable: they sent messengers to France to offer the throne of England to Prince Louis. Louis duly accepted and at once set sail for the south-east coast. John had received warning of the coming invasion but the fleet he assembled for the necessary naval engagement was scattered by a storm. Louis landed with his men at Sandwich, in May, and the barons and their armies rallied to his side.

With so much at stake – so much to gain – Alexander headed south once more, quickly retaking Carlisle. The scent of victory had blown far to the north and the young King of Scots did what no other Scottish monarch had done before or since: he marched an army all the way to Dover. His plan was to cut a deal with the French, annex the northern territories and rule them as King of Scots.

All of it seemed within his grasp. He swept south in pursuit of the English army, gaining momentum all the way. As he had hoped, he joined up with the French forces and together they laid siege to Dover Castle, the key to England itself. In all the wars with England no other Scottish king ever came so far. His head must have swelled with every day that passed. There he was, just seventeen and on the brink of fulfilling his family's longest-held ambition. Half of Britain was nearly his.

Only fate could stop him now and stop him it did. With Louis poised to march in triumph towards London, word reached the rebels of a development none of them could have foreseen. King John was dead, of dysentery. The death of the English monarch might have been good news for Alexander; but in fact the opposite was true. With John out of the way, the justification for the barons' war evaporated. The king was dead, long live the king – and that meant rallying around John's nine-year-old son Henry III.

Far from fighting on with Louis, the barons – their rebelliousness replaced with opportunistic patriotism – now turned on the would-be usurper. The French prince and his countrymen were soundly defeated at London and at Sandwich. As the French disappeared over the horizon, so too did Alexander's dream of ruling the north of England. While they were fighting their king, the barons had regarded the young Alexander as a vital ally; now that they had rediscovered their love of the crown, he was an alien threat. Those northern barons who had so recently sworn allegiance to him now turned against him.

There was no longer any talk of a deal for Alexander; all of his ambitions fizzled out. In time, Henry III reissued 'Magna Carta', with all references to the King of Scots carefully omitted. To make matters worse, even the Pope had entered the fray on England's side. Despite John's death, Alexander had initially been keen to fight on; and in a demonstration of his continuing will had invaded Northumberland during the spring and summer of 1217. But then, word reached him that he and his leading churchmen were being excommunicated by Honorius III. The 'fox-cub', his tail between his legs, had to surrender Carlisle in return for absolution. In the final indignity he presented himself at Northampton in December, where he paid homage to the child-king Henry III of England.

In the depths of his humiliation and disappointment, Alexander journeyed to Arbroath Abbey, to contemplate the grave of his father. Like the Lion, the 'fox-cub' had tried and failed to make northern England a part of Scotland. Perhaps it was in some or other moment of quiet thought in the abbey grounds that Alexander began to understand the lessons that would shape the rest of his reign. At heart – when there was a stark choice between the child Henry and the French prince – the English barons had known instinctively who their king was. But Alexander must have wondered then ... could the same be said for the nobles of Scotland?

Beyond the reach and limits of Alexander's demesne, other peoples lived other lives. But there was a fundamental split *within* his kingdom as well. In the south the land was dominated by the families of French descent that had been invited into Scotland by the early Canmore kings. Kings like Edgar and David I had grown up in England, witnessing at first hand how Norman culture had transformed the southern kingdom into one of the most powerful and sophisticated in Europe. When they had opened Scotland's doors to the incomers, they had hoped to draw north more of the same seeds of success and prosperity.

The immigrants had duly brought with them the European ways so coveted by kings of Scots. They also supported the Canmores in their decision to import the reformed monastic orders – Augustinians, Benedictines, Cistercians, Tironensians and others – and had paid for the building of the great abbeys and monasteries that had changed the face of the land. But in the north and west were the sons and daughters of the old Gaelic families that had been there at the start, helping to lay the very foundations of the young kingdom. Once they had been at its beating heart, but by Alexander's time the Gaelic elite had been sidelined. Where once they had helped run the kingdom, now they held titles like 'Divider of the King's Meat'. The upstart Norman lords, by contrast, were made 'Chancellor' and 'Constable of Scotland'. One chronicler of the time wrote: 'The modern kings of Scotland count themselves as Frenchmen in race, manners, language and culture; they keep only Frenchmen in their household and following and have reduced the Scots to utter servitude.'

So it was that the Gaelic nobles had long since taken their leave of the court of the Canmores, preferring to create their own realms beyond the reach of the kings. It was in these semi-independent territories – Galloway in the south; Argyll, Ross, Sutherland and Caithness in the north – that rebellious thoughts and dreams like those of the MacWilliams, and their kinsmen the MacHeths, had taken root. Beyond, in the Hebrides and the Northern Isles, were those who looked to Norway for their overlord.

Alexander surveyed his kingdom and found it too messy for his liking. It was time for a new approach, a new deal. Rather than backing one side over the other, as his predecessors had done, he struck a balance between Norman innovation and Gaelic tradition. In Alexander's Scotland, both worlds would be allowed to flourish. The Gaelic warlords and their families were duly invited back in from the cold. In return for a share of the top jobs and titles, they would fight the king's battles. With their help he would bring all of Scotland to heel, territory by territory.

Alexander married Henry III's sister Joan in 1221. This was the most prestigious match secured by any King of Scots in a hundred years and demonstrated to observers abroad – and perhaps as importantly, to those at home – that here was a ruler who registered in the consciousness of the wider world. In the same year he asked to be anointed and crowned by the Pope's representative. This was a watershed moment as well. The inauguration of Scottish kings had always been an event of the secular, rather than the spiritual world. Everything about the ceremony was earthy – a marriage to the rock itself. Now Alexander was asking that God himself bless his hold on the crown, a privilege already enjoyed by kings of England and France. His request was turned down – due in no small part to English objections – but it was a matter he would never let drop.

Within weeks of his wedding he was in Inverness, crushing a rebellion. Later the same year he was at similar work in Argyll.

In 1222, opponents of royal authority murdered Bishop Adam of Caithness by roasting him to death. The men who set the fire, henchmen of the Earl of Orkney, claimed Adam had brought it upon himself with his heavy-handed attempts to bring the local Church into line with practices further south. But Alexander, receiving the news while preparing to go on pilgrimage to Canterbury, saw it differently. Adam of Caithness had been put in post by the king's father and the grisly murder was therefore an act of rebellion against the crown. Alexander set aside his plans for peaceful contemplation and headed north instead, gathering an avenging army as he went. The perpetrators were rounded up and savagely dealt with.

The Western Isles, too, received Alexander's violent attentions. After a period when Norwegian influence there had been on the wane, the energetic and forceful King Haakon IV had ascended to the throne of Norway in 1217. He was determined to keep a tight rein on the islands and actively encouraged his subjects there to resist any and all attempts at assimilation by the King of Scots. Undeterred, indeed emboldened by his successes elsewhere, Alexander attacked the sea lords of the Isles – the start of a campaign for conquest that would continue for the rest of his reign, and beyond.

It was while Alexander was in this mood – unwilling to brook any challenge, any threat to his plans for outright domination – that the MacWilliams clashed for the last time with their nemesis. The murder of the baby girl in the market square in Forfar was a shocking act even by the brutal standards of the day. It was also politically pointless: the MacWilliam hopes of a return to the throne were dead before she was born. But this King of Scots was nothing if not thorough. The snuffing-out of her life, specifically the way in which he had chosen to do it, was remembered for generations, just as Alexander had hoped it would be.

True to his word, he rewarded those warlords who fought for him and helped him extend the reach of royal will. Farquhar MacTaggart, a Gaelic leader in Ross, had been knighted and granted an earldom by Alexander for his bloody suppression of an earlier MacWilliam rising in 1215. Elsewhere the king's own hand-picked men, scions of the old Gaelic elite among them, were eventually made earls of Sutherland, and of Caithness; lords of Badenoch and Lochaber. Galloway, too, was brought under direct royal control. Of the thirteen earldoms that existed in Scotland in 1286, eight of them were in the hands of sons of the old Gaelic elite.

Gaelic leaders were encouraged to adopt Anglo-Norman ways, but without shedding too much of their old distinctiveness. They became knights, built castles, married into prominent Anglo-Norman families. In time, many of them would hold lands in England as well. Unlike in England, where the Norman takeover had been aggressive – and complete – in Scotland the Anglo-Norman culture was something that could be dipped into, acquired as it suited.

More effectively than his father, perhaps more effectively than any King of Scots before him, Alexander II forged Scotland into something like the geographical entity we know today. But his most lasting achievements were more profound, affecting the way Scots regarded themselves.

He had sought the blessing of the Pope, of God, for his crown. Having had his first request for holy oil turned down in 1221, he asked again in 1233 – only to be refused once more. He may well have made more requests but his failure in the end is not important. What mattered was his contention – his certainty – that the kingdom of Scotland should be put on the same footing as those of England and France. Then in 1237 he scored his greatest success. By the Treaty of York he secured a permanent and lasting border between Scotland and England for the very first time. To get it he had to surrender for ever all claims on the northern territories but now England recognised a fixed line between the River Tweed and the River Solway. Implicit in that recognition was acceptance by the King of England that the kingdom of Scotland actually existed as a free and independent country. It would be fought over time and again in years to come – but it was there and it remains essentially unchanged to the present day.

One kingdom. Scotland. Everyone north of the Border was subject to one king and that made them one people – Scots. Now and for ever they could say: 'This over here is Scotland – that over there is England. And we are different.' This was the legacy of Alexander II.

He was fighting to extend royal control right up until the moment of his death. Although he secured a southern border in 1237, he never gave up plans to shape the western limits of his kingdom to his liking as well. Argyll was finally brought to heel in 1249. In the same year he had turned his attention once more to the Western Isles. He was with his huge fleet and army at Oban, ready to do battle with the forces of Haakon IV of Norway, when he was taken ill. He died on the little island of Kerrera, in Oban Bay, on 8 July. He had been King of Scots for thirty-five years.

There would be no attack on sea lords that year. The Scots forces drifted homewards and the body of the king was taken to Melrose Abbey where, in accordance with his wishes, he was buried near the high altar.

He was succeeded by his only son, the seven-year-old Alexander III. Joan of England, daughter of Henry III, had produced no children by the time she died in 1238. Her replacement had been found not in the English house, as Henry might have wished, but in France. No doubt the English king was not a little alarmed to find his ambitious neighbour had wed Marie de Courcy, daughter of the man who had commanded Prince Louis' forces against his father in England in 1216–17.

The production of male heirs was the single most important job of medieval kings and in 1241 Marie gave birth to Alexander. When trouble brewed between Scotland and England once again in 1244, the infant prince became part of the solution. The peace negotiations that avoided any actual conflict between the kingdoms that year included his betrothal to Henry's daughter Margaret.

Like his father before him, Alexander III was crowned at Scone, sitting upon the Stone of Destiny. That he had come into his kingship while still so young might have been a problem – especially following hard on the heels of a monarch who had achieved so much by the very force of his own personality. But the Scottish nobility and Church rallied protectively around the boy. Within a year his great-great-great-grandmother Margaret was made a saint – Scotland's only royal saint. It seemed a good omen.

In 1251 the ten-year-old king travelled in some splendour to York for double celebrations. First he was knighted by Henry and then married to little Margaret, herself just eleven years old. A marriage between the King of Scots and the daughter of the King of England; to onlookers it must have seemed to usher in hopes of a new time of peace between the old enemies – even the prospect of a union of the crowns.

The period of Alexander's minority ended on his eighteenth birthday in 1259. He had been guided by those nobles closest to the throne, notably the Comyn family, who held lands from the crown in Badenoch and Lochaber as well as in the south-west. But from the moment he came fully into his kingship he showed no lack of self-confidence, or direction. By 1261 he had focused his attention on the territory his father had been eyeing at the moment of his death. Royal envoys were sent to Norway to put pressure on Haakon to come to terms over control over the Western Isles, but when their efforts failed Alexander took the initiative.

Word reached Norway the following summer that a Scots force had attacked Skye. By 1263 Haakon had mustered his fleet and was on his way south to settle the matter. There was a show of strength and intent by the Norwegians, followed by attempts at diplomacy and a peaceful settlement. The eventual, seemingly inevitable battle – at Largs on 2 October – was a damp squib, if truth be known. The job of disabling the Norwegian fleet had been accomplished, not by the Scots but by a great storm off the coast of the town the previous week. By the time the survivors got down to confronting the Scots army gathered to greet them, they had little appetite left for the fight.

If there was a victor, then it was the Scots; but the battle had been inconclusive. Haakon and the remnants of his fleet turned their backs on the Western Isles and withdrew to Orkney, where he became ill at the end of October. He took to his bed in the Bishop's Palace in Kirkwall, and died. The Battle of Largs had decided nothing by itself. But the death of Haakon put a new complexion on things. The fire went out of any lingering desire to retain territories that were, anyway, so far from the homeland. In 1266 the Norwegians agreed the sale of the Western Isles to the Scottish crown, on condition that the kings of Scotland would respect Norway's hold on Orkney and Shetland.

It has been argued by some that Scotland entered a golden age in the second half of the thirteenth century. There was certainly prosperity. Economies across Europe enjoyed a boom period – one as inexplicable as that which came to an end in 2008 – and Scotland shared in the good times. By then the country had a population of perhaps 500,000. Although the majority of people still lived in the countryside, the burghs that had been established by David I had come on apace. Towns on the east coast, like Aberdeen, Berwick-upon-Tweed, Dundee, Edinburgh, Elgin, Inverness and Perth, thrived within a commercial network that took in all the countries encircling the North Sea. To the west, the urbanised populations of towns like Ayr, Dumfries, Glasgow, Irvine and Renfrew traded with Ireland and the towns of western England. Wool was a major commodity, much of it collected from the huge flocks maintained on the Southern Uplands by the great Cistercian houses. Fish, timber and animal hides were also profitable and exported in considerable quantities. Scotland was beginning to thrive.

The wedding of Alexander and Margaret had been a dazzling, golden affair – the Scots had made sure of that. Their intention had been clear: to pitch Scotland as an equal partner, an equal kingdom. Among the honoured guests had been one prince who would cast a long-legged shadow across the whole of Britain. He was Margaret's brother – now Alexander's brother-in-law – Prince Edward.

Heir to the throne of England, he possessed a potent mix of qualities. He had all the overweening sense of superiority that had directed his father and grandfather – but coupled with rare intelligence and military skill. If all of that did not make him dangerous enough, he was shot through with cold-blooded cruelty and a taste for messy violence. The English historian Matthew Paris, perhaps the finest chronicler of the thirteenth century, recorded a telling incident from Edward's youth. Angered by a slight, the prince had sent a henchman to attack a man, cut off his ear and gouge out an eye. With a palpable sense of gloom and foreboding Paris wrote: 'If he does these things when the wood is green, what can be hoped for when it is seasoned?'

What indeed. Edward channelled his violence into warfare and grew into a skilled practitioner of the art. In 1266 he went on crusade alongside King Louis IX of France. His bravery in the fight for the city of Acre – and the glamour of a near-fatal wounding at the hands of a Muslim assassin – added greatly to his prestige. It was on his journey home to recover his health that he learned of his father's death, and by the time he was back in England to claim his throne he was being hailed by some as a new Richard the Lionheart. But if Edward's life had all the glow of a 'Boy's Own' story, his Scottish brother-in-law was soon in the midst of a Greek tragedy. Alexander's wife, Margaret of England, died in 1275. By then she had given Alexander three children – two sons and a daughter, and the succession seemed secure. In the spring of 1281 it was announced that their daughter Margaret was to marry King Erik II of Norway, a move designed to bring the two countries closer together. But before the nuptials could take place, Alexander's eight-year-old younger son, David, took ill and died. It was a body blow and a cause of great lamenting; but, for all the sadness, at least the future of the throne remained safe in the hands of the elder brother, Alexander, Prince of Scotland.

The wedding of Margaret and Erik took place in August and little over a year later the royal couple were expecting their first child. But on 9 April 1283 came the news that Margaret had died giving birth to a daughter.

The infant, a sickly child, was named Margaret after her mother. Back in Scotland, the House of Canmore went into mourning once again. All of this was surely bad enough – a family bereft, its two survivors wondering at the course of events that had taken away mother, son and daughter. Then Prince Alexander took ill as well. He was newly married and there must have been hopes at first that a son and heir would soon follow, a return to good fortune. It was not to be. On 17 January 1284, the Prince of Scotland died.

King Edward was moved to write declaring his shock and sadness at all that had befallen his brother-in-law. Alexander's reply suggests a genuine fondness between the two men: 'You have offered much solace for our grief by [saying] that although death has ... borne away your kindred in these parts, we are united together perpetually, God willing, by the tie of indissoluble affection.' For any man, the loss of all of his children is too much to be borne. But a king cannot be like other men – not when the future of his crown and country is at stake – and Alexander had to set about the business of starting again. In the short term, his granddaughter Margaret – called the 'Maid of Norway' – was accepted as heir to the Scottish throne. An act of pragmatism on the part of the rulers of Scotland, it nonetheless caused much unease. Scotland had never had a female monarch and among the magnates were men who wondered what the future might hold if the crown were to be handed to a woman. Furthermore, several of them believed they had better claims on the throne themselves.

They were consoled by the knowledge that Alexander was still in the prime of life: plenty of time for him to find a new wife and to father more sons. Broken-hearted or not, the king duly set his stall out at the international marriage market, and within two years had found and married a new young wife. She was French, Yolande of Dreux, and to her now fell the duty of producing a boy child to make safe the Canmore line. Alexander was understandably keen to be with his bride as much as possible. So it was that on the night of 18 March 1286 he set out from Edinburgh Castle into the teeth of a howling gale. He had spent the day with the lords of his council and as the business drew to a close they urged him to wait for morning and, hopefully, better weather.

But Alexander had more to think about than rain and wind. Twenty-three-year-old Yolande was waiting for him in the royal manor of Kinghorn, on the other side of the Firth of Forth, and he had other duties to perform. At Dalmeny the ferryman tried to turn the king away, saying the 2-mile crossing to Inverkeithing was too dangerous. Alexander teased the man, asking him if he was scared. 'By no means,' the ferryman answered: 'it would be a great honour to share the fate of your father's son.' At Inverkeithing he was met by one of the town bailies and offered lodgings for the night. But by now Alexander was too close to his goal to think about stopping. Shrugging aside the offer, the king mounted a horse and set out into the storm accompanied only by two 'bondmen'.

Whatever actually happened on that journey has been lost to history. All that is known for certain is that, somewhere along the treacherous cliff-top path leading to Kinghorn, Alexander became separated from the other riders. He never reached the royal manor. Next morning, 19 March 1286, the last of the Canmore kings was found dead on the beach beneath a high point known today as the 'King's Crag', his neck broken. Scotland was without a king and her future lay in the feeble grasp of a three-year-old girl.

The following month there gathered at Scone a parliament of all the most senior churchmen and most powerful nobles in the land. They at once swore allegiance to little Margaret of Norway and vowed, under pain of excommunication, to keep Scotland safe and peaceful for her. A provisional government was established and six 'Guardians of the Community of the Realm' put in place. They were two bishops – Robert Wishart of Glasgow and William Fraser of St Andrews, two earls – Alexander Comyn of Buchan and Duncan MacDuff of Fife and two barons – John Comyn, Lord of Badenoch and James the Steward.

It was also decided by the parliament that Edward of England should be invited to offer his help and advice in maintaining the peace and security of Scotland. It made sense: the Maid of Norway was the granddaughter of Edward's sister, making her his grand-niece. For him, the future of Scotland was a family affair. At first the English king's involvement was a welcome presence in a time of need. Soon after Alexander's death, those nobles with the strongest claims on the throne had been sabre-rattling in a way that might have pushed the country into the abyss of civil war. Robert Bruce, Lord of Annandale and grandfather of the future Robert I, was noisily declaring his rights and it was the presence of Edward I on the sidelines, as much as any efforts by the Guardians, that stabilised the situation.

Negotiations got under way then to arrange a future marriage for the Maid of Norway and Edward's son and heir, Edward of Caernarvon. The protracted talks culminated in the Treaty of Birgham, of 1290. Hopes were high that a child born of such a marriage would assume the crowns of both kingdoms – it was a glimmer of optimism for a country that had lived through four years of darkness. The future seemed certain once more. The terms of Birgham even made it clear that the kingdom of Scotland should be 'separate, apart and free in itself, without subjection to the English kingdom'. King Edward viewed the matter differently. A master of the law, he well understood what his dynasty stood to gain from such a marriage. Medieval women, after all, were property. In the eyes of the law, what a woman owned belonged to her husband. Once she married Prince Edward, the Maid's Scotland would belong to England.

Untimely death, however, still stalked the blood of the Canmores. Little Margaret, six years old by then, was on her way to Scotland in October 1290 when she was struck down by illness – probably seasickness. Her ship docked at Orkney to give her a chance to recover, but she died there. Her body was returned to Bergen for burial while the shattering news of her death travelled south.

Edward may have been irked by the development at first, after all those drawn-out negotiations to arrange marriage, but he quickly saw it as an act of divine providence. With the death of Princess Margaret, the clear line of succession to the throne was broken and rival claimants were free to contest the matter. Robert Bruce of Annandale had staked his claim soon after Alexander's death – but there was a second, equally strong contender in the form of John Balliol of Barnard Castle.

It says a great deal for the wisdom of the Scone parliament that neither of these men had been chosen as a Guardian. Both had enough military clout at their disposal to enable them to back their claims on the field of battle, and it fell to the Guardians to act quickly enough and decisively enough to prevent the country tearing itself apart. With this in mind they sought out a man they felt had the relevant mastery of the law to enable him to offer sage advice; a man who commanded international respect, whose word would be listened to; a man who was, anyway, almost family. They asked Edward.

The English king called for a parliament to be held on 6 May 1291, to settle the future of the Scottish crown. The location he chose for the gathering was Norham Castle, on the English side of the River Tweed and the Scots immediately smelled a rat. The Treaty of Birgham had made it clear that no parliament to discuss Scottish affairs would be held outside Scotland. Now Edward proposed to decide the very future of the kingdom in England. As far as the Guardians were concerned, it was not right. While they stalled on the Scottish side of the river, Edward raised the stakes. Not only did he continue to insist the parliament be in Norham, the heavily fortified home of Anthony Bek, Bishop of Durham, but also he said the proceedings would not start until the Guardians and the claimants to the throne had acknowledged his position as superior overlord of Scotland. It was a stunning move and the Guardians reeled back from the blow.

Bishop Wishart of Glasgow was the first to regain his balance. To Edward's face he stated the independence of Scotland: 'The Scottish kingdom is not held in tribute or homage to anyone save God alone,' he said. These were brave and defiant words from a brave and defiant man, but Edward shrugged them off. Then he raised the stakes once more: in addition to Bruce and Balliol, he had found eleven other likely claimants for the throne. Robert Bruce was the first to crack under the pressure, driven no doubt by his desperation to gain the throne, but in the end all twelve claimants submitted to Edward. Balliol was the last to do so. On 12 June, Bishop Wishart himself, along with the rest of the Guardians, swore fealty to the English king as well.

So began what has become known as 'The Great Cause' – the bid to decide the rightful heir to the Scottish throne, with Edward as judge. In hindsight it was always a foregone conclusion. Sheer devilment had inspired the English king to round up the eleven newest claimants, but only two men had credible cases to make: Bruce and Balliol. In years to come the Bruce family would rewrite history to justify their actions, but the fact remains that in 1291 John Balliol had the superior claim. Ancestors of both men had married into the royal line when they wed daughters of David, Earl of Huntingdon, youngest son of King Malcolm IV. Robert Bruce (later known as the Competitor) was the grandson of Isabella, David's youngest girl. John Balliol was the great-grandson of Margaret, his eldest daughter.

With considerable effrontery, Bruce tried to argue that his claim was stronger because he was a whole generation closer to David. But he and everybody else gathered around the table in Norham Castle knew that in thirteenth-century Scotland it was all about primogeniture – being descended from the elder branch of the family. Since Balliol was great-grandson of the eldest daughter, the throne was his. Despite this simple fact, there followed seventeen months of talking, arguing and adjournments before he was officially named as the successor on 6 November 1292.

For Edward the result was a detail and of little real interest; he had already secured oaths of fealty from everyone in the room. On 17 November, Balliol accepted Edward as his overlord once more. Shortly afterwards, Balliol travelled to Scone and there, on 30 November, seated upon the Stone of Destiny, was inaugurated as King of Scotland. In fact, it was from Balliol's time onwards that the stone took on its most famous name. If it was called anything up until that point it was more likely 'The Stone of Scone'. Balliol was the last King of Scotland to be crowned upon that lump of sandstone.

With the stone beneath him and Edward above as overlord, Balliol was literally between a rock and a hard place. Edward I was one of the most powerful kings in Europe. He was also supremely smart, a master tactician of both politics and war. For the duration of his reign, that unluckiest of Scotland's kings was bullied and humiliated by his liege lord at every opportunity. If subservience to the English king was not bad enough, Balliol also had to endure the ill-will of the Bruce family and all their supporters. By any standards, the new king was in a hopeless situation. For a while the maltreatment was mundane – Edward as back-seat driver, taking day-to-day decisions out of Balliol's hands. But in 1294 Edward demanded the service of the king and the entire Scots army to help prosecute the English war in Gascony.

For Bishop Wishart and the rest of the Scottish leaders this was the last straw – the Scottish King to do military service for the King of England? Unthinkable. They assembled in secret in Stirling and agreed upon the formation of the so-called Council of Twelve, comprising four bishops, four earls and four lords. It was also agreed that this new team of Guardians would not be answerable to Balliol; he would be a figurehead, nothing more. The real power would lie with the most powerful members of the Council, namely the Comyns of Badenoch.

The Council understood from the start that they needed help from outside. In July 1295 a secret delegation was sent to win backing from Philippe IV of France, Edward's enemy. The result was a commitment to mutual support between the two kingdoms called the Treaty of Paris, but known fondly by Scots to this day as the 'Auld Alliance'. In the end it never really generated much in the way of help from France, but in principle it guaranteed that if England were to attack either kingdom, then the other would rise to its defence. Word of the Treaty – the treachery – reached Edward later the same year. He was furious. The kingdom he had so recently subjugated without spilling a drop of blood was now signing secret deals with his sworn enemy!

In Scotland there was a sense of excitement. With the prospect of military back-up from across the Channel, Balliol gave the order for the Scots host to assemble north of Selkirk on 11 March 1296. The Bruces, first among the contenders to submit to Edward at Norham, were conspicuous by their absence. Balliol immediately ordered that their lands in Annandale be made over to John Comyn, his own father-in-law and the Bruces' arch-rival.

As soon as Edward sent his troops into France, a Scottish force crossed the Border and attacked the English garrison at Carlisle. It was a show of commitment to the Treaty of Paris, but it had sown the wind. The people of Berwick reaped the whirlwind. Edward crossed the Tweed at Coldstream with a force estimated at 30,000 men and cavalry, far and away the largest army that had ever been sent north. Berwick was Scotland's wealthiest burgh and an obvious target. Easter celebrations were drawing to a close when nervous sentries keeping watch on the flimsy timber fortifications spotted the outriders of the English force. Word had reached them weeks before that English soldiers had been mobilised in the northern territories, and now here they were.

Since there was no purposeful defence to be offered in the face of such a host, the garrison surrendered at once. Edward and his men swiftly took possession. What followed was one of the worst atrocities in the history of medieval Britain. A chronicler recorded how 'for two days streams of blood flowed from the bodies of the slain, for in his tyrannous rage he ordered 7,500 souls of both sexes to be massacred ... mills could be turned round by the flow of their blood'. Edward had wanted nothing less than wholesale slaughter. The orgy of killing only came to an end when the frantic pleading of local clergymen moved Edward to show some semblance of pity for those traumatised men, women and children still alive. Out of an original population of almost 13,000, fewer than 5,000 were still breathing when Edward's men put their swords away.

As things turned out, the rape of Berwick was just a warm-up. With a reputation for massive violence preceding him, Edward made a gruesome advance through the heartland of Scotland. A Scots force had taken Dunbar Castle from its English garrison and by the end of April John de Warenne, Earl of Surrey had arrived to put the place under siege. The main body of the Scots army advanced to try and drive them off on 27 April, only to be cut to pieces by better-trained English heavy horse and infantry. Whether the rout was as bloody as the English chroniclers said – they claimed as many as 10,000 Scots dead – it was the end of the war.

The Scottish resistance collapsed like wet sand. During the course of the next few weeks the castles of Edinburgh, Perth, Roxburgh and Stirling opened their doors to English troops. Balliol wandered all the while seemingly unsure what to do. At the beginning of July he sent Edward a grovelling letter in which he admitted his fault: 'we have by evil and false council, and our own folly, grievously offended our lord Edward … we … have surrendered to him the land of Scotland and all its people'. Next he formally renounced the Treaty of Paris, before finally handing himself over to Edward like a guilty child. It was hardly surprising that he had tried to hold out against the inevitable. He had a lot of explaining to do. Under the terms of his sworn oaths of fealty, he was Edward's man – and yet he had conspired with the French and attacked English soil. In Edward's eyes he was nothing more than a defaulting vassal who would have to be punished.

Unfortunately for the Scots king – or rather the *former* king, as Edward had been calling him ever since the Scots army had mustered north of the Border the previous month – Edward would not be content with mere surrender. What he wanted was a show. It was therefore with all possible theatricality that King John of Scotland was literally stripped of every vestige of his rank. First paraded before Edward as a penitent, he then had the royal insignia ripped from his vestments, earning him the nickname that has trailed behind him ever since: 'Toom Tabard' – empty suit, King Nobody. Broken and humiliated, he was sent first to the Tower of London and ultimately to exile in France.

Edward behaved as though racking his brains for every way to humiliate and eviscerate the land he had newly conquered. He took the regalia – the crown jewels – from Edinburgh Castle. He took the Black Rood of St Margaret, holiest of all of Scotland's relics. So that the Scots might never again make a king of their own he took the Stone of Scone – the Stone of Destiny – and sent it to be a centrepiece of the shrine of Edward the Confessor, in Westminster Abbey. A bureaucrat to the tips of his fingers, he had the royal records – the paperwork detailing his new acquisition – inventoried, boxed up and put aboard a ship bound for England. They never made it; the ship sank and a priceless collection of irreplaceable documents was lost. Senior nobles were rounded up and sent into imprisonment south of the Border. The most prominent of those who had fought for Balliol – and for the independence of the kingdom – now shared the fate of the monarch. Scotland was not just without a king, it had been comprehensively stripped of all those who might foment further rebellion.

For several weeks in the summer of 1296 Edward toured the land, making sure to be seen in every burgh and every royal castle as far north as Elgin. While he was making his presence felt, his administrators were at work putting together a document that would go down as the most notorious and shameful in Scottish history. Edward wanted every significant landowner to pay him homage, to accept him as liege lord, and so it was that around 1,900 of them put their seals to what has become known as the 'Ragman Roll'.

Erstwhile competitors for the throne – Bruces and Balliols; bishops, senior clergy and the heads of religious houses; great noble families like Comyns and Stewarts; tenants-in-chief; under-tenants; knights great and small – it amounted to nothing less than a collective handover of the independence of Scotland. By the time all the seals had been fastened to the end of the roll, the best part of 2,000 ribbons gave the thing a ragged appearance, hence the name (the Ragman Roll also gave rise to the word 'rigmarole', meaning something lengthy and complicated).

Historians – not to mention self-styled patriots and rebels down through the intervening centuries – have made much of the fact that one name in particular does not feature on the Ragman Roll. Until 1296 or so, William Wallace was just an obscure squire, living on land at Elderslie, near Renfrew. His elder brother Malcolm was actually the holder of the land, but still the absence of both men's names from the list of local notables is surprising. Edward's men were uncommonly thorough, taking the seals and oaths of lesser men than the pair resident at Elderslie; so it seems unlikely they were considered too lowly for inclusion, and more likely that the Wallaces refused to toe the line – a first small spark of defiance.

In any event, the winter of 1296 was one of the country's darkest. Edward left Scotland in the charge of two trusted lieutenants – John de Warenne, Earl of Surrey as Governor and Hugh de Cressingham as Treasurer – and set off for home. He had, he thought, bigger fish to fry in France; Scotland was a done deal. As he crossed the Tweed back into England he quipped 'A man does good business when he rids himself of shit.'

For a few weeks, maybe a couple of months, the Scots reeled from all that had been visited upon them. But, if Edward really thought that an atrocity, a battle, a wagon-load of trophies and a ragged roll of paper was all it took to wring the last ounce of fighting spirit from the northern kingdom, he was terribly wrong. Still befuddled by the speed of events, the Scots paid the first instalment of monies required by Edward for his endless war in France. But by the spring of 1297 they had regained their senses, and their defiant tendencies. Despite his best efforts, Cressingham found the money was drying up. Instead of collecting taxes to pay for the wages of his staff and the occupying forces, he faced the prospect of explaining to his master why England now had to pay for the privilege of its overlordship in Scotland.

The first spark of real resistance was struck in the Gaelic north. It was a small act of defiance, a single standard raised against Edward, but all at once it began to spread. The top layer of society had been decimated by Edward's judgment upon them – either imprisoned or cowed into submission. But among the 'middling sort' – lesser landowners but not short on pride – there grew a concerted objection to paying for English adventures across the Channel. Resistance was unco-ordinated and sporadic at first, but soon there were many fires burning. What would happen if the flames were to be brought together in a firebrand?

Bishop Wishart was still at large and so too was James the Stewart. These two served for a time as a focus for rebellion, and were joined by a third – Robert Bruce, twenty-two-year-old grandson of Robert Bruce, the Competitor. That Bruce the younger should have stepped out into the light as an opponent of King Edward in 1297 is surprising to say the least. When the Bruces had failed to muster for the invasion of England the year before, their lands had been made forfeit. Driven south, they renewed old oaths of allegiance to Edward and only regained their holdings in Annandale as a result of the English conquest. What they had in Scotland now they owed to Edward; and yet here was young Robert declaring an urge to bite the hand that had fed him. Whether it was latent love of the land of his birth, or the very start of a long-term strategy to take the throne, he stepped up to the fight in Scotland's darkest hour, for a little while at least.

But all of them – Wishart, Stewart, even the Bruce – were shortly to be eclipsed by a brighter light by far. The Stewarts held lands around Renfrewshire and had done since the time of David I. It was from within the Stewart retinue then that William Wallace, the knight from Elderslie, emerged blinking from the darkness of obscurity. Sometime in May he found reason to kill the English sheriff of Lanark, William Hesilrig. According to Blind Harry's *Wallace* (or to give his book its full title, *The Actes and Deidis of the Illustre and Vallyeant Campion Schir William Wallace*), Hesilrig had cruelly murdered Wallace's wife, and so brought down upon his head the knight's righteous vengeance. Whatever the motive, Wallace certainly cut the sheriff down – and into pieces – in an act widely seen as the start of his war against the English occupation of Scotland. And it was not just the sheriff. Wallace and his men butchered every Englishman they could lay their hands on.

William Wallace . . . *The* Wallace . . . For many he is the ultimate freedom fighter, for others a terrorist. He is the enigmatic hero who appears from nowhere to liberate his people and to shape history. The Wallace story is one of the defining legends of Scottish identity and the epitome of Scotland's story. And yet, with all the mythologising, we have lost sight of Wallace the man: a remarkable man, but a man nonetheless.

After making a name for himself at Lanark, Wallace launched a surprise attack at Scone on the court of the English justiciar William Ormsby. He was accompanied on the raid by Sir William Douglas, a maverick former governor of Berwick Castle, and together they so surprised Ormsby he barely escaped with his skin intact. Furthermore, and of greater value, he left behind a great deal of cash. Now Wallace had a fighting fund.

Where he had learned, or honed, his fighting skills is not known. This, the most revered of Scotland's folk heroes, seems to emerge onto the field of battle ready-made for victory. That it was dangerous to get on his wrong side was beyond question; how he got that way we will likely never know. When it came to the business of war Wishart, Stewart and the Bruce, by contrast, were proving ham-fisted at best and downright craven at worst. After a farcical encounter with an English force near Irvine in July, Wishart and Stewart were taken prisoner. Bruce – willing, like a cockerel on a weathervane, to turn whichever way the wind blew – promptly renewed his vows of allegiance to Edward, yet again.

Wallace, though, was still very much at large and increasingly the popular focus of the rebellion. It may well be that Wishart had actually succeeded in at least one way: by drawing the attention of the English forces towards himself in Ayrshire – and by spinning out the terms of his surrender – he bought time for the Elderslie knight. An English chronicler wrote that the bishop 'caused a certain bloody man, William Wallace, who had formally been a chief of brigands in Scotland, to revolt against the king, and assemble people in his support'. That is certainly what Wallace did. He was a hit. But the people who flocked to his side – who loved him before the end and died for him and with him – were not of noble blood. Wallace's army was a mix of ordinary people, humble folk – 'the middling sort'. They were precisely the sort of people who had had first-hand experience of Edward's policies of wringing as many taxes and fighting men from Scotland as he could.

Those who rallied to Wallace might have been enthusiastic, and numerous, but for the most part they were unfamiliar with the arts of war. If his army was to stand any kind of chance against Edward's battle-hardened men-at-arms and heavy horse, he needed to give them the time and the space in which to train. By July he had them within the dappled clearings of the Selkirk Forest, instilling iron discipline and teaching them to fight in schiltrons – hedgehog-like formations made of tightly packed men armed with long spears. Wallace's men were also imbued with something that cannot be taught, and which is never carried among the weaponry of an invasion force: the determination to fight for the homeland.

Alexander II had given the Scots a united kingdom with a border, as well as a sense of who they were. During the course of the single decade that followed the death of Alexander III, all of that had been swept away. The people of Scotland looked south and saw that King Edward of England had already crushed the princes of Wales. Welshmen had been conscripted into his armies, made to fight in foreign lands, and now that king proposed to do exactly the same thing with Scots. It was this prospect, of being swallowed without a trace by an alien land and forced to fight a stranger's wars, that had tipped the Scots over the edge.

Wallace's army was not the only Scots force preparing to fight. North of the Mounth a nobleman's son named Andrew Murray had also been striking blow after blow against the enemy. He was no newcomer to the fight either. Together with his father he had joined the battle against Warenne's forces at Dunbar. Both of them had been captured, but Murray had made good his escape from imprisonment in Chester Castle and headed north, his blood still up. His fight-back had begun when he led a successful attack of hastily assembled warriors against an English garrison in the mighty stronghold of Castle Urquhart on the shore of Loch Ness. After that triumph his rebels had driven the English from castle after castle in the north-east.

They came together, the knight and the nobleman's son, towards the end of the summer. By then, Edward's lieutenants in Scotland had become vaguely aware they might soon have more to deal with than guerrilla raids and rabble-rousing. In fact, word was reaching Warenne and Cressingham that there was at large now in southern Scotland what could only be described as a rebel army – a peasant army led by nobodies, but an army nonetheless.

Edward was busy preparing for more fighting on the other side of the Channel and it seems he could hardly bring himself to raise his head from his maps of France. Over his shoulder, with a dismissive wave of his hand, he said efforts should be made to support the garrison in Stirling Castle. Those two characters Wallace and Murray should be rounded up and put to the sword. Scotland was conquered after all; it should be a trifling matter.

Confident the rebels would offer little more than a training exercise for English heavy horse – standing targets to be mown down like grass – Warenne and Cressingham moved north. They passed through English-held Berwick with its newly built curtain wall down to the river, a bone-white symbol of arrogant dominance. The troublesome Scots were already at Stirling, on the northern side of the River Forth. Warenne was first to arrive at the castle and, keen to get his men into position to settle the matter, made his way to Stirling Bridge to survey the only point at which the otherwise difficult and treacherous river could be crossed dry-shod.

He was met by James the Stewart (a dismal flop at Irvine alongside Bishop Wishart) and Malcolm, Earl of Lennox, another Scot ingratiating himself with Edward. That these serially duplicitous characters – the various Bruces included – avoided having their throats cut by some honest soul on one side or the other, is an enduring mystery to me. Even Edward was exasperated by the grasping self-interest of the Bruces. After Dunbar, the younger Bruce's father had asked the English king if he might have the Scots throne now. 'Have we nothing better to do,' came Edward's withering reply, 'but win kingdoms for you?' Stewart and Lennox said they would try and persuade Wallace and Murray to come to terms but their offer, like their worth as Scotsmen that day, amounted to nothing.

Warenne took himself off to bed and slept so long he missed the first deployment of his own men across the bridge. Since their commander had overslept, they were recalled. Once he had got up and breakfasted they were sent over for a second time, but Lennox and Stewart trotted into sight once more and the English forces were called back yet again. Warenne had thought they might have made good on their promise of a peaceful settlement, but he was to be disappointed.

Wallace and Murray had gathered their forces on the slopes of the rocky eminence known as Abbey Craig – the site nowadays of the Wallace Monument – and must have looked at those English comings and goings with amazement. Then from their high ground they spotted the approach of another party of horsemen. This time it was a pair of Dominican friars sent by Warenne to see if the Scots would come to terms. Wallace told them: 'Tell your commander that we are not here to make peace but to do battle to defend ourselves and liberate our kingdom. Let them come on, and we shall prove this in their very beards.'

Warenne and Cressingham cared little that a battle now seemed imminent. They had a couple of hundred knights and mounted men-at-arms, backed by several thousand well-armed foot soldiers, many of them Welsh. The Scots force a mile or so away at Abbey Craig had similar numbers, but they were hopelessly outgunned in terms of horse and armaments. The English commanders were advised then of the existence of a ford across the Forth, perhaps a mile upriver. The horses could cross there and move into a position from which the Scots might be outflanked. This was sound tactical advice but the Englishmen were impatient to let their forces in amongst the rebels, and saw no need anyway for such precautions. Warenne ordered his men to begin crossing the bridge.

Up on Abbey Craig, Wallace and Murray could not believe their luck. The old timber bridge (destroyed after the fighting and long since replaced by one of stone) was only wide enough to allow two or maybe three horses to ride across abreast. It was going to take half a day to get the army across. Cressingham, hugely fat and probably recognisable from a mile off, was among the first to trot over, smug arrogance radiating from every fold and roll.

The first sense of unease was not long in coming though. First the horsemen found the ground on the far bank a little on the soft side – too soft for easy deployment of any kind of massed, cohesive charge. Secondly, and even more troubling, they were milling about in a bend of the river. The Forth below Stirling Castle is all lazy meanders and loops and it was into one such watery noose that the English horse and the first of the foot soldiers had willingly slipped their own necks.

To their left lay the only hope of advance: a narrow bottleneck of dry land between two stretches of the Forth. They had their backs to deep, fast-flowing water and there was no other way out except the way they had just come, back across the crowded bridge. If it was a trap, it was one of their own making. The English chronicler Walter Guisborough wrote: 'There was, indeed, no better place in all the land to deliver the English into the hands of the Scots, and so many into the power of the few.' Guisborough's words, with their echoes of Churchill's, tell it just about right. Perhaps the first flutterings of panic were felt then in the guts of a few of the foot soldiers as well. As the lumbering heavy horses moved around them in mild confusion, snorting and champing at their cruel bits, their riders unable to see what should be done for the best, some of the men could hear the howling approach of the Scots. The horses' ears had pricked up first, alive to the distant hubbub of many armed men on the move.

Wallace and Murray had waited until perhaps half of the English army was across the river, crowded into the river bend with nowhere to go, and had then given the signal to advance. On had come the Scots at a confident jog – lesser gentry, countrymen, ordinary folk with extraordinary hopes – and the English could only wait upon their arrival. What followed was bloody slaughter.

Cavalry without order and room to deploy are little more than sitting ducks in the face of advancing schiltrons. Foot soldiers without orders will fare no better. Horses screamed as long spears were thrust home. Riders were hauled from saddles and messily dispatched. Cressingham too, unable to escape the mêlée, was pulled to the ground and butchered. The skin was later flayed from his great, bloated corpse. He had tried to tax the very skins off Scots' backs after all, and now they offered the same service in return. Wallace would have part of it fashioned into a sword belt.

Warenne never crossed the bridge. Together with the lucky half of the force he watched the butchery helplessly, with wide eyes. He was an older man, in his late sixties, and cannot have witnessed many reverses like this one. Accepting there was nothing to be done but flee, he ordered the destruction of the bridge and made first for the castle.

A few of the embattled English and Welsh had got back by swimming clear of the fighting. Among them was a Yorkshire knight with the luxurious and memorable name of Sir Marmaduke Tweng. Warenne hastily put him in charge of Stirling Castle while he himself fled for the Border. Behind him on the Carse of Stirling lay at least 100 dead knights and several thousand foot soldiers. True to their treacherous and unreliable natures, Stewart and the Earl of Lennox had changed sides. Having seen the way things were going for the visitors, they had scuttled away to join in the looting of the English baggage train.

Here was something far greater than could have been hoped for by even the most recklessly optimistic Scot. The English war machine – supposedly invincible, that had smashed the Welsh into submission, that was famed across Europe – had been taken apart piece by piece. Not just a victory, but a stunning, staggering victory. Scots ears were rendered briefly deaf – not by the battle's roar but by the sudden rush of blood to the head. For the English survivors, hardest of all to swallow was the fact that they had been sent running for their lives by peasant amateurs – *Scots* peasant amateurs at that. And for the first time, Edward would have to pay attention to the name William Wallace. One thing was already certain: he would never forget it.

The remnant threads of the Scottish nobility, either languishing in imprisonment, fighting for Edward in France or hiding from the fight behind the sick-note of the Ragman Roll, were stunned too. In a desperate bid to ride the unexpected tsunami of patriotic fervour, smuggle themselves somehow into the midst of the celebrations, they made Wallace Guardian of Scotland. In a separate impromptu ceremony at the church of Kirk o' the Forest, near Selkirk, he was dubbed a knight and thereby elevated at a stroke to the nobility. His able accomplice Murray, son of nobility and Wallace's social superior, would have been an easier choice for the Scots magnates, but he had died of awful wounds sustained amid the gilded victory.

Exactly when he had succumbed is not known, although he was certainly dead within a couple of months of the fighting. His name is alongside that of Wallace on a letter written in Haddington, in East Lothian, on 11 October 1297. It was sent 'To the Senate and Commoners of Lubeck and Hamburg' to try and persuade the trading nations of the North Sea that it was business as usual in Scotland: 'we ask you to make it known among your merchants that they can now have safe access with their merchandise to all harbours of the Kingdom of Scotland, because the Kingdom of Scotland has, thanks be to God, by war been recovered from the power of the English'.

Despite the triumph and the lionising of Wallace, there were still those who could not stomach the idea of Scotland being led by an erstwhile commoner. What could such a man know of politics and of the needs and wants of kings? Then there was the more glaring fact that while the Battle of Stirling Bridge had bloodied Edward's nose, it had also made him very, very angry. Before there could be any hope of returning King John to the throne of Scots – Wallace's sworn objective – the wrath of the English king would have to be faced.

Edward had indeed taken the reverse personally. But Stirling Bridge had been embarrassing rather than tactically significant in terms of settling Scotland's future. Throughout the rest of 1297 and on into the spring of the following year, he was personally tied up with his war in France. But by

May 1298 he was home and laying plans to crush the rebellion, and this Wallace, once and for all. Rather than leaving it in the hands of underlings, he would get the job done himself.

Wallace had not been resting on his laurels all the while. After Stirling he led his men on a punitive raid into northern England. Here, too, Scotland's Guardian revealed his own taste for ruthless violence. The soldiers of his large and unruly army were not prevented from butchering and pillaging whomever they found in Cumbria and Northumberland. Even men and women of the cloth – none was spared.

In July, Edward crossed the Tweed at the head of a massive army – 1,500 mounted knights and men-at-arms and more than 10,000 soldiers. He also brought archers, recently armed with something new – the longbow. For all the muscle and technology at his disposal, Edward was not to have things all his own way. As he advanced through southern Scotland he encountered a land laid waste by Wallace's policy of scorched earth. Invading armies were largely dependent on what could be gathered from the lands around them and, as the days and weeks passed, an air of desperation spread through the English and Welsh ranks. Tensions between men of two different and traditionally opposed nations spilled over into bitter fighting.

By the start of the third week in July, Edward's army was encamped a few miles outside Edinburgh. Rations were short and hopes of a delivery of fresh supplies into the port at Berwick had been dashed by bad weather. The would-be avengers of Stirling Bridge might tear themselves apart before the Scots could even be brought to bay.

Edward was facing the prospect of a frustrating, even humiliating withdrawal when word reached him that Wallace and his force had been spotted just 20 miles away, at Falkirk. Determined the opportunity would not be missed, Edward force-marched his men towards what he hoped would be a final showdown. English and Welsh blood was already up; the anti-Wallace propaganda machine had gone into overdrive in recent weeks and the soldiers believed they were in pursuit not of a man, but of an ogre who wanted to skin them alive.

The sight of the English approach can only have been a mixed blessing at best for Wallace. It might have been better for him had Edward begun a frustrated march for home – at least then they could have been harried and tormented as they headed south through a wasted land. Now a pitched battle was in prospect. He had managed victory – resounding victory – at Stirling just the year before. Perhaps it was best to get it over with, while

Scots spirits were high. Now, though, he was without Murray, a man often painted by history as the real tactical and military genius of the rebellion. Wallace was the heart and soul of Scotland, but would he also pass muster as her commander-in-chief?

It was too late in the day for fighting by the time Edward got his men within reach of the rebels, so they hunkered down in their thousands for an uneasy night of mumbled rumours and broken sleep. With the dawn of 22 July came orders to form up and face the monster. Wallace had his men arrayed in gigantic schiltrons – thousands of men packed shoulder-to-shoulder, long spears prickling in every direction. Between these hedgehogs was a body of Ettrick archers, commanded by Sir John Stewart and, roving around the fringes and ready to be unloosed whenever needed, were the horses and riders of the Scots cavalry. These were smaller beasts than those of fabled English heavy horse, their riders only lightly armed, but they might prove vital just the same.

The first charges by the English cavalry were galled by the stubborn resolve of the spearmen in their schiltrons. So long as order and discipline could be maintained, they made a formidable obstacle. No headway could be made by the infantry on either side and for a while it seemed deadlock might stifle any chances of a telling breakthrough. Wallace may even have found cause to hope his men might carry the day by dogged determination alone.

In the end it was the Scots cavalry that made the difference – by unceremoniously quitting the field. No explanation for their action was available on the day and none has surfaced since. In the absence of fact there have been rumours – of cowardice, of treachery – but in any event their departure made all the difference. Emboldened by having the field to themselves, the English horse now advanced towards the Ettrick archers. Where before the bowmen had been protected by the presence of the Scots cavalry, now they were exposed and dangerously static on the field. Under the command of their leader, Wallace's loyal follower Sir John Stewart, they bravely stood their ground. But the weight and purpose of the heavy horse was too much and they were soon cut down to the last man.

There was a first wavering then by the men of the schiltrons, helplessly watching the harvest of their comrades. Then English attentions turned upon them as well. Edward's archers stepped out from cover and directed their bows of the long red yew upon Scots foot soldiers for the first time. Accurate and deadly from many hundreds of yards distant, they rained darkening storms of iron-tipped shafts down upon the heads of the spearmen.

Like the Spartan 300 at Thermopylae nearly 1,800 years before, the Scots stood briefly in their sudden shade, and then fell for ever – revenge for what had been done at Stirling. It was a bloodbath. It was said the Scots fell like blossoms in an orchard when the fruit has ripened.

Pushed beyond endurance by the countless dead dropping around them, the surviving spearmen broke and ran. Before there had been stubborn, seemingly immovable schiltrons; now there were disordered scrums of frightened, traumatised men breaking and running for cover. The English cavalry completed the rout and Wallace and his surviving few fled the field.

Soon after Falkirk, Wallace resigned his role as Guardian. He stepped out of the spotlight for a time then, though the folk myths insist he carried on his fight from the shadows. He is supposed to have returned to his favoured guerrilla tactics, snapping at the heels and loins of the English wherever and whenever he could. And while the reins of leadership of the Community of the Realm were taken up by men like John 'the Red' Comyn, Robert Bruce the younger and Bishop William Lamberton of St Andrews, Wallace briefly left the country.

The return of King John remained the sole objective of the rebellion and Wallace made his way to the court of Philippe IV of France in hope of exploiting the Auld Alliance in Scotland's favour. Only young Robert Bruce had cause to dread the return of the king. The Bruces owed their hold on their Annandale lands not to Balliol, but to Edward. With that in mind, naked self-interest was always closer to young Robert's heart than any loyalty to his absent king. In the end, Wallace's efforts as a diplomat came to naught. Philippe was too busy it seemed, fighting and losing to the Flemish, to be bothered by requests to honour a promise.

By 1303, when Edward found the energy to return to the job of crushing the rebellion, Scotland was a nation alone. The Community of the Realm of Scotland quickly realised the cost of more war would be too much for the country to bear. They sought terms. Even Edward, in his sixties now and tired, had lost the stomach for it all. Apart from anything else, the wars in Scotland had taken an enervating toll on his finances and by 1304 he just wanted to draw a line under the whole sorry affair.

Most of the Scots nobles were to be left more or less alone, their lands intact. William Wallace, however, could not be forgiven. While Edward lived, his grudge against the leader of brigands could never die. At a parliament ordered by Edward at St Andrews in March, Wallace was made an outlaw. Some 129 Scottish landowners accepted Edward as their liege lord at the same time. Among those bending the knee was Robert Wishart, Bishop of Glasgow. Robert Bruce was tucked safely at Edward's heel as well. The document they signed up to was called 'The Ordinances of 1305' and in truth it quietly marked the completion of Edward's second conquest. There was no mention of a kingdom, far less a king of Scotland. In fact they signed in meek acceptance of Edward's truth – that they held territory now in a place to be described merely as a 'land'.

Wallace was on the run, eking out an existence in the caves and forests of his homeland. Edward turned the screws tighter and tighter. Those who had been Wallace's friends and followers were bullied into turning traitor to him. He was finally captured and handed over to the English by Sir John Mentieth, uncle of Sir John Stewart who had died for Wallace at Falkirk. In the evening of 3 August 1305 he was surprised and taken in a house at Robroyston, outside Glasgow. Transported to London, he was presented before Edward's judges in Westminster Hall. Supposedly in mockery of his ambitions, he was made to wear a crown of laurel leaves.

Wallace had never claimed the crown. He had fought only and always for King John but the English judges cared about their own truth and no other. There was no trial. Wallace was an outlaw and therefore already condemned. The words of the indictment that echoed around the walls and rafters of the great hall were just sound effects for a royal command performance. Edward did enjoy his shows.

Wallace had notoriously committed killings, they said. Arson, destruction of property, sacrilege – Edward was master of the law and he was showing off. Wallace had assumed the title of Guardian and had seduced his fellow Scots into an alliance with the French. Only at the utterance of the words 'treason' and 'traitor' did Wallace raise his voice in reply. He had never in his life sworn allegiance to the English king – his name, after all, was absent from the Ragman Roll. 'How am I a traitor,' he demanded to know, 'when England is foreign to me?' Edward's judges were unmoved, of course. When King John had sworn allegiance to Edward in return for his throne, they said, he had done so on behalf of every one of his subjects. Wallace was trapped in the web of Edward's legal arguments, the outcome a foregone conclusion.

It was 23 August 1305 and with the sentence of the court ringing in his ears, Wallace was marched outside. The butchery of Scotland's finest patriot was performed on a spot across the road from the modern Smithfield Meat Market. In accordance with the conventions demanded by a traitor's death, he was first of all throttled at the of end a hangman's noose. Once he had regained full consciousness his genitals were cut from his body. The knife was used then to open his abdomen so that his stomach, intestines and lungs could be 'drawn' from inside him. His heart was last, wrenched from his chest and held aloft for the appreciation of the crowd. Finally he was beheaded with a blow of the executioner's axe. His head was exhibited upon a spike on London Bridge. His corpse was cut in four and the quarters sent for public display in Newcastle, Berwick, Stirling and Perth.

The destruction of the body was a deliberate and calculated act. It was Edward's hope that without a body to be buried, a grave for mourners to gather round, the man would soon be forgotten. Of course the opposite was true, and the Wallace legend is immortal.

In the end, his mission on earth had failed. King John of Scotland was king in name only, his nobles imprisoned or under oaths of fealty to another. Edward I, Hammer of the Scots, had won every battle that mattered. Scotland in 1305 was nothing more than a region of England. But there was another battle, a battle without end. Far from winning it, Edward was blind, deaf and dumb even to its existence. It was the battle for the people of Scotland.

In his fixation with the crown of Scotland, Edward had underestimated her folk. He had torn the heart from one of them, but hundreds of thousands more were beating still, and loudly. Patriotism – the love of country – was not the cause of Scotland's wars of independence, but their product.

Edward's determination to crush them had served only to define for the Scots who they really were.

CHAPTER FOUR

BISHOP MAKES KING

'Put not your trust in kings and princes. Three of a kind will take them both.'

General Robert C. Schenck

Duplicity – double-dealing, along with cunning and cruelty – these more than honesty, courage and honour, it seems, are the defining characteristics of kings and princes . . . and of men who would be kings.

General Schenck commanded Union armies in the American Civil War. He was at both battles of Bull Run and fought 'Stonewall' Jackson in the Shenandoah Valley. He was also a card player – draw poker mostly. His book of rules is at the root of the game's popularity on this side of the Atlantic. Having survived that war, Schenck understood as well as anybody how a civil war tears apart families and friendships: brother turns against brother; father makes war on son. As a poker player of some prowess he also knew that while a face card might look impressive, it was next to useless on its own. In poker, as in war, it was about strength in numbers.

So it was with Scotland's kings and Scotland's wars.

After Wallace's defeat at Falkirk he was replaced as Guardian of the Realm by two major noblemen. Robert Bruce, Earl of Carrick and John Comyn, son of the Lord of Badenoch, were two of a kind. Both were young – in their twenties – both ambitious in the extreme. Each was the representative of his family, and their families were the most powerful in the land.

The Comyns – lords of Badenoch and earls of Buchan – supported the royal claim of John Balliol, Badenoch's uncle. The Bruces of Annandale – bitter rivals of Balliols and Comyns alike – backed themselves.

John Comyn and young Robert Bruce also had a dilemma in common.

Both families held lands not just in Scotland but in England as well – vast tracts of territory in the case of the Comyns. They held these lands directly from the English king and paid him homage for them as a result. Were either of them to give up territories and break their ties to Edward they would at once cut themselves off from the wider world of feudal society. Such a move might make it easier for a Comyn to support a Balliol; it would simplify things for a Bruce in pursuit of the crown. But by limiting their ambitions to Scotland they would make of themselves big fish in a very small pond.

It was complications like these that made the rivalries between the Scottish dynasties in the fourteenth century so unforgiving, so cruel and so relentless. It certainly explains the bitter spat between Bruce and Comyn when they clashed at a council of war in Peebles in 1299.

With Wallace out of the country on his diplomatic mission, Sir David Graham, a Comyn supporter, had laid claim to the absentee knight's lands and possessions. Graham claimed Wallace had failed to give any warning to the Guardians of his planned absence in a time of war – and that his belongings were for the taking as a result. Wallace, however, was a supporter of the Bruces and young Robert decided to take the slight personally. Strong words between Bruce and Comyn descended into outright violence, with Comyn finally grabbing his rival by the throat.

The constant scheming and strategising – what to do for the best, for the future – also caused violent splits within families. Son might disagree with father over whom to support, what line to take; brother might fight with brother for the same reason. The eldest and therefore the heir might favour the status quo; the younger, with less to lose, might choose a more reckless path in pursuit of power and riches. One English chronicler wrote: 'in all this fighting the Scots were so divided that often a father was with the Scots and his son with the English, or one brother was with the Scots and another with the English, or even one individual was first on one side and then on the other'.

As the summer of 1305 gave way to the gloom of autumn and then the darkness of winter it might have seemed as if the sun would never return to Scotland. Edward of England could certainly have been forgiven for thinking he had snuffed out the last lights of the northern kingdom.

Edward was a game player too – not cards, but chess. Invented by the Persians long before, the game had been brought to north and west Europe by the Vikings at the end of the first millenium. All about long-term strategy mixed with subtle feints, misdirection and lightning-fast attacks, it was the perfect training for a military strategist like the King of England. The end game was the death of the king – *Shah mat* in Persian, literally 'the king is dead', hence 'check mate' in English – but leaving him with nowhere to go, no moves left to make, worked just as well.

King John of Scotland was out of the game. Broken and defeated, he had been boxed into a corner by Edward's bishops, pawns and *rukhs* – his war chariots. Even more gratifying for Edward, at least in the short term, had been the outmanoeuvring and total destruction of King John's troublesome knight, William Wallace. Edward the chess master – he had won because he was the better player. Scotland was a conquered province and would be governed like any other. Her nobles were left in peace, more or less. Edward let them keep their homes and their titles, as long as they first bowed down to him as king. The iron fist of war was covered with the velvet glove.

The game was not over: at least, not the long game. There were still pieces on the board and, unbeknown to Edward, some of them were still moving. Some of them, in fact, had moved in overlooked corners of the board while Edward was too engrossed in his torment of the king and the knight to notice what the Scots bishops were up to. For practical purposes, he had lumped Scotland's senior churchmen in with her nobles, leaving them alone in their great houses and estates just as long as they acknowledged him as the dominant power. But behind the English king's back, two bishops were involved in a long-term strategy so convoluted – of such Byzantine cunning – even he would have had to offer grudging admiration.

By 1305 Robert Wishart of Glasgow, a stubborn bulldog of a man, had been fighting for Scottish independence for the best part of twenty years. He had made some of his moves in full view of the English king – even standing up to him during the Great Cause – but he was just as likely to favour underhand conniving. William Lamberton, Bishop of St Andrews was another double-dealer, a strategist on a par with the English king himself.

If Edward had known them better he would have strung them both up alongside Wallace. Aside from the individual personalities of Wishart and Lamberton, they held by far the richest of Scotland's eleven dioceses. Argyll, Caithness, Galloway, Moray, Ross and the rest . . . they varied enormously in terms of population, size and wealth; but these nine together did not add up to the clout, military and financial, of St Andrews and Glasgow. As

Bishop of St Andrews, William Lamberton had his principal palace as well as another nine or ten manor houses besides; these were not just church-men, they were magnates.

In the Borders, the Cistercian houses of Coldingham, Dryburgh, Jedburgh, Kelso and Melrose had grown enormously rich through the lucrative trade of sheep farming. Wool production was a thirteenth- and fourteenth- century goldmine for the Church and with wealth had come vast lands.

As rich and powerful landowners, existing in a world apart from other men and women, the bishops had always attracted the attentions of the kings of Scots. Keen to be involved with them – for spiritual and for practical reasons – the monarchs did their best to keep a hand in the appointment of new bishops. For the most part, this interference was tolerated. It was a symbiotic relationship that mattered, more than any other, to both parties. The powerful influence of the Church in general – and of the dioceses of St Andrews and Glasgow in particular – was demonstrated by the selection of those bishops as two of the six Guardians of Scotland following the death of Alexander III in 1286.

The Scottish bishops were also working from an older rulebook than that of the English king, one that enabled them to see the game through different eyes. Central to every move and argument they would make was the independence of the Scottish Church – specifically, its independence from England.

Some of their confidence stemmed from the Quitclaim of Canterbury, the document signed by Richard the Lionheart in 1189. It had made null and void the humiliating Treaty of Falaise of 1174, by which William the Lion had accepted the English king Henry II as his overlord. But finding himself short of funds for crusading in 1189, Richard I had willingly sold back Scotland's independence for 10,000 merks. Implicit in the Quitclaim was Scotland's spiritual as well as temporal freedom – the King of Scotland was free of England's domination and so was the Church.

As far as Scotland's bishops at the time were concerned this merely underlined a judgment they had received the year before, from the Pope. In 1188, a delegation of Scottish churchmen had visited the Vatican in search of a clarification. The question they had asked, in light of the Treaty of Falaise, was: Who is in charge of the Scottish Church – the Pope in Rome or the King of England? Pope Clement III had been in no doubt and issued a Bull stating that the Scottish Church answered directly to the Apostolic

See – in other words, to the Pope himself. From that moment, Scotland's bishops saw Scotland, and Scotland's Church, as 'Rome's special daughter'. While bishops in England were subject to their archbishops in Canterbury or York, their Scots counterparts had no one standing between themselves and the Pope.

By the turn of the fourteenth century, however, there was a glaring problem. The independence of the Scottish Church depended upon the existence of a Scottish kingdom, of a Scottish *king*. If there were no king – if Scotland were to become no more than a province of England – then the bishops' privileged position would cease to exist. No more the hotline to their holy father. Soon they would be bending the knee and paying the tithes in York or Canterbury. The notion of Rome's special daughter would disappear like a dream upon the moment of waking. Men like Wishart and Lamberton, another two of a kind, understood perfectly well that they and their colleagues now faced that rude awakening. Balliol was in exile in Europe, in the custody of Pope Boniface VIII, and Scotland's fate was blowing in the breeze like a toom tabard.

As recently as 1299 the Pope had restated his direct authority over the Scottish Church. But King Edward – leaving no stone unturned in his bid to prove English overlordship – wrote a carefully worded letter to the Pope the following year. As part of his argument he quoted the origin myth of the English, as recorded by Geoffrey of Monmouth in the twelfth century. The English, he said, were descended from Brutus, a Roman consul who had conquered the island of Britain in ancient times; in fact the very name 'Britain' was derived from Brutus. Since the English were there first, went the logic, they must have precedence over the Scots. It was a bold and colourful argument and it inspired a reply in kind from the Scottish bishops.

In the summer of 1301 a small party of Scottish priests travelled to Italy to make their case in person. The Pope was in his summer residence in the hill town of Anagni, his birthplace, 50 kilometres south-east of Rome. It was there that the Scottish bishops made their first subtle moves in the defence of their homeland. The delegation was led by a wily churchman named Baldred Bissett. Hailing originally from Stirlingshire, he was an expert in Church Law; and with the very future of Scotland and her Church at stake he would need every ounce of his experience and guile.

He made his case. If the English had a version of ancient history, so did the Scots: they were descended from Noah and had started out in Israel. When Israel had fallen to the Assyrians, his descendants fled the land among the 'Ten Lost Tribes of Israel'. After much wandering they reached Scythia, near the Black Sea. One of their number, a prince of Scythia, married an exiled Egyptian princess named Scota. It was from Scota that the Scots had acquired their name, said Bisset, and the upshot of all this was obvious: the Scots were something very old, something other. How could they be subject to England, when England was foreign to them?

Next he reminded the Pope of Scotland's status as Rome's special daughter. Given the behaviour and intent of Edward I of England, said Bissett, that daughter was in urgent need of her father's protection. Then he turned to the recent past: the English king had wickedly mistreated Scotland's legitimate king. Edward had exploited Balliol's forced absence – and Scotland's resultant weakness – by committing boundless atrocities against Scots both clerical and lay, noble and peasant, male and female. Bissett called upon the Pope to free Balliol and let him return to Scotland as the rightful king.

It worked. Pope Boniface ordered Balliol's release and let it be known that in his eyes Balliol was the 'illustrious King of Scots'. Back in Scotland, the Guardians began to issue edicts in the name of King John Balliol once more. The success of Bissett and his team, however, was short-lived. Despite the studious efforts of so many – to clear him a path all the way back to his birthright – Balliol did not have the stomach for the job. He was ensconced in his family estate in Picardy and in no mood to return from there into Edward's firing line.

There would be further setbacks. In 1302 Boniface would push too hard against the wrong man by issuing his most famous judgment, the Bull *Unam Sanctum*. The Pope was the supreme power on earth, it said, and therefore greater than any king. Among those who took extreme exception to the claim was Philippe IV of France, who went so far as to make war on the Pope – even taking him prisoner, in 1303. (He was later released, but died within a month; his views on the independence of Scotland and her king died with him. It was after this grievous affront that the papacy moved to Avignon.)

All the hard work of the Scots bishops was undone. They had staked everything on winning the backing of Boniface VIII and while they held his full attention they had been able to count on his support. But once he found himself fighting for his own survival, his concern for the well-being of his special daughter slipped his mind. And while the Vicar of Christ tried to fend off the King of France, Scotland found herself alone in the world.

Edward, meanwhile, was contemplating the necessity of reinvading Scotland. But before the war machine could be got into motion, another redoubtable Scots churchman made his move.

Sometime in the autumn of 1302 William Lamberton, Bishop of St Andrews since 1297, travelled to Paris on Church business. He was part of a delegation of priests and other worthies, but perhaps he made sure to be alone when he met with a fellow Scot, resident in the city at that time. John Duns Scotus was just thirty-seven when he received his visit from Lamberton, but was already seen by some as the greatest theologian of his day. Little is known about his early life but it is thought he was born in Duns, in Berwickshire. He became a Franciscan, was ordained at St Andrews Church in Northampton in 1291, and during his short life of just forty-three years taught theology and philosophy at Oxford and Cologne, as well as in Paris. Central to his thinking was the importance – the primacy – of the individual and it was this tenet that had moved Lamberton to seek the counsel of Duns Scotus on the matter of the King of Scotland and the individuals of the Community of the Realm.

Every bit as much as the world of the twenty-first century, that of the fourteenth was governed by a rule of law. Emperors, kings and even popes might make fast and loose with its strictures as and when it suited, but all of them would have at least paid lip service to the fact. It was undoubtedly in the interest of the first two groups to assert the rights – indeed the inviolable, God-given rights – of kings.

Lamberton's problem – Scotland's problem – was that King John was a lame duck. What the bishop wanted to do was have him sacked and put another man in his place. Historian Dr William Russell has done more than consider the possibility of a meeting between Lamberton and Duns Scotus. He believes that it was from Duns Scotus that Lamberton gained the argument, and the confidence, for a move to overthrow the legitimate King of Scots and to replace him with another. According to Dr Russell, when Lamberton sought a legal case for backing the Bruce over Balliol, Duns Scotus did not disappoint him. The real root of royal authority, said the theologian, had nothing to do with inheritance. A king whose power was legitimate was king because his people granted him their consent, and if that consent were to be withdrawn for any reason then the man was king no more. By his refusal to return to his throne even when it was offered to him without conditions, John Balliol had committed the medieval equivalent of gross professional misconduct. The 'people' – effectively his employers – were within their rights to sack him and choose someone else.

This way of thinking had echoes and resonances of the time of the ancient kings. In the distant past, among the Gaels and the Picts, had been the question of *febas* – a Gaelic word meaning 'worth'. Even in those days, descent from some dynasty was a prerequisite, but it was not the only or even the most important qualification of a candidate for the kingship. The surviving followers of the royal household cared at least as much that the new king would be worthy of the position; if in their eyes the dead king's eldest son was not, they would choose some other man as their ruler.

Scotland, indeed the land before Scotland, bequeathed to the modern world one of the foundation stones of lawful government – the people's right to choose who they will be governed by. The problem was, of course, that until very recent times 'the people' meant a relative handful of the richest and most powerful men in the land.

Soon after his meeting with Lamberton, Duns Scotus would write at length about rulers having a moral obligation to those they sought to rule. He said a king was chosen not by God, nor did he have supreme power just by dint of owning more land than anyone else. According to Duns Scotus a rightful king was selected by the community around him. As long as he satisfied that community he was entitled to rule, but as soon as he failed them he could be deposed and replaced. In fourteenth-century Europe, these were truly radical ideas. It is tempting to think, like Dr Russell, that they crystallised into a definite form for Duns Scotus after the conversations he had with Lamberton in Paris in 1302.

The Bishop of St Andrews returned to Scotland a happier man, secure in the knowledge that he had the justification for removing the king from his throne. But time was running out. While Lamberton set about the task of persuading others of the rightness of his cause, Edward was preparing for the final conquest of his restless northern neighbour.

Stirling Castle was the last stronghold to fall to Edward during the spring and summer of 1304. He had saved it to the end as a showpiece finale – revenge for Stirling Bridge seven years before. Between the last week of April and the last week of July the Scots garrison under the command of Sir William Oliphant put up a dogged resistance. Edward flung everything he had at the walls, even providing the ladies of his court with a grandstand view of the bombardment by his siege engines.

The greatest of these was a monstrous catapult, a *trebuchet* he called

'Warwolf'. It had taken twenty-seven wagons to carry its component parts to Stirling and the town's defenders had had to watch while it was constructed beneath their castle walls. Once it was completed, Edward used it to launch huge stone balls as well as earthenware jars of 'Greek fire' onto the terrified inhabitants. Here was a medieval weapon of shock and awe. In spite of the battering by Warwolf and the rest of the English king's armaments, the garrison held out. Only when they finally ran out of food did they open the doors to the enemy.

While Edward was distracted by the pounding of Stirling Castle, two of his sworn vassals slipped quietly away. Robert Bruce had been at the English king's side, obediently watching his master at work. Lamberton, too, his travels completed, was in attendance at the pleasure of the king. Within sight of the castle – close enough to hear the relentless bombardment – the Bishop of St Andrews met with the future King of Scotland, on 11 June 1304. The venue for their secret assignation was Cambuskenneth Abbey, beside the River Forth and less than half a mile from Stirling.

It was a turning point in the history of a nation. When Balliol had been chosen as king, there were two other families with strong claims upon the throne. The Comyns were related to the Balliols by both blood and marriage, and had honoured family ties in surrendering their own rights. Lamberton knew that John Comyn was a scrupulous man, a doer-by-the-book. It would be difficult to persuade such a man to wrap himself up in business that looked and smelled like – in fact was – the usurpation of the throne. But there was of course another family and another claim. The 6th Earl of Annandale, son of the Competitor, had died just two months before. Now his son had assumed the mantle and, along with the lands and the name of his grandfather, he had inherited the ambition. The seventh Robert Bruce was, like Lamberton, a vassal of King Edward. But his loyalty to the family claim upon the throne of Scotland was greater by far.

In spite of his unshakeable conviction as to the rightness of his claim, however, this Bruce had as yet no idea how to go about acting upon it. But Lamberton did. There at Cambuskenneth they put their names to a bond, 'of mutual friendship and alliance against all men'. Given the importance, the treacherous intent of the document, its wording is wonderfully vague: 'They have agreed faithfully to be of one another's counsel in all their business affairs at all times and against whichever individuals ... and that neither of them should undertake any important business without the other of them. They will mutually warn each other against any impending

Knap of Howar village, Orkney

Skara Brae village, Orkney

Bennachie, Aberdeenshire

Broch of Mousa, Shetland

Calanais stone circle, Lewis

A reconstructed crannog, Loch Tay

Dunadd, Kilmartin Glen, Mid Argyll

Iona Abbey, Iona

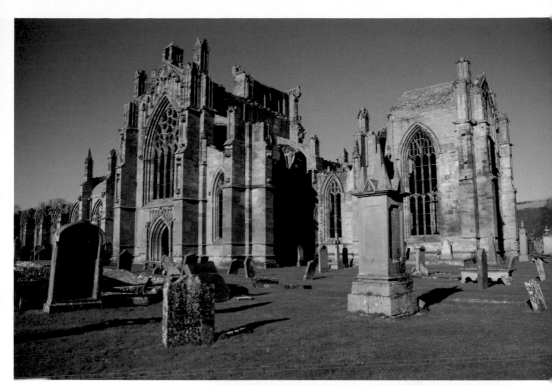

Melrose Abbey

Edward I

The Ragman Roll

The Coronation Chair, Westminster Abbey

Cambuskenneth Abbey, Stirling

Stirling Castle

The Declaration of Arbroath

Pilkington Jackson's statue of Robert I, Bannockburn

danger and do the best to avert the same from the other.' Nowhere is there any mention of what the contract was really about: that Lamberton and the Scottish Church would work with the Bruce to make him King of Scotland. Of course, committing any such plan to paper would have been a suicidal move. Secrecy was vital. With this in mind, the penalty for the failure of either party to observe the terms of the bond was set at the fantastically high sum of £10,000.

The deal struck, silence agreed, both men departed the shadows of the abbey and returned to the pressing business of being Edward's loyal servants. All the while the English king's 'Ordnance for the Governance of the land of Scotland' was being prepared, while a price was being put on the head of William Wallace, both Lamberton and the Bruce continued to kneel before their liege lord. For the Bruce, the continued quiet subservience was a tall order. Lamberton had pressed upon him the need for patience, the need to behave obediently and normally until the moment was right to move towards the throne. Clearly, Lamberton intended that *he* would be the man to make that decision. The Bruce, however – already twenty-nine and not known for his patience – had other ideas.

He managed to put up a front and hold things together for around eighteen months. It is supposed by some that during that time he may have entered into some kind of quiet discussions with his rival John 'the Red' Comyn about who should be king. Both men would have understood that the Bruce's claim was legally the stronger, by far. But to win agreement from the most powerful family in the land he sought to govern, he must have suggested there was something in it for the Comyns as well. It is possible the Bruce offered up his own lands in exchange for a promise of Comyn backing, but in the event any such details were about to be swept away.

On Thursday, 10 February 1306 the Sheriff Court was in session at Dumfries Castle. This was about Edward's justice of course, but the king was ill and lying on his sick-bed in an English monastery. Everyone else of any importance for miles around, though, was in attendance.

Under such circumstances it would have been quite natural for both Robert Bruce and the Red Comyn to be there. Their seats were local and it would have made sense for the two noblemen to get together for a conversation about future plans. It is even possible that Lamberton and the other bishops had given their sanction to the Bruce quietly raising the matter of their support for him as the new king of Scotland. Whatever was on the official agenda is unknown, but the two met in a Franciscan priory near the River Nith, a building known to history as Greyfriars Church. Both men were accompanied by their followers and there may have been some tension in the air. Meetings between the pair were not always cordial, after all.

Despite any understandable nervousness, it was quite appropriate for the Bruce to get together with his rival and try to persuade him of the newly assured legality of replacing one king with another. It did not make sense, however, for the Bruce to kill him. But kill him he did. Perhaps at the vital moment it was a final declaration from John Comyn of his continued and defiant support of Balliol that pushed his opponent over the edge. The Bruce made at least one – probably the first – of the wounds with his own blade. As Comyn buckled, his men stepped in with swords drawn. Bursting from the church, Bruce shouted to one of his followers, Sir Roger de Kirkpatrick, that he thought he had killed Comyn. 'I'll make sure,' replied Kirkpatrick, rushing inside to finish the job. The words 'I mak siccar' are the Kirkpatrick family motto to this day. (Whether this happened or not matters less than the way in which it has become fixed in folklore. At the very least it is a literary device that shows the Red Comyn's murder was a drama in two acts.)

In a further blatant act of rebellion, the Bruce and his followers broke up the Sheriff Court, sending everyone away. This was bad enough – a barefaced challenge to Edward's authority – but killing a fellow nobleman was infinitely worse. The sin itself was deadly, but the place in which he had committed the crime – God's house – placed it beyond redemption. The man who would be king had stepped into the abyss. By letting his anger and frustration get the better of him, he had made an executive decision that compromised for ever the pact with Lamberton. In that moment he had moved from being the likely heir to the throne to a man facing ruin, both temporal and spiritual. He faced perdition, the destruction of his immortal soul.

There was no time for grief or regrets. Whether or not he was beset by fears about eternity, Bruce at once set about the business of claiming his kingdom with a will. By his own hand he took control of the castles of Ayr, Dalswinton, Tibbers and Dumfries. Rothesay Castle on Bute was taken on his behalf by his ally Robert Boyd of Cunningham; other fortresses within reach of his own lands were either taken or made over to him.

Within weeks of the murder Bruce was in Glasgow. Wishart, Lamberton's

co-conspirator in the bid to replace Balliol, understood that success had
depended upon waiting for the death of Edward. The English king was old
and increasingly frail; it might only have been a matter of months or at
most a few more years. Now the Bruce had made all of that irrelevant. By
his one sacrilegious act he had imperilled everything – even the very hope
of ever again making Scotland an independent kingdom. But Wishart was
sage enough to see that none of that mattered any more. If anything were
to be salvaged from the wreckage of Greyfriars Church, they would have
to move at once, maintain the unwanted and yet undeniably powerful
momentum created by a fusillade of blows in a distant priory.

He absolved the Bruce of all guilt for his crime and wrung from the
penitent a pledge that he would remain obedient to the wishes of the
Scottish Church. It was a reminder of his pact with Lamberton; a shameful
reminder of his crime. It was a tug on a leash, worn now and for ever. The
fiery cross – the ancient call to arms – was sent across the land. Wishart,
the old war horse, climbed into the pulpit and preached as though his own
immortal soul depended upon the veracity of his words. He told the faithful
that this Robert Bruce was to be King Robert I of Scotland. They must give
battle for him now, give up their lives for him if required to do so, because
this was to be nothing less than a crusade. He is your *king*, the bishop
thundered, *fight for him!*

Just six weeks after felling his rival in Dumfries, Bruce was at Scone to
don his crown. When word of the event reached Edward, he may have taken
some comfort from knowing the Scots lacked even the tools with which to
make a king: he had the Stone of Destiny, the Black Rood of St Margaret
and all the regalia of sword, sceptre and crown – he even had in his
custody the sixteen-year-old Earl of Fife, whose ancient privilege it was to
inaugurate the King of Scotland.

The bishops, however, had the man, and they made him king just the
same. Wishart produced a set of royal robes, carefully hidden away for just
such an occasion, so the Bruce will have looked the part. His second wife,
Queen Elizabeth, was at his side. In the absence of the Earl of Fife the crown
was placed upon Robert's head by Isabella of Fife, Countess of Buchan. Her
husband, the Earl, was a cousin of the murdered Red Comyn. He was not
a little put out by Isabella's betrayal and it was a move that in time would
cost her dearly. The available records show that among others present
were four earls and three bishops: Lamberton, Wishart and David Murray,
Bishop of Moray (three of a kind – the better to shape a winning hand). It

was Friday, 25 March 1306. King Robert I was thirty-one years old.

Lamberton was certainly in attendance two days later when he celebrated a High Mass. If the new king took the opportunity to pray for help and protection from the Almighty, then he had more than his own hide to worry about. There were his followers and anyone else who had acted or spoken up in his support. He was the eldest of ten children: four brothers – Edward, Alexander, Thomas and Neil – and five sisters – Mary, Christian, Matilda, Margaret and Isabella. There was also his eleven-year-old daughter Marjorie, by his first wife, Isabella, who had died giving birth to her. Bruce's actions imperilled them all and their fates in the months and years ahead would hang around his neck like a servant's yoke.

So much for crowns and ceremonies and brave words: King Robert faced not just the prospect of defending his realm against Edward of England, but also the more pressing necessity of taking ownership of his realm in the first place. The Comyns, too, were the descendants of kings, mightier by far than Bruce and his traditional supporters, and he had murdered their son and heir. Also rising to seek vengeance were the Balliols and all their followers. Robert could call himself king if he wanted, but proving it in the hearts and minds of the people of Scotland – from the lowliest, to the Community of the Realm – was something else entirely.

King Robert returned first of all to the ancestral Comyn lands in the south-west, and set about making them secure. Bishop Wishart put aside the trappings of his office and captured Cupar Castle for him, 'like a man of war'. But there was a storm coming. Edward I had appointed his own man in Scotland: Red Comyn's brother-in-law, the able and experienced troubleshooter Aymer de Valence, next Earl of Pembroke. This wet-work by forces loyal to the English king would be like nothing yet endured by the Bruce, or by anyone else. On Edward's orders, Pembroke had 'raised dragon' – the dragon banner telling all who saw it that the men riding beneath had suspended all customs of chivalry. There would be no quarter for any that stood in the face of them. Only their positions as senior churchmen saved the necks of Lamberton and Wishart. Both were captured and imprisoned.

The English had recaptured Cupar; they had swiftly taken Perth as well. In an attempt to seize the initiative, King Robert offered pitched battle there in June. With a recklessness bordering on the stupid, he set no sentries around his makeshift camp among trees near Methven as he and his men settled down for the night. With chivalry set aside, Pembroke and his force –

bolstered by Comyn supporters – thought nothing of launching a surprise night attack against the king. Less a battle than a rout, Bruce and a few hundred of his followers were lucky to escape the carnage with their lives.

For most of those taken prisoner by the English, only the grisly deaths allotted to traitors awaited them. King Robert I of Scotland was a fugitive on the run. After Methven he headed towards the north-west, and suffered a further defeat at Dalry, near Tyndrum. With nothing left to do but keep running, he sent Elizabeth, their daughter Marjorie and the rest of the womenfolk towards the far north. The hope was that they would make it all the way to Orkney, from where they could take ship to Norway. Robert's sister Isabella was the widow of King Erik of Norway (she had become his second wife after the death of Queen Margaret, while giving birth to the Maid of Norway) and the promise of a sanctuary with family beckoned. It was not to be. The women were captured at Tain and handed over to Edward.

King Robert was luckier, being able to draw upon all his powers of endurance. With every other avenue blocked to him, he turned towards the south-west. Eventually, though, he simply ran out of road. Having reached the sea, he turned around and looked back at his kingdom. He had been king for mere months and now he was poised to leave his realm in the hands of his bitterest foes. Left behind too were his wife and daughter, his brothers and sisters, his bishops and all those who had stepped up to the fight alongside him. Discretion is said to be the better part of valour, however, and for now the king's only real course was to disappear. And so he put to ship and vanished into thin air.

Back on the mainland, Edward indulged himself in a spectacular orgy of cruelty and slaughter. Dozens, scores of Robert's supporters were executed, and in all manner of ways. His own brother Neil was butchered like William Wallace. Many more were dispatched the same way. John of Strathbogie, Earl of Atholl had been captured while trying to lead Robert's womenfolk to safety. He was sentenced to hang. When it was pointed out to Edward that Atholl was his kin, the king ordered that his gallows be raised so that he might hang higher.

It was in his treatment of two of Robert's women that Edward revealed the true temperature of his vengeful wrath. He had two cages built, one each in Roxburgh and Berwick castles. Robert's twenty-four-year-old sister Mary was imprisoned in the first and Isabella, Countess of Buchan – who had placed the gold circlet on the king's head – in the second. The cages were hung from turrets, in public view, and may have been open to the elements. Both remained in those conditions until at least 1310, when it seems they may have been moved into convents. Edward initially sentenced little Marjorie, just eleven or twelve years old, to the same fate. Just in time he relented and sent her to a convent instead. Queen Elizabeth was placed under house arrest in Holderness. She would not see her husband again for eight years. Her sister-in-law Christian Bruce was sent to a convent.

Apart from any other privations he suffered during his six-month vanishing act, surely none would have bitten more deeply than hearing one by one of the fates of his family and friends. King Robert – King Hobbe, as the English now dismissively called him – was a religious man. He had been excommunicated by the Pope after his murder of the Red Comyn and now the news of every agonising death must have intensified any feelings of doubt about the rightness of his quest: misfortunes such as these might be signs of God's displeasure – perhaps God did not want him to be king.

Precisely where he spent those most painful months of his life is not known. Dozens of caves up and down the western coast of Scotland and even northern England are supposed to have given shelter to the King of Scots at some point during that winter of 1306–7. Perhaps he was in the Hebrides, or in Ireland. Ardnamurchan is a current favourite, but the truth of it may never be known. Maybe King Robert himself thought the details of his humiliating forced absence best forgotten. It was Sir Walter Scott who pulled together all the strands of myth and hearsay about the travails of the Bruce in 1828, in *Tales of a Grandfather*. It was also Scott who gave him a spider for company:

> Bruce was looking upward at the roof of the cabin in which he lay; and his eye was attracted by a spider, which, hanging at the end of a long thread of its own spinning, was endeavouring, as is the fashion of that creature, to swing itself one beam in the roof to another, for the purpose of fixing the line on which it meant to stretch its web. The insect made the attempt again and again without success; and at length the Bruce counted that it had tried to carry its point six times. It came into his head that he had himself fought just six battles with the English and their allies and that the poor persevering spider was exactly in the same situation with himself . . .

The parable of the spider was not invented by Scott. There is a much older storytelling tradition, spanning many cultures, about their industry and perseverance. Spiders and caves come up again and again, often in tales to comfort children. One old fable has the holy family fleeing Herod's men soon after Christ's birth. They take shelter in a cave and a spider, understanding the importance of the child, spins a web across the cave mouth to make it look as if no one has entered in a long time. Overnight the strands are covered by glittering frost and by the time the soldiers arrive, the illusion is complete. Tinsel is hung on Christmas trees in memory of the crucial role played by another spider and another web.

The message of Scott's spider was factual enough. During the winter of 1306–7 King Robert faced a stark choice: whether to give up or fight on. Giving up could hardly have been attractive: he could flee all the way to Norway and move in with his sister, make a life for himself, but that would leave the rest of his family and all of his supporters at terrible risk. It would leave his brother's death – and so many more besides – unavenged.

Wherever he drew his inspiration and determination from, it must have been a deep well. For when he returned to the fray in the spring of 1307 all that greeted him at first was more death, more grief and more frustration. His plan of attack had been two-pronged: he sent two of his brothers, Alexander and Thomas, to Galloway with a small force. Captured almost at once, their men were either killed or taken prisoner. Alexander and Thomas were summarily executed.

King Robert landed on the Ayrshire coast, near Turnberry Castle, where he had been born thirty-two years before, with a few score Irishmen and Hebrideans. The English were everywhere and once again he was forced to hide in the wilds of his own kingdom. In spite of it all – the deaths of two more brothers included – he dug deep into his store of self-belief. He had no intention of following Wallace to an early grave and so set about making the most of what physical resources he had. Denied force of numbers, he formed his handful of knights and his few hundred spearmen and foot soldiers into a tight guerrilla unit, as described in the *Scotichronicon*:

> Let Scotland's warcraft be this: footsoldiers, mountains and marshy ground; and let her woods, her bow and spear serve for barricades. Let menace lurk in all her narrow places among her warrior bands, and let her plains so burn with fire that her enemies flee away. Crying out in the night, let her men be on their guard, and her enemies in confusion will flee from hunger's sword. Surely it will be so, as we're guided by Robert, our lord.

Just when he and his men needed a result in their favour, they came up trumps, in March 1307, by surprising and driving off a much larger English force, at Glen Trool, in Galloway. The enemy had been commanded by Aymer de Valence, Earl of Pembroke, and in May, desperate to crush the troublesome 'King Hobbe', he offered pitched battle in Ayrshire. Contrary to all the precepts of guerrilla warfare, the offer was accepted. But what Pembroke could not know was that his opponent planned to mould the scene of any encounter to suit his tools. While the English knights looked forward to galloping across some level field – and they were all around them in the gently rolling landscape of Ayrshire – the guerrilla leader selected the one location for miles around that would fight for him. He chose Loudoun Hill, a volcanic plug of rock marking the eastern end of the Irvine Valley. A decade before, William Wallace had attacked and overpowered an English baggage train in its shadow, but the ill omens of the place passed Pembroke by.

The Scots got there first and, while they waited for the English, they set to work. They would be uphill from the enemy, with their backs to the crags but, even so, there were crucial modifications to be made to the ground. King Robert ordered the digging of three great trenches on the slopes below them. These were filled with sharpened stakes and then carefully camouflaged so as to be invisible to approaching horsemen.

All was ready by the time the 3,000-strong English force came into view – knights, mounted men-at-arms and infantry. If Pembroke had imagined having no more to do than unleash his heavy horse and have them run down the 600 or so Scots ranged against him in neat but comparatively flimsy lines, he was shortly to receive a crash course in the art of war. The knights duly charged, making the ground shake in the traditional manner, and clattered straight onto the traps.

Horses and men, hundreds of them, were skewered on the stakes. Scots spearmen advanced sharply downhill and put the bleating mass of them out of their misery. Then they advanced again, stepping over the corpses into the confused tangle of men and horses trapped between fallen comrades and foot soldiers to the rear. They speared them as well. Now at last had come a chance for the Scots to snatch some revenge, to remind themselves of the metallic stink of enemy blood. So shaken were those English forces not yet engaged, they simply made a run for it. John Barbour described it all in his epic poem *The Bruce*:

> The king's men met them at the dyke
> So stoutly that the most warlike
> And strongest of them fell to the ground.

Then could be heard a dreadful sound
As spears on armour rudely shattered,
And cries and groans the wounded uttered.
For those that first engaged in fight
Battled and fought with all their might.
Their shouts and cries rose loud and clear;
A grievous noise it was to hear.

With hindsight, the Battle of Loudoun Hill was the moment when King Robert revealed himself for what he truly was – a brilliant tactician and a winner.

Five days later a Scottish noble on the English side sent a letter south, reporting on the effects of Loudoun Hill upon morale north of the Border: 'Bruce never had the good will of ... the people so much ... as now. It seems that God is with him, for he has destroyed King Edward's power'. As far as the English were concerned, King Hobbe had become a bad dream, largely through his refusal to die. A prophecy was circulating too, an old prophecy of Merlin's that had risen from the depths of the past to live again. It said that when 'The Covetous King' was dead, the Scots and Welsh would unite and assume the full lordship of the whole of Britain. Before his death, Edward would have the heads of two English churchmen who said the advent of King Robert was the second coming of Arthur – to unite all the Celtic peoples of Britain. But who was to blame for all this doom-mongering? Who was sowing the seeds of doubt among the English, while at the same time giving the people of Scotland a hero to believe in? Who else but the bishops of the Scottish Church. They had chosen him in the first place and now they were keeping the faith, as bishops are paid to do.

Edward I – Longshanks the Lawgiver, slaughterer of Scots – was old and weakened now, weakened by time and ceaseless warring. But he was ready to stab at Robert Bruce and his Scots from hell's very heart. Frustrated beyond words by the failure of his generals to get the job done, he struggled northwards himself at the head of yet another army. Ill-health made it a journey of many months and by July 1307 he was still south of the Border, at Burgh-on-Sands on the English side of the Solway Firth. Scotland could be clearly seen across the silt brown waters but it was, and in some fundamental sense always had been, beyond his reach. The Covetous King died on 7 July.

His son, Edward of Caernarvon, replaced him on the throne. Time would tell that he had all of the old man's aspiration to be seen as Scotland's overlord, but almost none of the military abilities or appetites required to make it a reality. History has been notoriously unkind to the 'weak and foolish' Edward II – 'chicken-hearted and luckless in war'. In his defence it must be said that he inherited enormous debts accrued during his father's endless wars in Scotland and France. His people were heartily sick of the expense – and the taxes – and the last thing they really wanted was to see the new king carry on where the old one had left off.

Longshanks had been so desperate to be in at the finish that he left his son explicit instructions. His heart was to be embalmed and sent on crusade, but his bones were to be placed in a sack and carried on campaign in Scotland until the work there was done. Young Edward had other ideas. He joined up with the army and crossed the Border with them, but did little more than tour the south-west receiving the homage of some of the local worthies. Content that he had done enough in the short term just by showing up, he turned the force around and headed south. He would leave the Scots in peace, by and large, for the next three years.

Thankful for the breathing space, the reinvigorated King of Scots turned then to matters domestic. He had proven his point with the English – shown that he was to be taken seriously on the field of battle if nowhere else. But his own realm was full of doubters – aggressive, embittered doubters at that. The Comyn family and their supporters, loyal still to Balliol, were too numerous to be ignored. King Robert turned upon them with a vengeance that would have brought a smile to Longshanks' old face.

The task was made easier by the military incompetence of the Comyns. They were rich and commanded the loyalty of many – of that there was no doubt – but as leaders of men they lacked the warrior's mentality. But King Robert did have it. The Comyn heartlands lay in the north and for the rest of 1307 he ground relentlessly towards them, his reputation riding many leagues before him. One by one his enemies' strongholds fell to him: Inverlochy Castle near modern Fort William; Urquhart Castle on the shore of Loch Ness; Inverness Castle.

He had formulated his strategy in advance: his was an army on the move, travelling light. He had no use for castles and so those he took, he took apart. Defenders slain, defences smashed, wells filled in. They were no use to him and he would make sure they were no use to the Comyns, the English or anyone else. He razed Nairn to the ground. By November he had stamped his authority right up the Great Glen and across the north-east, where he was joined by Murray, Bishop of Moray – another man of God with a job on the side as a man of war.

It was while he was riding high – and roughshod over his opponents – that he was laid low for the first time by the mysterious illness that would blight the rest of his life. It was nameless to those around him but it left him desperately weak, hardly able to move. Since it had no name, it had no cure. The campaign stalled in Buchan, in Comyn territory, leaving the king no alternative but to order a withdrawal into the wilds. John Comyn, Earl of Buchan and cousin of the murdered Red Comyn, was close by with a sizeable force. Yet it seemed that, sick or not, some kind of luck stayed with the king. No Comyn attack ever came and King Robert was taken to recover at a nearby castle.

Some had thought he might die, consumed by grief and guilt perhaps, as well as by his malady. But with the spring of 1308 came signs of recovery. He was still weak, but sheer bloody-mindedness got him back on the road. Buchan had dug himself in on top of Barra Hill, between Inverurie and Old Meldrum. There was, and is, an old Iron Age hill fort up there and perhaps the earl and his men felt secure behind its ruined ramparts. If they did, they were sorely mistaken. In the end it was fear that did the trick – the Buchan men's fear of the Bruce reputation. In short order they fled the fort and fled the field. John Comyn, last of his family with any hope of defying a king, fled too – all the way to England. He was dead within the year.

There was no one left to protect the Comyn lands now, but that was not enough for Good King Robert. There was still a debt to be paid it seemed, and only he would say when the books were straight once more. He marched to Duffus Castle, a Comyn stronghold near Elgin, and utterly destroyed it. He visited upon Buchan a devastation that might be described as apocalyptic. Every village, every settlement was burned. Such was the mayhem wrought upon the territory in 1308 that the land was left barren for a generation or more. But it was not the farmland the Bruce damaged: burning the crops would just have improved fertility. Rather it was the people he punished, and the animals they tended. Every man, woman and child that came the Bruce's way was put to the sword. Buchan was barren because there was no one left alive.

And after all that, while the Bruce's hands were still slick with the blood and brains of his people and their children, the Pope lifted the ban of excommunication and welcomed King Robert back into the fold. It was therefore with the reassurance that even sacrilegious murder and the whole-sale slaughter of infants would not close the door to heaven for a king that he started 1309 determined to get on with the business of governing his kingdom.

He summoned a parliament, his first, at St Andrews. The cathedral there was nearing completion after 150 years and King Robert chose the brand new venue to air some brand new ideas. They were contained within what was essentially an open letter. It is not a famous document, but it should be. Known as 'The Declaration of the Clergy', it enshrined for the first time the bishops' take on what had been gleaned from Lamberton's conversations with John Duns Scotus in 1302. It declared nothing less than that 'the people' had *chosen* their king: 'And by the knowledge and consent of the same people he was received as king so he might restore the defects of the kingdom and correct things needing to be corrected, and might steer those that lacked guidance. And by their authority the aforesaid king of Scots was solemnly endowed with the kingdom, with whom the faithful people of the kingdom wish to live and die.'

It certainly had a ring to it, and to twenty-first-century eyes it has the look of a revolutionary manifesto. But in 1309 'the people' were the important people like the nobility and the senior clergy – the Community of the Realm – rather than the drinkers down at the Drover's Arms. In truth 'The Declaration of the Clergy' was written *for* the common people, not by them, because those 'people' were meant to listen to it. As well as being sent to the Pope, it was preached in churches the length and breadth of the land. It was copied, shown around, repeated endlessly. It was the party line and it came direct from King Robert's ever-faithful supporters: the Scottish Church.

Bluff and bluster notwithstanding – even well-written bluff and bluster – the sheer scale of the task of establishing him as the undisputed monarch was becoming clear. By military skill and cold-hearted violence he had crushed the most visible opposition. By the Declaration he had made clear the legitimacy of his position. But in the eyes of many he was a *soi-disant roi*, a so-called king.

In order to make his position unassailable, both for himself and for a male heir, he would have to complete three tasks. First he had to secure the loyalty of all of Scotland's nobility, while at the same time ejecting the English; second, he had to force or persuade the King of England to recognise the independent status of his throne; third, he would have to set about the business of fathering a male heir. With his wife still in captivity in England, job number three would simply have to wait. Before all of that, he began the expulsion of the English and the retaking of the great fortresses of Scotland. He raided south of the Border as well, using the north of England as a bank from which he could withdraw funds for his campaigns.

The work forged his warriors into an ever-tighter unit. His senior commanders – men like James 'the Black' Douglas – had remained at his side throughout, inspiring yet more confidence among the men they led. And King Robert never seemed to put a foot wrong. Always he had denied himself the vainglory of pitched battle, remembering to use stealth, guile and surprise as his principal weapons. His resultant success at ousting English garrisons from Scots strongholds was astonishing. In January 1313 he took Perth, in February Dumfries, between May and June the Isle of Man.

King Robert felt strong enough by the end of year to issue an ultimatum to those nobles still denying him their outspoken support: they had twelve months to make up their minds or face the consequences. All the while, his persecution of the English in Scotland continued. Sir Thomas Randolph, the king's nephew, captured Roxburgh Castle in February 1314 and then completed a truly memorable double the following month by taking mighty Edinburgh Castle as well.

When it came, the biggest gamble was made not by King Robert, but by his brother Edward. In the same month that Robert had retaken Man, Edward was put in control of the siege of Stirling Castle. With the king out of the way, the English constable of the castle, Sir Philip Mowbray, offered Edward a deal: if an English force had not arrived to lift the Scots siege by Midsummer's Day – 24 June 1314 – he would hand over the keys. Edward agreed at once ... and Robert was furious. This was counter to every strategy that had brought King Robert so far. He had always used the element of surprise to gain the upper hand over superior numbers. Now his brother had forced him into a situation where Edward II could work towards a specific date! On 24 June 1314 the King of England would know where the King of Scots would be – at Stirling Castle readying his forces to try to drive off the massed might of the English war machine. There was no way King Robert could allow the English to retain their grip on Stirling.

His un-asked-for predicament also presented an opportunity to deliver another kind of surprise, a surprise of a different order of magnitude. Here he had been, working away for years, grimly retaking his kingdom stone by stone. Despite his success, none of it had served to proclaim him as unquestionable, beyond the reach of any challenger. A victory over the English in the shadow of Stirling Castle, however, might do that for him at a single stroke . . . might make of him a legend.

Still he hedged his bets, kept his head. He had his men on site well ahead of the English, training and training again in the arts of the schiltron. They were in 'the park', acres of open woodland stretching south from the castle. It was ideal territory for men on foot. The trees offered one kind of natural protection, especially from cavalry, while the nearby 'carse' – the boggy floodplain of the River Forth, off to the east – presented another. Since time immemorial, the few miles of solid ground beside the castle rock had offered the only guarantee of dry feet for men and animals travelling north or south. It was this that made the rock so important: whoever held it controlled the coming and going. The Romans had appreciated the fact, and had built a road leading straight to it. It was along this same, already ancient thoroughfare that King Robert expected his foe to advance.

With this in mind, he had had his men dig hundreds of metre-deep pits either side of the road. Camouflaged out of sight with turf and grasses, they presented a lethal hazard to men and horses at full tilt. Above all else he was allowing himself to remain undecided about how deeply to commit to the fight. On paper, a pitched battle with the English was beyond him and regardless of what his brother had agreed he was keeping open as many options as possible. Were the enemy to advance in formation up the line of the road, they would see the Scots ahead of them and loose their heavy horse. The pits would gall the advance and enable the Scots spearmen to get in among them. It might not add up to a total victory, but it would serve to bloody King Edward's nose at least.

When the English army finally came into view, on 23 June, it was a sight to behold. No doubt King Robert felt vindicated for having mixed such a measure of caution into his thinking. It was a force as large as anything sent north since the glory days of Longshanks himself. Thousands upon thousands of them: knights, mounted men-at-arms, longbow-men, foot soldiers. There were fabled names too – like Sir Giles d'Argentan, third best knight in all of Christendom. Accurate reckonings are non-existent but best guesses suggest 15,000 men on foot and up to 3,000 horse. They certainly outnumbered the Scots, perhaps by as much as two to one. But while Edward II had been able to summon impressive numbers, they had been assembled at the last minute. His men had finally come together as a single unit only days before – quite a handicap in the face of an enemy that had at its core a hard-bitten team of men who had been learning and growing together for long years.

The fighting that first day, the last before Midsummer, was mostly an untidy affair. None of it worked out as King Robert had planned. Instead of galloping headlong into the leg-snapping pits, the English knights circled around the body of the Scots forces, looking for openings that did not exist, losing tempers and lances in the process. But one event, up near the road, will be remembered as long as there is a Scotsman left alive.

An English knight named Sir Henry de Bohun, nephew of the hereditary Constable of England, Sir Humphrey de Bohun, was trotting in line with his fellows when he spied an unexpected target: a mounted knight wearing a golden crown. Here was immortality in the making, a chance to defeat the King of Scots in single combat. Lowering visor and lance, he spurred his war horse out of the formation and galloped forwards. It is hard to imagine that poor deluded de Bohun ever stood a chance. King Robert was alone right enough, and mounted on a pony rather than a war horse. But he had been fighting and killing as king for seven relentless years; fighting and killing to protect his lands and name and title for a lifetime before that. He had lost brothers and friends to the English butcher's slab and hangman's noose. His wife, daughter and sister were imprisoned, along with the bishops who had offered him his throne. He had fought his way all the way back from a cave to a kingdom.

As de Bohun bore down on him, King Robert judged the moment and moved aside. He stood up in his stirrups, holding his favourite battleaxe with both hands. It was with the weight of all he had suffered at English hands that he brought the mill-sharpened weapon down upon his young adversary's helmeted head. The axe shaft snapped in two and de Bohun's head was cleft from crown to chin. When King Robert trotted back to rejoin his nobles they scolded him for taking such a risk. He replied only that he was sorry about his axe.

The long summer evening drew to a close and both sides withdrew, the Scots into the cover of the trees and the English onto the sogginess of the carse. During the night that followed, a Scots knight who had been fighting for Edward changed sides. He trotted into the Scots camp and said English morale was dangerously low. A swift attack at first light might just carry the day for the Scots.

24 June was a Sunday and the Scots celebrated Mass in the half-light of

dawn. The English were still half-asleep when word spread that the enemy was on the move. This was a disappointment. The English had hoped the Scots might have taken the opportunity to drift away to their homes during the night, content to have settled at least some scores. Instead they looked up towards the trees and saw Scots spearmen stepping out of the shadows by the thousand, dropping to their knees. Edward joked that the enemy had come to ask his forgiveness. A traitor Scot, Sir Ingraham de Umfraville, corrected him: 'They want forgiveness – not from you, but from God, for what they are about to do.'

Just as it had for Wallace at Stirling Bridge all those years before, the land fought for King Robert as well. Down on the floodplain, within loops of a Forth tributary stream called the Bannock Burn, the English cavalry could not deploy. Rather than achieve any kind of order, they just got in each other's way. Archers too – some of the same who had been so effective at Falkirk – were hemmed in by stumbling horses and foot soldiers. The English strength in numbers proved meaningless. Only a narrow front of cavalry and infantry had their faces towards the Scots – and those Scots were advancing towards them at a trot, armed with long spears. It was a bloodbath that turned the Bannock Burn dark red.

Those English that could extricate themselves from marsh, stream, river and Scottish spearmen took the only sensible option and made a run for it. King Edward ran too, all the way to the castle. Turning up at the gates, he found them barred against him. With more sense than his king, Mowbray had seen what way the wind was blowing. From the battlements he told Edward he had no forces to protect him, and urged him to head for home. Humiliated, Edward did as he was told. The Battle of Bannockburn, 23–4 June 1314. King Robert I had his legend.

Back on the battlefield, the Scots busied themselves rounding up prisoners – and a valuable haul it proved too. King Robert was able to exchange some of them for those he had lost in 1307. Robert Wishart, seventy-four by then, and blind; his daughter Marjorie and his sister Christian; best of all, he had his queen returned to him as well. Like the rest of them, Elizabeth had been eight years in captivity. The empty years had left their mark, adding yet more to the sum of the king's grief.

The legend of Robert the Bruce and Bannockburn, though, would never grow old. The passing years have only burnished the glory of it. But it was and is a glory that blinds us to bleaker facts. It had been a luminous victory, but when all was said and done it was just another battle, another bloody

Sunday. The English were all but evicted from their squats north of the Border, but the English king was not one inch closer to acknowledging an independent Scotland.

For the next four years, the Scots raided northern England again and again. It became almost an obsession for King Robert, an obsession born of desperation to secure English recognition of his kingdom before it was too late. Robert Bruce was in his late forties, his health damaged by long hard years of tough living and ceaseless fighting. He had no heir as yet and for a while it must have seemed to Edward that he had only to wait for the inevitable.

King Robert turned his attentions further afield, invading Ireland and raising his surviving brother Edward to the kingship in 1316. Still the raiding of the north of England continued. They blackmailed, they raped, they burned. After several attempts, Berwick was reclaimed from English hands in 1318. Any satisfaction at the gain was tempered by the loss of Edward Bruce in battle in Ireland in the same year. It was all in vain – Edward II took no notice because he did not have to.

What the English king lacked as a warrior, he made up for with his skills as a politician. In a move that must have been galling for King Robert, a king made by bishops, Edward had turned to the Church for help.

Pope John XXII, newly ascended to the Holy See, wanted all the major crowned heads of Europe to join in a new crusade against Islam. With such grand plans at the forefront of his thinking, he was ill-disposed towards any monarch who might be accused of causing trouble for his neighbours, of disrupting Christian unity. In 1318, word reached the Scots that King Edward had managed to paint them black in the eyes of the Pope. The Holy Father had been persuaded that the Scots were to blame for all their years of war with England. King Robert, his lieutenants and his bishops were all excommunicated. Furthermore, every English priest was ordered to hold a service, three times each day, during which the very name of the King of Scots was cursed. Once again the fate of the Scottish crown was in the hands of churchmen. And once again the Scots bishops rose to the challenge.

In April 1320 a Scottish knight set off for the papal court. He was, in a sense, a postman. He carried with him three letters. One was from King Robert, one from the bishops and the last from the nobles of Scotland. Only the nobles' letter survives. It is likely it was composed in the chancellery at Arbroath Abbey, founded by William the Lion. In 1320 the Declaration of Arbroath, as it has come to be known, was a hard-nosed reply to all of King

Edward's spin. It was signed by the nobles and magnates of the realm, fifty-one of them, but it was not written by them. It is more likely to have come from the hand of Abbot Bernard, Chancellor of Scotland and based at Arbroath.

Popes were required to sit for hours listening to one petition after another from disaffected souls scattered the length and breadth of Christendom. Abbot Bernard clearly had in mind the need to jolt his boss from his daydreaming and so used every literary gun in his arsenal.

The Declaration begins with a rehash of Baldred Bisset's origin myth of the Scots. They are an ancient people; Scotland is Rome's special daughter. So far, so familiar. Next it follows the line of the Declaration of the Clergy of 1309 – that Robert the Bruce 'by due consent and assent of us all' had freed the Scots from the weight of the English yoke.

By now, Abbot Bernard's blood was up: if this King Robert were to submit in any way to English rule, then the Scots would *drive him out* (a bald statement guaranteed to rouse any sleeping pontiff). They would drive him out: 'and make some other man who was well able to defend us our king; for as long as but a hundred of us remain alive, never will we be brought under English rule. It is in truth not for glory, nor riches, nor honours that we are fighting, but for freedom – for that alone, which no honest man surrenders but with life itself.'

Abbot Bernard then asks the Pope, begs him indeed, to look with fatherly eyes upon the plight of Rome's special daughter. Even the words of Tacitus' Calgacus are there in the echoes, when the Holy Father is asked to intercede on the Scots' behalf and command Edward II 'to leave in peace us Scots, who live in this poor little Scotland beyond which there is no dwelling at all'.

As a final thought, the Pope is asked to see things from the Scottish perspective: it was the English, not the Scots, who were making excuses to avoid going on crusade; the Scots were just fighting for recognition as an independent kingdom. And for as long as the English made it impossible for either king to lead warriors against the forces of Islam, innocent Christians would continue to die. If the Pope failed to act, then *he* would be responsible for the consequences, said the Scots. The loss of lives and perdition of souls would lie at the Pope's feet.

Viewed with modern eyes, the Declaration of Arbroath is a stunning document. As an elegant declaration of independence, it is without equal. It was not, however, an overnight sensation in 1320. At the very most, all it achieved at the time was a turn of the screw, nudging the Pope in the right direction without actually changing his mind.

King Robert was not even completely secure at home. He had recently weathered the 'Soules Conspiracy', a dangerously potent attempt to knock him from his throne. The plot took its name from the involvement of the hereditary butler Sir William Soules, but was in reality a symptom of a deep-seated infection. Edward Balliol, son of the exiled king, had turned up at the English court. For Balliol and Comyn supporters slumbering in the north, this was a supply of oxygen over glowing embers. Even after fourteen years on the throne, after all he had endured and achieved, there were plenty of Scots ready to try to bring King Robert down. That he survived the crisis – just as he survived everything else – was a testament to his stubbornness, and his luck.

In 1321, Edward II offered to seek terms for peace with the Scots. The French king had applied pressure; so too had Pope John, moved in part perhaps by the Declaration. Bamburgh Castle on the Northumberland coast was nominated as the location for the talks and the envoys from both sides gathered there in March.

It was a farce. Once again the English repeated their claims of over-lordship. The Scots replied by rereading their own, dog-eared origin myth. Now they could stir in a generous helping of the Declaration – and just for good measure they said Edward and his Plantagenet dynasty were illegitimate. The family line stemmed from the 'foreign usurpation' of 1066, by a *soi-disant roi* the Scots called 'William the Bastard'. The legitimate claim on the English crown was that of the House of Wessex, they said, whose sole living representative happened to be King Robert I of Scotland.

A few spiteful jibes aside, it was the same argument on a different day: nothing achieved, nothing settled. For King Robert it was Groundhog Day – to be endured for the next six years. Every time his bishops came close to securing concessions from the papal court, Edward's men would make last-minute moves to ensure they were slapped down. In 1323, in a bid to bring an end to the raiding, the English king signed a thirteen-year truce with Scotland; but it contained no cessation of the age-old claims of overlordship.

5 March 1324 was different, a break from the norm. The thirty-five-year-old Queen of Scotland gave birth to a healthy baby boy, David. King Robert was nearly fifty and by the standards of the day it was close to miraculous. Scotland had her male heir but her king was no closer to having an

acknowledged independent kingdom to pass on to him. The breakthrough, when it came, was one King Robert could hardly have hoped for in his wildest dreams. On 20 January 1327, King Edward II of England was deposed by his long-suffering wife, Isabella of France. Their fourteen-year-old son was crowned Edward III the following month but it was Roger Mortimer, Isabella's lover, who was the *de facto* ruler of the country.

Fate had removed one King Edward from King Robert's path in 1307. Now it had removed another and he was determined to take advantage. Though stricken yet again by his nameless illness, he laid siege to Norham Castle in August, while Moray and the Black Douglas attacked the fortifications at Alnwick and Warkworth.

King Robert was at Berwick, on 18 October 1327, when he let it be known what it would take for him to bring an end to the violence: the English king must acknowledge the independence of the Scottish crown in perpetuity and there must be a marriage between David and Edward's younger sister, the Princess Joan. Finally the force of King Robert's will was too much to be resisted – particularly by a regency government. In March 1328 Edward III duly announced that:

> we will and concede for us and all our heirs and successors ... that the kingdom of Scotland shall remain forever separate in all respects from the kingdom of England, in its entirety, free and in peace, without any kind of subjection, servitude, claim or demand, with its rightful boundaries as they were held and preserved in the times of Alexander of good memory king of Scotland last deceased, to the magnificent prince, the lord Robert, by God's grace illustrious king of Scots, our ally and very dear friend, and to his heirs and successors.

There it was: freedom and peace from England.

King Robert had won, but he had also lost. Queen Elizabeth lived long enough to know success was on its way, but she did not live to see it. She died just days before English envoys arrived at Holyrood Abbey, in Edinburgh, for the formal ratification of the Treaty of Northampton-Edinburgh.

The King of Scots was on his sick-bed too, tortured still by his chronic illness. But, for all that, he was well enough to hear the terms that meant his life's work was nearing completion. The treaty echoed all of the sentiments of King Edward's announcement the month before. It was almost beyond belief. Time had been rolled back to the days and the world of

Alexander III: the same and not the same. The world had changed, been made different by three decades of war.

King Robert's earls were in attendance, his bishops too. William Lamberton was there, old and frail. Without him, it is unlikely such a day would ever have come. As he watched the signing his mind would have gone back to marks made upon a different document, twenty-four years before in the conspiratorial silence of Cambuskenneth Abbey on the banks of the River Forth. Within two months of the signing of the Treaty of Northampton-Edinburgh he too was dead, his job done.

On 12 July the Princess Joan, who was six, and David, who was only four, were married in Berwick. It was a union of children but it symbolised peace. Peace at last: after thirty-two years of struggle and bloodshed. The Pope let it be known that he too recognised the Scottish throne and that the ban of excommunication had been lifted from King Robert.

With so much optimism and good will, a request was made on the king's behalf for something that every European monarchy of status already possessed: an ampulla of oil blessed by the Pope himself. Oil from such bottles was used to anoint kings during their coronation ceremonies. Any attempt to conquer or in any way interfere with the lands of a king who, by virtue of this oil, had been anointed by God, was a mortal sin. The kings of England had an ampulla; the kings of France as well. The Scottish kings never had, and they wanted one. An ampulla was no mere status symbol either – rather it was a bottle-full of independence from the King of England.

With so much accomplished – all of it against the odds – the ailing king might have been forgiven for granting himself a little peace. But it was beyond him. If peace were to be enjoyed, it would have to come from somewhere else, somewhere beyond his own reach. Like an indelible stain, his illness marked him out, in his own mind at least, as unclean. He lacked God's grace or he would be freed from his physical suffering.

How was he to square the books and pay the price demanded by his crown? So far it had been paid by others – wife, family, friends, bishops. They had bled for him and that blood was on his hands. But how was he to settle his own account? He paid a chaplain in Buchan to recite daily Masses for the soul of his brother Neil, the first to die. Elizabeth had been buried in Dunfermline Abbey, the last resting place of St Margaret, and money and favours were sent there too.

This is the truth of King Robert the Bruce and yet it slipped from plain view long ago. Instead his name is a fixed point, the nation's True North. If ever 'Scotland' lost her way she had only to take a bearing from 'the Bruce' and then the path ahead would be obvious once more. Yet the man himself spent his final years in a desperate search for proof that he had done right.

In the last months of his life his illness took permanent hold. He was dying, they said, and this time they were right. The shrine of St Ninian, at Whithorn in Galloway, was already an ancient place of pilgrimage – famed for its powers to cure the sick – and now King Robert turned to it for help. If the saint could not fix his body, perhaps he could ease the pain in his soul. Much too ill to ride, he travelled on a litter. The journey took several weeks but when he arrived he embarked at once upon five days of fasting and penance.

The return journey was easier and at last he was taken to Cardross, on the north shore of the Firth of Clyde, and to the house he had had built there three years before. Knowing that he had only days or weeks to live, he sent out letters requesting the presence of his earls and magnates. They duly gathered at his side and swore that, when the time came, they would do no less for his son and heir. 'Sirs, my day is far gone,' he told them. 'And there remains but one thing, to meet Death without fear, as every man must do. I thank God he has given me the space to repent in this life, for through me and my wars, there has been a great spilling of blood and many an innocent man has been slain. Therefore I take this sickness and this pain as a penance for my sins.' He asked that his embalmed heart be taken on crusade and James the Black Douglas, ever his most faithful lieutenant, was given the task.

King Robert I of Scotland was fifty-five when he died on 7 June 1329, in his house at Cardross. His heart was removed, as he had requested, and his body taken to Dunfermline Abbey where it was interred beneath a tomb in the middle of the choir.

The following year, the Black Douglas joined the crusade of the Spanish King Alfonso XI. He may have been in command of the body of Scottish and English knights that found itself outmanoeuvred by an overwhelming force of Moors at Tebas de Ardales on 25 August 1330. In any case, every man of them was slain. King Robert's heart was recovered from the field and returned to Scotland along with the bones of the Black Douglas. It was buried in Melrose Abbey.

David and Joan were enthroned as King and Queen of Scotland on 24 November 1331. There was no Stone of Destiny. Despite Edward III's promises to return it along with the Black Rood of St Margaret, both remained in Westminster. There was, however, an ampulla of blessed oil. For the first time, a King of Scotland was anointed by the grace of God and in the manner respected by other monarchies. King Robert had won his last battle.

Robert the Bruce is a statue now – many statues in fact, scattered across the land and the world. He gazes south from the esplanade in front of Stirling Castle, ever watchful in case the English approach over old ground. The most familiar is the one by Pilkington Jackson that sits on high ground at the Bannockburn Heritage Centre. Here is the Bruce at his most warlike, twice life size and astride a giant horse (an exact replica of it sits outside the Jubilee Auditorium in Alberta, Canada). But it is almost as if the fossilising began while he was still alive. In his last days he was paralysed by his illness. One observer noted, 'for he can scarcely move anything but his tongue'. He was being made fixed and unreal even as he died.

While he lived, his words revealed his humanity, his humility and his grief, 'through me and my wars, there has been a great spilling of blood and many an innocent man has been slain'. He understood his debt and was in no doubt about how much remained to be paid. Once he fell silent, the transformation to effigy was complete and for ever. There would never again be any mention of his consuming guilt, of the bishops who chose him and guided his every move across the checkerboard of nights and days; no words for the loss of brothers, friends, family. The legend of Robert the Bruce blurred the *medievalness* of all that had been done by him, and in his name.

Scotland was, at last, free and independent of English dominion – but the king who made it happen had been turned to stone. A fairy-tale curse for a king made myth. The rock of Scotland had claimed him for its own.

***

For most Scots living their lives in the fourteenth century, there were more telling developments than the triumphs and disasters of Bruces, Balliols and Plantagenets.

There is no denying that the ever-present threat of raids became a fact of life for people in the Borderlands – whether Scots or English – in the first four or five decades of the 1300s. And if it was not raids it was the depredations of full-scale war. With this in mind, society in that belt of territory either side of the Border certainly did evolve with a strongly militaristic feel. Powerful families in the debatable lands kept themselves on a war footing as a matter of course and their tenants readied themselves to defend hearth, home and livestock as best they could.

There were also those who had had as much to fear from their own king as from any foreign army. King Robert's crushing of his Comyn rivals in Buchan had caused devastation that was still being felt in the territory half a century later.

But away from the Border, and away from centres like Edinburgh and Stirling, war was much less of a concern, the power games of the mighty less distracting. For most Scots there were other matters to occupy mind and hands. For one thing, the climate was deteriorating, becoming colder and wetter. Better weather in preceding centuries had made existing farmland more productive. The resultant population growth inevitably meant many people had had no option but to move on to tougher land. Climate change, however, had begun to bring about a contraction of the population – which led in turn to an abandonment of the least attractive farmland.

As the fourteenth century wore on, the population was further reduced by outbreaks of plague, which first made landfall in Scotland late in 1349. It was this decline in numbers that brought about a change in many people's lives more profound than anything wrought by royal dynastic tussles. While Scotland had been more densely populated, land was at a premium. Those who owned the land controlled the wealth and the power; the landless, by contrast, lived only by the strength of their backs.

While population was high, labour was cheap and plentiful, keeping them poor and dependent. During the second half of the century, however, a correction took place that fundamentally altered the relationship between landless and landowner. For the first time in living memory, property values fell alarmingly. Those unhappy with their rent or other conditions had options that had never existed before. They could go elsewhere. Their labour was an increasingly valuable commodity and, for the more industrious among them, things were looking up.

The decades of uncertainty and then outright war that followed the death of Alexander III in 1286 had given Scotland's Guardians – and then her kings – a renewed obsession with the view to the south. The border-lands, and England beyond, took up most of their time, and this pre-occupation had unexpected consequences for those parts of the realm outside the beam of the spotlight.

By the time Alexander III died, the Western Isles had been part of Scotland for just twenty years. If the king had managed to stay on his horse and lived, he might have had more time to concentrate on bringing the new territory properly into the fold. His successors, freed from the burden of a war to keep a mighty enemy at arm's length, may have ensured that 'Scottish' ways reached and permeated the society of the Isles men.

Of course, that is not what happened. Instead the Western Isles were left to take care of themselves. While the Scottish kingdom on the mainland fought for its very survival from 1296 onwards, the Isles were increasingly open and receptive to ideas and mores imported from Ireland. The cult of the warrior was the dominant influence and, as the thirteenth century gave way to the fourteenth, it was the axes of the 'galloglasses' that came to dominate lives in the islands and on the north-western seaboard. And as the fourteenth century wore on, the dominant family of the Isles – the MacDonalds – began to look at more and more of the northern mainland of Scotland with hungry eyes. This, then, was the other side of Scotland – out of sight and often out of mind, making its own way. By the time Good King Robert was approaching the end of his battles – his enemies crushed and only his conscience left to trouble him – the far west was a land apart.

David II inherited a world made by war. Bannockburn and the Declaration of Arbroath had made a legend of his father. While Robert I lived, Scotland's future as an independent kingdom was assured. Even today many Scots hear the word 'Bannockburn' and their minds fill with grand thoughts of the ultimate Scots victory, proud Edward's army sent home to think again. Somewhere in their heads, a book snaps shut: end of story. The problem is that Edward and his army did think again, and so did the kings and armies that followed them. And what they thought about was coming back and carrying on where they had left off.

Little David might have fared better if his principal Guardian had lived longer. But by 1332, Sir Thomas Randolph, Earl of Moray, great ally and nephew of Robert the Bruce, was dead. At the same time, the English King Edward III reached adulthood and almost immediately began planning how he would right the wrongs and humiliations he had endured at Scots hands during his minority. The Treaty of Northampton-Edinburgh of 1328 stung most painfully of all, but he had also had to describe the King of Scots as 'our dear friend and ally' while promising to respect the boundaries that existed between the two countries in the days of Alexander III. Now the time had come to show Robert's heir just how much room there was to manoeuvre within the text of grand treaties.

Edward Balliol, the heir of King John, was still floating around the English court like a ship that had slipped its mooring. King Edward gave fresh impetus to his namesake by sending him north to rekindle the anti-Bruce feeling innate in the Comyns and their never-say-die supporters. Balliol also rounded up the so-called 'Disinherited' – those Scots who had lost lands thanks to the Bruce – and put them all aboard a fleet provided by the English king.

They landed in Fife in August 1332 and immediately marched towards Perth. A hastily assembled force they may have been, but they were driven by grudges that had been festering darkly for half a lifetime. On 8 August they were met on Dupplin Moor by a royalist force led by the Earl of Mar, the new Guardian of Scotland. The battle was a bloody disaster for King David's men. Geography and poor leadership conspired to leave his spearmen completely exposed to Balliol's archers. Thousands of them fell dead, Mar among them, and the resultant rout was total.

Scone had been witness to the coronation of King David and Queen Joan just months before, but Edward Balliol was able to step out onto Moot Hill and reclaim his father's throne. Scotland had two kings now, and who was the usurper was largely a matter of opinion. David had the throne from his father Robert, but Robert had claimed it from John Balliol, the rightful king. Ownership of the kingdom of Scotland had almost become a matter for lawyers or philosophers to decide.

In the end, right was less of an issue than ownership of a backbone and Edward Balliol was found wanting. No sooner had he donned the crown than he was on his knees swearing subservience to English Edward as his own and Scotland's overlord. Just for good measure, he handed over the whole of southern Scotland as a gift. Even more pertinently, he promised his master the return of Berwick – reclaimed by King Robert in 1318 – but added that the English king would have to come and take the place himself.

With the Earl of Mar dead, the Guardianship of Scotland had passed initially to Sir Andrew Murray, son of the Andrew Murray who had fought at the side of William Wallace at Stirling Bridge in 1297. But Murray was captured and stewing in an English prison when English Edward arrived near Berwick to claim his gift.

Archibald Douglas, brother of the Black Douglas, was Scotland's acting Guardian and leader of the Scots forces when they clashed with Edward's army at Halidon Hill on 19 July 1333. Like Dupplin Moor it was a disaster for King David's men. Douglas fell dead, along with three earls, hundreds of knights and barons, and thousands of foot soldiers. King David and Queen Joan were immediately sent to France for their own safety. English Edward was master not just of Balliol, but of Scotland too.

This Scotland, however, was different from any that had existed before. Every Scot knew and understood that Edward Balliol was a puppet, and they had suffered and learned too much in their wars of independence even to contemplate tolerating English dominion again. Guardian Murray was soon free and back in Scotland and under his leadership the Scots fought on. It was a war of attrition but the toll it took upon the people and the land only increased their determination to be rid of Balliol.

By 1337 Edward of England had become embroiled in war across the Channel, a big war that would preoccupy him and his successors for a hundred years. With too much to do in France, Edward lost interest in Scotland and Balliol, to such an extent that by 1341 it was safe enough for King David to return from exile with his queen. Always one to turn an opportunity into a problem, he managed to remain at large in his kingdom for five years before his still-youthful enthusiasm got the better of him. In August 1346, Edward scored his victory at Crécy – the work of archers who had probably perfected their skills against Scots at some point. When the French king, Philippe VI, called on his old ally Scotland to help him by invading England, David was only too happy to oblige. In the disastrous encounter that followed, he was taken prisoner and sent to the Tower of London. He would be a guest of his brother-in-law for the next eleven years.

The English spilled northwards; southern Scotland was theirs after all, the gift of Balliol. As for Balliol himself, he soon understood that his time as king had passed. Having quietly made his excuses, he left. He died in 1364.

When David was finally allowed home in 1357, he came back with a huge annual ransom to pay. His need for cash made him lean more heavily on the burghs in search of funds – and enabled them to increase their influence on the affairs of state as a quid pro quo. It was in the reign of David II, therefore, that the burghs secured their rights to send representatives to parliament, becoming the 'Third Estate'.

Of more significance – in the long term, certainly – was the enhanced status of the man who had assumed control of the country in David's absence. Robert Stewart was the son of King Robert I's daughter Marjorie, and therefore King David's nephew. His father had been Walter the Steward – holder of the hereditary title created by King David I – but by now 'Steward' had become Stewart. In 1318, years before David had even been born, Stewart had been designated as heir presumptive to the throne, on account of his mother. All these years later, it was the position he still held.

While his uncle languished in captivity, Stewart had busied himself building alliances with other powerful men of the realm, including the Douglases. He secured the marriage of his daughter to Good John Mac-Donald, of the Isles, making friends in the west. He twice obstructed his uncle's return to Scotland and by the time King David finally came home there was no love lost between the two men. David's queen, Joan of England, died without providing him with an heir and, despite his best efforts with subsequent partners, he never had a son. When he died suddenly, in Edinburgh Castle, on 23 February 1371, his nephew's moment had arrived. Robert Stewart was duly crowned King Robert II, at Scone, on 26 March the same year.

This first of the Stewart kings had arrived upon the throne late in life. He was fifty-five and he dedicated his remaining years to securing the future of his line. Sons and heirs duly poured forth. His eldest son, by his first wife, was John, Earl of Carrick, but there were to be plenty more. From two marriages he produced a total of five legitimate sons and eight legitimate daughters. There were at least eight bastard sons as well.

His approach to kingship was much like a boardroom takeover. The whole strategy was based on placing his own people – usually his own sons or sons-in-law – in as many of the top jobs as possible. His second son, Robert, was Earl of Fife; his third, Alexander, was the Lord, rather 'the Wolf' of Badenoch; his fourth was David, Earl of Strathearn and his fifth was Walter, Earl of Caithness.

While his fecund abilities to reproduce himself solved some problems, they created others to take their place. The Wolf of Badenoch earned his nickname from his own management style. Alexander, Lord of Badenoch, was the king's favourite. But he was the third son and therefore unlikely ever to succeed him. Off in his own wild domain he went native, acquiring the warrior sensibilities of the powerful local warlords. They kept their private armies of wild Highland men and so did Alexander. He indulged himself in private vendettas against other magnates and annoyed the Bishop of Moray so much he was preached against in Elgin Cathedral. The Wolf of Badenoch did not take kindly to hearing judgments laid against himself and burned the building to the ground.

Robert II's inability to control his son had brought about a palace coup. Forced from the throne in late 1384, he was replaced by his heir, John, Earl of Carrick, who was made Guardian of Scotland.

A bout of the old trouble – trouble with England – flared up again in 1385. Richard II was on the throne by then, and the hostilities were the customary raids back and forth. Finally the English pushed all the way to Edinburgh and razed the city before turning for home.

Robert II was seventy-four when he died in 1390. He could never have expected to become king and yet the crown came to him just the same. Unfortunately it was snatched away abruptly by his own son.

In 1388, two years before his father died, John, Earl of Carrick, had been kicked and nearly killed by a horse. He never fully recovered and was disabled for the rest of his life. Bad luck begets bad luck, they say, and it was decided John should shed his name, the better to avoid associations with John I – John Balliol, Toom Tabard. It was therefore as King Robert III that he was crowned at Scone on 14 August 1390. His infirmity undermined his reign from the start and nine years later his personal rule was brought bloodlessly to an end. He remained king but in the eyes of the magnates and nobles he was replaced as effective ruler by his son, Prince David, and younger brother Robert, Earl of Fife.

After a friendly start, relations between the two men turned sour. The Earl of Fife – who had been created Duke of Albany by his brother in 1398 – eventually took his nephew prisoner. Having gone so far, and realising that 'King' David III would likely want revenge at some point in the future, Albany decided he could never be let go. Prince David died in his uncle's castle at Falkland in March 1402, of starvation some said.

Broken-hearted and desperate, David's father moved to protect his last surviving son, James. Political manouevrings came to nought and finally the boy was put aboard a ship bound for the Continent. Friendly exile was his only hope of survival, but bad luck struck again and his vessel was boarded by opportunist English pirates off the Norfolk coast. The twelve-year-old prince was found cowering beneath a pile of stinking animal hides. Identified as a prize beyond price, he was handed over to King Henry IV of England. Once again, the future of the King of Scots was in English hands.

CHAPTER FIVE

LANGUAGE IS POWER

'From the lone shieling of the misty island
Mountains divide us, and the waste of seas;
Yet still the blood is strong the heart is Highland,
And we, in dreams, behold the Hebrides.'

The Canadian Boat Song

To try to understand part of the story of the rise and fall of the legendary, near-mythical Lordship of the Isles we visited a pub on the Isle of Skye called 'Eilean Iarmain'.

It was early evening and the place was full of Gaelic-speaking locals. Only one person, a Lewis man, was able to join in the chat without first asking everyone to speak English. It is a strange and vaguely unsettling experience to be in your own country and yet find yourself surrounded by fellow Scots whose language you do not understand. Beyond '*Ciamar a tha thu?*' – 'How are you?' – and a few place names like *Buachialle Etive Mor* – 'the Big Shepherd of Etive', in Glencoe – I am utterly lost among the Gaels. I would stand more chance of understanding and making myself understood in a pub in Paris, or Madrid, and that is saying something.

At one point a man asked, 'Why did some people want to destroy Gaelic? It's the first language we all had.' It is a good question, and one that lies at the heart of an uncomfortable truth.

Scotland is a place of two countries, two languages and two cultures. Most Scots do not speak Gaelic and whether or not they admit it to themselves, they have to view their country through the prism of a language that was once foreign to the land – English.

Scots Gaelic, like Irish and Welsh, hangs like a last apple of autumn from the old, Celtic branch of the Indo-European tree of languages. In the millennium before the birth of Christ, Celtic languages were being spoken right across western Europe. Scots Gaelic seems to be part of the cultural package that arrived with farming; indeed it is possible the hunter-gatherers had to pick up the new language in order to understand the business of farming in the first place.

Whether it came with the farmers themselves – a new population of settlers – or arrived just as new words that had been passed from person to person over great distances, hardly matters. The point is that Gaelic, or a language very similar to Gaelic, was spoken throughout the British Isles long before anyone gave a moment's thought to anything 'English'. As the man in the pub on Skye said, it is the first language we all had. The story of how that first language fell from grace is also the story of how modern Scotland became the country it is today, a country divided.

There is an old tale of a medieval Spanish traveller who came to Edinburgh to see the sights. When he got home someone asked him what was the most wonderful thing he had seen. The traveller thought for a moment and then answered: 'A grand man called MacDonald, with a great train of men after him, called neither duke nor marquis.'

By the time young James Stewart was being captured by English pirates off the Norfolk coast, the MacDonalds thought themselves '*Righ Innse Gall*' – the kings of the Hebrides. Along with the MacDougalls and the MacRuaries, they were descendants of Somerled, the Viking warlord who in the twelfth century had established a 'kingdom' stretching from the Isle of Man to the Butt of Lewis and from Kintyre to Knoydart. Norse-speaking Vikings they may once have been, but for reasons lost to time they had acquired the Gaelic language of their new home, gradually forgetting the tongue they had known before. The island kingdom, with its ancient traditions of seaborne warfare, had become part of the kingdom of Scotland in 1266. But that had not stopped the separate development of the unique culture of the Isles.

The MacDonalds had played the game well. While the MacDougalls backed the Balliol-Comyn camp during the battle for the throne, the MacDonalds backed the Bruces. When King Robert fled mainland Scotland, it is likely the MacDonalds took him in. He certainly led a body of MacDonald Isles men – galloglasses – at the Battle of Bannockburn.

The rise of the Bruces was therefore good news for the MacDonalds, but they remained much more interested in their own affairs than those of any

King of Scotland. While they continued to be a source of potential support for the Bruce line, they were less than impressed by how much territory the king was granting to his Stewart relatives – especially when his gift-giving encroached upon western lands they coveted for themselves. (The Mac-Donald resentment of all things Stewart had its roots with Somerled himself: he had watched with jealous eyes as King David I invited the Fitzalans, ancestors of the Stewarts, into Scotland along with Bruces and Balliols and the rest of the Anglo-Normans. Other immigrants bothered Somerled less, but those Fitzalans – those ' Stewards' – took up lands too close to his own for his liking.)

During the middle years of the fourteenth century, Good John Mac-Donald of Islay – the first to style himself *Dominus Insularum*, Lord of the Isles – had used guile and intelligence to return his family's holdings to something like the glory days enjoyed by Somerled. He had even been prepared to back Balliol claims during the reign of David II whenever he saw it could strengthen the MacDonald position. Duplicity is hardly exclusive to kings, after all.

At the same time, the Gaelic lands of the northern mainland also found themselves distanced from central government influence, but for different reasons. When the Bruce took his revenge on opponents like the Comyns of Badenoch and Buchan, and also upon the earldoms of Strathearn and Atholl, he failed to establish long-term replacements with ties to his crown. The local warlords who filled the vacuum were intent on building their own petty empires and happy to keep the kings at a distance. The Isles men and their galloglasses were also drawn to these areas – first as mercenaries and then as colonists – so that the culture of the Gaelic Hebrides took root in the northern mainland as well.

By the time the Stewarts were building their family firm during the reigns of Robert II and Robert III, a separate, independent world had grown in the untended wilds of the west and the north. Where those lands were held by MacDonalds, there was always an instinctive suspicion about Stewart intent. And while the Stewarts as a whole were bad enough, recent empire-building by Robert, Duke of Albany had been beyond the pale in Mac-Donald eyes. Albany and his kin had been spreading north for years, but when they turned their attentions to the vast and wealthy territory of Ross, it was too much for Donald MacDonald of Islay, son and successor of Good John, first Lord of the Isles.

On 24 July 1411 this enmity came to its horrifying conclusion at the battle remembered as 'Reid Harlaw'. Massed armies from both sides clashed on a hillside 20 or so miles north of Aberdeen and spent a day building heaps of slain. In its aftermath – a draw many said – Donald and his MacDonalds retreated all the way to the Isles. In time, only the bards knew the truth of it, but Harlaw stands to this day as the moment when the division – the split between Highland and Lowland – was made clear to the world.

This was the Lordship of the Isles that Alexander had inherited. The powers of his people had been curtailed somewhat, but the feud with Stewart Scotland was left as simmering embers. As the fifteenth century drew on, more and more people in the western Lowlands of Scotland began complaining bitterly about the savage activities of 'wild, wicked Highlandmen'.

Alexander MacDonald of Islay became Lord of the Isles in 1423. From his father and grandfather he had inherited a private army of perhaps 10,000 men and a fleet of more than 100 'birlinns' – state-of-the-art sea-going galleys descended from the same longships their Viking ancestors had used to terrorise Scotland in centuries past. In fourteenth-century Scotland it was far quicker to move men and materials by sea than by land. By controlling the western seaboard – and Alexander did, unquestionably – he still wielded extraordinary power and influence.

The beating heart of his territory was at Finlaggan, on Islay. A visit to the place now is a sombre experience. What was once the hub of a vast territory is little more than a handful of ruins and barely discernible earth-works. The little island in the loch, which was once the site of the Great Hall where all the important business of the day was conducted, seems too small ever to have been the scene of anything that mattered. But matter it did; and when Alexander, Lord of the Isles summoned his men to his side, they came running.

The most noticeable characteristic of Finlaggan, given its role as the capital of an empire, is the lack of fortifications. There were grand buildings, luxurious and impressive by the standards of the day, but no battlements, no encircling walls. This more than anything testifies to the power of the Lords of the Isles. Such was their unchallenged status within their own territory they had no need to defend themselves. By the time Alexander came to power, the Lordship had enjoyed an unbroken century of internal stability.

With that peace, and under the patronage of the MacDonald lords, there was a flourishing of the arts – of sculpture, music and poetry:

Do Mhac Domnhaill na ndearc mall
Mo an tiodhlagudh na dtugam,
An corn gemadh aisgidh oir,
A n-aisgthir orm 'n-a onoir.

Ce a-ta I n-aisgidh mar budh eadh
Agam o onchoin Gaoidheal,
Ni liom do-chuaidh an cornsa:
Fuair da chionn mo chumonnsa.

To MacDonald of the stately eyes
Is the gift of what I am giving,
Greater than the cup – though a gift of gold –
In honour of what to me is given.

Though I got this cup free, as it were,
From the wolf of the Gaels,
It doesn't seem that way to me:
He received my love as payment.

These MacDonalds of the Isles then were a looming, sometimes troubling presence for the kings of Scots. For as long as there were amicable relations between the crown and the men styled King of the Hebrides, there was nothing to fear. But no king of the mainland – and certainly not a Stewart king – could sleep easy in his bed while the MacDonalds roamed the islands and Atlantic seaboard at will with 10,000 men in 100 longships.

Perhaps, more than anything else, they represented the old world, the world of before. Their ties to Ireland were close. They were of the Gaels who had unified the country long ago under the likes of King Constantine II of the House of Alpin. That first kingdom had been called Alba, the Gaelic world for the whole of mainland Britain. In a kingdom where primogeniture counted for so much, were not the Gaels 'firstborn'?

The Lords of the Isles also maintained the age-old ties to Iona. They carefully solicited the good will of St Columba's spiritual descendants and for generations had made a point of being buried in the abbey grounds. Alexander MacDonald and his ilk were old-school Scots, the originals. He showered the abbey of Iona with money and treasures, but if these actions were born out of fear for his everlasting soul, then that was pretty much his only fear. For Alexander, *Ri Innse Gall*, was a king in his own land – a land in which there *was no king*.

James Stewart – James I – had been born in 1394, the youngest son of Robert III and his wife Annabella. The death of James's elder brother David, Duke of Rothsay in 1402 at the hands of his uncle Robert Stewart, Duke of Albany, had made him heir to the throne. Robert III's councillors were David Fleming and Henry Sinclair, Earl of Orkney. Both men initially worked hard to establish a loyal following around the young prince and so raise his stock above that of his uncle's Albany Stewarts, but in so doing they managed to fall foul of the powerful Douglas family in the Borders.

A disastrous clash with the Douglases in 1406 caused Fleming's death in battle. It was Sinclair who took young James to the fortress of the Bass Rock in the Firth of Forth then, to await his departure into exile – the departure that put him into the hands of King Henry IV of England. Within days of his capture, word reached James of the death of his father. For what it was worth, he was King of Scotland.

King James I would spend the next eighteen years in captivity south of the Border. In his absence, Albany was made Governor of Scotland. Albany's son Murdoch was also a captive of the English, and the Duke would spend much more time and energy seeking the release of his own son and heir than that of his young king. Henry IV, and then his son Henry V, made it clear to the Scots that if they wanted James back they would have to accept English overlordship. It was the same old game the English always tried to play. Forget the Bruce, they said – give up your independence. But the Scots, with Albany at the helm, refused to adopt the role assigned to them. They were managing without a king and would continue to do so. Why, in any case, would Albany go to any great lengths to secure the return of the king and so end his own time as Governor? Murdoch Stewart was released in 1415 but James was going nowhere.

Left to brood upon his own redundancy, it is hardly surprising that James came to admire the achievements and aspirations of the courts of the Henrys. Although he began his time in England as a prisoner in the Tower of London, and in the castles of Nottingham, Pevensey, Kenilworth and Windsor, he was gradually made welcome in the king's household. He grew to adulthood as part of English court life and his outlook and attitudes were permanently altered as a result.

For one thing, he came to support the claims Henry V was making in France. Abandoned by his own folk, he may well have felt moved to celebrate his host's victory at Agincourt in 1415, and he was with the English king when he laid siege to the strategic town of Melun, 30 miles south-east of Paris.

Melun, as it turned out, was an acid test of sorts for the young King of Scotland. His loyal subjects had come to the aid of the French Dauphin, the future Charles VII. Albany was honouring Scotland's age-old alliance with France and thousands of Scots troops had crossed the Channel under the command of Archibald Douglas, Earl of Wigtown and John Stewart, Earl of Buchan and Albany's relative. Hundreds of Scots were in Melun when Henry laid siege to the place in November 1420 with 20,000 men. Quite reasonably under the circumstances, the English king told James to order his subjects to surrender – and James obliged. Kings like Henry V expected and received unquestioning obedience. It was the English way.

James had either forgotten – or perhaps had not even had time to learn – that the Scottish way was different. In Scotland the kingdom and the king were two different things; loyalty to one did not necessarily mean loyalty to the other. And after all, the kingdom of Scotland had been functioning for years without a king. The Scots at Melun saw no reason suddenly to defer to orders from a monarch they simply did not know. To a man, the Scots soldiers kept on fighting to defend the town. The 700 French and Scots defenders clung on for four months. The English dug tunnels and mines under the town walls in hope of making them fall down. But the defenders dug counter-mines, breaking through into the English tunnels and engaging their tormentors in desperate hand-to-find fighting in the claustrophobic darkness.

In the end, it was starvation within the walls that made the difference. And when the English finally got inside the town, Henry had his heart set on revenge. The disobedient Scots were singled out, rounded up and executed. Notionally they were being put to death as punishment for betraying their king but for James it was humiliating. King of Scotland he might be, but his title and rank had counted for nothing when it came to trying to get his own way with his own people. He learned from Henry V of England that kings had to make themselves in their own image. It was an active and dynamic business. Rule was a verb not a noun – it was about what you did as much as who you actually were.

Melun 1420 was a lesson King James never forgot. He had been made to act as the puppet of the Auld Enemy and had been openly defied by his subjects in the process. In many ways it was the siege of Melun that made him the kind of king he became – impatient, inflexible and intolerant.

Henry knighted James on St George's Day 1421, further underlining his 'Englishness' and during the summer of 1424 he married Joan Beaufort, niece of Cardinal Henry Beaufort and a relative of King Henry VI.

Henry V had died on 31 August 1422 and in his wake James's position had entered a new phase. As an inheritance the King of Scots was always valuable, both in terms of ransom money and as a bargaining chip. It was money that formed the basis of the negotiations the English happily entered into with the Scots for the return of their king in 1424, but with the powerful and charismatic Henry V replaced on the throne by his much less impressive son, the English had suddenly found a reason to make friends in the north. The last thing they needed, in their weakened state, was any trouble from Scotland and so in March the sum of £40,000 was agreed for James's return. By April he was on his way back home – a stranger to a strange land.

He had not been entirely cut off from his homeland during his captivity. Henry had allowed him to maintain a household and he had been visited down through the years by those Scots who wished to establish ties with their monarch, exiled or otherwise. But he was still an enigma to the majority of the magnates and nobles who now had to wait and see just what kind of a king they had got for their £40,000.

Put simply, there was nothing in it for the greatest of them. Robert, Duke of Albany and the principal thorn in King James's side, had died in 1420. His son Murdoch was acting as regent for Scotland and clearly had nothing to gain from the king's return; and Murdoch's son Walter had openly opposed James's release and so had no wish whatsoever to see his rightful monarch north of the Border. Archibald Douglas, Earl of Wigtown, controlled much of southern Scotland and even held the keys to Edinburgh Castle and Holyrood Abbey: what would King James have to say about that?

And then of course there was Alexander MacDonald of Islay. As Lord of the Isles he had a kingdom of his own and no wish to have some other monarch throwing his weight around again. He was also eternally watchful of the activities of the mainland nobles – as concerned by any moves any of them might make as he was about the agenda of the homecoming king. And as the son of his father, he was also ever watchful of anyone called Stewart.

James was crowned at Scone on 21 May 1424 and he only had to wait three months until he took delivery of the best coronation gift imaginable.

On 17 August the Scots armies of Archibald Douglas and John Stewart were utterly destroyed by the French at Verneuil. It was troops from the same force that had so humiliated James at Melun and the knowledge that the rest of them had been cut to pieces must have gladdened the king's embittered heart. At a stroke, the power of the Douglases and of the Stewarts loyal to Albany was seriously undermined.

James had had Murdoch's son Walter imprisoned as soon as he got home, and after Verneuil he felt empowered to go much further. On the one hand he played the other magnates off against one another: in a blatant snub to the Earl of Mar, an Albany Stewart, he gave the earldom of Ross to Alexander MacDonald. For the Lord of the Isles it was sweet revenge for Reid Harlaw. Mostly, though, James indulged himself in the destruction of the Albany line. 'Bob's your uncle' had meant suffering rather than advantage for the young king, but the old man himself was in the ground and out of reach of vengeance. His descendants were in James's hands, and they would not be long in following him to the same destination.

In March 1425 Murdoch, who was James's own cousin, was arrested along with his other son and thrown into prison. The Lord of the Isles – no doubt enjoying his role as Earl of Ross, but wary just the same – was in attendance at the parliament in Stirling that year when Murdoch, Walter and Alexander of the Albany Stewarts were put to death. At the same time, James took back the keys of the castles of Stirling and Dumbarton, along with control of the Albany earldoms of Fife, Lennox and Menteith.

Back home in Finlaggan, Alexander MacDonald would have had a great deal to mull over. Perhaps he summoned his warlords to his island hall to talk about what the future might hold for the Gaelic Lordship while there was a Stewart king in the east. While their hunting dogs sniffed out scraps in the fire-lit shadows, the Isles men would have had time to wonder how much of Scotland would be left once the new master had had his fill.

There was more to King James than a taste for revenge. He claimed his kingdom had gone to seed in his absence, that it was a garden run wild and in need of pruning. But as well as displaying his hard edge, he was determined to demonstrate to the magnates that he also had all the bearing of a cultured, sophisticated European monarch. His pet project in this regard was the building of Linlithgow Palace, the like of which had never been seen before in Scotland. Here was no fortress, but a Renaissance-style royal residence instead. Linlithgow made its point not through strength, but through the display of wealth. His aim was nothing less than the elevation of the very idea of kingship.

Before James I, the Scottish nobles and bishops – the Community of the Realm – had been in the habit of regarding the king as first among equals. The thinking of Duns Scotus, revealed in the Declaration of the Clergy of 1309 and the Declaration of Arbroath in 1320, made it quite clear that the king depended on his 'people' for his power. As long as he scratched their backs, they might scratch his. But James Stewart had learned the craft of kingship not in Scotland, but in England. Standing at the shoulder of rulers like Henry V, he had come to believe that a king's power was total.

The uplifting wave of the Renaissance had also washed over this Scots king, leaving an educated and accomplished man in its wake. Among his talents was a gift for poetry and in one work, 'The Kingis Quair' – 'The King's Book' – he described the moment when he fell in love. Traditionally the words are thought to have been inspired by his queen, Joan Beaufort, but the object of his affections is never named:

> And therwith kest I doun myn eye ageyne,
> Quhare as I sawe, walking under the tour,
> Full secretly new cummyn hir to pleyne,
> The fairest or the freschest yong floure,
> That ever I sawe, me thoght, before that houre,
> For quhich sodayn abate anon astert,
> The blude of all my body to my hert.

Here is James as love-struck young man, but the lines reveal something else, of much greater significance: his mother tongue.

Scotland in the fifteenth century was a blur of different languages and dialects and James Stewart spoke Scots. The dialect of the Lowlands, it was a distinctive vernacular with Anglo-Saxon roots. It was the tongue he would have learned and used for the first twelve years of his life and he must have missed its sweet sound during his long captivity. That he chose to compose his great work in Scots is a measure of how much it meant to him.

Only half of James's kingdom was Lowland; only half of his people spoke Scots. Those living in the rest of the land, the Highlands and the islands, and Galloway, spoke Gaelic. Gaelic was still dynamic, still culturally powerful. It was the first language we all had. Its sound echoed and reverberated from the rocks themselves. Within Gaelic Scotland there was no stronger voice than that of Alexander, Lord of the Isles.

This latest of the MacDonalds knew all too well what his 'kingdom' was – and what it had been during the time of his forefathers. He had Ross now, a gift from the king that gave him a footprint on the mainland stretching all the way from the rocky Atlantic coastline in the west to the rich farmland of the North Sea in the east. It made Alexander one of the most powerful landowners in the kingdom. But as Calgacus had said to his Caledonians fifteen centuries before, a rich foe excites the greed of powerful men.

King James was powerful but, unfortunately for his nobles, no longer rich. All that palace-building had left him short of cash and he was, after all, a king with a price on his head. He still owed his erstwhile captors, the English, for his freedom and money that ought to have been sent south to help meet his ransom payments had gone instead on gold leaf and fine stonework. In 1424 parliament granted James the right to raise taxation to pay for his ransom but even this failed to satisfy his many needs.

He turned instead in the direction of the rich men of his kingdom, and it was upon Alexander MacDonald, and Ross, that his gaze fell most piercingly. James began by trying to stir up trouble within the Lordship, as though to destabilise it. When this tactic failed to produce the desired results, he summoned Alexander to a parliament in Inverness, in 1428. Alexander arrived in good faith, along with his mother, Mariota, and fifty or so of his nobles. As soon as they stepped within the walls of Inverness Castle, however, they were rounded up and made prisoners in the tower. Even Mariota was manhandled and abused, dishonoured in front of her son. James the poet was inspired once more. Having seen the MacDonalds carted off in chains, he is said to have entertained his men with some off-the-cuff verse:

Let us take the chance
To conduct this company
To the tower with care
For by Christ's death
These men deserve death.

As well as Alexander and his following, James had also imprisoned several others of the most powerful men of the northern territories: Angus Dubh MacKay, of Strathnaver, leader of 4,000 fighting men; Kenneth Mor, John Ross, William Leslie, Angus de Moray – all leaders of 2,000 men each. The king had celebrated his return to his kingdom by destroying the

Albany Stewarts; now he was marking the cards of yet more of the influential men of his kingdom. It was a high-handed, absolutist approach to the Community of the Realm that would lead, in the end, to his undoing.

In the short term, he got what he wanted and needed: the wealth of Ross. He executed some of his prisoners but not Alexander, who was set free with a theatrical display of leniency within a few months. The Lord of the Isles showed his gratitude by gathering his fighting men to him and razing most of Inverness to the ground. The king, suitably outraged, raised a huge force of his own and headed north with it to terrorise those loyal to the Lordship. In August 1429, Alexander found himself with no more moves to make and he surrendered to James at Holyrood Abbey. With echoes of the humiliation of Toom Tabard, the Lord of the Isles was stripped to his underclothes in front of the king. He was made to drop to his knees and hand over sword, title and lands. Disgraced, he was led away then into captivity within the mighty East Lothian fortress of Tantallon Castle.

If James thought that was an end to the trouble in the west, he was terribly wrong. The kingdom of Scotland had shown time and again that she could hold herself together while her kings languished in captivity. The same was true it, seemed, of *Ri Innse Gall*. While Alexander gazed out of the windows of his prison cell towards the slate-grey waves of the Firth of Forth, men of his ilk were gathering on the waterways of his own kingdom. Dispossessed he might have been, but from every corner of his erstwhile realm his supporters gathered. The longships were on the move, under the temporary leadership of his young kinsmen Donald Balloch and Alisdair Carrach, and heading swiftly in the direction of the royal army camp at Inverlochy Castle, an old Comyn family stronghold near the head of the Great Glen.

As their bards would tell them, urging them onwards:

A Chlanna Cuinn, cuimhnichibh,
Cruas an am na h-iorghaile:
Gu h-airneach, gu h-arranta,
Gu h-athlamh, gu h–allanta,
Gu beodha, gu barramhail,
Gu brioghmhor, gu buan-fheargach,
Gu calma, gu curanta,
Gu crodha, gu cath-bhuadhach,

Gu dur is gu dasannach,
Gu dian is gu deagh-fhulang,
Gu h-easgaidh, gu h-eaghnamhach,
Gu h-eidith, gu h-eireachdail . . .

Children of Conn, recall now,
Courage in time of combat:
Be attentive, audacious,
Agile, ambitious.
Be bold, beautiful,
Brawny, belligerent,
Contemptuous, courageous,
Clever, combative,
Deliberate, destructive,
Deadly, enduring.
Be eager, expert,
Well-equipped, elegant . . .

A great wrong had been committed against their kin – but more than that, the independence of the Gaelic west had been threatened. Now the Islesmen's birlinns landed by the score, downriver from Inverlochy Castle near the site of modern Fort William. They made their way silently along the riverbank until they were within sight of the king's army.

A force of bowmen led by Alisdair Carrach was already in position on high ground overlooking the royalist camp. Seeing the approach of Donald Balloch and his men Carrach gave the order to unleash a hail of arrows. The royal troops, commanded by Alexander Stewart, Earl of Mar – the same who had fought the MacDonalds to a standstill at Harlaw – were taken completely by surprise. It is said that Mar was in the middle of a game of cards when word first reached him of the enemy's approach. He dismissed it, saying he 'knew very well the doings of the big-bellied carles of the Isles'. Maybe he did and maybe he did not – but their arrows seemingly came as a bolt from the blue. With the iron-tipped shafts still in the air, the main body of the Islesmen charged full tilt, bellowing their battle cries into the dark. It only took a few minutes, after which 900 royal troopers lay dead. Their card-playing commander had fled into the mountains behind the camp and so lived to tell his tale.

James was keen to press on with his campaign to bring the Islesmen to heel, and asked parliament for the necessary funds. But reverses like

Inverlochy, coupled with the greater, enduring defiance of the Highlands, had damaged the king's reputation. The Community of the Realm were also all too aware of how much money James was lavishing on his lifestyle of palaces and of patronage of the arts. They made it clear they were disinclined to throw good money after bad and obstructed the king's attempts to finance yet more adventures in the north. It seemed to the king then that it was as dangerous to have the Lord of the Isles in captivity as it was to have him roaming with his warriors. Alexander was promptly released from his imprisonment and returned to his hearth at Finlaggan, none the worse for his ordeal. In fact, he was victorious. His lands and titles were given back to him; so too, crucially, his prestige. The Lord of the Isles was back on top and it was the king who was left to look to his laurels.

Fortunately for James, he *had* succeeded in securing the future of the Stewart dynasty. After a long and worrying period when only the junior, Albany branch of the family had produced male heirs, Queen Joan was finally delivered of twin boys on 16 October 1430. The elder, Alexander, died in infancy, but the other, James, survived as a promise for the years ahead. In the same year, the king betrothed his six-year-old daughter Margaret to the French Dauphin Louis, son of Charles VII. This was a prestigious match for the Stewarts and ushered in a renewed Franco-Scottish alliance.

Soon after the wedding itself, in 1436, James felt bold enough to launch a campaign to try and regain the two Scottish castles that had remained in English hands since the supine reign of Edward Balliol – Roxburgh and Berwick. Despite lavish, almost theatrical preparations the resultant effort was farcical. Far from reducing the walls of Roxburgh, James's specially commissioned cannons did little more than make a lot of noise. Word of an advancing English army prompted the Scots into a hasty withdrawal. For certain of his magnates this latest expensive – not to mention failed – foray was the last straw. James had been shown to be profligate, and militarily weak. His final release of the Lord of the Isles had left him bleeding respect as well.

The king and his household were lodged in a Dominican friary in Perth when a group of conspirators made their move to rid themselves of their burdensome monarch. Led by Sir Robert Graham, nephew of the Earl of Strathearn, and Sir Robert Stewart, grandson and heir of the Earl of Atholl, they approached the bedroom of the king and queen on the night of 21 February 1437. The alarm was raised and James had time to prise up a floorboard and drop down into a sewer below. The board was put back in place and a first search by the traitors failed to find him. But in a crushing irony, James had had the end of the drain blocked up just days before – because he kept losing tennis balls down it. He therefore had nowhere to go and a second search of the bedroom revealed where he was hiding.

One by one the conspirators dropped down into the stinking dark. James, ageing and out of condition but still a danger when brought to bay, dispatched the first of them with just a knife. Finally Graham himself went down, armed with a sword, and dealt his king a fatal blow. Emboldened, the rest piled into the attack. When the body was hauled back up into the bedroom it was found to have sixteen deadly wounds upon it.

It is likely Graham and the rest had meant to kill the queen too. But in the confusion, and injured though she was, she made good her escape. Most important of all, given the conspirators' intentions to try and seize some degree of power, she also had little Prince James with her. Together with those of her followers who had escaped Perth, she made it to the security of Edinburgh Castle.

Scotland held its breath. The killing of a king was a shocking, almost sacrilegious act. But the kingdom had learned how to live with absent kings – dead or otherwise – and a royal party did its best to rally to Queen Joan's side. The conspirators were rounded up. Stewart was flogged before a crowd for three days, with a red-hot iron crown jammed down upon his head. Only the executioner's axe finally eased his pain. There was more blood besides. The little prince was crowned King James II on 25 March 1437. The coronation took place in Holyrood Abbey – Scone was too dangerous, seated as it was in the heart of territory controlled by the Earl of Atholl, the traitor Stewart's grandfather. The Earl himself, Walter Stewart, was parted from his head as well, for good measure, and his earldoms of Atholl and Strathearn added to the royal demesne.

Despite the ghoulish savagery of the punishments dealt out to the conspirators, there was no denying that the move against the king had left the Stewarts looking vulnerable. Much of the damage – to his name and to the kingdom as a whole – had been done by James while he still lived. By the time of the king's murder, the nobility too were a weakened presence. Lords and barons had been bullied and cowed by the king's attempts to finance his court and his ambitions. Several had died in France fighting the English in the cause of the Auld Alliance and two more were prisoners in England as security for James's unpaid ransom. As a consequence of the rule of

James I the central, royal administration of the country was confused at best and dangerously exposed at worst.

The MacDonalds, by contrast, appeared unassailable. By the time Alexander died in 1449 his empire, stretching from coast to coast, was still intact. He was buried, not on Iona like his forefathers, but in the rich mainland soil of Ross. From beyond the grave the Lord of the Isles was not only reinforcing past claims but also hinting at ambitions for the future.

For the Stewarts, that future lay in the hands of a boy king. Archibald, Earl of Douglas, a grandson of Robert III and James's closest male relative, was made regent. He died of plague after just two years and was succeeded as Earl by his teenage son William. Still there was no firm, consistent hand on the kingdom's tiller. While James remained a minor, other families sought positions of power in his shadow. On 24 November 1440, Sir William Crichton, keeper of Edinburgh Castle and Sir Alexander Livingston, keeper of Stirling Castle murdered the young Earl William Douglas, then sixteen, and his younger brother, David, in front of the king.

James had grown close to these Douglases – even idolised the young noble – and in their jealous spite, Crichton and Livingston had kidnapped the boy king and made a macabre spectacle of the killings. Having invited the Douglas boys to a dinner at Edinburgh Castle, they seized the pair and held a kangaroo court at which they were accused of treason. The boys begged on their knees for their lives but were beheaded while the weeping king looked on in horror. James grieved and the event has been remembered to this day as the 'Black Dinner'. But it was in fact a grim foretaste of the fate awaiting a future Douglas. William and David had suffered the consequences of coming between the king and ambitious men with eyes on their own advancement. In future, it would be the king himself who posed an awful threat to the powerful Borders earldom.

The future of the MacDonalds, meanwhile, depended on the success or otherwise of Alexander's son, John. He took his father's place as Lord of the Isles in 1449 after an inauguration ceremony wrapped in all the lyrical mysticism of anything ever witnessed at Dunadd in the days of the ancient Gaelic kings of Dal Riata. Clothed all in white – symbolising his innocence and integrity, that he was a light for his people – John would have stood upon a large rectangular stone. With one naked foot placed into a footprint carved into the rock – 'denoting that he should walk in the footsteps and uprightness of his predecessors' – he would have been handed a white rod, demonstrating his right to rule. He would also have received his father's sword – symbolic of his duty to protect his people.

> True my praising of MacDonald, hero I'm bound to, hero of every conflict,
> Sun of the Gaels, face of Colla's descendant, around the Bann's borders, swift his galleys,
> Meath's confusion, wolf of Islay, root of bounty, each land's defender,
> None grew up around him but kings and queens, true these judgements, true my praising.

He was being handed a heavy mantle, and the praise of the Gaelic bards only made it harder to bear. Some said he was more suited to the life of a priest than a leader of men. But leader of men he was, whether he liked it or not. And where should he take them? There were always those around him, within his own family, who wanted to see the continued expansion of the Lordship. John tended to believe there was more to be gained in the short term from consolidating an empire he considered overstretched already. He opted for the status quo.

Just as John took his place as Lord of the Isles, so James II came fully into his kingship. He was no longer the boy who had cowered in tears while the Douglases were murdered in his name. He had been born with a bright red birthmark covering half of his face and by 1449 he had earned a reputation for a fiery temper to go with it. They nicknamed him 'James of the fiery face'.

His marriage the same year was a glittering triumph for the newly empowered king and for his lineage. His bride was Mary of Gueldres, niece of Philip the Good, Duke of Burgundy and one of the wealthiest and most powerful men on the Continent. James stepped up to the altar of Holyrood Abbey with Mary on 3 July, and in so doing took his place at the top table of European power. Mary was a trophy bride, and her uncle's choice of wedding present underlined the fact. Philip of Burgundy was an international arms dealer and, along with several other impressive pieces of ordnance, he sent James a great cannon he had had made in the town of Mons in the same year the young king had entered his majority.

Mons Meg was a fiftheenth-century weapon of shock and awe capable of firing 20-stone balls the best part of 2 miles. Used in anger against a stone castle, she would have been truly formidable, but her real power was in the prestige she bestowed upon her owner. Given the physical difficulty of moving such a monster any distance, of getting her into position to attack a fortress, Mons Meg was always impractical as a weapon. But for a young king on the make she was the equivalent of owning a space shuttle. By her very existence, she projected the King of Scotland into orbit. And James II was a man in need of every ego-booster he could lay his hands on. He was thin-skinned, prickly and paranoid, apt to rise to any slight, real or imagined. Some of his sensitivities were understandable: to the north and west of his personal seat of power lay the lofty, independent-minded Lordship of the Isles; to the south was the territory of the 'Black' Douglases, for long the most powerful family in the Borders. King James felt trapped between them.

When he learned that William, the 8th Earl of Douglas, had signed up to a pact of friendship with John, Lord of the Isles and Alexander, Earl of Crawford, all of his face burned red. The Douglases had for long been the major power in the Borders. The Lords of the Isles were similarly important in the scheme of things and it made sense for both to agree an alliance of mutual support with another powerful magnate, namely Crawford. But the king did not see it as an innocuous handshake between men of influence; he saw it as the first move in a conspiracy to threaten his throne. Like the boy left out of the team, he was hurt and angry. But in the case of James II, there was more to it than that.

In February 1452 he invited William Douglas to dinner at Stirling Castle. William was a fifteenth-century pin-up, a man of the world with an international reputation and the vast family wealth to back it up. He was also shrewd, in the manner taught to his ilk by hard lessons in betrayal. Smelling a rat, thinking the king had more in mind than a conversation about fine Burgundy wine and big guns, he requested and received a letter from James guaranteeing safe conduct for himself and his entourage. Despite the precautions, it was the dinner party from hell. The king was jumpy and volatile and William was understandably edgy himself. The fact that the two men – one a twenty-seven-year-old playboy, the other a twenty-two-year-old king of all he surveyed – had been drinking all day did not help. Only one thing seemed certain, and that was trouble.

Late in the evening and full of drink, James pressed William to break his bond with John MacDonald. When William refused, the king leapt to his feet. He was at boiling point. He called William a traitor and, drawing a knife from his sleeve, plunged it hilt-deep into his foe's body. As the blood flowed, the king's courtiers seized the moment and rushed to gather round the mortally wounded earl. Time and again they stabbed and hacked at him. Legend has it that when the frenzy was over, William's lifeless body was flung from a first-floor window into a garden below. True or false, the place is called the Douglas Garden to this day. When William's followers recovered their master's corpse, they found it had twenty-six separate stab wounds. The head had been cleft in two with an axe.

By any standards it was shocking behaviour for a king, a brutal violation of all notions of honour and trust. William's followers tied a copy of James's signed letter of safe conduct to a horse's tail and led the beast through the streets before ransacking the town. But James had shown he was a monarch to be taken seriously.

James wanted the lands and wealth of the Black Douglases and he did not mind getting his hands dirty in the process. Military and political manoeuvrings during the three years that followed the murder ended with William's brother and heir, James, driven into permanent exile, with the loss of all his lands. Two more Douglas earls, brothers of Earl James, were executed and their lands confiscated by the crown.

Big guns, rich and powerful friends and relations in high places, murder: King James had the will and the clout to get whatever he wanted. For the Lord of the Isles, it was a nightmare scenario: was he to be next on the king's hit list?

James completed his takeover of the Black Douglas lands by 1455, the same year the English royals and nobility began the business of tearing themselves apart in their War of the Roses. In 1460, the red rose of the ruling House of Lancaster hung its head with the news that King Henry VI had descended into one of his occasional bouts of insanity. He was taken prisoner by the Yorkists and later replaced on the throne by Edward IV.

With his southern neighbour in turmoil and its rightful king deposed, James of Scotland decided the time was right once again to try to retake the castles of Roxburgh and Berwick. The Lord of Isles, desperate to show his loyalty, loudly pledged that he and his men would fight 'one league mile' ahead of the main royal army. As it turned out, it was a vow he would never have to keep.

James was at Roxburgh Castle on 3 August 1460, in the middle of a long, hot summer campaign, when word reached him that his wife, Queen Mary, was about to arrive for a visit. Excited by the news, he gave orders to prepare one of his cannons to fire a salute in her honour. He was standing close by the weapon when the gunner put fire to it. A fault in the casting, or maybe over-use that hot day? Who knows. In any case the gun tore itself apart, sending lethal lumps and shards of metal flying in all directions. King James II, just twenty-nine, was dead.

He left a widow and five children – two daughters and three sons. The eldest of the boys was the nine-year-old James, Duke of Rothsay and on 10 August he was crowned at Kelso. Roxburgh Castle had fallen to the Scots two days before.

Once again Scotland had a boy Stewart king on the throne and once again the magnates and other men of influence stepped into the power vacuum in hope of personal gain.

Just a year after the late king's death, an emissary arrived at Ardtornish Castle, overlooking the Sound of Mull. Resident there was John, Lord of the Isles and the messenger had an exciting and dangerous proposition to make. He had been sent by the exiled Black Douglas, but the puppet master behind the whole enterprise was Edward IV, the Yorkist King of England. The Lancastrian Henry VI was in exile in Scotland, along with his wife and son. Mary of Gueldres was playing power games and had offered sanctuary to the runaway royals.

What Edward IV was proposing, via the mouthpiece of a Black Douglas lackey, was a plot with more potential explosive power than any cannon James II had ever coveted: John MacDonald was to join forces with the Black Douglas and together they would rise in rebellion against James III. Once the takeover was complete, they could share Scotland between them – John would have the north and the Black Douglas the south. For his part, Edward IV would secure his grip on the English throne. There was one condition, however, the condition English kings always had in mind when thinking about Scotland: John and the Black Douglas would need to accept Edward IV and his heirs as overlords.

The Lord of the Isles agreed to the proposal and the condition. It was treason and he knew it. James II must have been spinning in his grave: now his old paranoia looked like prophecy. Never as politically astute as his predecessors, John was anyway under huge pressure from within his own family. The majority view within the MacDonalds seemed to be to return to the business of expanding the family territory – and this offer from the English king seemed like a dream come true. They were subject in theory to the King of Scotland, but look how seriously they had taken that state of affairs. Switching allegiances to another distant king seemed like a small price to pay.

John's illegitimate son Angus Og, Young Angus, got the bit between his teeth at once. Before the ink was dry on the paper he was out demanding that taxes owed to James III should be paid now to the MacDonalds. Something fruitful might have come of it all, had not James III decided to cancel his family's support of the House of Lancaster. As it turned out, Edward IV had only ever needed, or wanted, a diversion in the north and now that his rival for the throne had been cut adrift by the Scottish crown, he did not need Scotland, or anything Scottish, any more. The Black Douglases were already in exile in England and out of harm's way, and John was left alone to face the consequences.

Finally summoned before the king, John was put through a humiliation that echoed his father's treatment at the hands of James I. Kneeling before his liege lord, he was ritually stripped of his lands and titles. He had wanted only to be like his father and this was the bitter fulfilment of that wish. But John's humiliation was about more than just a personal failure. The repercussions of that single, irrevocable wrong move would be felt much more widely, rippling down through the centuries to affect Scotland to this day.

Like his father, John kept his head. He also kept some of his lands – but not the mighty earldom of Ross, or territories in Knapdale and Argyll. The loss of such prizes was too much for the rebellious young bloods within the family. They wanted land at any cost. Most strident of all the voices that rose in criticism of the chastened Lord of the Isles was that of Angus Og. James and his parliament had even sought to appease this most bellicose of John's relatives. Illegitimate though he was – and therefore legally entitled to nothing of his father's in the event of his death – parliament named him as John's heir. It was not enough. Angus became the hub around which John's opponents could gather. They listened while he harked back to the old days: Alexander's days, when MacDonalds feared no one on earth; when they had put their torches to Inverness and routed a royal army at Inverlochy. Were the sons of those MacDonalds supposed to roll over now?

Folk myth has it that sometime in 1481 Angus turned up at his father's hall with a troop of armed men. There was a terrible argument and John – Lord of the Isles – was flung unceremoniously out of his own home and forced to spend the night sheltering under an upturned boat. When news spread that Angus was seeking to overthrow his father, the Lordship erupted into full-scale civil war. There were those minded to follow the young pretender, but just as many who stayed by John's side. The birlinns that had made the Lordship now gathered to tear it apart.

The opposing forces met in the Sound of Mull and amid the disastrous violence could be heard the death knell of a whole ancient world. The place is called 'Bloody Bay' now and Angus Og is supposed to have emerged from its carnage as victor. But in truth, there were only losers. Angus won the battle but it was a defeat for the whole of the Lordship. Something more than men died that day: the idea of a strong Gaelic world – a coherent entity that could deal on equal terms with the rest of Scotland – died too.

The rock of Scotland is endlessly on the move, tectonic plates grinding mindlessly past one another on the way from somewhere to elsewhere. From time to time there is a jolt, a judder great enough to be felt through the feet or heard like distant thunder. Bloody Bay was a seismic moment too. The hairline crack between Highlands and Lowlands became a yawning chasm, too wide ever to be bridged again. Once, it was all Gaelic – the first land and the first language we all had. For long after other tongues arrived, giving new names to old places, the Gaelic world had remained part of the centre, the heart. It was a crystalline vein running through the collective identity of all Scots. All in an instant that day in the Sound of Mull, Gaelic Scotland became something else, something different – something threatening and something 'other'. The future was changed in that same moment.

King James had troubles of his own as his reign drew on. A sixteenth-century chronicler said he 'lost the hearts of many of his lords'. He certainly seems to have developed a habit of taking advice from men other than of noble birth – astrologers, philosophers, stonemasons and the like – and his leaders felt themselves slighted. He suffered, too, from a general failure to understand the way his kingdom had always worked. Where previous, more popular kings had circulated among their nobles, seeing and being seen, James III preferred to stay at home, in Edinburgh, mixing with his small inner circle of close acquaintances.

He had married Margrethe of Denmark in July 1469. In lieu of her dowry, her father King Kristian had mortgaged Orkney and Shetland. Both sets of islands had come under the Danish flag when Denmark took over control of Norway, which still owned the islands, and it is likely Kristian meant to keep up his repayments. For his own reasons he failed to do so and in 1472 James III claimed them for the Scottish crown. As well as completing the map of Scotland we know today, the union of James and Margrethe also produced three sons to secure the future of the dynasty – two named James and one called John. When the elder James was a year old, he was promised in marriage to the Lady Cecilia, daughter of the Yorkist King of England Edward IV.

It was part of a policy James had, of cultivating good relations with his southern neighbour, that went down badly with some of his nobles – especially those in the Borders for whom fighting the English was a profitable and enjoyable way of life. Part of being Scottish, especially Borders Scottish, was hating and fighting the English. What the king seemed to have in mind was anathema.

In 1480 King Edward demanded that young James be sent south for the marriage, but his father hummed and hawed. At that moment James's brother, Alexander, Duke of Albany, travelled south instead and presented himself before the English king. He promised to overthrow his brother – with Edward's help – and replace him on the throne. The job done, he would grant all of southern Scotland to Edward, along with his oath of allegiance. Not one to look a gift-horse in the mouth, Edward duly gathered a huge English invasion force and sent it north.

Spurred into action, King James led his own army south. He got as far as Lauder, in July 1482, before a farcical *coup d'état* was attempted by some of his nobles. In the huff about non-nobles in positions of command in the army, they took the law into their own hands, cancelling the invasion and kidnapping the king. James was frog-marched all the way home and shut up in Edinburgh Castle. He must have been livid. After mysterious negotiations that may have involved Queen Margrethe and the elder Prince James, the king was triumphantly released – by his brother Albany! The affair has gone down in history as the 'Lauder Lynching' and the alleged involvement of his eldest son may explain the sour relations that existed between the pair for the rest of the reign.

Another rebellion against the crown in 1488 culminated in the confusion of the Battle of Sauchieburn, on 11 June. With the king on one side of the clash – close by the site of the Battle of Bannockburn, outside Stirling – and the son and heir on the other, the scene was set for tragedy. In circumstances that have been lost to history, King James III was cut out from his retinue and murdered, perhaps with the collusion of the future James IV.

The new king was crowned at Scone on 26 June. Whatever the truth of his involvement with his father's death (it was rumoured that ever after he wore a belt of heavy iron links around his waist as penance for his share of the guilt), he is remembered as the most charismatic and charming of the

Stewart kings. He inspired affection as well as respect but he did have one troublesome trait in common with his predecessors – overweening ambition and desperation to make a mark the whole world would notice.

When the Spanish ambassador Don Pedro de Ayala visited James's court in 1497, he was struck by the self-assurance of the Scottish king. He was a man who, the Spaniard remarked, 'esteems himself as much as though he were Lord of the world'. Personal vanity aside, James IV was behaving in a way pioneered to some extent by every James Stewart before him. Whether by politics or by violence – or by display of wealth – this latest of the Stewart kings was in the business of showing the aristocracy that he sat alone on top of the pyramid of power.

At the beginning of the fifteenth century, the grandest of the grand families of the realm had been able to rival the king when it came to display. Most notable of all, the Douglases had risen to the point where their chivalry, wealth and all-round glamour were talked about and admired even in the courts of western European kings. Back home in Scotland they had established themselves as the kingdom's principal defenders against aggression from the south. Before James II took his murderous action in 1452, he had watched with envious eyes as William, the 8th Earl of Douglas paraded his wealth before admiring crowds while on an ostentatious pilgrimage to Rome in 1450. By the second half of the century, the picture had changed for ever. Never again would there exist a noble family able to turn on the style with anything like the brio and excess of the royal family.

The business of making knights was not the exclusive preserve of the monarch either. But with the rise of the James boys came the enhanced value of receiving a knighthood from the king rather than from any other member of the aristocracy. It was all part of a steady and insidious process that changed the role of king from first among equals to a position of unassailable, unchallenged dominance over all. There could be only one.

To complete the process, James IV had embraced the ideas and symbolism of the Renaissance more enthusiastically and more intelligently than anyone else. In 1496 he made it compulsory for all landowners to pay for their sons to be educated, and it was also during his reign that the foundations were laid for the creation of the Court of Session. He spent phenomenal sums building a navy, to defend the realm against English ships. When his flagship, the *Great Michael*, was launched in 1511, she was the largest vessel afloat.

Where his father had been awkward around people, preferring the company of intimates, James IV was a glittering showman who attracted exciting characters to his court. John Damian, Abbot of Tongland, in Galloway, was one of the most fabled. As well as promising to turn base metals to gold, he claimed he had learned how to fly. His one and only demonstration of his command of aeronautics ended in comical disaster. Wearing feather-covered wings, he leapt from the walls of Stirling Castle – landing in a midden that limited his injuries to a broken leg. His patron was much more successful at rising above all other men. His court shone with luminaries from all branches of science and the arts. Almost as a by-product, he created the Stewart 'brand'.

Falkland Palace was already a royal retreat, having been acquired for the crown from the local landowner in the fourteenth century. It had once been a fortified building – the castle in which the 1st Duke of Albany had left his nephew David, heir to the throne of Robert III, to starve to death. But from the start of the sixteenth century, James IV set about its trans-formation into an elegant Renaissance hunting lodge. By the time he had finished with it, Falkland Palace was among the finest residences in the country. Visit the place now and you notice that the interior decoration features thistles – everywhere you look, in fact. James had acquired the thistle as the symbol, the logo of the Stewart dynasty. It was a brilliant choice and in time it came to symbolise not just the Stewarts, but Scotland as well. The two – family and crown – had become one.

James was a political visionary. He wanted to create a whole new Scottish identity. But it was a very specific, even limiting identity: no more would Scotland operate as a loose alliance of regional and family loyalties. Loyalty was to be owed, first and foremost, to the king.

As part of the process of unification, James saw to it that one language rose to dominance – and that language was his own Scots. The same Spanish ambassador who had noted the esteem in which the king held himself also reported that he spoke eight languages. The Spaniard referred to one of these as 'the language of the savages'. The tongue he was describing, in such disparaging terms, was Gaelic, and James IV was the last Scottish king to speak it.

James's enthusiasm for all things Renaissance inspired him to encourage the introduction of printing to Scotland. Sometime between 1507 and 1508, the first printing press in the kingdom was established in Edinburgh's Southgait (a part of the city known now as the Cowgate) by Walter Chepman and Andrew Myllar. Myllar had learned the skills of printing in

Rouen, but had returned to set up a business in his homeland. Edinburgh merchant Walter Chepman had the money and, more importantly, the ear of the king. The surviving copies of Chepman and Myllar's first books are among the most prized items in the collections of the National Library of Scotland. One published work in particular, the so-called *Flyting of Dunbar and Kennedy*, gives an intense flavour of the battle for supremacy between the Gaelic and Scots languages.

William Dunbar was a priest, legal clerk and makar or poet to the royal court of James IV. As such he would have been required at times to see the world through the eyes of his patron and to compose lines that would please him. Walter Kennedy, Dunbar's opponent in the poetic 'duel', or 'flyting', hailed from a part of Ayrshire that was still predominantly Gaelic-speaking in the early years of the sixteenth century. Dunbar challenges Kennedy to a war of words by using the most insulting terms he can find in his lexicon. And central to his attack is ridicule of Kennedy's mother tongue:

> *Iersch brybour Baird, vyle beggar with thy brattis,*
> *Cuntbittin crawdoun Kennedy, coward of kind,*
> *Evill farit and dryit, as Denseman on the rattis,*
> *Lyke as the gleddis had on thy gule snowt dynd;*
> *Mismaid monstour, ilk mone owt of thy mynd,*
> *Renunce, ribald, thy rymyng, thow bot royis,*
> *Thy trechour tung hes tane ane heland strynd,*
> *Ane lawland ers wald mak a better noyis . . .*

Irish [i.e. Gaelic-speaking] rascal bard, vile beggar with your rags,
Pox-ridden craven Kennedy, coward like your kin,
Ugly and dried up, like a Dane on the rack,
As if a buzzard had feasted on your yellow nose;
Misshapen monster, mad every full moon,
Renounce your rhyming, you scoundrel, you just rave,
Your treacherous tongue has taken a Highland strain,
A Lowland arse would make a better noise . . .

Dunbar was a poet and in the context of this flyting he aimed to win approval, and hopefully financial reward, from his king. He bore no real malice towards his fellow makar Kennedy, another popular face at the court of James IV in any case; he was just delivering words he knew his patron would enjoy.

It was King James who had the cultural, political and social agenda. He was looking to push Lowland Scots forward as the official language of the people and the kingdom of Scotland and to do that he had to popularise his own tongue in the furthest reaches of his kingdom. Under James IV earthy, everyday Scots became the language of literature and law – and therefore of power. Gaelic, meanwhile – the 'Highland strain' – grew tainted. The mother tongue of half of James's subjects it may have been, but as far as Lowlanders were concerned it was the language of traitors and outlaws.

Chepman and Myllar may have pioneered the trade of printing, but they were followed and copied by others. Soon there would be printers turning out books and pamphlets on all manner of subjects – religious texts included – and the steady proliferation of the printed word would soon have huge cultural impact.

While the king and his fellow Lowlanders found ways to come together and celebrate their culture, the folk of the Highlands and Islands made only war upon themselves. Without the glue of a cohesive Lordship to hold everyone together, Gaelic society tore itself to pieces. It became a self-fulfilling prophecy as desperate men turned themselves into the living embodiment of 'wild, wicked Highlandmen' – the bogeymen who had already haunted Lowland imaginations for generations.

Everyone in the wild west was out to grab whatever he could. In the bloodletting, old scores were settled: Angus Og, the upstart son who had tried to wrest control of the Lordship from his father, was strangled to death by one of his own followers, an Irish harpist named Dairmaid O'Cairbre. O'Cairbre in turn was tied between two horses and ripped apart. It was a time remembered by the Gaels as *Linn nan Creach*, or the raiding time. The Highlands and Islands descended into the chaos of lawlessness. James IV must have looked on with grim satisfaction as the territory that had for so long defied the men of his blood now drowned in its own. In the end, the Lordship of the Isles visited upon itself a fate no king could ever have inflicted – it ate itself.

By 1493, even the crown had seen enough disorder and death. James IV was still in his minority but either he or his advisors were astute enough to see that decisive action against the troublesome northerners might help him kill two birds with one stone. For one thing, it might distract or otherwise refocus the nobles, still jittery about the manner of the old king's death. The killing of a king was always bad news and the whiff of blood was somewhere around the new man on the throne. Secondly, any attempt to 'daunt' the

Lordship – ringleaders of the troublemakers – would give the rest of Scotland something to unite behind. For James, it was a win-win situation.

The lands of the Lordship were soon declared forfeit to the crown and the title was taken for the king himself. To mark his new-found dominance he organised a tour of his latest acquisitions. It must have been a sweet taste upon the Stewart tongue: the last time a king of Scotland had ventured by ship into the labyrinth of the Hebrides, he was on the run. But, unlike Robert the Bruce nearly 200 years before, James IV arrived in the island kingdom not as a fugitive but as overlord.

Sometime in 1494 Finlaggan itself was abandoned as the administrative centre of the Lordship. John's failure was complete. For the hundreds of years that the Lord of the Isles was the hub of the Gaelic heartland, the 'Kingdom of the Hebrides' was secure. By failing to maintain control, John had let centuries of tradition and certainty slip through his fingers. He lived until 1503, but by then he had withdrawn completely from public life into one of penance and prayer.

1503 was a memorable year for James IV for altogether different reasons: his marriage to Margaret Tudor, daughter of Henry VII of England. Henry and James had been on reasonably amicable terms for years and the prospect of a lasting peace between their two countries required a celebration. Both monarchs signed the Treaty of Perpetual Peace in 1502 and on 8 August the following year the thirteen-year-old princess was married to the thirty-year-old King of Scotland.

James spent a royal fortune on five days of feasting, pageantry and parties at the Palace of Holyroodhouse, as well as three days of tournaments and jousting. According to some accounts, the English guests were unimpressed. As one chronicler had it, they 'returned into their countrey, gevynge more prayse to the manhoode, than to the good manner and nurture of Scotlande'. It was ever thus but, carping aside, it marked another spectacular advance by the Stewart dynasty. This had been a marriage with a difference.

Henry VII was an old man by the time he attended the event they called 'the Marriage of the Thistle and the Rose'. He was the first of the Tudor kings of England and his family's hold upon the crown was less than secure. Richard III, the last Plantagenet, had died on the field of battle, at Bosworth in 1485. It was Shakespeare who was to paint him as a villain and the Tudor claim on the throne was easily disputed. Marriage into the long-established and illustrious Stewart line was therefore a coup for the new English royal family. It was just the kind of good news Henry VII needed as part of a rolling campaign to paper over the cracks and reassure his subjects that he was rightfully in charge. James IV brought the Tudors much-needed legitimacy in the eyes of European royalty as well. It was an extraordinary reversal of fortune. The Stewart dynasty, whose sons had once been hostages and political prisoners of the English, had emerged as major power brokers. It was they who made the reputation of their royal rivals in the south.

An undeniable fondness for the ladies had brought James more than one illegitimate child before his marriage to Margaret. With Marion Boyd he had Alexander, in 1493, who would be educated by the great Humanist scholar Erasmus before being made Archbishop of St Andrews, by his father; with Margaret Kennedy he had James Stewart, in 1499, whom he made Earl of Moray. The first three children from his marriage, two boys and a girl, died in infancy. But on 10 April 1512, another James was born, the future James V. Once more, the dynasty was secure.

While the Stewart court blossomed, the MacDonalds of Islay knew only grief and sorrow. Giolla Coluim Mac an Ollaimh, a friend of Angus Og and poet to the Lordship, wrote:

> It is no joy without Clan Donald,
> It is no strength to be without them,
> The best race in the round world,
> To them belongs every goodly man ...

> Brilliant pillars of green Alba,
> A race the hardiest that received baptism,
> A race that won fight in every land,
> Hawks of Islay for valour,

> A race without arrogance, without injustice,
> Who seized naught save spoil of war,
> Whose nobles were men of spirit,
> And whose common men were most steadfast,

> It is no joy without Clan Donald.

The bard's lament was in vain. The original is written in Gaelic, of course, and without a translation would mean nothing to all but a few tens of thousands of Scots. This is James IV's greatest coup. You do not have to kill people to deny them power, to deny them rights. You have only to take away their words, make them silent. He who remains silent, after all, is deemed to have granted his consent. By now, the rise of Scots – and of English – had made Gaelic an incomprehensible babble to all but a handful.

The Highland Boundary Fault Line cuts through the heart of Scotland. From coast to coast it divides the country into two distinct parts – one that is Highland and one that is Lowland. It is a neat division, perhaps too neat. It is easy to think that the differences between the Gaelic Scots' identities are somehow set in stone. But that sense of separation is only a few centuries old. It is history, not geography, that divides Scots. Scotland's split personality is the result of a family struggle that pulled the kingdom apart. From being fully-paid-up members of the Scottish project, the Gaels were made rebels and outsiders. Ironically, they delivered the *coup de grâce* to their own necks. Scotland could not continue to be diverse. It had to become a single political entity – and maybe a single cultural entity as well.

It was the Stewarts who drove this new vision of the Scottish kingdom. In their eyes, Scotland was now secure in its independence and established on the European stage. But it was only the beginning of what they had set out to achieve. In the years to come, their ambitions would truly take flight.

***

With the MacDonalds humbled and the Lordship nominally in the hands of the king, there was a power vacuum in the Highlands and Islands. James IV of Scotland might now be Lord of the Isles as well, but the day-to-day running of the place had still to be undertaken by someone on the ground.

Life for the lumpen majority continued as before – in the Highlands and in the Lowlands – lives in both being dictated by the cycle of farming and by the force of law as administered by local landlords via barony courts or something similar. But though families like the Campbells of Argyll and the MacKenzies of Kintail did their best – often with royal sanction – to stamp their authority upon the 'wild west', the stubborn ghosts of the MacDonalds still haunted the land. The spectre of lawlessness was not likely to be exorcised by the behaviour of royal lieutenants like Gordon, Earl of Huntly, or Argyll, men more interested in feathering their own nests than establishing a fair and functioning society.

For the people of the Lordship, the central problem was the orientation of the king. Robert I had understood and valued the people of the west; so had Robert II, the first of the Stewarts. But thereafter, men like the

1st Duke of Albany and all the subsequent Stewart kings had tended to sense only strangeness and trouble in the Highlands and Islands. Their preoccupation with, and preference for, the southern half of the kingdom left the ordinary people of the Lordship out on a limb long before the fall of the Lord himself.

James IV spoke Gaelic, and seems to have been interested in the language from an intellectual point of view. But he was a dilettante in matters more serious to his health than linguistics.

The Treaty of Perpetual Peace of 1502 lived up to its name as long as the elderly Henry VII was still breathing. But his death in 1509 ushered in more turbulent times. Where old Henry had been content to spend his last years in peace, his athletic and forceful young son Henry VIII was quickly out of the blocks.

All across western Europe the main political talking point was the rise and rise of France under Louis XII. When Ferdinand and Isabella of Spain joined forces with the city of Venice and with Pope Julius II in a 'Holy League' against Louis, Henry VIII was more than happy to engage – leaving his Scottish brother-in-law in a difficult situation. On the one hand the Treaty of Perpetual Peace demanded brotherly love from James. But on the other, his chivalric heart had to consider his kingdom's much older tie to France. The Auld Alliance had begun during the reign of King John Balliol, and Louis had taken pains to remind James of its obligations as soon as Henry VIII became involved with the Holy League.

James's hand was finally forced in 1513 when Henry invaded France. Louis demanded help from his auld ally and his wife sent James a ring from her own finger along with a letter begging her 'champion' to 'take but three paces into English ground and break a lance for my sake'. King James handed over at least some responsibility for decision-making to little James, and started preparing to invade Northumberland.

A greater handicap than his chivalric sensibilities, however, was his dilettante's understanding of war. As long ago as 1497, Don Pedro de Ayala had reported to his master and mistress, Ferdinand and Isabella, that the King of Scotland was 'courageous, even more so than a king should be. I have seen him often undertake most dangerous things . . . He is not a good captain because he begins to fight before he has given his orders.'

Louis had sent seasoned advisors to instruct James and his men in the use of the most fashionable new weapon of the day – Swiss pikes measuring well over 20 feet in length. James rounded up the largest Scots army ever to invade England, as well as a truly awe-inspiring and hugely expensive artillery train. He sent forth the navy as well, the *Great Michael* included.

So far, so impressive, but James was a relatively inexperienced warrior. And as he crossed into Northumberland he approached the man Henry VIII had entrusted with the security of his realm – Thomas Howard, Earl of Surrey. Surrey was seventy years old but a battle-hardened commander who had seen it all and done most of it. James and his thousands were lumbering towards a predator.

The battle that ensued, between Flodden Edge and Branxton Hill on 9 September 1513, was all about hubris and bad tactics. Having arrived first and fortified Flodden Edge with his heavy guns, James allowed himself to be taunted and goaded into leaving his defences to face Surrey in pitched battle on the slopes of Branxton Hill.

Success for the Scots depended on their massed schiltrons of spearmen, armed with their unwieldy pikes, maintaining tight formations. Had they had time to practise properly, their sheer force of numbers might have carried the day. As it was, what should have been tight hedgehogs of men all but fell apart in tragic confusion as they clattered down the slick slope of Branxton Hill. Arriving at the bottom in a shambles, and faltering in soft ground, they were little more than a huge, unruly mob. English troops armed with shorter, but more easily handled bills – large axes perfectly designed for making matchwood of Swiss pikes – stepped into the confused mass of Scots and cut them to pieces.

King James, leading from the front, as was his custom, was easily felled. Dying alongside him were his illegitimate son, Alexander, Archbishop of St Andrews, two bishops, two abbots, nine earls, fourteen lords of parliament, hundreds of knights and thousands of spearmen. James had been a hugely popular king and those who had gathered so eagerly to his side paid dearly for their love of him. Even the head gardener of Stirling Castle lay among the fallen. The English losses were dwarfed by comparison.

It was a military disaster the like of which not even the Scots had ever suffered before. The king himself, their shining Renaissance prince, had been butchered before his men's eyes.

'The Flowers of the Forest', written in the eighteenth century, commemorates it best:

> At e 'en in the gloaming, nae swankies are roaming,
> 'Bout stacks wi' the lasses at bogle to play,

> But each one sits drearie, lamenting her dearie, –
> The Flowers of the Forest are a' wede away.

Once again the kingdom of Scotland was in the hands of an infant. James V was crowned in the Chapel Royal of Stirling Castle on 21 September 1513. Within a year his mother, Margaret Tudor, had met and married Archibald Douglas, 6th Earl of Angus. But the loss of an adult king, followed by the arrival on the throne of a child, was almost business as usual for a Scotland well used to adversity. The magnates and the Church fell into their familiar roles, vying with one another for control of the young monarch.

In August the dowager queen surrendered her sons, James and his younger brother Alexander, to the newly appointed regent – John Stewart, 2nd Duke of Albany (and son of Alexander, who had once promised southern Scotland to Edward IV of England during the reign of his elder brother James III). In October she gave birth to the Lady Margaret Douglas, future Countess of Lennox and eventually the mother of Henry Stewart, Lord Darnley, second husband of Mary Queen of Scots.

James V had a tough act to follow. Not only had his father been glamorous and charismatic, he had also been a successful and effective monarch. His death at Flodden had conferred upon him the legendary status enjoyed by hero kings like Robert the Bruce. For these reasons, James V tends to exist somewhat in the shadow of an icon, who would always be impossible to live up to. Despite all this, he too was a successful ruler, shrewd in his relations with his magnates and often intelligent in his use of power. He was also interested in the lives and conversations of the common folk of his kingdom. By the Castle Rock in Stirling is a district known then and now as Ballengeich. It was the king's habit to wander incognito among his subjects, sitting with them in their taverns and listening to the craic – so that he earned the nickname 'the good man of Ballengeich'.

The architectural remodelling of Scotland that had started under James IV was continued and taken to new heights by his son. James IV had seen to the construction of the Great Hall at Stirling Castle, but it was James V who created the magnificent Renaissance palace there, a building unique in all of Britain at the time.

On 1 January 1537 he married Madeleine of Valois, daughter of King François I of France. Henry VIII had been keen for James to marry his own daughter Mary, and by sidestepping the English offer James had forcefully aligned himself and his country with his southern neighbour's great and implacable rival. After the promise of peaceful union that had grown between the two countries after the Marriage of the Thistle and the Rose, James was choosing instead to keep a distance between himself and England.

Madeleine died within months of arriving in Scotland, and James immediately returned to France for a replacement. In yet another coup – and a further snub to England – he received as his second bride Marie de Guise-Lorraine. Henry VIII himself had sought to add her to his collection of wives (a lucky escape there) and her loss to the King of Scotland must have irked him severely. In contrast to the frail and sickly Madeleine of Valois, Marie was a formidable woman and an able partner. A daughter of one of the most powerful families in Europe, she was also highly intelligent, politically astute and a shrewd operator in a world of men. James had chosen well.

Like all the Stewart men, he was well able to father children. By multiple mistresses before his first marriage he had sired a brood of illegitimate sons and scattered them like cuckoos into the comfortable nests of senior Church jobs around the kingdom. With his queen he fathered two legitimate sons – James, Duke of Rothsay and Arthur, Duke of Albany; but far from securing the dynasty, they brought little more than heartbreak. Both boys died in April 1541, James at just under a year old and Robert within days of his baptism.

King James had had the wit and guile to exploit the weakness of the Church as it began to squirm in the heat of Europe-wide religious dissent. The teachings of Reforming preachers like Martin Luther – and of Humanist scholars like Desiderius Erasmus – had posed awkward questions for the Church and raised calls for change.

Henry VIII had already severed his own and his kingdom's relationship with the Pope, but over matters related more to the bedroom than to any questions of faith. Furious at the Holy Father's refusal to annul his marriage to his first wife, the Spanish Catherine of Aragon, he had declared himself 'the only Supreme Head on Earth of the Church in England'. He had since begun to apply pressure to his nephew, the King of Scotland, to put a similar distance between himself and the Pope, but James was astute enough to see an opportunity. With the Pope anxious to keep Scotland under his wing, James was able to extract huge financial rewards for his continued fidelity. In Scotland, the plight of the men of the cloth was therefore intensified by James V's demands for money.

To raise the necessary funds, the great religious houses were forced to 'feu' their lands and demand cash rent from their many tenants. For those who could afford the rent – and the up-front payment known as a 'grass-um' – there were certain advantages. As long as they continued to meet the rent, their land belonged to them and their heirs in perpetuity. But for those unable to get onto the property ladder, as it were, the business of feuing became a massive bone of contention and the cause of unbearable hardship. Of course it had not been the Church's idea, and it is ironic that a straw that broke the camel's back and hastened calls for the Reformation in Scotland grew out of James V's fiscal policies. From a religious standpoint James was not in the least interested in rocking the boat; and yet it was his demands for money to secure his obedience to Rome that forced the Church to behave in a way that alienated too many of its faithful.

Relations with England broke down completely in 1541, the year of his sons' deaths. Margaret Tudor died in November, severing a familial tie to Henry, and by the following summer the armies were on the move once more. At the Battle of Solway Moss, on 24 November 1542, an invading Scots army was roundly thrashed, with many of the nobles taken as prisoners.

The king, weakened no doubt by the deaths of his heirs and by yet another drubbing from the English, retired to Falkland Palace and took to his bed. He died, either of cholera or dysentery, on 15 December. Just the week before he had received the news that his queen had given birth to a third child, at Linlithgow Palace – but a daughter rather than the son his line so desperately needed.

For the first time since the death of Alexander III in 1286, the throne was in the hands of an infant girl. Little Mary Stewart was the future of Scotland and on his deathbed her father made a gloomy prediction: 'It came wi' a lass …' he said, referring to the way the Stewarts had first got their hands on the throne through Marjorie, daughter of Robert the Bruce, and her marriage to the Steward, '… and it'll gang wi' a lass.'

Born on 8 December 1542, she was just a baby when she was crowned Queen of Scots in the Chapel Royal of Stirling Castle on 9 September 1543. The date had been chosen deliberately – the thirtieth anniversary of the Battle of Flodden – and the ceremony dripped with moment and sig-nificance. She had to be sat upon her mother's knee to receive the crown and the anointing, and it was said that when the sceptre was held near her, she reached out and clutched it with her tiny hand. The observers were delighted by her seeming enthusiasm for the task ahead.

CHAPTER SIX

PROJECT BRITAIN

'Then that little man in black there, he say women can't have as much rights as men, 'cause Christ wasn't a woman! Where did your Christ come from? Where did your Christ come from? From God and a woman! Man had nothin' to do with him.'

Sojourner Truth, Woman's Rights Convention, Ohio, 1851

'Woman is ever a fickle and changeable thing.'

Virgil, *The Aeneid*

Stirling Castle is to me the most impressive and romantic fortress in all of Scotland – easily superior to that of Edinburgh. A lot of my affection comes from living in its shadow, but context is everything and really it is the setting, in the centre of one of the most stunning views in the whole country, that adds unequalled grandeur to the stones and stained glass of the buildings themselves. The Ochil Hills provide the backdrop, their colours changing moment by moment at the whim of sun and cloud. It is across the almost unnaturally flat floodplain of the Carse, at the Ochils' feet, that the silver ribbon of the River Forth winds absent-mindedly, as though having forgotten where it is supposed to be going.

The real genius of the natural design is in the presence of two great craggy ridges that rear up out of the Carse like ancient, battered sharks' fins. On top of one of them, Abbey Craig, is the Wallace Monument, erected in the early nineteenth century by Unionist Scots living in self-imposed exile in London. On the other is Stirling Castle. Writing in the early nineteenth century, the geologist Dr John MacCulloch had this to say:

> Who does not know Stirling's noble rock, rising, the monarch of the land-
> scape, its majestic and picturesque towers, its splendid plain, its amphitheatre
> of mountain, and the windings of its marvellous river; and who that has once
> seen the sun descending here in all the blaze of its beauty beyond the purple
> hills of the west can ever forget the plain of Stirling, the endless charm of this
> wonderful scene, the wealth, the splendour, the variety, the majesty of all
> which here lies between earth and heaven.

Quite so. The Great Hall of James IV, with its coat of lime harl, shines like
a nugget of pale gold from within the battlements, the *pièce de résistance*.
Restored to its original glory in 1999, after years in a more work-a-day
incarnation as a barracks for men of the Argyll and Sutherland Highlanders,
it is a beacon and magnet for the thousands of visitors who make a tour of
the castle every year.

Less familiar by far is a little detail of masonry cut into the battlements
above the Douglas Garden – scene of the infamous murder of William, the
Black Douglas, by King James II. Here the view is out over the Haining
Field, where tournaments were held in the days of the Stewart kings. The
battlements are chest high, but at knee height there is a little spy-hole,
maybe six inches across, cut through one grey block. It has been neatly and
deliberately made but you might not even notice the thing unless it was
pointed out. It is also highly unlikely that you would ever imagine it was
put there in the 1540s to let little Queen Mary – then just a toddler and
being kept hidden from her great-uncle Henry VIII, lest he seize her as a
bride for his baby son – look out over her realm.

Mary, Queen of Scots, the most mythologised woman in the nation's
history, was dynastic dynamite from the moment she was born. All her life,
her importance lay not in who she was, but *what* she was. The daughter of
the King of Scotland *and* the granddaughter of Margaret Tudor, sister of
Henry VIII, she had the blood of both ruling dynasties, Scottish and
English, in her veins. And so from the moment she was first held above the
bloodied sheets of the royal bedroom in Linlithgow Palace, where she had
been born to Marie de Guise-Lorraine, wife and queen of James V, she was
a prize beyond price. By the time she was old enough to stand and take in
the view through that little spy-hole in the battlements of Stirling Castle,
she was wanted as a bride in royal courts across Europe.

The view from the spy-hole was narrow, fixed and immovable. In time
Mary would give birth to a son with a quite different outlook – one wider,

more all-encompassing and revolutionary than anything his mother ever dreamed of. But that is a long story and it starts at the very moment a sweating, anxious midwife inspected her mistress's new-born child and found she was holding not a son and future king, but a daughter and future queen.

The news of the birth of a baby girl was received with great interest by James Hamilton, 2nd Earl of Arran and a great-grandson of James II. A Prince of the Blood, he was heir presumptive and would ascend the throne were Mary to die before she had time to produce legitimate offspring. Should she live there was the secondary hope of acquiring her as a wife for one of his kin. The de-facto leader of a Henry-backed, pro-English party in Scotland, Arran was appointed governor and regent for Mary in January 1543. He soon revealed that while the blood of kings ran in his veins, he had all the upright backbone of a snake – he certainly lacked the strength of character required honourably to navigate a sea troubled by the riptides of Reformation and prowled by brooding leviathans like King Henry VIII of England.

Sixteenth-century Scotland was especially susceptible to a virus like religious reformation. James IV had made it law for landowners' sons to be educated, a move that caused a manifold increase in the literate population of the country. Added to this was the impact of his decision to encourage the introduction of printing; Scotland became a fertile breeding-ground for the germs of new ideas. By the time copies of William Tyndale's English translation of the Bible began circulating in the 1530s, the Church's days as the unquestioned source of all religious knowledge were numbered.

Some of the demand for the Church to change its ways undoubtedly grew out of the discontent felt by poor people forced to look at an institution grown rich beyond belief. Church and crown had long been in each other's pockets, sharing the spoils of power; but a Scottish population bearing the burden of feuing found it galling to be lorded over by fat, wealthy churchmen, many of whom seemed to spend their spare time fathering broods of children by assorted lady parishioners.

In the end, however, it was the natural hunger for knowledge – for answers and understanding – that fuelled the calls for revolution. People who had long desired access to the word of God had been thwarted by the priests' stranglehold on literacy. Only the churchmen could read Latin and so the common people needed their priests to explain everything. The advent of books and pamphlets, written in everyday language, changed all of that for ever. Tossed by so many undercurrents, Arran could not decide which way to jump. On the one hand he tried to take advantage of the appetite for religious reform that followed the death of James V. But he and his advisors finally lost their nerve in the face of what suddenly seemed like an avalanche of 'heretical' literature and issued a blanket ban.

More troubling than the sale of seditious books though was the looming presence of Henry VIII. Ageing and in pain from various ills, he was a lion with toothache – driven by his misery into hunting easy prey. The infant Mary was as toothsome a morsel as he could have hoped for and Arran was no protection for her.

Mary's father had resisted Henry's calls to join him in defying Rome, and every other powerful monarch in Europe seemed wordlessly united in opposition to the English king. Scotland remained a back door through which any of his Catholic enemies, acting alone or in concert, might launch an attack. Feeling vulnerable and isolated, Henry saw his grand-niece as a way to shut and bar that door for good. If he could secure her as a future bride for his own baby son, Edward, Scotland would effectively be his.

Arran had been keen to curry favour with the English king and by 1 July 1543 he had signed the kingdom up to the Treaty of Greenwich, betrothing Mary to the English prince. But then his lack of a spine let him down. After all his sycophancy, he suddenly noticed the scent of Anglophobia in the air. To many within Scotland – from the grandest to the lowliest – Henry's advances stank of the age-old English belief that Scotland was theirs anyway; over-lordship had shown its face after it had been lurking all along. The memory of Edward I and of his machinations during the short life of his grand-niece the Maid of Norway moved through Scotland like an unquiet ghost.

Arran fell between two stools, failing comprehensively to back either the pro-English or the pro-French camps. Before he could find a third direction to run in, Marie de Guise-Lorraine made her own definite move. Backed by the pro-French, pro-Catholic Cardinal Archbishop of St Andrews, David Beaton, the dowager queen asserted her God-given control over the country. By the end of 1543 the Scottish parliament had thrown out the Treaty of Greenwich and realigned the kingdom with the auld ally, France. It was against this backdrop that little Mary had been crowned. Arran, vacillating and concerned only to preserve his own hide for future duplicity, was nonetheless 'the second person of the realm' – and, as such, allowed to carry the crown at the coronation.

The Scots' change of heart, their refusal to hand over Mary, made Henry VIII as angry as he had ever been. Diplomacy having failed him, he turned to violence and in May 1544 sent tens of thousands of soldiers north in a two-pronged invasion. Edward Seymour, Earl of Hertford attacked the city of Edinburgh, ordering wholesale murder and rape. With innocent blood pooling in the streets, Hertford's men then set the place alight. Holyrood Abbey was desecrated and destroyed, along with the Palace of Holyroodhouse. Only Edinburgh Castle itself managed to resist the onslaught. The second English force crossed the border at Coldstream and destroyed the great abbeys of Dryburgh, Jedburgh, Kelso and Melrose. Hundreds of civilians were raped and murdered, their homes destroyed. It was Sir Walter Scott who coined the phrase 'the Rough Wooing' to describe Henry's clumsy attempts to get his hands on the toddler Queen of Scots. It was murder, rape and wanton destruction choreographed by a psychopath blinded by rage.

While Scotland's commoners suffered and died by the thousand, the most craven of her nobles slunk to the murderer's side. Matthew Stewart, another grandson of James II and 4th Earl of Lennox, turned up in Henry's court offering his services. He was duly appointed Lieutenant for the north of England and all of southern Scotland, with the promise of the governorship of the whole country to follow. Lennox had once been considered as a future husband for little Mary, but now he was presented with the hand of Lady Margaret Douglas, daughter of Margaret Tudor and the Earl of Angus, her husband after the death King James IV. Lennox was not alone in his treachery. Either by threats of violence or the promise of jam tomorrow, Henry won over hundreds of Scots to his pro-English campaign.

Corrupt and dissolute, rotting from the inside, King Henry VIII died in the Palace of Whitehall on 28 January 1547. His orgy of violence had succeeded only in creating piles of dead and smoking ruins where towns and abbeys used to stand. The independent spirit of Scotland too was always annealed by fire, and emerged toughened yet again. The Reformation, though, which had been of interest to Henry only in so far as it enabled him to get his own way with his subjects and his crown – and to bed the women of his choice – had come on apace in Scotland.

Only a gambler with deep pockets and a crystal ball would have backed the Protestant horse in the first half of the sixteenth century. People wanted to see the Catholic Church reform a little – appear more sympathetic and honest, maybe – but its wholesale destruction was not the objective of most Scots. History up until the middle of the sixteenth century would have made it seem more likely Scotland would follow the French, rather than English, path and remain resolutely faithful to Rome. But events that unfolded north of the Border during Henry's last months set in train the hitherto unthinkable.

Between late 1544 and early 1546, the sermons of a Reforming preacher called George Wishart had been filling churches across Scotland. In February 1546 Cardinal Beaton had him arrested, tried and sentenced to a revolting death. Beaton was as corrupt, venal and licentious a man as ever donned a surplice – owner of many mansions, immensely rich and the father of un-counted children from scores of mistresses. This guardian of the faith ordered Wishart to be strangled and then burned in St Andrews, in front of Beaton's fellow men of God. Gunpowder had been packed into the condemned man's clothes to ensure spectacular and spiritually enlivening fireworks.

If Beaton thought he had nipped something in the bud, he was wrong. On 28 May a group of Protestant landowners from Fife burst into Beaton's palace and hauled him from his bed – and from the arms of one of his many lovers. He was messily butchered, his genitals cut off and stuffed into his mouth before being put into a barrel and dumped in the bottle dungeon of St Andrews Castle. In sixteenth-century Scotland, forgiveness and brotherly love were low on everyone's agenda. The killers holed themselves up behind the battlements and sent for help from England, which never came. Henry was followed onto the throne by Edward VI; but of more significance for the Protestants in St Andrews Castle were events unfolding across the Channel.

King François I had died and his son Henri II ascended to the Valois throne on 25 July 1547. At his shoulder were the relatives of Queen Mary – the Guises – and French ships and men were soon dispatched to deal with the trouble in Fife. The castle was pounded into submission, the rebels within rounded up and imprisoned. Among them was a young preacher called John Knox – once a sword-wielding bodyguard of Wishart, now a latent firebrand. Along with many of his colleagues, he was sentenced to serve his time as a slave chained to an oar aboard a French galley.

Distractions like Beaton and the Protestant 'Castilians' notwithstanding, the Rough Wooing continued unabated. Chief advisor to the young King Edward VI was Edward Seymour, brother to Jane, uncle to Edward, Earl of Hertford and more recently Duke of Somerset. Having washed his spear in the destruction of Edinburgh in 1544, he returned to the bloodletting after Henry's death with renewed vigour.

Far more Protestant than the old king had ever been, Somerset awarded himself the task of getting his hands on Mary. He was every bit as committed to a marriage between the King of England and the Queen of Scots, and took another army north with a view to forcing compliance from the northern kingdom. On 10 September 1547 at Pinkie, east of Edinburgh, he inflicted a devastating defeat on a Scots force commanded by the ineffectual Earl of Arran.

He followed up his victory by establishing English garrisons at bases all across Lowland Scotland, but like Henry VIII before him he was shortly to find that the real prize was beyond his grasp. Understanding at last that the might of England was too much for them to withstand much longer, Mary's advisors had entered into negotiations with the French. In return for military aid, they signed up to the Treaty of Haddington, on 6 July 1548, promising the little queen's hand in marriage to the Dauphin of France, François, eldest son of Henri II and his queen, Catherine de Medici.

Mary Stewart, just five years old, had spent her life in hiding. While her mother and the rest of the adults around her engaged in the politics that would shape her destiny, the little girl was moved from safe house to safe house. Much of her childhood was spent in Stirling Castle, and it was in an atmosphere of constant danger and uncertainty that she was forced to exist.

Temporary respite from it all began on 29 July 1547, when she stepped from the harbour wall at Dumbarton onto a ship sent by her French father-in-law to be. Her mother stayed behind to ensure she would one day have a kingdom to return to. The five-year-old was accompanied instead by a governess and the 'four Maries', the daughters of four of the ladies of the court – Mary Beaton, Mary Fleming, Mary Livingston and Mary Seton. It was not love that had motivated the French king to step into the middle of the bloodbath that was the Rough Wooing. Mary Stewart, Queen of Scots and of English royal blood as well, was simply a fantastically valuable store of royal genes.

Henry VIII never had persuaded the Pope to annul his first marriage, to Catherine of Aragon. As a result, every Catholic king in Europe could dismiss Henry's subsequent marriages to Anne Boleyn and Jane Seymour as worthless. Apart from Mary Tudor, his daughter by Catherine, his children were illegitimate. In Catholic eyes at least, neither Edward nor Elizabeth – his daughter by Anne Boleyn – could rightfully sit upon the throne. Henry himself had sought to erase Elizabeth's mother from the story of the Tudors, first divorcing her and then cutting off her head. Elizabeth had even been declared illegitimate by an Act of Parliament. Only Mary Tudor, therefore, stood between Mary Stewart and the throne of England.

If love was not the motivation for King Henri to spirit Mary away to a childhood in his Valois court, it was at least a part of what his attraction finally became. The magnificent châteaux of the Loire Valley were Mary's refuge, and almost from his first sight of the little girl for whom he had gone to war, Henri confessed himself smitten. 'She is the most perfect child that I have ever seen,' he said. She was given a warm welcome in his many homes; in fact Henri treated her like one of his own. She lived in the royal nursery alongside her future husband, the Dauphin, receiving a wonderful Renaissance education in literature, rhetoric, music, dancing, falconry, horse-riding and sport. By the time she reached adulthood she had mastered classical Latin and Greek, along with French, Spanish and Italian. Little golden-haired Mary was a precious jewel – and within the glittering Valois court she shone brightest of all.

François, her betrothed, was a year younger and small for his age. He had a stutter and was said to be a clumsy little boy. By contrast, Mary was tall and graceful, with pearl-white skin and hazel eyes. An insight into her personality comes from the reports of the affection she showed François. Whatever his shortcomings, she loved him – like a little brother at least.

It is impossible to imagine the impact on Mary of the sophisticated, effortless elegance of the Valois court. Her father James V had admired French style, and no doubt his remodelling of Stirling Castle, Falkland Palace and the Palace of Holyroodhouse were inspired by his desire to make his two French wives feel at home. But there was no disguising the culture shock that would have been experienced by a little Scots-born girl leaving Stirling and taking up residence in the châteaux of the Loire.

If the Renaissance had had its impact on Scotland, then it was as nothing compared to its effect on France by the second half of the sixteenth century. The town of Amboise, where Mary spent many of her French years, had been the last home of no lesser a Renaissance figure than Leonardo da Vinci, invited there by François I in 1517. That the great man himself had chosen to spend his remaining time there gives some sense of its comforts and attractions. Wrapped in the silken grandeur of Henri's court, Mary's education was indeed second to none. But as well as all those classes in poetry and needlework, she listened while her destiny – her birthright – was whispered to her like a lullaby.

In 1550, Somerset's control of Scotland collapsed, a financial burden too great to be borne any longer. Over in France, Henri celebrated the English withdrawal and used it as an opportunity to tell the world of the rightness of Mary's claim to the crown of England. But with Edward VI on the throne and his elder half-sister Mary Tudor waiting in the wings, any possibility of Mary Stewart adding the kingdom of England to her collection must have seemed remote even to ambitious Valois eyes.

Then, in 1553, events took an unexpected turn with the death of fifteen-year-old Edward, after a long illness. Mary Tudor duly followed him onto the throne and married the Catholic King Philip of Spain. Suddenly England was nominally Catholic again and unhappy Mary added 'Bloody' to her name by burning Protestants.

Scotland, meanwhile, had been turned into a de-facto French colony. Henri was her protector and French troops were in charge of the kingdom's defence. In 1554 Marie de Guise-Lorraine was made regent for her daughter. For the Catholic House of Valois it must have seemed as though God himself was beginning to smile upon their dreams. On 24 April 1558, fourteen-year-old François and fifteen-year-old Mary were married in the Great Hall of the Louvre Palace, in Paris. Before promising herself to François, however, she had put her name to a secret contract, a sort of pre-nuptial agreement. By its terms she agreed that were she to die without producing a child, the crown of Scotland would pass to her husband. She had given Scotland away.

By the year's end, the stakes had risen yet again, and all at once the lullaby of Mary's rights to the English throne began to sound more like a call to arms. 'Bloody' Mary was dead and onto her throne had stepped Elizabeth I. Here was the opportunity the French had been waiting for, yet might never reasonably have expected to see: Elizabeth had been conceived before Henry had even put a ring on Anne Boleyn's finger. In the eyes of Valois France, and all of Catholic Europe, she was illegitimate as a daughter and as a queen.

Mary Stewart's French family now stoked her imperial ambitions to boiling point. God had already chosen her as Queen of Scotland, they told her. One day, she would be Queen of France as well. Now, with a bastard on the throne of England, a third crown was within her reach. If she could get her hands on it a single, all-powerful empire would stretch from Scotland in the north to France in the south, with England in between. It would be a vast, Catholic empire that would dominate western Europe. Was not that what God had in mind for Mary, they whispered insistently in her ear. Was not the triple crown her God-given right?

Within the year the second crown – that of France – fell into her lap when Henri II fell from his horse, in July 1559. Fatally injured while jousting, his death made the frail and sickly François King of France. With Mary at his side he ruled for less than two years. He contracted an ear infection sometime towards the end of 1560 and died on 5 December. By all accounts Mary, who had doted on him, was heartbroken. But she had lost more than a little husband and the crown of France. Henri had been blatantly unfaithful to Catherine de Medici, his frigid queen and the mother of both François and his younger brother and heir, Charles IX. With François gone, Catherine wanted nothing whatever to do with his widow or with her power-hungry relatives. At a stroke, Mary found herself unwelcome in her French home and her principal allies, the Guises, exiled from the court.

Mary's glittering life and fabled future had changed before her eyes like a fairy tale turned bad, and she and her husband had reigned long enough to learn some harsh lessons about the wider world as well. Just as it had in the rest of Europe, the Protestant Reformation reared up like a wave in France, threatening to wash away Catholic monarchs such as Mary and François. The floodwaters of change reached all the way to the gates of Château d'Amboise itself, when a group of French Protestant lords had attempted to capture the young king. The royal couple were unhurt, but Mary witnessed the bloodbath that followed the capture, trial and execution of the would-be religious revolutionaries. She would have seen – and smelled – the bloodied corpses that were hung from the balcony of the château as an example and a warning.

Elsewhere, the Protestant tide had continued to rise. Freed from his galley in 1549, John Knox had settled in England. But when Edward died in 1553, 'Bloody' Mary soon made it an unpleasant place for a Protestant activist to try to make a home. He fled across the border in 1555 and swiftly began stirring those Scottish congregations happy to have a revolutionary at their head. He won a certain amount of support among the Scottish nobility – including Mary's illegitimate half-brother, Lord James Stewart.

For some of the ordinary folk of Scotland, Knox's words and promises where like a match to tinder. Many had been impotently stewing about the corruption endemic in the Church: of royal bastards squatting upon lucrative senior positions; of crippling rents charged for feued lands by fat, venal abbots; of Church services delivered in Latin, that none but the priests could understand. Knox's new world order promised to sweep all of that away. Driven by his incendiary preaching, Protestant mobs would eventually set themselves the task of attacking centuries-old churches and ripping out the iconography and idolatry of ages. Unspoken grudges and grievances found their voice in Knox – and their preferred means of expression was soon the thuggish violence of the mob. But in 1555 he was still years away from lighting the blue touch paper.

He had not had it all his own way, and during the last years of her life Mary's mother played an intelligent political game. Her prime motivation at all times had been to safeguard her daughter's hold on Scotland and as the 1550s had progressed, that had required considerable skill. News of Mary's marriage to François was soon followed by the revelation that she had promised him the right to rule the land if she should die before him. Yet Marie de Guise-Lorraine still managed to steer a course through waters troubled by the very real threat that Scotland might one day be annexed by France.

Until just the year before her death, the dowager queen's efforts helped ensure that support for the Reformation remained limited, and in 1558 Knox had stomped huffily back to Geneva where, surrounded by like-minded bigots and zealots, he felt safe enough to write *The First Blast of the Trumpet against the Monstrous Regiment of Women*, his misogynistic rant against female rulers like the regent and her daughter.

Only in 1559 did Knox and his Protestant nobles, known as the Lords of the Congregation, succeed in deposing Marie as regent and replacing her with the Earl of Arran, a magnate with all the integrity of an especially wealthy conman. (When the French king had assumed the mantle of protector of Scotland after Somerset's abandonment of the Rough Wooing in 1550, Arran's support for the plans to wed Mary to the Dauphin were bought with the gift of the duchy of Chatelherault, a title still borne proudly by his Hamilton descendants. If honour and trustworthiness are the marks of higher species, then Arran, son of immeasurable privilege, Duc de Chatelherault and Prince of the Blood, was a single-celled organism.) Knox had returned to Scotland via a stint in England. He had been brave enough to shout about 'monstrous' women while ensconced in Geneva, but was disinclined to fight against the sisterhood in an England now ruled by Elizabeth I.

A revolution had begun to take place, but despite Knox's woman-hating fantasies it was about politics and paperwork rather than any intention to depose Catholic Mary Stewart. Even when the Lords of the Congregation removed the regent from office, they did so under the convincing guise of loyal nobles acting for the leadership of 'the second person of the realm' – Chatelherault – on behalf of Queen Mary and King François, sovereigns over the water. Back in Scotland, and given a relatively free reign, Knox had turned his volume up to maximum. He had bellowed about the evils of

Popery and of the idolatry of the Mass and the mob duly attacked church buildings in Perth and St Andrews.

Protestantism had been accepted as the official religion of England that year, and the Lords appealed to their neighbour for military support. (Sensing a change in the wind, Catholic Chatelherault and his son steered a Protestant course.)

In late October, the Lords of the Congregation gathered in Edinburgh and agreed among themselves that the rule of the regent, Marie de Guise-Lorraine, was over. Now they wanted help from England to back them up. But despite the apparent logic of supporting the bold Protestant Reformers north of the Border, English Elizabeth was instinctively appalled by the prospect of challenging a sister-queen. It took the determination of her chief advisor, William Cecil, to win her round by arguing that nothing less than her own personal security – and that of Protestant England – was at stake.

Setting aside her natural horror of meddling in another's realm, Elizabeth finally sanctioned military intervention in Scotland in December 1559. By the Treaty of Berwick, signed on 27 February the following year, she promised Lord James and his fellow Lords that her intention was only to protect the ancient rights and liberties of Scotland for the sake of Queen Mary.

Events continued to move quickly, and matters began to slip increasingly beyond Mary and her mother. After the strength and charisma of the reign of Henri II, François and Mary looked like – and were – ineffectual children at the mercy of scheming adults. Guise power had depended upon Henri's gravity at the centre of his court and feeble François was no substitute. Mary's relatives were being spun away from the centre by the centrifugal force of change.

In July 1560 England, Scotland and France signed up to the Treaty of Edinburgh. In reality, François and Mary had nothing to do with it until the ink was already dry on the paper. By its terms they accepted Elizabeth I as rightful Queen of England and dropped for ever their own claim on the throne. Mary for her part refused to ratify the treaty, as did her husband. Indeed, while still Queen of France she began to come into her own. When Nicholas Throckmorton, Elizabeth's ambassador to France, met her that summer even he – a fire-breathing Protestant – confessed himself charmed.

Had she had more time, it might have all have been very different. While imbued with the confidence of two crowns, still shining within the Valois court, she was able to treat Elizabeth as an equal. But when François died his miserable, agonising death Mary found herself alone in a world turned suddenly cold ... and fraught with real physical danger.

With the French rug torn from beneath her feet she was never quite so steady again. No longer welcome in the land where she had spent her gilded childhood and early adulthood – where she had ruled as queen – she turned and looked instead towards the land of her birth. How distant Scotland must have seemed to her then – especially since her mother had died that awful year as well, on 11 June 1560, just as negotiations for the Treaty of Edinburgh had got under way. No longer a land offering the solace of a mother's love, it had also been thoroughly washed over by the same Reforming tide that had endangered her own and her husband's life.

Inside the tiny Magdalene Chapel in Edinburgh's Cowgate, not far from the building where Chepman and Myllar had had their printing press, the leaders of Scotland's Reformation gathered together for the first time, on 20 December 1560. Built between 1541 and 1544, Magdalene was the last Roman Catholic chapel built in the city prior to the Reformation. Perhaps because it was set aside as the cradle of the new order it features the only surviving examples of pre-Reformation stained glass in the entire country still in their original location.

Cold winter sunlight filtered by those four roundels, showing the arms of Scotland and of Marie de Guise-Lorraine among others, fell upon the faces of Knox and his fellows as they declared themselves the architects of all-encompassing reform. They started with religion but in truth they wanted to reach out and touch every part of every person's life. Like that from a December sun, it was a chill and revealing light they generated in their little chapel. Some of what they had to say could hardly fail to take the form of a direct attack upon their absentee monarch and Mary's most loyal supporters – who had dominated the country on her behalf – were to be driven from power.

Knox meanwhile preached measures as extreme as anything heard outside John Calvin's Geneva. He had approved of all he had heard during his stay within earshot of the radical Frenchman. In the world according to Calvin, and therefore Knox, blasphemers and witches would be put to death. Adulterous women would be drowned, men beheaded. Were a child to raise a hand against its parent, the offending limb would be cut off. In order to make the Scottish religious revolution secure Knox wanted nothing less than death for anyone found practising the Catholic Mass. He also preached that any Catholic monarch could, and should, be thrown from power: and he meant Catholic monarchs like his own, Mary Stewart. And yet now she was coming home.

From earliest times there had been something of the feminine about Scotland. Smaller and physically weaker than the mannish presences around her – first the Romans; the Vikings; the Anglo-Saxons and then England, France and Spain – yet desired by all of them; easy on the eye; lacking wealth in her own right but no less attractive for lack of funds; cool, aloof and infuriatingly independent against all the odds. In the end they wanted her just because no one had managed to get her.

Some would-be suitors tried sweet words, deception or downright lies, but all ultimately relied on force against a resistance they imagined would soon melt into their insistent arms. In Mary, those elusive feminine qualities of Scotland had finally been made flesh and bone – young, leggy, beautiful, intelligent, chic flesh and bone. The kingdom that had stubbornly resisted every advance was never more attractive to foreigners than when it was represented on the world stage by a female performer, by Mary Stewart. Now all those lothario states could seek to wed Scotland *herself*. Given life as Mary, Queen of Scots, the nation had suddenly become even more desirable and, perhaps, truly attainable for the very first time.

Mary Stewart knew all too well the nature of the pheromone she was giving off. By dint of her descent from Henry VII, she offered suitors a chance to claim the throne of England as well. She was therefore the most maddeningly alluring woman most of them had ever lived to see. That she was a Catholic in a Europe flirting with Protestantism only added an extra *frisson* to the whole affair. Poor little Scotland was a femme fatale.

The first, urged on by his father Philip II of Spain, was Don Carlos. Mary was not interested. Don Carlos slunk away but was followed in short order by James Hamilton, the new Earl of Arran and son of Chatelherault. Young Arran had made the grievous – and unforgivable – mistake of asking English Elizabeth to marry him first and was swiftly shown the same door as the Spanish prince. Then it was an almost unseemly rush by the dukes of Ferrara and Bavaria; the King of Sweden; the King of Denmark – even Ferdinand I, Holy Roman Emperor, looking for a wife for one of his sons. There were other sorts of offers as well. The Catholic George Gordon, 4th Earl of Huntly and the murdered Beaton's replacement as Chancellor of Scotland, urged Mary to sail to Aberdeen where he would meet her with a Catholic army. Together they would ride south and sweep the Protestant Reformation before them.

In the end, it was the soft words of her Protestant half-brother, Lord James Stewart of the Lords of the Congregation, that won her over and set her on a collision course with destiny. If she would accept that Scotland was now a Protestant country, he said, she could return home safe in the knowledge that she was free to practise her own religion in private. It was a sage suggestion by Lord James – most Scots were still Catholics in private if not in public, and would continue to be so – but also a dangerous one. Rabid Calvinists like Knox were as likely to accept the continued practising of Mass as they were to shake the devil himself by the hand. But despite the way post-Reformation history was painted until recently, the change from Catholicism to Protestantism in Scotland was a process rather than a Damascene event. By 1561 *The First Book of Discipline* had emerged as an owner's manual for the new religion, but it contained strong meat, too strong for many. Once the Treaty of Edinburgh came into effect and the French troopers withdrew from Scotland, any nascent fear of Catholics went with them.

The ship carrying Mary back to the land of her birth sailed into the estuary of the River Forth on 19 August 1561. The little flotilla was almost a week ahead of schedule and there was no welcoming party. A few rounds from the ship's cannon promptly made the good people of Edinburgh aware that something momentous might be about to happen, and by the time the Queen of Scotland stepped ashore in Leith a small but suitably appreciative crowd had gathered.

Glamorous and captivating she might have been to those first onlookers, and to those who watched her make her progress to the Palace of Holy-roodhouse. But within a matter of days she was to have the first clash with the realities of a Reformed Scotland – one that would set the pattern for her relationship with her kingdom for the rest of her reign.

On 21 August she had her first meeting with Knox and she asked him why her subjects should obey him rather than their queen. Straight to her face he questioned her right to rule Scotland: for one thing she was Catholic, he told her, and Scotland was not, any more – and for another, even more offensive to Knox, she was a woman.

Although Lord James had promised her the right to receive Mass in her private chapel, Knox and his ilk had different ideas. With Mary inside at prayer, and Lord James standing outside the door with his sword drawn, the firebrand preacher turned up with a mob. Someone lunged for the door; there were threats to drag the priest outside and kill him. Lord James stood his ground and the thugs withdrew, but the following Sunday Knox climbed into the pulpit of St Giles' in Edinburgh, to preach hellfire. 'That one Mass was more fearful,' he thundered, 'than if 10,000 armed men were landed in any part of the realm, of purpose to suppress the whole Protestant religion.'

Despite the white heat of his words, Knox was as yet unable to light a fire strong enough to consume Mary. Fuelled by his fervent Calvinism, he had moved faster than anyone else in the country. By the time he looked over his shoulder, he was too far ahead to be taken seriously by sane people. Young as she was – just nineteen – Mary initially proved herself up to the job of tackling and holding at a distance the extremism of the minority.

No doubt her half-brother Lord James was responsible for the direction of some of her first steps, but there can be no denying that Mary was a graceful mover across the stage of power. It was also the case that the social and political infrastructure of Scotland was unable to change overnight. *The First Book of Discipline* demanded root and branch reform, but the powers that be had to be – and were – pragmatic. Like any major change, it required new people to replace old in the many key jobs forming the knots in the net holding society together. It also had to be financed; and the nobles enjoying the funds they received from the Catholic Church were, unsurprisingly, disinclined to asset-strip the golden goose.

Mary spent a great deal of her time travelling around her realm, getting to know a country and a people she had last encountered when just a five-year-old. The powerful regional magnates were easily won over by her beauty and charm and she exploited an ancient truth of Scotland – either by instinct or by instruction from others – that old loyalties to kin and crown ran as deep, deeper perhaps, than obligations born of a new religion.

She could be frightening too. As 1562 drew to a close she saw to it that Huntly, who had urged her to don the mantle of Catholic figurehead and ride over the Protestants like an avenging warrior, was brought down and executed. Lord James, whom she made Earl of Moray as a demonstration of her trust, was her agent – but the will was as much Mary's as anyone's.

It is when you visit the castles and manor houses she must have toured herself in those first months that you encounter a moment from Scotland's history that stays with you: Mary was back home and making a success of things. But she had been Queen all of her life – and surrounded for most of it by the opulence of the French, not the Scottish court. All those years of her childhood and adolescence she had had an ambition to be Queen of

Finlaggan, Islay

Linlithgow Palace

Falkland Palace

The Great Michael, ship of war

James IV of Scotland

Mary, Queen of Scots

John Knox

Henry Stewart, Lord Darnley

James VI

Lochleven Castle

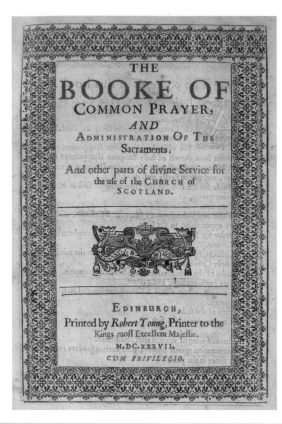

The 1637 Book of Common Prayer

St Giles' Cathedral, Edinburgh

The National Covenant

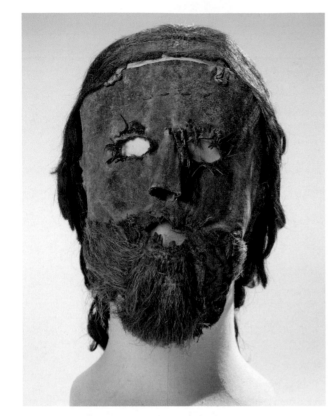

Peden's mask

Bass Rock

England first implanted in her imagination and then fanned into flame. Now, after all of that, could she really reconcile herself to a life lived on the edge of the world?

This, then, is part of the conundrum at the heart of the story of Mary, Queen of Scots. Was she really the committed Catholic monarch, desirous above all to follow her faith even if it must mean being forever out of rhythm with the beat of her nation's heart? Or is there a clue in the role she took in the destruction of Huntly … a glimpse of an altogether different, grander agenda that was the truth of the matter all along?

It has been suggested that Mary's Catholic convictions were slightly less than genuine and that she used the glamour and theatricality of her faith to disguise her driving ambition to replace Elizabeth on the throne of England. Soon after her return, she had begun asking Elizabeth to acknowledge her as heir to the throne. But Elizabeth had only prevaricated and dissembled, promising to answer eventually but never doing so.

Elizabeth was almost a decade older than her Scottish cousin: still unmarried and still without a legitimate heir of her own. The English queen wanted it both ways. In order to produce the heir who would continue her branch of the Tudor dynasty, she would have to submit to a husband and so compromise the integrity of her rule. By avoiding such a climb-down, she would ensure her unquestioned authority while at the same time condemning her line to extinction. In 1588 she would tell her soldiers at Tilbury that she had 'the body but of a weak and feeble woman but … the heart and stomach of a king'. If those were Elizabeth's sentiments in 1561 when Mary came home, an apology for being female, then it was yet another trait that put her at odds with her sister-queen.

Mary had no such qualms and gamely set out to survey the field for a suitable husband. (This behaviour can only have added to Knox's rage. While he was almost prepared to tolerate Elizabeth – who seemed at least to be keeping herself pure, rather than leading on helpless men – Mary was ready to mate and to breed.) More than any mere husband, after all, she was intent on finding a man to match or even enhance her bloodline, letting her fulfil her dynastic potential. And all the time she perused the marriage market she softly but insistently pushed for an answer from Elizabeth on the question of her place in the line of succession.

A lot of the suitors she had rejected with a flick of the hand while she was still in France gamely offered themselves as suitors once more. Word spread across Europe that the Queen of Scotland was actively in pursuit of a match and now, even more ardently than before, the likely suspects came forward again.

Don Carlos of Spain was first back into the glare – and was allowed to remain optimistic for longer than anyone else. Then there was Archduke Charles of Austria, son of the Holy Roman Emperor; but like the doltish younger Earl of Arran before him he had made the mistake of offering himself to Elizabeth as well. Charles IX of France, the thirteen-year-old brother of her first husband, was in the running for a while, but Mary's frosty relations with her mother-in-law, Catherine de Medici, made him a long shot. Even Queen Elizabeth herself tried to play cupid, first offering and then practically insisting that Mary should take Lord Robert Dudley as her husband. But – and unbeknown to the likes of Knox – Elizabeth had thoroughly road-tested him (while his first wife was still alive, come to that) and the Queen of Scots was less than thrilled by the offer of her cast-off.

The man Mary settled on – a love match, in fact, at least as far as she was concerned – shocked and surprised just about everyone. He was seventeen. He was tall and beautiful to behold. By all accounts he was quite the huntsman and, like Mary, an enthusiastic and talented dancer. He was Henry Stewart, Lord Darnley, son of the Earl of Lennox and Lady Margaret Douglas. Since his mother was the daughter of Margaret Tudor, young Darnley was Mary's own cousin – and right behind her in the succession to the English throne. Like Mary herself Darnley was, and always had been, dynastic dynamite.

The crushing irony of it all was that it was Elizabeth's fault Mary ever set eyes on him. The Lennox family had been resident in England, an enforced residence in fact, and Darnley had been a guest of Elizabeth's court. Like every other woman with a pulse, she had taken a shine to him and liked to have him play music for her. When she decided to release the family from their cradling in England, Elizabeth asked her cousin Mary if she would find a home for the Earl and his Countess north of the Border and out of her hair. What it seems she had not counted on was that Darnley would travel north as well.

Still promoting Dudley as her choice for Mary's husband, she was somehow blind and deaf to the dynastic threat posed by a union between two cousins descended from Henry VII. Darnley was Scottish by name, but English by birth – a qualification likely to make him acceptable to English subjects and the English parliament. Like Mary he was Catholic, but he wore it lightly – an affectation with which to accessorise his dandy outfits. When Darnley's qualifications are examined even casually, it almost beggars belief that Elizabeth did not do more to keep him away from husband-hungry Mary. As it was she failed even to prevent Darnley visiting Scotland, and there meeting the Queen of Scots for the first time.

Disastrously as it turned out, it was while Darnley was doing the rounds in Fife that word finally reached Mary of Elizabeth's judgment on the vexed question of the succession. She had made a decision ... not to make a decision. She would only settle the matter once she had herself found and married a husband. Mary was devastated and furious, and promptly fell in love with Lord Darnley. After a whirlwind romance it was announced they were to be married. Jolted out of her absent-mindedness, Elizabeth bridled. Since Darnley was English-born, he was her subject. She protested that her permission for him to be married to the Queen of Scotland had neither been sought nor granted.

That a queen as intelligent and shrewd as Elizabeth I could have made such apparent blunders in relation to Mary and her husband-to-be is hard to believe. At the very least she might have been happy to note that Mary had kept it in the family, marrying a local noble rather than uniting her kingdom with that of another European monarch. She would surely also have seen that by raising the stock of the Lennoxes – a family who did not have to look far within Scotland to find enemies – Mary was storing up troubles for herself in the future.

Her angry words, genuine or not, fell upon ears deafened by a combination of lust, mischief and sheer bloody-mindedness. Mary quickly showered Darnley with titles and had it proclaimed in Edinburgh that once they were married he would be made King of Scotland. There was also the tricky matter of kissing cousins to consider: technically Mary and her fiancé were too closely related and a special dispensation ought to have been obtained from the Pope.

None of it was enough to stop the runaway bridal train, though, and on Sunday, 29 July 1565 the pair were wed by Catholic rite in Mary's private chapel in the Palace of Holyroodhouse. Having married in haste, however, there was soon little for the Queen of Scots to do but set about some leisurely repentance. (Knox was strangely quiet, perhaps because he had found a distraction of his own. The great critic of the monstrous regiment of women had celebrated the start of his fifties by having a relationship with a sixteen-year-old girl, the daughter of a friend.)

Everyone knows the Mary and Darnley match was a troubled one. But in a drawer of the National Museum of Scotland in Edinburgh there is tantalising evidence of just how quickly Mary realised her mistake: a coin struck in July 1565, to commemorate the marriage, features the happy couple face to face and gazing into each other's eyes. The inscription has Darnley's name before Mary's, apparently indicating his superiority within the relationship. Very soon, however, these were recalled. The replacements that followed firmly reasserted Mary's dominance and put her husband in his place. Too late, Mary had come to her senses.

In spite of her earlier proclamation that Darnley would be king, Mary forever withheld the so-called 'Crown Matrimonial' from him. He might be her husband and consort, but he did not rule. The boy was livid. Already a loose cannon, given to boasting in public about returning Scotland to 'the true faith' of Catholicism, the news that he would never wear a crown infuriated him. But if he was an embarrassment, in one key respect it no longer mattered – because he had already performed the most important task of all by making his wife pregnant. Ever one to snatch defeat from the jaws of victory, however, he even seems to have made an attempt to undermine that single, worthwhile achievement of his spoiled and dissolute life.

Dangerously angry and often drunk, he was easily persuaded to join a group of nobles plotting to kill Mary's private secretary and confidant, David Rizzio. An effete Italian, he had attracted the ire of those who had found themselves out of favour at court following the elevation of Darnley and his family. Mary's half-brother Lord James, Earl of Mar was among them and they quickly convinced themselves that Rizzio was an English spy or an agent of the Pope. A plan was duly hatched to take matters, and control of the queen, back into their hands. Darnley was stupid enough to go along with them and add his dubious sanction to the plan.

The deed was done on the evening of 9 March 1566 and it unfolded in tragi-comic style. Mary was heavily pregnant by then and sitting with Rizzio and others in her private chambers in the Palace of Holyroodhouse when several of the plotters burst through the door. Patrick, Lord Ruthven shambled and clanked to the head of them. Aged, overweight and sweating profusely from a fever that would shortly kill him, he was wearing armour under his cloak and on the point of collapse when he managed to gasp a request that the private secretary be handed over to them.

Mary refused and Ruthven slumped against the door frame, desperately trying to remain upright, but the mob had spotted Rizzio hiding behind his mistress's skirts. Squealing in a trembling falsetto voice, he was dragged out, hauled into an adjoining room and messily murdered with as many swords and knives as it was possible to stick into his body.

Fearing that she might be next, or that the intention all along had been to terrify her into a miscarriage, Mary fled from the palace – and from Edinburgh. Together with some of her staff she managed to ride on horseback all the way to Dunbar Castle, where she was joined by a man who would shortly share her destiny. James Hepburn, 4th Earl of Bothwell, was a maverick noble. Yet whether by accident or design he had remained faithful to his monarch and now rode to her side like a knight in shining armour. It was a decision both of them would live to regret, but for now she was glad just to have a soldier of proven skill and bravery – he had fought with valour in skirmishes in the Borders and all across Europe – as her principal bodyguard.

The crisis of the Rizzio murder behind her, Mary's attitude to her husband turned harder still. In all practical respects she had him at arm's length but, lest anyone think the child she had carried was illegitimate, she ordered him to her side when, on 19 June 1566, she gave birth to their son, James. His Catholic baptism in the Chapel Royal of Stirling Castle was followed by a lavish and hugely expensive party. Darnley stayed well away and the job of welcoming the guests fell to Bothwell.

The party was held over three days in the Great Hall and Mary had ordered the construction of a huge round table as the centrepiece for a celebration designed to make a key political point. For the benefit all the English guests the Queen of Scots was conjuring up the memory of King Arthur. Little James was hailed as 'Little Arthur' and the message was clear: this was the boy who would be king of a reunited Britain. The visiting English ambassador was suitably offended by the Scottish royal family's claim to be the future rulers of the whole of the British Isles. It was indeed a provocative gesture ... but it was also realistic.

Time was running out for Elizabeth. She was well into her thirties and it was becoming less and less likely she would ever have a child of her own. If she did not – or simply could not – where would that leave the throne of England? The answer to that question, however bitter it might taste in English mouths, was simple: in Scotland's hands. Mary might well miss out on the English crown but her rightful and lawful claim on it remained. Baby James would inherit that right. For a while at least Elizabeth seemed to acknowledge the inevitable and to be on the point of naming Prince

James as her successor. Until, that is, his mother's poor choice in men undid her yet again.

Darnley had had bouts of ill-health both before and during his marriage. There has been dark talk of some or other sexually transmitted disease, syphilis maybe, but whatever it was it laid him low once more in the winter of 1566–7. After all he had done to her, Mary remained fond enough of her husband first to visit him at his residence in Glasgow and then to have him brought back to Edinburgh where she could oversee his care.

Her fondness did not go so far as bringing his nameless disease anywhere near the prince, and Darnley was put up in a house in a part of the city known as Kirk o' Field. In the early hours of 10 February 1567, the building was blown apart by the ignition of gunpowder packed into the basement by person or persons unknown. Darnley survived – in fact he may have got wind of what was going on in the minutes before the blast and climbed out of a window – but he did not live on for long. His partly clothed body was found in the garden. He was unmarked by the explosion and had been strangled or suffocated. One of his servants was discovered dead nearby.

Mary had spent the night in the Palace of Holyroodhouse as usual, but she did not escape the fallout of the blast that killed her husband. No one was ever convicted of the crime but it was widely rumoured that nobles close to the queen – perhaps her new best friend Bothwell – had carried out the deed with her blessing. However the Queen of Scots conducted herself in the aftermath of hearing the news, it seems she failed to convince anyone of her grief. Henry Stewart, Lord Darnley had been King of Scotland in all but name, and yet there was no state funeral to mark his passing. There was hardly a funeral at all. Word had it that his corpse had been dumped at night inside the walls of Holyrood Abbey. He lies, supposedly, among the rest of the dead there; but, while they have gravestones, he has nothing. No one knows for sure where he was buried.

His sordid death changed everything for Elizabeth – and, therefore, for Mary too. The English queen declared there would be no more talk of the Stewart place in the line of succession until Mary could be cleared of any involvement in her husband's murder. But that could not and did not happen. Bothwell was being named as the killer in every pub in Edinburgh and, a month later, Darnley's father was allowed to bring a case against him. The eventual trial was a farce, the courtroom stacked with Bothwell's supporters. Once everyone had gone through the motions, he was loudly acquitted.

Mary was understandably rattled. If she herself was innocent, then the only logical conclusion was that the murder had been committed by some of her own nobles. These were the very men with whom she sought to govern – so how was she to perform the business of government, knowing there was a killer in the room? Even such depths of confusion and uncertainty, however, can neither explain nor excuse what Mary did next. With rumours still circling above her like vultures, and with Elizabeth watching her every move for signs of guilt, she married the man nearly everyone had named as the killer: James Hepburn, Earl of Bothwell.

Some said he kidnapped and raped her and that she only married him to preserve what remained of her honour. Whatever the truth of it all, whatever the attraction, she became his wife in a Protestant ceremony on 15 May 1567 in the Great Hall of the Palace of Holyroodhouse. Maybe by then she honestly believed he was the only noble she could rely on, if not actually trust.

Within days of the news breaking, Scotland teetered on the brink of civil war. A group of nobles led by Lord James, Earl of Mar came together as the 'Confederate Lords' and pledged to free their queen from Bothwell's clutches. It was no more than a gloss on plans for a palace coup.

Husband and wife were side by side at the head of an army on Carberry Hill, near Musselburgh, on 15 June to meet their opponents. There never was a battle. Mary lost her nerve and sued for peace on condition that Bothwell could leave the field. He was granted safe conduct and, after saying farewell to his wife, he left for Dunbar. They would never see each other again and, after many more adventures and intrigues, he would die in prison in Denmark in April 1578.

If Mary thought she would be welcomed back into Edinburgh by a sea of happy, smiling faces, she was sorely mistaken. Instead, her subjects gathered on the streets and hung from windows to call her a whore and demand her death.

The Protestant nobles who had defied her had no real interest in killing her. Regicide was usually more trouble than it was worth and it was enough just to get her out of their sight. After a last, desperate, tear-soaked night in her palace she was hustled out of the city. She had last seen her son, then a ten-month-old, in April, and perhaps she hoped to be reunited with him. It was not the case. She was taken instead to Lochleven Castle, in Perthshire, and imprisoned there. She would never see James again. Mary had once beheld her kingdom through the spy-hole cut for her through the battlements of Stirling Castle. Now she viewed it through the windows of a prison. Within a few weeks of her arrival, she suffered a miscarriage; in all likelihood the little lost twins had been fathered by Bothwell.

Just over a year after she had lost so much at Carberry, a group of hardline nobles led by the young Lord Ruthven and Lord Patrick Lindsay took a boat across to the island on which Lochleven Castle stood. They planned to take even more from her – and used threats of death to get their way.

The Confederate Lords now wanted nothing less than her abdication and her replacement upon the throne with her own infant son, whom they now controlled. Weakened by losses of many kinds, she defied them for as long as she could. Even though she did indeed sign it all away on 24 July 1567, she made it clear she was acting under duress. 'When God shall set me at liberty again, I shall not abide these for it is done against my will', she told them.

With unseemly haste, little James was crowned just five days later. It was the worst-attended Scottish coronation of all time. The congregation, in the Church of the Holy Rude in Stirling, sang the 110th Psalm, in which the Lord gives dominion to the king: 'The Lord at thy right hand shall strike through kings in the day of his wrath'. Knox the firebrand, freed at last from the woman he despised above all, preached the sermon: 'And he brought forth the king's son, and put the crown upon him, and *gave him* the testimony; and they made him king and anointed him'. For all his frothing bluster, and the story of the justifiable murder of monarchs, from 2 Kings 11, it had not been unusual to see an infant given a crown: the Stewarts did that all the time. But there was something momentous about the events of 29 July 1567, a turning point in the history of Scotland: for the very first time a King of Scotland had been crowned in a Protestant ceremony.

Mary managed to escape from her prison in May 1568 and was quickly able to gather a huge army. She had heard the wrath of the mob in Edinburgh, and been briefly cowed by it, but the truth remained that a majority of the nobility preferred to side with the queen than with the Confederate Lords. Scotland had a natural tendency towards the status quo, and was drawn towards it yet again, like filings to a magnet. Mary's half-brother, Moray, had been made regent and he it was who led the force that faced up to her at Langside, then a village outside Glasgow, on 13 May. He was short on nobles but by his side were Lennox and also James Douglas, 4th Earl of Morton and a committed Protestant. Moray had also mustered a force numbering several thousand soldiers, but noticeably fewer than Mary's.

Archibald Campbell, 5th Earl of Argyll was Mary's commander and it was military incompetence – his and that of her other lieutenants – that handed overwhelming victory to the veteran battler Moray. Mary fled the field. Had she stayed in Scotland, she may well have been able to build on her support and try again, especially since Moray's control of the situation was shaky at best. But it seemed she had had enough. Not only did she flee the field, but she also fled her kingdom. Crossing into England via the Solway Firth, she threw herself on the mercy of her sister-queen. It was the start of the second half of her life – and nineteen years as a prisoner of Elizabeth.

The last obstacle to the Protestant Reformation having disappeared at last, the hardliners felt free to take a more fundamentalist approach to Church governance as well. Now came the rise of Presbyterianism, whereby each local church is governed by its own elders, or *presbyters*. Calvin had taught Knox about 'the elect' – meaning that, at the beginning of time, God had chosen all those who would be saved. These predestined, *pre-saved* people would naturally come together as congregations – and so the elders would be their natural leaders. It was all very convenient. At the top of the pyramid of command sat the General Assembly, where the decisions affecting the running of the Church as a whole could be made by representatives of each presbytery, or group of elders.

Convenient and effective it certainly was for churchmen like Knox, but it brought the Church straight into conflict with the crown. The symbiotic relationship between the king and the Church had evolved in such a way that the monarch exercised a degree of control over his churchmen by appointing his favourites to the top jobs. Presbyterians like Knox wanted nothing to do with bishops and archbishops, and by doing away with them they severed the link between Church and crown. This was a move that was never going to go down well with kings, definitely not with Stewart kings.

Knox was undeterred and, together with those nobles who shared his views, he ploughed his furrow. Moray and the Confederate Lords had the king in their power and a priority was to prepare him to rule a Protestant kingdom. He had been baptised as a Catholic but with his coronation a line had been drawn separating the past from the future. Given that James might one day rule a Protestant England too, nothing was to be left to chance. Little James's education, therefore, was placed in the hands of Scotland's leading scholar. George Buchanan had been a close confidant and advisor of Mary's from the moment of her arrival back in her kingdom in 1561, but he had soon become one of her fiercest critics. It was now his job – his mission – to turn her son against her as well.

It is impossible not to feel sympathy for the little boy. He never knew either of his parents and spent his childhood under governors and other adults who cared only for his blood, not his heart. His uncle, Moray, had been made his regent but it was Buchanan who had day-to-day control over his life. A fine scholar he may have been, but his approach to childcare was draconian. The Countess of Mar was one of those charged with the prince's care and, after witnessing the start of one particularly savage beating by Buchanan, she stepped in and accused him of going too far. 'I have whippt his erse,' he retorted, 'you may kiss it if you want to.' Kisses were never something little James received. Instead he suffered Buchanan's attempted brainwashing. It was the tutor's objective not just to educate the boy in literature and mathematics, but also in what Protestants and Presbyterians saw as the limits of royal power.

In 1579 he published *De Jure Regni Apud Scotos* – 'The Powers of the Crown in Scotland' – and sent it to James as an aide-mémoire for kings. 'I have sent you this book to steer you through the reefs of flattery,' he wrote, 'that it may not only admonish you but keep you to the path that you have once embarked upon and, if you should stray from it, rebuke you and drag you back again'.

Couched in affectionate language it may have been, but still there is no mistaking Buchanan's intent – and that was to continue to control the young prince. What he wanted, in fact, was to make a puppet king.

Within the text of the book itself Buchanan reiterated sentiments that had their roots in the Declaration of the Clergy and the Declaration of Arbroath of the fourteenth century. He wrote that if a king acted in such a way that he caused the people to despise or distrust him – if he reigned like a tyrant – then the people would be justified in getting rid of that king. In sixteenth-century Scotland 'the people' increasingly referred to the Protestant Church and its noble backers.

All the while the king was being prepared to rule, his Guardians continued to fight off his mother's supporters. Mary was imprisoned, and as time went by it looked less and less likely that Elizabeth would ever let her go; but those loyal to her fought on regardless.

Moray was assassinated in 1570. His successor to the role of regent was Darnley's father Lennox, James's grandfather, and he too was killed the following year. Eventually it was lack of hope that undid the 'Marian' party.

Edinburgh Castle was the last fortification in the country holding out in the name of the queen and it too succumbed to the inevitable in 1573. The civil war was over.

Since 1572 the regent had been James Douglas, Earl of Morton and one of those who had fought against Mary at Langside. During his first six years in the post he was able to bring a degree of stability to the realm that had been painfully lacking during the years of war, but he was undone in the end by an adolescent crush.

It began in 1580 with the arrival in Scotland of a Frenchman named Esmé Stuart, sieur d'Aubigny (lacking a 'w' in their alphabet, the French had found their own way of spelling Mary's surname). A cousin of James's father, he was therefore the only 'family' the young king would ever get close to, and it appears the boy was soon besotted with his elegant, dashing, thirty-something relative. Esmé returned the affection (some said it was even a consummated love affair for a while) and was soon showered with titles and privileges.

In 1581 Esmé used his position to accuse Morton of having been involved in Darnley's murder, and the regent was swiftly tried, convicted and executed. James's undoubted love soon caused Esmé more trouble than it was worth, when a group of jealous nobles lost patience with being passed over in favour of the foreigner. In August 1582 they kidnapped the king and bundled him into captivity in Ruthven Castle, near Atholl, in Perthshire. William Ruthven, Earl of Gowrie was the ringleader of what became known as the 'Ruthven Raid'. What nobles need and desire most is the ear of the king, and with Esmé around they had been shut out. The death of Morton was the last straw – even Queen Elizabeth had grown anxious about the level of influence being wielded over the King of Scotland by a man with Catholic leanings. It was with her support, therefore, that James remained in captivity, in one fortress or another, for almost a year. Deprived of the king's protection, Esmé soon saw the wisdom of returning to France.

Is it any wonder that James VI grew up to be a man who trusted himself above all others? Denied his parents, abused by his Guardians, used a pawn by those who sought power for themselves and, finally, given a taste of his mother's endless captivity – it should be no surprise that while weeks turned to months behind one locked door or another, he listened to his own voice.

Buchanan had been determined to make James accept that he was subject to the will of others, not least the will of the Protestant Church and its pet nobles. What he helped to create, ironically, was the very thing he most feared – a king who had learned to look after himself, who put himself first when no one else would. Buchanan and his brethren took a helpless baby boy and made of him an absolutist king.

James managed to escape the Ruthven Raiders in June 1583. While he gathered supporters and rode towards Edinburgh to reclaim his independence and his kingdom, Ruthven and his cronies sailed for France. Having gained a hold on the reins of power, he never let them drop and the Protestant Church began to suffer for its treatment of him. Knox had died in 1572 and was replaced at the head of the Reformers two years later by Andrew Melville. Regarded by historians as the real brains of Scottish Presbyterianism he was, however, no match for James. Not just a successor to Knox, he was also a close friend of Buchanan's and his eventual collision with the king was inevitable.

James was as convinced as any of his predecessors of his God-given right to rule and, having long since grasped the Reformed Church's intention to make itself independent of any monarch, he acted swiftly. All of Buchanan's published works – including his handbook for supine kings – were banned. The authority of the bishops was also loudly reasserted and the king was named supreme at the top of the hierarchy. Melville and his supporters fled the country.

With his position at home secure, James was able to cast his eye further afield. Like his mother before him he began to press Elizabeth for a ruling on his place in the succession. But despite the fact that she was allowing her dynasty to wither on the vine of her own squandered fertility, she refused to go beyond extending the hand of friendship.

The test of that friendship – upon which Scotland's hopes of securing the English throne now depended – came in 1586 with a plot to kill Elizabeth and replace her with Mary. Hatched by Sir Henry Babington – publicly Protestant but privately Catholic, a Recusant in other words – it was an elaborate plan to liberate Mary, land a Catholic army on the south coast of England and then sweep northwards to London and triumph. It was nothing less than a plan for a holy war and Babington managed to get a letter outlining the details smuggled into Mary's hands.

Imagine how her mind might have been working by now, after nineteen years spent practising her embroidery. Once upon a time she had been promised a triple crown, a Catholic empire with honours and titles beyond dreams. All of that was gone and, widowed twice over, she had not even her son's love to cling to. Every letter and gift she had tried to send him had been turned back by her captors. She had learned from others how his mind had been poisoned against her by Buchanan, her one-time friend and confidant. There was nothing more to lose but life itself and what was that anyway without liberty?

She put pen to paper and wrote to Babington advising him that he would need foreign help before he might attempt her rescue. The murder of Elizabeth was something for his own conscience, she told him. Of course the letter never got there. Intercepted by the agents of Elizabeth's 'spymaster' Sir Francis Walsingham, it was passed to the queen.

There is a legend from Babylonian times that the lion and the unicorn hate each other. While the unicorn represents spring, the lion is the symbol of summer and so their fight is eternal. An English nursery rhyme recalls the age-old animosity not just between spring and summer, but between Scotland – represented on the coat of arms by a unicorn – and England, represented by a lion:

> The lion and the unicorn
> Were fighting for the crown;
> The lion beat the unicorn
> All around the town.

Legend also had it that the wild unicorn could only be tamed by a virgin – and, in Elizabeth, England had its virgin queen. She finally tamed her unicorn by accepting that Mary was guilty of an act of treason and sentencing her to death.

All of this left the King of Scotland in a cleft stick: should he take up the cudgels in defence of the mother he had never known and risk annoying Elizabeth enough to cut him out of the succession? Or should he meekly accept her will and risk the possibility of the Scottish people rising in rebellion? The solution he came up with would have impressed even the most duplicitous of his ancestors. Ambassadors were dispatched to London with clear instructions: 'The one to deal very earnestly both with the queen and her councillors for our sovereign mother's life; the other that our title to that Crown be not pre-judged.' He also wrote to Elizabeth suggesting he would cut himself off from England were she to go ahead and kill Mary, but his language was always tempered, lacking any note of real threat. The implication was that he would be disappointed, more than anything else. Perhaps merely exiling his mother would satisfy Elizabeth, he said.

Mary, Queen of Scots was beheaded in the Great Hall of Fotheringhay Castle, in Northamptonshire, on 8 February 1587. She departed this life in the guise of a Catholic martyr, wearing a long black dress with a blood-red petticoat beneath. Years before she had embroidered a motto into a chair: 'En ma fin est mon commencement' – 'In my end is my beginning'. The chair and the sentiment stayed close by her until the end, like a premonition. It took two blows of the axe to separate her head from her body and afterwards every trace of the act was cleaned away, all her clothes and other mementoes burned. Her body was embalmed, placed in a lead coffin and eventually interred in Peterborough Cathedral, at night and by Protestant rite.

Edward I had tried to eliminate all thoughts and memories of William Wallace by tearing the patriot's body apart and scattering it across England and Scotland. But in so doing he created the very myth and martyr he had hoped to avoid. The same was true of Mary. Fascinating, beguiling and frustrating in life, she became infinitely more potent in death. English attempts to make her disappear only succeeded in making her unforgettable and unforgotten. (A quarter of a century later James would have his mother's coffin exhumed and moved to Westminster Abbey. The tomb he prepared for her there was more elaborate and impressive by far than that which holds the remains of Elizabeth I.)

Regardless of any legality associated with the execution, Elizabeth felt personally tainted by it. In an attempt to wash the damned spot from her hands she wrote to James claiming his mother's death had been a mistake, almost an accident. James's reply made it plain he cared more for his own future than for his mother's passing. In her end, was his beginning too. 'I dare not wrong you so far as not to judge honourably of your unspotted part therein,' he wrote, 'so, on the other side, I wish that your honourable behaviour in all times hereafter may fully persuade the whole world of the same. And, as for my part, I look that you will give me at this time such full satisfaction, in all respects, as shall be a means to strengthen and unite this isle'.

In public James mourned but in private he continued where Mary had left off – pressing Elizabeth to name him as her heir. She would not. Determined not to lose control of Scotland, as his mother had, he turned his attentions to matters closer to home. This was an intelligent king and he understood that his homeland needed him as well. Here was a kingdom that had been through turbulent decades of change: Reformation, Mary's quixotic rule, the flagrant power struggles of his minority. Aged twenty-two, he tightened his grip on the reins of power. For a wife he chose Anne, Princess of Protestant Denmark. Scotland rejoiced, not least because the match proved a fruitful one. In time, the fecund Anne would produce seven children for James, three of whom survived to adulthood. There was the eldest (and favourite) son, Henry, the Princess Elizabeth and a spare heir, Charles.

Like his grandfather and great-grandfather, he gathered an elegant court around him. With memories of his childhood education still vivid, he turned to the self-help books of his age in pursuit of greater wisdom. He obtained a translation into Scots of *The Prince*, Niccolò Machiavelli's near-legendary treatise on statecraft and the getting, keeping and exercise of power. If he did not know before, he would have learned from *The Prince* that a king must have the skills of a fox and also a lion. His self-education worked and, in stark contrast to his mother, he became a monarch who ruled not with his heart but with his head. In 1598 he wrote his own treatise on kingship, the *Basilikon Doron* – 'The Royal Gift'. The recipient of the gift was his eldest son Henry, Duke of Rothsay, then just four years old but already the apple of his father's eye.

Where James did resemble Mary was in his ambition. And, although Elizabeth held out, her refusal to promise him her crown became increasingly irrelevant. All he had to do – and the English queen's advisors accepted this even if she didn't – was to outlive her. Frustratingly, given the context, Elizabeth I lived longer than any English monarch before her. But at least her staying-power gave James time to think and plan; and what he came up with was something more radical and revolutionary than any mere takeover of the throne of the Tudors. It was a vision, and James believed its time had come.

Good Queen Bess was sixty-nine when she died on 24 March 1603. She had ruled England for forty-four years – long enough to give stability and a sense of national identity after the short reigns of her half-brother and half-sister. But the queen was dead ... long live the king. The ring was slipped from her still-warm hand and entrusted to a messenger, reaching James just three days later. The message the ring accompanied was a summons to London and to the very seat of power. The kingmakers wanted him to travel with all possible haste, but James took his time, savouring the moment as he made a triumphal tour of his promised land. Those moments belonged to one of the most accomplished kings Scotland had ever produced, a king who loved peace over war, knowledge over ignorance, tolerance over persecution.

When he reached London he boarded a barge to carry him the last few miles along the Thames to Westminster. What moment in all of Scotland's history could have matched that one? James was approaching the seat of power of his nation's most ancient foe. The English had been the enemies of his blood, the people who had murdered, raped and burned his subjects for generations, centuries. English kings and queens had sought to dominate his nation for more than 300 years and yet now they were offering him everything they had to give – throne and crown.

James VI of Scotland was made James I of England on 25 July 1603, in a ceremony in Westminster Abbey. He sat upon St Edward's Chair, the same that had been commissioned by Edward I in 1301 and which contained the stolen Stone of Scone, the Stone of Destiny. It was the first time a Scottish king had sat upon the stone since the ill-fated John Balliol in 1292.

It was a momentous occasion – and James had a grand idea to match. What he proposed was much more than mere union of the crowns. His vision was of the nations united, one Great Britain. For his subjects there would be common citizenship, a common religion, common laws. He would sit at the top of it all as emperor, ruling a union of two equal nations.

It was that word 'equal' that caused the first of many problems with his grand design: how, asked the English, could Scotland be described as the equal of England? The southern kingdom was bigger, richer, more developed, stronger, superior in every way. What benefit would there be, they asked, in accepting parity with poor little backward Scotland?

The English objections were not the only ones. When James had departed Scotland to take up his new crown, he had bid his people a fond farewell and reassured them he would be back every three years. He would return just once, in 1617, but the Scots smelled a rat long before that. What they feared more than anything else was a loss of their identity, and of their independence. If the Scots had learned nothing else in three centuries and more of struggle, it was that their independence was sacred. Uncounted thousands of them had fought and died to win it and secure it – and yet now their own king was proposing that their kingdom should be swallowed up by that of the Auld Enemy. To many Scots it sounded like betrayal.

It seemed the only person in favour of a Great Britain was King James himself. The idea eventually went before the English parliament in 1607 and was rejected out of hand.

With the king ensconced in London, hordes of his fellow countrymen took the high road south to join him. There had always been the occasional Scot in the capital but now they seemed to be everywhere. James surrounded himself with Scottish advisors. His bedchamber, where matters could be discussed so effectively, was full of them. English courtiers felt like foreigners in their own court. They talked among themselves about how the incomers were on the make, and stingy. And as the criticisms grew louder, so the Scots closed ranks around their king.

English Catholics were among those with a particularly powerful grudge: they felt James had let them down. Here was a king who had been baptised Catholic, who was the son of a martyred Catholic queen. He had shown tolerance of Catholics in his native land and had suggested he would do the same in England. But James had encountered rabid opposition to any talk of extending the hand of friendship and, reluctantly or not, had quietly cut them adrift.

When Catholic conspirators packed gunpowder beneath Parliament in 1605, their specific target was not the institution itself but the monarch within it. Guy Fawkes had become expert in the use of gunpowder while serving as a soldier in Europe. Caught red-handed, he initially refused to tell his captors anything. Broken on the rack, he gave up everything – including the truth that the plan was to blow Scottish James all the way back to Scotland. The plotters had the names and addresses of every significant Scot in London as well. What they had intended was the ethnic cleansing of the whole city.

With his dream in tatters – threatened by terrible violence and rejected by parliament – James resorted to signs and symbols. Soon after arriving in London he had had a number of flags designed, attempts to unite the saltire of Scotland with the English cross of St George. The Union flag was the ultimate product of his doodling, but during his own lifetime it served as no more than a reminder of what might have been.

For centuries English kings had clung to a prophecy that told them King Arthur would return one day to unify Britain. Time and again the image had been invoked to justify English attempts to subdue Scotland, to be recognised as overlord. In one of the great ironies of history, it was Scotland's own 'Little Arthur' – James VI – who had finally fulfilled it. His achievement was remarkable, but within it were the seeds of new trouble.

By 1603 the people of Scotland had a strong sense of their identity as an ancient and independent nation. Waves of invaders had been defied. Alongside Wallace and Bruce they had fought for and won their freedom, developed a unique and distinctive court and forged a place in Europe. But the union of the crowns was more than just another step along the road. It was the decisive turning point in Scotland's history.

***

King James I and VI has gone down in history and legend as 'the wisest fool in Christendom'. The story goes that he never said a foolish thing nor ever did a wise one. For long, historians were disparaging about the first man to rule the kingdoms of Scotland and England together, and certainly his later years saw him succumb to one ailment after another.

We remember dead kings more fondly when, like some of James's predecessors, they die young and beautiful:

> ... Smart lad to slip betimes away
> From fields where glory does not stay ...

Instead, poor James suffered all the inevitabilities and indignities of old age, from arthritis, to piles, to the loss of all his teeth; and it was these physical failings as much as anything else that helped leave behind a picture of a failed king. But he was also a man of great intelligence, even a peculiar, self-preserving kind of wisdom. And because he so valued the role of kingship – a gift from God – he strived to live up to an idealised view that, by the end, was becoming distinctly unfashionable in some quarters.

It seems extraordinary now but having a Scot on the English throne after all those years of fighting off the Auld Enemy caused joyous celebration in Scotland for only a short time. It was all very well that King James VI had finally got his hands on the ancient prize, but to most Scots – and most English people as well – the reality after the honeymoon was an anticlimax. Scots in Edinburgh worried that the loss of the court to London would take the shine off the city as a place of glamour, and of gratuitous spending. Elsewhere there were slow-burning concerns for Scots about how the future would take shape. It was all very well while Scottish James sat upon the English throne – he had spent all his life in Scotland and knew well the place and the people, their likes and dislikes. But what would happen once he was gone and they were ruled by a king strange to them?

Scotland was, anyway, a kingdom that had grown used to the absence of the monarch. It had been a regular pattern down through the past three centuries and the mechanisms were in place to cope. James was in London, but he was theirs too. Short-term fascination with the novelty of a king of two countries soon faded from the forefront of most people's minds.

James famously observed that he could rule Scotland with his pen, but some of his ideas led inevitably to the drawing of swords. By the 'Statutes of Iona' of 1609, he tried to bring 'peace' to the still-barbarous islands of the west. James had been meddling in the strongholds of Gaeldom since the 1590s, an old Stewart hobby. He tried to bring what he regarded as civilisation to the whole of the island of Lewis by leasing it to Lowlanders in 1597, 1605 and 1607, and the project failed every time under furious assault by the locals. By the Statutes he tried to force the chieftains to lead their people away from their ancient traditions and towards a lifestyle James regarded as more fitting for his subjects. Underlying it all was a determination to replace Gaelic with English and, while the new rules did little to impose Lowland ways on the folk of the islands, the damage done to the old language was irrevocable.

It was also in 1609 that James invited his Protestant aristocracy to establish 'Plantations' in Ireland. Soon there were thousands of Protestants in Ulster and the consequences of their presence in the north of the island resonate across the British Isles to this day.

In 1598 James had written the *Basilikon Doron* for his son Henry. It was all he understood about the craft of kingship and it is interesting to wonder what use the eldest son might have made of the father's undoubted intelligence. But Prince Henry died in 1612, breaking his father's heart. When James himself died on 27 March 1625 it was his younger surviving son, Charles, who ascended to the thrones of Scotland and England in his stead.

Unlike his handsome, athletic older brother, Charles I stood barely five feet tall in his silk-stockinged feet and was always studious and pious rather than physical and outgoing. He had been born in Dunfermline and was such a sickly little lad he had to be left behind at first while his father travelled south to claim the throne in 1603. So wary was he of people that he came across as aloof and distant. To many, even those closest to him, he often seemed charmless and abrupt. He stuttered too, and was slightly lame.

The *Basilikon Doron* – the Royal Gift – had passed from Henry to Charles and there is no doubt that he took the role and his destiny very seriously. He was like his father in many ways, though a much less talented, less defined version of the original. But he certainly took on board the central contention of his father's book – that that he was a 'little god' set upon the throne to rule over other men.

CHAPTER SEVEN

KING JESUS

'They're all crazy. They're all crazy except you and me. Sometimes I have my doubts about you.'

Martin, *Dracula*, 1931

A Scottish Presbyterian man is headed for a new life in Australia when his ship hits an uncharted reef and sinks. Alone of all the passengers and crew he survives the wreck and swims to a little uninhabited island. Twenty years later another liner is blown off course by another storm and onto the same reef. This time a handful of survivors make it into a lifeboat and they row themselves to the Scotsman's island.

He greets them warmly and takes them on a tour of their new home. They soon realise he has worked hard to create a comfortable, civilised life for himself.

'This is my house – complete with running water,' he says, walking them past a well-built timber building with a roof of palm leaves.

'Here's my garden and my vegetable plot,' he says, smiling broadly. 'I can grow fruit as well, anything I want – the climate is so wonderful.'

'And over there – slung between two palm trees – is my hammock, where I like to watch the sun set each evening.'

One of the survivors takes a minute to gaze around and then points to a stone building on a nearby hill.

'And what's that?' he asks.

'Oh, that's my church,' says the Scotsman.

Another survivor points to an almost identical building right beside the first one.

'And that?' he asks.

'That,' says the Scotsman, 'Oh . . . that's the church I don't go to.'

You almost have to be a Scot to get the joke. Its humour lies in the religious bigotry that still cuts right across the country like an infected wound. As it turns out, it is an old injury.

In seventeenth-century Scotland everyone was a religious bigot. The Episcopalians distrusted the Presbyterians. The Presbyterians in turn treated the Episcopalians with contempt. At least they had Calvinism in common. Both sets of Calvinists loathed the Catholics and the Catholics kept their heads down, secure in the knowledge that all Protestants were going straight to hell anyway. South of the Border, in England, were the Anglicans. For those of the Reformed Scottish Kirk, these unfortunates comprised nothing less than 'a synagogue of Satan'.

Even within the separate cliques, the members tended to distrust each other. Each man and woman was encouraged to believe that he or she alone was responsible for ensuring they were doing things the way God wanted. The neighbours had to be watched as well, to ensure they were not slipping either. Everything and everyone was under scrutiny, all the time. This was bad enough – providing citizens with a new stick with which to beat themselves and their neighbours – but the obsession with faith, and its correct practice, also provided a licence for dangerous levels of nosiness into other kinds of behaviour.

Seventeeth-century Scotland was a time and a place of unprecedented intrusion into people's private lives, in search of signs of immorality and wrongdoing, real or imagined. King James himself had been fascinated by witches and witchcraft, even going into print on the subject; and hundreds and then thousands of men and women were being burned and drowned for alleged involvement in the dark arts. It was not just Protestants either: as the Catholic Church went into full counter-Reformation mode, after the panicky house-cleaning inspired by the Council of Trent in the middle years of the sixteenth century, her kingdoms began to put witches to the flame as well.

Homosexuality was persecuted with renewed vigour. James VI, whose own personal relationships with men were often the subject of tittle-tattle, wrote in the *Basilikon Doron* that sodomy was among those crimes that 'ye are bound in conscience never to forgive'. Earthly vices like drinking, music and drama were increasingly frowned upon. Eventually they banned the celebration of Christmas and Easter as 'superstitious observation and licentious profanation'.

The Reformation of the Kirk had begun in the 1560s and by the time Charles I replaced his father on the throne in 1625, many Scots believed they had created the most perfectly Reformed Church in the world. Scots men and women of all classes were finding unbridled rapture in their closeness to God. Through the act of worship alone, they found, they could come face to face with their Maker. They therefore valued, above all other things, the very specific ways in which they practised their Protestant faith. No deviation could be countenanced or tolerated; the risk of losing touch with God was too much to be contemplated.

The atmosphere was intensified by a pervading belief – indeed the absolute certainty – that the apocalypse was at hand. Jesus would very shortly return to earth to judge the quick and the dead and create a new heaven and a new earth. This was, therefore, no time to change a winning formula. Every Protestant in Scotland, Presbyterian or Episcopalian, had reason to believe they were among the Elect. They had been predestined for heaven by God at the beginning of time and so God help the man – or the king – who might seek to meddle with that perfection and that closeness at such a time. Trials on earth – ridicule, abuse, torture or death – were as nothing compared to the prospect of upsetting God in heaven. The stage was set for drama.

It is untrue that King James I and VI was 'the wisest fool in Christendom who never said a foolish thing nor ever did a wise one'. His son Charles did indeed ignite the touch paper of war with his tinkering with the stuff of worship – but largely because he lacked James's theological brilliance. It was the reign of King James that produced the book that has had more influence on the English language, and therefore upon the world, than any other work – even those of Shakespeare. It would provide the context for the civil wars that would consume James's son. Its prose has shaped and informed the very language of movements as profound as the independence of the United States of America and the campaign there for civil rights. No literary accomplishment before or since has come so close to perfection. The King James Bible was the result of seven years of work by more than fifty scholars tasked by the monarch with producing a new translation based on the original writings and the various translations already in existence at that time.

From the very start of his reign in England James had been pestered by those determined to maintain or even increase the distance between the Anglican faith and the Catholicism of Rome. Like the Presbyterians in

Scotland, the Puritans in England wanted no interference by bishops in Church business; they demanded assurances from their new king that he would bar bishops from seeking to intercede between God and man.

James had endured a childhood of religious brainwashing, and had been altered for ever as a result. George Buchanan, the royal tutor, had beaten the Protestant faith into the young king. The intention had been to ensure his obedience to the Reformed Kirk, along with a lifelong aversion to the Catholic faith of his mother. Ironically, it created a king convinced of his own unique place in the scheme of things: he was anointed by God and therefore set above other men. By the time he arrived in London in 1603 he was utterly and unshakeably convinced of his right to rule. He was also determined to rule over a unified kingdom, one in which his subjects would share one set of laws, one language, one culture – and one religion.

Thanks to Elizabeth I, James inherited an England in which the king mattered, where his power was unchallenged. Ireland was Catholic and her subjects therefore answered to the Pope. But from James's point of view, Scotland was only a little better. When he bade his fond farewell to the old country in 1603, promising to return soon, he was turning his back on a Scotland conquered by Presbyterianism. There the Kirk elders were all too anxious to lecture him and tell him he had no right to meddle in Church business. Small wonder that respectful England and the Anglican Church seemed like a blessed relief by comparison. That is not to say he was without his religious tormentors south of the Border; the Reformers there were every bit as vocal, if less confident about browbeating the king. In England, respect for the role of monarch gave James more room for manoeuvre.

Harassed by Puritans and bishops alike, he summoned a conference in 1604 so that the many sides of the debate could be aired. Although he tended towards the Puritan angle at first, he was never going to give up his own vision of an overarching, unified kingdom of which he was the keystone. With considerable guile, he placed the burden of proof in the Puritans' hands. It was up to them, said the king, to find the evidence for their claims within the pages of the Bible. If they could show that God himself objected to the existence of bishops, then he would take the appropriate action. The Puritans could not do so, and James summed up the findings of the so-called Hampton Court Conference with a neat, four-word slogan: 'No Bishop, no King'. James saw himself at the top of a hierarchy, with his authority over the Church administered on his behalf by the bishops. Any attack on the authority of the bishops was therefore an attack on the king himself.

James would subsequently force onto the General Assembly of the Kirk the 'Five Articles of Perth', by which he sought to make the Church of his homeland much more like that of his English subjects. The Scottish Church was to be brought into line with the English, 'so neir as can be'. It was very much the case that, by then, James was seeing himself as leader of England and the English Church first – and King of Scotland second. It was a model that would be followed by his son, a much less talented builder.

A by-product of the Hampton Court Conference, however, was James's new translation of the Bible. Translations into English of 'The Word of God' had been in existence since the time of John Wycliffe in the late fourteenth century. The flaming torch was passed to William Tyndale in the sixteenth century, who was eventually strangled to death for having had the temerity to make and preach from his own translation. It is his profound and elegant work that was to form the basis for the King James Bible, published for the first time in 1611.

Today English is the language of the Internet, and therefore the predominant tongue of the modern world. Its foundation is the Bible and the man who laid that foundation was the first Scottish King of England. This work, then, was surely one wise thing achieved by that often-maligned monarch: the teachings of the Christian faith were placed securely into the public domain, sanctioned by the king, and thereby informed the debate that led in due course to the very creation of democracy. It is no fiction either to say the King James Bible laid the basis for a belief that would help shape the world ever after – the certainty for many that God was an Englishman.

Unfortunately for Britain – and ultimately for the man himself – Charles I lacked all his father's considerable store of wisdom. Charles shuffled awkwardly onto the throne. His father had been a meddler, no one would question that fact; but he had also been a skilled political survivor. Charles merely read the *Basilikon Doron* and expected everyone to respect its teaching – he needed no one's consent and could rule as he saw fit.

For a king destined to rule a Protestant country, his choice of queen was hardly likely to endear him to his subjects either. On 1 May 1625 he had married the Catholic Princess Henrietta Maria, the fifteen-year-old daughter of Henri IV of France. It was a good match for Charles – they would have a happy marriage and she would bear him plenty of heirs – but it provided too much ammunition for those critics who would say his heart belonged to Rome.

Raised in England since he was a toddler, Charles had grown into a very English king. He dearly loved the Anglican faith and saw it as a happy medium, one that found a common-sense route between the twin extremes of Catholicism on the one hand and the various versions of Calvinism being espoused by groups of fanatics all across Scotland on the other. He made his first visit to his homeland in 1633, for his belated coronation as King of Scotland. He might not have bothered to come home at all; but despite repeated requests from him, his countrymen had refused to send the Scottish regalia, or crown jewels, to London. So it was with some reluctance that he turned up in Edinburgh.

He did not like the thought of Scone either, the traditional crowning-place of Scottish kings. He found the little chapel there far too small for his visions of grandeur and opted for the capital instead. The ceremony was conducted in the old abbey church at the Palace of Holyroodhouse in Edinburgh. Right from the outset, Charles showed a lack of forethought and sensitivity when it came to handling his fellow countrymen. He was accompanied by William Laud, whom he had appointed as Archbishop of Canterbury, and the Anglican gloss on the coronation was obvious. Charles even declared that the High Kirk of St Giles' was henceforth to be recognised as an Anglican cathedral – anathema to Presbyterians.

Not content with riling the clergy of his homeland, he proceeded to upset the other body upon whom successful rule depended: the nobility. At a parliament held in his presence he made a point of observing who voted for what and openly jotted names into a little black book. Parliament was sacred, independent; what was to be made of a king who seemed to be taking such an interest in who agreed with him there, and who did not? He put bishops on the Scottish Privy Council as well, taking yet more power from the nobles and seeding it elsewhere.

In 1636 Charles issued the 'Code of Canons', a set of laws designed, much like his father's Five Articles of Perth, to bring the Scottish Kirk into line with the Anglican Church. And tired as he was of the mechanisms of his parliaments – stocked with nobles who actually *disagreed* with him sometimes – he opted for tying up the countries with the help of acquiescent churchmen. He loaded the Scottish Privy Council with bishops, and thereby put out of joint the noses of nobles who saw themselves being passed over for the jobs and power that had once been their right.

But if all this was getting people hot under the collar, their temperatures were pushed to boiling point the following year when he ordered that a newly revised English prayer book was to replace that of the Scots in Scottish kirks. The New Book of Common Prayer for Scotland was published in 1637. As a work of literature, it had been carefully thought out. Although both Charles and Laud had had a hand in its writing, Scottish bishops had been invited to ensure it enshrined as much as possible of Scottish practice. What stuck in Scots' craws was that it had been forced into Scottish churches without any discussion or vote by either the Scottish parliament or the General Assembly. It was a clumsy, autocratic act by a clumsy, autocratic king. (Laud's fate – he was beheaded in 1645 – would be a grim foretaste of what lay in store for Charles.)

It fell to James Hannay, Dean of St Giles, to mount the pulpit on Sunday, 23 July 1637 and open the new prayer book for the very first time. The Bible is explicit about it being only he who is without sin that is entitled to throw the first stone. History has nothing to say about who flung the first *wooden stool* at Hannay, but legend declares it was one Jenny Geddes, a venerable and well-known costermonger of that parish. As part of what was in all likelihood a well-orchestrated act of rebellion against the thin end of the wedge of Popery, the elderly but vital lady in question is said to have listened to the first utterance from the English book before hurling colourful abuse, and then her seat, at the hapless Dean. More abuse followed from more of the congregation, along with more stools, until eventually armed men had to be summoned to drag out Jenny and her fellow rioters. They continued their rowdy objections in the street outside.

Elsewhere, in churches across the land, similar events unfolded. By one simple act, Charles had applied a match to a store of combustible material that had been years in the gathering. The protestors were quick to organise themselves – further evidence that the riots had been carefully planned – and soon petitions were rolling into Edinburgh from around the country demanding withdrawal of the book. Keen to find a scapegoat other than the king, the protestors took to calling it 'Laud's liturgy'.

A rebel parliament was formed, with representatives of the nobility, the lairds, the burgesses and the ministers taking their places at one of four tables. A fifth table was occupied by delegates from the other four and acted as a kind of executive committee. 'The Tables' sent formal word to Charles, asking him to backtrack on the prayer book and on other matters relating to the governance of the State and the Kirk, but their calls fell upon deaf ears.

In response to the royal snub 'The Tables' set a few of their members to work composing a very special document. It was to be a contract between God, the king and every Scots man and woman committed to the cause. Since it self-consciously called to mind the deal struck between God and the survivors of The Flood, it became known as the National *Covenant*. It was a pledge to defend Scotland's rights and to declare precisely what would and would not be tolerated by Scots on matters of Kirk and State – and it was signed by tens of thousands. Among its principal authors were two of Scotland's brightest and most fanatical minds: churchman Alexander Henderson of Fife and the twenty-five-year-old Edinburgh lawyer Archibald Johnston of Wariston. For such creative men the document they produced was a seemingly endless, graceless tract full of Acts and clauses and lacking any kind of cadence or flourish. Perhaps they hoped to put Charles to sleep with it.

It comprised three parts: first a repudiation of Catholicism; second a rehash of all the legal protections for Presbyterianism that had come and gone since the days of Knox; and third a series of demands for a free parliament (free of the king's interference, that is), along with a return to Presbyterian-controlled government of the Kirk. 'We promise, and swear by the Great Name of the Lord our God, to continue in the profession and obedience of the foresaid religion: that we shall defend the same and resist all these contrary errours and corruptions, according to our vocation, and to the uttermost of that power that God hath put in our hands, all the days of our life.'

Leaden and dull it surely was. It deliberately took for granted the fantasy that Charles I understood that his role was to protect the Presbyterian faith. By this sleight of hand the National Covenant sought to sneak rebellion in through the back door.

What mattered, though, what resonates into the present with a note as clear as a bell, is the response it provoked from the people of Scotland. By 28 February 1638 the first copy of the National Covenant (also called 'The Nobles' Covenant') was available for signing in Greyfriars Church in Edinburgh. One of the first to take up the pen was a man whose name would become synonymous with the fight between King and Covenanters – that of James Graham, 5th Earl of Montrose; but he would be followed by hundreds more.

If a flood brought about the first Covenant, then the second Covenant caused another. This time the torrent was made of people, as copies of the document were circulated all around the country for signatures. Before the end, folk were signing their names in their own blood. Here was the price to be paid by a King of Scots who had put England and the English Church first. It was no longer to their king that Scots looked for a symbol of their unique identity, but to their Kirk.

For an impassioned young man like Archibald Johnston of Wariston, this response was wholly appropriate. Believing the Reformed Scottish Kirk was as close to perfection as anything on earth, he looked on at the mass commitment to the terms of the National Covenant with nothing short of rapture. He called it 'the glorious marriage day of the kingdom with God'. Wariston was a Presbyterian's Presbyterian. For all his outward certainty about the rightness of the cause, inwardly he was a seething, tortured mass of self-doubt. His family had selected his wife for him, and on first meeting her he had been pleased to note that disease had left her with a disfigured face; no one could think he was marrying to satisfy any lustful thoughts. In his troubled heart he knew that only 'King Jesus' was perfect. From that perfection came grace – grace to be worked towards by every humble sinner – and according to Wariston it was up to each man and woman to look inwards in search of imperfections that could be put right.

As part of his ceaseless project of self-improvement Wariston wrote a diary in which he recorded his daily attempts to keep himself upon the road to salvation. Even though years' worth of jottings have been lost, the surviving work runs to thousands of pages. They tell how he attends anything up to three sermons a day; how he constantly talks to and questions his very soul; how he lives in fear of failure to reach the mark. But while Wariston's diaries are undoubtedly unusual – exceptional, even – the discipline that guided his pen was felt by many. The crucial point is that Presbyterians were prepared for the imminent arrival of King Jesus. King Charles was just another soul in danger of damnation and no right-thinking Presbyterian was about to risk being dragged down by him into the abyss. There was a part of every human soul that no king could ever touch.

Wariston had attended a meeting to discuss the new prayer book in May 1637. When he got home he wrote in his diary that it was 'the very image of the beast'. When it was finally put into use on that fateful 23 July, the result was a foregone conclusion. The Bishop of Brechin managed to preach from it that day; but he had taken the precaution of climbing into the pulpit and thumping down two loaded pistols, one on either side of the new prayer book.

For Wariston and his ilk the rebellion of the National Covenant was the only course open to them. The first Covenant had been between God and his chosen people. In the Old Testament, the chosen people were the Jews – but it was an article of faith for Christians that the coming of Jesus Christ had changed the terms of the Covenant. Now God's chosen people were the Christians, but what sort? The Protestant Reformation had rejected the universal power of the Pope, so it certainly was not the Catholics. Anglicans, in their synagogue of Satan, were scarcely any better. Every virtuous person could plainly see that God's chosen people were none other than the faithful members of the Scottish Presbyterian Kirk.

On Sunday, 18 March 1638, Wariston and his family attended their second church service of that day, at Currie parish kirk, north of Edinburgh. It was to be an opportunity for the parishioners to sign the Covenant and the minister duly explained that the basis for the document had been derived from the Bible itself. Then he told the congregation to rise to their feet and join him in making their covenant with God. Wariston would later confess to his diary how:

> ... as they stood up and lifted their hands in the twinkling of an eye the influence of God's spirit fell upon them all, melted their frozen hearts, watered their dry cheeks, changed their very faces: the minister was almost suffocated by his own tears, and then all the people fell down on their knees to mourn and pray ... Lord, let me never forget that I was an actor in this. There is a very near parallel between Israel and this church – for we are the only two nations sworn unto the Lord.

More than a thousand copies of the National Covenant survive. It is a document of the most profound importance, symbolising the moment when Scots were encouraged to regard their homeland not as a kingdom, but as a nation state. Within that state men and women were citizens rather than subjects and as such they had rights – *human rights* – to follow their own religious beliefs, regardless of what the king might tell them – to do whatever was necessary to save their own souls. There on the pages, sometimes written with the practised ease of educated gentlefolk, sometimes in an unsteady scrawl by hands more used to tools than pens, are the signatures of every class of Scot. Lords and ladies, ploughmen and peasants: grand or humble, man or woman, it mattered not. In the eyes of God, after all, every soul weighed the same.

This was a marvel. For the first time in history the ordinary men and women – the mass of us – were briefly visible. History tends to be about a handful of kings and queens, and the elite who have their favour, rather than the countless thousands of folk who lived, and live, unremembered lives. Scratched uncertainly onto the parchment of the National Covenant is the first documented proof of our existence.

Some of the signatures were pressed from their owners. In those febrile times, when neighbour watched neighbour and dark suspicions and gossip were whispered, it was hard to resist the will of the majority, regardless of personal conviction. To refuse to sign was to risk being seen as sinful, even Popish. In the north-east of Scotland the bishops held sway over a stately Church of the sort that pleased King Charles. But Covenanting agents were duly sent north to bring to bear whatever pressure was necessary to secure the signatures. Once a citizen had made his or her mark, it was impossible to unmake. How do you end a contract with God? It created an almost unbearably oppressive atmosphere, a terrible weight for any nation to try to live beneath. In such a world it was all too easy for extremism and fundamentalism to take root and to grow. And from fundamentalism it was but a short step over the line into madness.

Charles was fully aware of the antics of the so-called 'Covenanters'. He made threatening noises, perhaps believing that his subjects would simply bow to his will. He even issued his own version of a Covenant, in which he denounced Popery but said little else of note. The Kirk dismissed it out of hand – the king had never signed their Covenant and they would not be signing his – and the Covenanters declared they were ready to die rather than break their promise. James Hamilton, Marquis of Hamilton was sent north to settle the matter. Charles told him: 'I give you leave to flatter them with what hopes you please.'

Hamilton arrived at Glasgow Cathedral on 21 November 1638 in time for the Kirk Assembly. If he and his king had been labouring under the misapprehension that the National Covenant was the product of a talking shop, then the lord and his master were in for a shock. The Covenanters were armed, dressed for war; the bishops had found discretion to be the better part of valour and were conspicuous by their absence. Once Hamilton had taken his seat, the doors of the cathedral were locked behind him. He would be listening to the proceedings whether he wanted to or not.

Alexander Henderson, co-author of the Covenant, was elected moderator of the Assembly, with Wariston as its secretary.

Even within such a gathering, the speakers were not yet preaching to the converted. There were dissenting voices that questioned the rightness of what was being asserted. In a carefully stage-managed act, designed to silence all opposition, Wariston produced registers from the earliest days of the Reformed Kirk. Long since believed lost, they provided the young firebrand lawyer with apparent proof that bishops had always been abhorrent to the souls of true Presbyterians.

After a long, hard day in front of the blast furnace, Hamilton was permitted to leave. Every member of the King's Privy Council left with him except Archibald Campbell, 8th Earl of Argyll. Like Montrose, the name of Argyll would shortly be graven deeply into the story of the Covenanters.

During the following days every trace of Charles's hand was erased from the Scottish Church. The Code of Canons was thrown out, along with the new prayer book. The existing bishops were deposed and the very office of bishop abolished. Charles had had ideas for changes both to Church architecture and holy vestments: these too were rejected as though they had never been. King Jesus was everywhere and King Charles was nowhere. Wariston confessed to his diary: 'We shall extend the royal prerogative of King Jesus the son of God above all others, perhaps extend his kingdom through all the borders of earth. For it is true that our Scots kirk in its rediscovered perfection will be a pattern for other nations, for its purity of doctrine and worship, its government of God's house and church'.

Running invisible, but undeniable, behind rapturous pronouncements like Wariston's was the electric charge of a declaration of war. Scotland was in revolt against the Crown and Charles quickly understood he would need to send an army to regain control of the northern kingdom. Ironically for a King of Scots, it was an English army that he had to dispatch to quell his countrymen. This was the First Bishops' War, of 1639, and it was a disaster for Charles. The Scots rebels had formed their own army, headed by the mercenary soldier Alexander Leslie, a veteran of many successful years leading fighting men on the Continent. Summoned home, he brought battle-hardened officers along with him and these formed the backbone of the Scots force that confronted Charles's Englishmen and forced them to sue for peace after just a few weeks of skirmishing.

A Scots parliament met in June 1640 – in a further defiance of the king's wishes – and confirmed the decisions made in Glasgow Cathedral in

November 1638. The world according to Charles had been completely unmade. He summoned an English parliament to try to secure the funds for yet more military action, but was defied there too. Many Englishmen had grudges against the king, similar to those of the Scots, and Charles angrily dismissed the gathering after just three weeks. It has gone down in history as the 'Short Parliament'.

Despite a shortage of funds Charles sent a second army north for what is remembered as the Second Bishops' War. It was as dismal as the First for the king. Having taken control of key castles in Scotland, the Covenanting army led by Leslie and Montrose crossed the border into England. By October Charles had faced the inevitable and called a truce – even having to submit to the humiliation of paying the Scots the best part of a third of a million pounds to cover their expenses for the time they had had to spend occupying his southern kingdom!

Despite the successes, the Covenanters were in fact a divided force in Scotland. Argyll was a man with a grudge against everything that moved. He had seized the reins of the Presbyterian movement and by 1641 was demanding that Charles be deposed once and for all. State government should assume full power, he said. Montrose, among the first of the sig-natories of the National Covenant, was quietly horrified. His head was Presbyterian but his heart was with the king and, together with a small cadre of like-minded nobles, he attempted to unseat Argyll. Their mild-mannered putsch failed, however, and Montrose was thrown in jail. The battle lines between the two men had been drawn.

In the autumn of 1641 Charles travelled to Edinburgh to address par-liament. He tried and failed to appear as a beneficent peacemaker and by the time he left for London Scotland was even more fully in the control of Argyll's rebel government. Montrose and the rest of the nobles sympathetic to Charles's position languished in prison while Argyll was made a marquis and Leslie ennobled. Just to compound Charles's woes there was soon a Catholic rebellion in Ireland – brought under control only by the use of Scots Protestant troops.

Charles appeared to be, and was, increasingly weak and embattled. His united kingdoms were unravelling and every move he made seemed to be the wrong one. In the short term he had to come up with the money to pay the bill of the lately departed Covenanter army and again summoned the English parliament. Emboldened by the king's plight, they were in defiant mood. They would sit for thirteen years in total, earning the nickname of the 'Long Parliament'. Far from easing Charles's troubles, they added to them by passing a 'Grand Remonstrance', a patronising document that blamed 'Popish' bishops for royal excesses on the one hand while seeking to hobble the king's personal power to rule on the other.

As autocratic as ever, Charles attempted to arrest his tormentors – principally two Puritan MPs, John Pym and John Hampden. His move was too late and too slow and both men evaded capture. Charles looked foolish and impotent. Finally realising the gravity of his situation, he fled London and on 22 August 1642 he raised the Royal Standard in Northampton in hopes of rallying support. The English part of the civil war – a war that really began in Scotland and lasted there for far longer – had begun.

Everyone knows the outcome of the 'English Civil War' – Cromwell and his dour Parliamentarians defeat the flouncing Cavaliers and cut off the king's head. But for the first few months of that conflict south of the Border, the result was a long way from certain. In fact until 1643 it looked, for much of the time, as if Charles and his Cavaliers would carry the day by panache alone. Best of them all was dashing Prince Rupert of the Rhine, Charles's own nephew. Rupert's mother was Elizabeth Stewart, Charles's sister and widow of Frederick, one-time Elector of the Palatinate and briefly King of Bohemia. So brief was their reign, a matter of months, that Elizabeth was known affectionately ever after as the 'Winter Queen' and the romance of that title rubbed off on her handsome, long-haired son. Under his leadership, Charles's cavalrymen managed to live up to the textbook ideal of the Cavaliers.

After nearly a year of inconclusive fighting, both king and English parliament appealed to the Scots for help. It seemed a divine opportunity for the bigots of the north, and it was; but at first the Covenanters failed to agree on a course of action. Direct opposition to a king was always a touchy subject and there were those in the Covenanting ranks who fought shy of actually attacking their anointed monarch. It had always been easier to misdirect their opposition – to make it look as if it was the royal advisors who were at fault and that it was therefore an act of loyalty to the Crown to seek to try and free him from such evil influences.

In the end, the hardline anti-Royalists within the Presbyterian party were triumphant. They would indeed send a huge Scots army to fight on behalf of the English parliament. But there was a clause in the agreement, a massive clause: in return for military support, England would have to accept the terms of a document the Scots called 'The Solemn League and Covenant for Reformation and Defence of Religion, the Honour and Happiness of the King and the Peace and Safety of the Three Kingdoms of Scotland, England and Ireland'. Catchy though that title undoubtedly was, the agreement the English signed is usually referred to just as the Solemn League and Covenant and it committed them to reforming the Anglican Church into an exact replica of that in Scotland. It amounted to nothing less than a Scottish Presbyterian takeover of Britain. 'Every plant which my heavenly father hath not planted shall be rooted out.'

The Scots were as good as their word. Since the humiliation of Charles at the end of the Second Bishops' War of 1640, followed by the quelling of the Irish Catholics, their army of 20,000 men had been kept in a state of readiness for further action. By the time they marched south to lend a decisive hand at the Battle of Marston Moor in 1644, they were a professional force to be reckoned with.

Back in Scotland, however, it was a different story. Montrose had been freed soon after Charles left Scotland after his joyless visit to parliament in late 1641. Opposed to Argyll personally – as much as to the hardliners in general – he was now an out and out Royalist, determined to restore Charles to his rightful place at the pinnacle of the ziggurat.

While Presbyterians and Parliamentarians basked in the glow of crucial victory at Marston Moor, the first of many, a legend was being written in the hills and glens of northern Scotland. Montrose and his supporters had begun a Royalist fight-back in March 1644, but with little success. In the August of that year, however, they were joined by Alastair McColla MacDonald, a twenty-one-year-old giant of a man with a fighting reputation to match his build. They called him Colkitto, a corruption of the Gaelic for left-handed, and he had crossed to Scotland from his home in Antrim with 2,000 warriors and a thirst for Campbell blood.

Like his men, Colkitto was Catholic and since he was a MacDonald, Argyll's Campbells were the enemies of his blood. On arrival in the west of Scotland he was joined by a thousand Highlanders and set off at once on a bloody rampage through the Campbell lands. None was spared. By the time he joined forces with Montrose at Blair Atholl his name was a byword for awful violence and it was as an avenging host that the combined armies set out to tackle the Covenanted zealots of Argyll.

First they defeated a much larger Covenanter army near Perth in September, before indulging themselves in a brutal ransack of the town. Aberdeen was next. Once again the army placed in their path was the greater in numbers, and once again it was crushed and brushed aside. The Irish Catholics and Highlanders then tore the place apart. As invariably happens when religion is involved, the victors easily cast aside any notions of humanity – the better to rape and murder and burn. Montrose and Colkitto presided over an orgy of violence against innocent civilians that damned for ever any claims they might have had to righteousness.

The secret of their military success lay in a tactic that had sprung fully formed from the cruel imagination of the giant Irishman. For decades to come the mere mention of 'the Highland charge' would be enough to make would-be opponents' blood run cold. Having got within range, the Highlanders would swiftly fire a single round before dropping their muskets, taking up their broadswords and charging pell-mell into whatever hapless ranks were arranged against them. It was their custom to throw off their plaids as well, to make running easier. Who would dare to stand still, trying to reload a musket with shaking hands while a half-naked, howling horde, committed to death or glory, came on wild-eyed and roaring? Not the Covenanters in the months between 1644 and 1645, that much became clear.

With blood drying like rust upon their blades, Colkitto and his countrymen parted with Montrose after Aberdeen and headed off into the west in search of reinforcements. It was Montrose alone then who had to face the consequences of their campaign so far. Argyll himself was coming, enraged by news of the slaughter of his Campbell brethren, and utterly convinced the Royalist forces would soon be in his grasp. But Montrose proved wily as well as brave and led his small force into the hills and out of reach.

By the time winter set in fully, Colkitto had returned with thousands more MacDonald clansmen and, while the weather did its worst, so did they. Rewriting the rulebook of military tactics as he went along, Montrose led his men on forced marches that ought to have been beyond human endurance. While Argyll and his forces made plans for one sort of battle, 'the Great Marquis' found ways to outflank and outmanoeuvre them at will and to deliver wrathful surprise attacks that soon littered the hills and glens with more Covenanter dead. He appeared as though from nowhere to slaughter a predominantly Campbell force at Inverlochy, in February 1645. In May a Covenanter force tried to take Montrose and Colkitto unawares outside the village of Auldearn, near Nairn. The surprise attack nearly worked but the Royalists replied with almost maniacal bravery and dash, breaking the Covenanter attack and smashing the force to pieces. There was another stunning victory at Alford, near Aberdeen, in July and then the bloodbath of Kilsyth on 15 August where 3,000 Covenanters fell beneath Royalist swords.

Montrose's run of victories made him seem invincible – that was the word they were starting to use about him in the Covenanter ranks – but in truth it was all form and no substance. The Marquis had all the dash and flair to make a dozen warriors seem heroic, but he was just one man. He had military brilliance in spades but he faced a whole ideology, a religious and political movement that would not be denied by a single brave soldier.

Colkitto was gone now and, whatever else he might have been fighting for, it was never the Protestant cause of his unlikely bed-fellow. If he had a vision at all, it was of the rebirth of MacDonald dominion in the Isles. His thirst for Campbell blood would never be slaked and he had taken his men away for more killing in the west. He would not see Montrose again, returning instead to Ireland where he died, bloodied sword still tightly clasped in his left hand, in 1647.

In England the tide of war had long since turned in favour of the Parliamentarians. On 14 June 1645 the Royalist heart had been finally broken on the field of Naseby. Leslie was freed to take his Presbyterian soldiers back towards home and it was at Philiphaugh, near Selkirk, on 13 September 1645 that the mercenary met the artist. At last the religiously inspired machine of the Covenanters proved too much for Montrose. After five luminous victories in a year it took just one defeat to reveal that he lacked strength in depth. Beneath his will to win a fight there was nothing else. Leslie was at the head of a many-geared juggernaut and it drove the Great Marquis off the road. Hauled from the rout by his followers, he fled the field – and Scotland too.

In May 1646 Charles had faced up to the inevitable, but with one last card to play. Handing himself over to the Scots at Newark, he dared them to betray their king face to face. If he thought his presence among them would teach them the error of their ways, he was to be bitterly disappointed. Far from being cowed by him, they whisked him off to Newcastle and there tried to force him to sign the Covenant. It demanded that he accept a kingship limited by laws – that he would agree to establish in the three kingdoms a Presbyterian Church to which he would be subject like every other man. In short they were asking him to give up his sense of himself, nothing less than his soul.

Whatever other qualities he possessed, Charles had within himself a core of stubborn bravery. More than anything else, he believed it was his Christian duty to see the errors of his subjects' ways and lead them back to the path of righteousness by his own example. He rejected the appeals, the begging and the threats and in January 1647 his countrymen gave up in disgust. With £200,000 in their pockets from the English parliament (rather more than thirty pieces of silver) they turned their backs on their king for ever and set out for home.

Charles was notionally under the guard and protection of a force of moderate Presbyterians, but once the main Scots army had departed there was nothing to keep out the New Model Army of Oliver Cromwell. Into Newcastle they marched, their battle cry of 'Lord of Hosts' on their lips, and took hold of the king with a grip that would not be broken. Here was the rub, in fact. Their eyes filled with rapturous tears and visions of religious union – of Scotland, England and Ireland coming together as a new Israel. The Scots were blind to reality. The English Puritans had been ready to agree to anything that would gift them the military might necessary to secure final victory, even a Solemn League and Covenant. But once they had checked and mated the king, their game was won and all bets were off.

In the aftermath of the king's capture, the Covenanters found yet another way to split in two. Blinking into the light of political reality, realising the English had never had any intention of meeting either their financial or their spiritual obligations to their erstwhile brothers in arms, they ran out of reasons to stick together. Faction split from faction. There were many who continued to favour finding some way of working with Charles, but these so-called 'Engagers' only enraged the hardliners. They came to final grief at Preston, between 17 and 18 August 1648, when Cromwell's radicals utterly destroyed an invading army of Scots moderates and drove them not just from the field of battle but from the political realm as well.

Fresh from his victory, Cromwell crossed into Scotland in October and, with Argyll at his side, mopped up the last of the humbled Engagers. In his own mind Cromwell was convinced the blame for this second war was all Charles's – a product of his stubborn refusal to bow to the will of the people.

In Scotland it was 'the people' who were in the ascendant. The Engagers had been dominated by the nobility, but their hardline opponents – the 'Protesters' – were drawn from the rank and file. From their spiritual heartland in the south-west of Scotland they rose as one and marched towards the capital. Edinburgh was soon theirs and so too the Kirk. Argyll threw his lot in with them, as did Wariston. Now 'the people' saw themselves as God's own and there would be no toleration whatever of backsliders, or of opponents of any hue.

'Scotland is in her flower,' wrote a leading Protester. 'There is no family so obscure that the General Assembly cannot probe its sinfulness. No scandalous person can live, no scandal can be concealed in all Scotland because of the strict correspondence between ministers and congregation. The only complaint of profane people is this: they have no liberty to sin.' They called it the 'Rule of the Saints', and yet it was a world in which children were prosecuted and jailed for failing to honour their parents; where executions were a daily occurrence; men, women and children flogged, nailed by their ears to posts, holes bored in their tongues. In later years Covenanters would look back on it all as the Golden Age.

With no one left in their way, and Scotland's radicals knee-deep in their neighbours' blood and guts, the king's implacable foes in England took the final step. Cromwell had the whip hand and persuaded those around him that Charles had committed High Treason. He had intercepted a letter sent by the king to his wife in which he had outlined his approval of the noble Engagers' motives. Cromwell had known ever since that the king would not bend.

On a December morning in 1648, Colonel Thomas Pride took up a position with his regiment on the steps of Parliament in London. Whenever a Member with known sympathies for the king arrived, he was arrested and excluded. This was 'Pride's Purge'. Before it there were 489 MPs in the English parliament; by the end of it there were fewer than 200 and none of those would speak for the king. The 'Long Parliament' was over and what was left became known as 'the Rump'.

On 4 January 1649, the Rump passed an Act declaring that the king would indeed be tried for treason. The trial began on the 20th and from the start Charles refused to defend himself – he refused even to recognise the jurisdiction of the court or the very charge itself. But his stubborn pride made no difference. Tried and convicted, the anointed king was beheaded outside the Palace of Whitehall on 30 January 1649. Soon after, the Rump would abolish the very estate of monarchy, and with it their own crime of regicide.

As a gout of royal blood spurted across a black-draped scaffold in London, so a wave of ice-cold water splashed into the face of Scotland. The nation awoke from a religiously induced coma and Scots eyes beheld a truth blindingly obvious: by killing the King of England, the English had killed the King of Scotland too. This was too much to be borne. Sickened at last by their own radicalism, even the harshest of the fanatics knew instinctively that Cromwell had gone much too far. Souls were at stake here after all. What was God to make of the cold-blooded murder of a king? And while the English had decided there was no need for a monarch, the Covenanters believed *absolutely* that their perfect nation depended upon the existence of a king – a Covenanted king.

From here it looks like nothing less than mass hysteria, the madness of an entire people. And yet, five days after the head of Charles I fell, the people of Scotland proclaimed his son their new monarch. If they had settled for him being King of Scots, they might have got away with it. Instead they insisted he was King of England and Ireland too. Had they kept Charles II to themselves, Cromwell would likely have contented himself with the role of Protector of an independent, post-union republic of England. As it was, he saw their proclamation of his nemesis' son as king of three kingdoms as a dangerous challenge to the purity of his vision.

News of the execution of the king had also reached the ear of the Marquis of Montrose. With the son hailed as successor, the Great Marquis was spurred into action once more – indeed, one of Charles's first acts following his proclamation had been to name Montrose Lieutenant-General of Scotland and task him with invading the country in advance of his own homecoming.

Montrose had been four years on the Continent and sailed from Sweden to Orkney in March 1650. As things turned out, he should have stayed away. He managed to raise a force of committed but untrained and largely clueless Orcadians and crossed over to mainland Scotland in April. Intercepted by a Covenanter force at Carbisdale on 27 April 1650, his old skills deserted him and his force was soundly defeated. The young king-to-be promptly disowned him and left him to his fate. Betrayed and captured soon afterwards, he was taken to Edinburgh and executed as a traitor on 21 May.

When the assembled crowd caught sight of the Marquis that morning, they gasped. He was immaculate – dressed, it was said, like a bridegroom, with his long dark hair curled to Cavalier perfection, black suit, scarlet cloak and ribboned shoes. Before his head was parted from his body, he recited a poem he had composed the night before:

> Open all my veins, that I may swim
> To Thee my Saviour, in that crimson lake

Why are style, wit, panache and class so often the preserve of the vanquished – while the grey-faced wee men grind on to victory, powered by the irresistible force of their mirthless drudgery?

It was more of those wee men who accompanied Charles on his homecoming voyage, badgering him about the evils of the world. Imagine now that utterly joyless voyage out of Continental exile in June 1650. The Scots still wanted – indeed, still insisted upon – a Covenanted king. And so all the way over in the boat he was bullied, harangued and lectured about the evils of his father and of every king before or since. They assured him he was a sinner and that he had a long road to travel before he would be worthy of sitting upon the kind of throne they had in mind.

Driven to distraction and then into submission, he duly signed the Covenants. He was still aboard his ship, docked at the mouth of the River Spey, when the commissioners went aboard with pen and paper in hand. Charles would not even be allowed to set foot in Scotland, it seemed, until he had been bent into shape. With his signature drying upon the document, Charles was transported south, to Falkland Palace, where he spent days and weeks being lectured about his duties and obligations as a Covenanted king. They made him compose a penitence and rumour has it he wrote in it that he was sorry he had ever been born.

Cromwell came north with an army of 11,000 men. He wrote to the Scots: 'Is everything you say infallibly agreeable to the Word of God? I beseech you in the bowels of Christ think it possible you might be wrong. There may be a covenant made with death and hell.'

Had the Scots made the most of their battle-hardened army, they might have turned Cromwell back. He was soon pushed all the way to the sea, at Dunbar, and turned round to find the doughty Alexander Leslie bearing down on him at the head of more than 20,000 men. The Protector might have been grateful just to be allowed to slink away, back across the Border to think again. But instead it was at this moment that Archibald Johnston of Wariston decided the Covenanting army must be purged of all ungodly elements. Leslie protested, but Wariston declared that 'God can do much with a few'. The ungodly elements turned out, in the main, to be the professional soldiers upon whom so much depended. By the time the purge had been completed, the Covenanters still outnumbered the English by almost two to one, but they were an army of amateurs.

Cromwell could not believe his luck and promptly broke out of Dunbar on 3 September 1651, killing 4,000 Covenanters and taking 10,000 prisoner. The survivors ran for their lives, all the way back to Edinburgh. When they delivered their news, the men of both the town council and the Kirk Session promptly fled. English troops arrived soon afterwards and proceeded to loot the town.

The Rule of the Saints was over and the Covenanting movement was split yet again – this time between the do-or-die Protesters and the 'Resolutioners' who would find ways to work with the Stewarts once more. It was the Resolutioners who crowned Charles II at Scone on 1 January 1651. Argyll set the crown upon the young king's head and then sat back to enjoy a sermon that reminded them all that 'a king hath not the power to do what he pleaseth'.

Moderate or hardline – it mattered not a jot to Cromwell what sort of Presbyterians he had to deal with in Scotland. He let them have a honeymoon period while he endured long months of illness after his victory at Dunbar. But by the summer of 1651 he had the Scots on the rack yet again. There had been no shortage of volunteers ready to rally around the new king and the Royalist army was thousands strong by the time Charles led it over the Border into England to try and regain his southern kingdom.

He was deluding himself. Cromwell was the master and when the forces finally met at Worcester on 3 September 1651, not even Leslie's skills were enough to make a difference. Charles had to go into hiding, running like a whipped dog from Cromwell's men for several harrowing weeks before finally boarding a ship to France in October. He would be gone for eight years, while Cromwell placed the pitch-black shadow of his hand across the face of Britain.

The three kingdoms were brought together in a hellish union over which he presided with the title of Lord Protector. To his face men addressed him as 'your Highness', but behind his back many called him a tyrant and a usurper. He charged Scotland £10,000 a month for the privilege of being occupied by his English garrisons. After the requisite soul-searching, Wariston sided with the new regime and was rewarded with the title of Lord Clerk Register, chief record-keeper of the Scottish government. There was hell to pay as well. Wariston's own son, young Archibald, went mad. At first it seemed he was just struggling with his faith, but gradually, and before his father's eyes, his sanity unravelled like wet knitting. He stopped wearing clothes, he rolled in the ashes of the fire, he made up his own rituals and ate his own excrement.

Cromwell died on 3 September 1658, the anniversary of his victories at Dunbar and Worcester. He wanted his son Richard to replace him, make the governance of Britain into a family business, but 'Tumbledown Dick' lacked the conviction of the old man. The reins of power slipped through his fingers and he fled into exile on the Continent.

Charles II was restored to the thrones of Scotland and England in May 1660. Soon it was as though Cromwell and his Commonwealth had never been. In Edinburgh there were scenes of wild celebration, drunkenness, many-gun salutes. The new king was as close to a perfect opposite of his father as was humanly possible. Over six feet tall, good-looking and laid-back. A louche dilletante. He liked his luxuries and his comforts and most of all he liked his women. In 1662 he married the Catholic Infanta of Portugal, Catherine of Braganza. She gave him no children but Charles sired plenty elsewhere. His mistresses were innumerable, the near-legendary Nell Gwynn among them. After the austere, pious leanings of his father, followed by the misery of the Commonwealth, the Restoration period of Charles II swept across much of Britain like a breath of fresh air.

For a man who had been driven twice into exile by enemies who wanted his head, he had grudges to settle as well. Cromwell's mouldering corpse was exhumed from its resting place inside Westminster Abbey and trailed through the streets of London before being hanged. The head was then cut off and stuck on a spike while the rest of the corpse was flung onto a midden to rot. As many as possible of the men who had put their names to the death warrant of Charles I were found and executed.

Even Argyll, who had placed the crown on Charles's head at Scone, was put to death on the 'Maiden', a killing machine much like the guillotine. As unrepentant as Montrose had been, he addressed the crowd – but with rather less élan. 'God has laid engagements on Scotland: we are tied by Covenants to religion and Reformation: those yet unborn are engaged to it, in our baptism we are engaged to it, and it passed the power of all Magistrates under heaven to absolve a man of an oath to God.' Right or wrong, dashing or devout, his head was parted from his shoulders just as easily.

No doubt it was guilt that inspired Charles to order the exhumation of Montrose's bones. These were then made the focus of an elaborate state funeral in Edinburgh before being interred beneath a marble tomb in St Giles' Cathedral.

For Charles's detractors, and they were many, there was much to complain about. Most worrying of all was his religion. He wore it casually, but it was High Anglican in flavour, even Romish. Some said he was a Recusant, a secret Catholic. And then there was his younger brother James – there was no need for rumours about him because he was openly Catholic.

For a country scarred and misshapen by years of civil warring and ghoulish self-flagellation, the religion of the monarch was not the prime concern for most people. Normality was what they craved, a return to something like the world before the horror; and it seemed there was even a need to seek forgiveness for the worst excesses of the Presbyterian project itself. Keen to get in on the act, the Scottish parliament set about the familiar business of making laws to ban things. For now it was outdoor prayer meetings they decided to prohibit, the so-called 'conventicles' that were cropping up like mushrooms in the quiet places of the land.

As the government sought to restore 'normality', Episcopalianism was somehow rehabilitated along with all the other old habits. Unbelievably in the context of a country that had torn itself apart in its apparent desperation to be rid of meddlesome bishops, they were being allowed back in from the cold. For many of those still committed to Presbyterianism – particularly the die-hards in the south-west – there was no alternative but to leave the churches and take their faith into the untainted hills that were, anyway, closer to God in heaven.

Everyone was still a bigot; madness was still abroad in the land but wearing different clothes. The English parliament declared the Solemn League and Covenant unlawful. Those in public office were required to swear an oath rejecting it and surviving copies were collected and handed over to the hangman for burning. Paperwork was being executed. Madness.

The Kirk was controlled for now by the Resolutioners and they wanted to know where they stood with the new king. The man chosen to meet Charles on their behalf was James Sharp, minister of Crail. He was no accidental choice either: he was from Banffshire, where the form of the Church that had pleased Charles I was still popular. Even Cromwell had once regarded Sharp with suspicion, and had let him out of prison for a time. But the Resolutioners considered him a canny operator. What they wanted by 1661 was a guarantee that their moderate version of the Presbyterian settlement was safe. But it turned out they had chosen badly when they entrusted their fate to Sharp. Without their knowledge he had turned his coat, reinventing himself as an advocate for the return of the bishops. By the time he came back from London he was the new Archbishop of St Andrews.

As far as the Protesters of the south-west were concerned Sharp was in league with the devil himself. He was a traitor to their cause and his card was marked. For the moderates of the Kirk, he was just a disappointment. They watched as Charles II decided he would turn the clocks all the way back to 1633. He appointed more bishops and ordered that all ministers must swear an Oath of Allegiance to them, and to him. Of around 1,000 men of the cloth, 262 refused to comply.

One of them was Alexander Peden, minister of the parish of New Luce, in Galloway. Fired up by the Covenant, he had revealed a skill as a charismatic preacher and when he heard about Charles's Oath of Allegiance, he instantly baulked at it. Instead of signing, he took to his pulpit and preached from early morning until midnight. When he finally ran out of words, he stomped down the aisle and out of his church, taking his congregation with him. Slamming the door behind him, he said it should never be reopened but by a true Presbyterian.

Now was the heyday of the conventicles and Peden was soon among the most famous leaders of the movement. The Oath of Allegiance had driven at least 261 other preachers into the hills as well and in time the largest of the outdoor meetings were attracting congregations of up to 10,000 people. With such gatherings outlawed, the crowds took to arming themselves to fend off any government forces sent to break them up. Peden in particular seemed to have an uncanny ability to predict the arrival of the troops and make himself scarce, so they called him 'Prophet Peden'.

Soon he was a marked man, a target for those who wanted religion safely ensconced behind walls and doors approved by the king. But Peden was defiant, sleeping rough or moving from safe house to safe house. He made a mask of his own face that could be worn by an accomplice while he escaped. He learned to love the outdoors, the endless sky. The rocks of Scotland, bedrock of the nation, became his pulpit and it was his righteous wrath that kept him warm.

A year after Peden took to the hills of Galloway with his mask, a familiar face reappeared in Edinburgh, albeit unwillingly. The exiled Wariston had been tracked down and hustled home to face the music. He was senile, scarcely able to make sense for much of the time, but Charles would not be denied. On 22 July 1663 he was hanged. Before the deed was done he managed to pull himself together long enough to tell the waiting crowd he had meant no harm. His head was cut from his still-warm corpse and stuck on a spike beside the city gates.

Still the Protesters of the south-west refused to comply with Charles. In November 1666 around 3,000 conventiclers in Galloway rose in protest about the way government troops had treated one of their fellows. They marched towards Edinburgh with plans to hand over a petition outlining their complaint, but on the outskirts of town they were stopped and then brutally attacked by soldiers. Many were killed on the spot and scores more imprisoned, tortured or executed.

Even the king could see the so-called 'Pentland Rising' had been hopelessly mishandled and in the aftermath he began making tolerant noises towards the south-west. Prayer meetings could be held as long as they happened indoors. It was by such relaxed measures that the king gradually encouraged more and more stray sheep back into the fold. Increasingly his subjects accepted the return to a Church run by the bishops, and therefore subservient to the king.

The larger truth of the matter, of course, was that Charles was leaning more and more towards Catholicism. By the Treaty of Dover of 1670 he pledged to help Louis XIV of France in his war against the Protestant Dutch republic. In return, Louis would help Charles lead England back into the arms of the Pope. This was explosive stuff; and there were even well-substantiated rumours that Charles was about to reveal he had converted to the old religion. But Charles II kept his head. His subjects remembered all too clearly what had happened the last time a king had lost his head; and in a way it was the spectre of the murdered monarch that moved among them, oozing reproach and keeping the worst of them at bay.

The Protesters of south-west Scotland, with their conventicles now grown so large they looked more like musterings of armies than prayer meetings, kept the embers of rebellion smouldering. These folk the king could not and would not forgive, and his soldiers were sent to harass them, break them up and capture the ringleaders. Prophet Peden was found in Ayrshire in 1673 and flung into the dank depths of a new prison on the Bass Rock, in the Firth of Forth. He remained there with others of his kind for five years. In 1678 he was among sixty or so Covenanters sentenced to transportation and put aboard a ship bound for America. But they docked for a day or two in London and there the American captain learned of the reasons for their imprisonment and set them loose. At large once more, Peden made it all the way back home.

The south-west to which he returned was still home to rebels, but their numbers were thinning as more and more folk opted for a quiet life. But though fewer in number, the demands of the remainder were as strident as ever. On 3 May 1679 a band of Covenanters was lying in wait by the side of a road near St Andrews. Their intended target was the Sheriff of Fife, a hated suppressor of conventicles; but an altogether more significant enemy fell into their hands.

Archbishop Sharp ('Judas' Sharp) it was, who happened to be relaxing as best he could with his daughter, as their carriage bounced and jolted along the rutted track towards their home. The Covenanters pounced and, when they realised whom they had caught, they fell upon him and butchered him while his girl looked on in horror. The killers would say they had done no more than cut down a servant of Satan, but Charles sent in the troops.

At the head of the 150 dragoons tasked with punishing the wrongdoers was a thirty-one-year-old professional soldier called John Graham of Claverhouse. Dashing and bold, Claverhouse had won his spurs while in the service of William of Orange – Prince of the Dutch Republic, champion of the Protestant faith in Europe and the son of Charles's own sister, Mary. For his apparent appetite for punishing Covenanters in south-west Scotland the young Captain, who had so impressed Charles's Dutch nephew, would earn the nickname 'Bluidy Clavers'.

At his first real encounter, though, he was lucky to escape with his life. Running across an armed conventicle at Drumclog, in South Lanarkshire, on 1 June 1679, he found himself confronted by thousands of men, women and children, many of them armed. During a courageous advance by the Covenanter menfolk Claverhouse's horse was injured and bolted from the field, taking its rider with it. Panicked by the sudden departure of their leader, the dragoons broke and ran.

Emboldened by a victory that seemed like a gift from God, thousands more Covenanters rallied to the cause and gathered at Bothwell Brig, near Hamilton. With Claverhouse licking his wounds, a new government army was prepared and sent into action under James Scott, Duke of Monmouth and the eldest of Charles's many illegitimate sons. More interested in talking theology and splitting into factions, the rebels were hopelessly unprepared when Monmouth and his men set about them. After the victory of

Drumclog, the defeat of Bothwell Brig was especially hard to take – but it was total. Hundreds of them were slaughtered on the field and 1,200 or more taken prisoner and dragged off to Edinburgh to await justice. Around 400 were kept in a cage in Greyfriars churchyard.

It is said the Prophet Peden had prophesied the butchers yard of Bothwell Brig, and that from many miles away in Galloway he saw too the fate of the Greyfriars captives. They had done something to try to save their skins, he said, but the waves of the sea would be their winding sheets. In fact, most of the imprisoned Covenanters had signed the 'Black Bond' – a document, written for them, that declared they had acted in simple rebellion and would never again behave in such a way. As a reward their lives were spared. The rest, like Peden had been before them, were sentenced to transportation to the American colonies. They would not be as lucky as the prophet, however. Their ship, the *Croune of Orkney*, was caught out by bad weather and sank off the coast of the Orkney Islands. Fewer than fifty survived.

By the end of the year, there was a Stewart at large in Scotland once more – Charles's younger brother James, Duke of York. But if his family name summoned happy memories for some, his Catholic religion conjured fear and distrust. As the king wanted him to, James kept on with the harassment and the executions. Ironically, it was not his Catholicism that was the greater irritant; rather it was his determination to persuade moderate Presbyterians to accept the rule of bishops. It was this stance, rather than his religion, that drove the Covenanters to fight on – and by fighting, they continued to die.

It was into this atmosphere of intensified repression that James Renwick began to find his voice and his commitment to a martyr's death. A weaver's son from Moniaive, Renwick was always drawn to the Church, and to the Presbyterian faith in particular. In 1681 in Edinburgh he witnessed the mass executions of several Covenanters and was radicalised as a result.

It was already clear that James, Duke of York would succeed as king, and his commitment to religious oppression made his ascent to the throne a frighteningly unappetising prospect for men like Renwick. In 1681 the king-to-be forced the Scots parliament to pass the 'Test Act', which demanded an oath of loyalty to the king from all holders of public office, and soon Scotland descended into a sad horror remembered as the 'Killing Times'.

The Protesters were becoming a war cry that had no mouth or tongue. The ministers who had once stood among the hills and led the rebellious prayers had either been cowed into submission or had their heads on spikes by Edinburgh's Netherbow Gate. So when a group of them gathered at Lesmahagow to form an alternative government called 'The United Societies', Renwick was prominent and vocal among them. Now their calls for a return to the perfection of the Rule of the Saints could be heard once more. Prophet Peden wanted to be among them and returned from one of his regular periods of self-imposed exile in Ireland to preach in their support. But time had moved on and those committed to the cause had grown more radical. Renwick ridiculed Peden for valuing his own neck too highly – for staying alive when what was required was a martyr's death.

To prepare himself for holy war, Renwick departed Scotland for the Netherlands, where he was ordained as a minister. Returning to Scotland in 1683, he began to preach. He was also an author of what he called 'The Apologetical Declaration' – in reality less an apology than a declaration of war on all officials, judges, soldiers and ministers loyal to the king. For good measure it promised death to any who informed about the activities of the Societies. The royal response to the document came in the form of the 'Abjuration Oath'. Any man or woman could be stopped and, on pain of death, ordered to say 'God Save the King'. It was a simple enough phrase and guaranteed to save your life, but it was poison on the lips of Covenanters. None could say it and hold true to their deal with God.

These, then, were the Killing Times. During the course of a little less than a year, some eighty souls would be sent to their Maker for failing to ask God to save their monarch. In the context of the period, the number was small; but it was the arbitrary nature of the killings that was remembered. There were no trials, no juries. Men and women were simply stopped in their tracks and challenged. Failure to say four little words would be followed by a bullet to the head, or worse.

On 11 May 1685, two Wigtown women were singled out. Margaret Maclauchlan was over sixty and Margaret Wilson was just eighteen. One was already in custody for her outspoken opposition to the king, the other her regular visitor in prison. Both were frog-marched onto a beach near the town and tied to wooden stakes placed below the high tide mark. When the seawater was up to their chins and they were struggling to breathe, the soldiers waded in and asked them one more time to save themselves by saving the king. They refused and the men held the women's heads under the water until the struggling stopped.

Charles II had died of a stroke and James II and VII was king by then. It was like the good old days – or the bad, depending on your point of view – and the new king's attitude to kingship was the same: he was anointed by God and he sat above all other men.

In the same month as the drowning of the Wigtown women, three small ships set sail for the south coast of England carrying eighty-two men, 1,500 muskets and a few light field guns. It also carried James Scott, Duke of Monmouth and all his hopes of deposing his uncle and replacing him on the throne.

There had been an attempt in 1681 to prevent the Duke of York ever being king. A clever sleight of hand by Charles, in dissolving the parliament, removed the threat for a while. But the 'Rye House Plot' of 1683 – a plan to assassinate both Charles and James – had been more alarming. Protestant Monmouth had opted for exile in the Netherlands then and while his father remained on the throne he had been content to bide his time. He believed after all that his mother, Lucy Walter, had been secretly married to his father and that he was therefore the legitimate heir. It was only when Charles died and James took the throne that Monmouth decided to gamble everything on a shot at the kingdom. In Scotland the Earl of Argyll – son of the Argyll who had been executed by Charles – agreed to rise as well. Monmouth gathered his Protestant supporters and landed at Lyme Regis to start his rebellion. It was a fiasco followed by a tragedy.

For a start, Argyll's rebellion was nipped in the bud. Captured on his way to Glasgow, he was convicted of treason and beheaded on the Maiden. Like father, like son. Monmouth managed to raise an army right enough, but led them to final disaster on the battlefield of Sedgemoor on 6 July 1685. Monmouth was captured and executed, his soldiers either hanged or transported to the Americas.

It might have seemed God was intent on saving the king after all. In France, Louis XIV revoked laws protecting French Protestants from prosecution. Maybe the war that Charles II had planned with Louis, the war against the new faith, might come to pass. Perhaps time and tide would roll all the way back to an era and a place when all of Europe, Scotland and England included, was Catholic.

Regardless of God's plans for James, there was at least one Protestant left in Continental Europe who had no intention whatever of standing by while the kings of England and France joined forces in a Catholic-inspired union. William of Orange was James's nephew – and married to his daughter Mary. That made him a Stewart, or at least the next best thing. So as well as being Protestant, he had a legal claim on James's thrones. But for all the

Protestant intent over the water, James seemed secure. He began to surround himself with fellow Catholics, elevating them to as many positions of power as possible. Soon they were the majority on the Scottish Privy Council, running the burghs as well. And still his enemies were being harvested.

James Renwick, firebrand of the Societies, met the martyr's death he so craved on 17 February 1688. He was just twenty-six but there was a price on his head and an immaculate destiny in his heart. Contemptuous of the danger he faced, he came to Edinburgh and exchanged fire with government troopers before being captured by them. He was a man prepared to die, but before departing this earth he had some things to say.

Climbing calmly onto the scaffold he spoke at length. Scotland should be ruled by its Kirk, he said. Only a return to the Rule of the Saints was good enough; James was a usurper. He quoted liberally from the book of books. From Psalm 103: 'The Lord executeth righteousness and judgment for all that are oppressed ... As for man: his days are as grass: as a flower of the field, so he flourisheth ... To such as keep his covenant, and to those that remember his commandments to do them ... The Lord has prepared his throne in the heavens; and his kingdom ruleth over all'. And from Revelations 19: 'Come and gather yourselves together unto the supper of the great God; That ye may eat the flesh of kings'. 'Lord I die in the faith that you will not leave Scotland,' he said. 'But that you will make the blood of your witnesses the seed of your Church, and return again and be glorious in our land. And now, Lord, I am ready.' They hanged him then and as his body swung, life leaving him like a last prayer, he became as a pendulum marking the last moments of the king's reign.

Against all expectations, James's wife Mary of Modena, then in her forties, gave birth to a baby boy on 10 June 1688. For William of Orange and for James's Protestant subjects north and south of the border, this was too much. With the coming of little James Francis Edward Stewart, a Catholic succession was assured. William had been considering taking action for months and now he let it be known that invasion of Britain was his wish.

James had planted a Catholic tree on stony, Protestant ground. It had grown too tall too quickly and now a wind was starting to blow from the Continent. The tree was rocking on its shallow roots. William had his invasion force ready – 70,000 men – and for a while he had to wait for favourable winds. Then, on 5 November 1688, he made landfall to begin his 'Glorious Revolution'. Queen and heir fled the kingdom on 9 December and James VII and II, understanding which way the wind was blowing, followed on the 23rd.

It was 'glorious' and it was 'bloodless' too. By February 1689 the English parliament had passed the Act of Settlement, stating that no Catholic could sit on the throne. William and Mary accepted and on the 13th of the month were duly proclaimed King and Queen of England and Ireland. On 11 April 1689 they were proclaimed sovereigns in Scotland as well.

Something momentous had happened. King William II and III and Queen Mary were the first of a new breed of monarch. This was the advent of a *constitutional* monarchy – one in which the king could no longer and never again do as he wished. He was beholden to parliament instead. It was too much too soon for some. In Scotland John Graham of Claverhouse, 'Bluidy Clavers', was driven to war. In October 1688 he had ridden south with an army 13,000-strong to try and support his Stewart king. James was his personal friend – had made him Viscount Dundee, Lord John Graham of Claverhouse as reward for his suppression of the Covenanters – and he was sworn to fight for him.

When King James turned tail and fled his kingdom rather than face his tormentors, Dundee had to return home. He attended the Convention of the Estates of the Realm that gathered in Edinburgh in March 1689 to decide whether William and Mary or James Stewart should have their backing. Dundee found himself a lone voice in support of his friend and in the second week in April he sallied forth and raised the king's standard on Dundee Law. It was his declaration of war. On 27 July he led the first Jacobites to a famous victory on the steep slopes of Killiecrankie, near Blair Atholl, but paid for it with his life. Riding at the head of his men, he was felled by a musket shot and died at the very moment of his greatest triumph. There was support for the cause elsewhere, in the garrisons at Edinburgh Castle and on the Bass Rock, but within months the rising was over.

The remnant threads of the Presbyterian Kirk were knitted back together, a tattered garment still proudly worn. Despite King William's protests they rejected the rule of bishops and repealed the Act of Supremacy that made the king head of the Church. They abolished lay patronage and re-established the Presbyterian Kirk as the Church of Scotland. They could not go back to the Rule of the Saints – that much was no longer even a pipe dream. Instead they made an arrangement modern enough for us to understand:

the Church remained subject to parliament. The might of the king and parliament had seen to that. They had put a lid on religion.

Underneath that lid, religion simmered. In November 1690 the Kirk held its first General Assembly since 1653. Those who attended called it a General Assembly but those who stayed away – the Covenanters – refused to recognise it as such. Fewer than 200 ministers and elders attended, all of them from south of the River Tay. This was the Church of *southern* Scotland. In the north the old loyalties to the older kind of God-anointed king – to the Stewart dynasty and to a Church with bishops – remained in force. The split in the Kirk was a split across the country, an unhealed and festering wound. And the Stewarts, of course, were far from dead – only in exile, in France. They were not a problem solved, rather a problem pushed aside.

In the nineteenth century, monuments to the dead Covenanters spread across southern Scotland. The Victorians saw the Covenanters as martyrs who had died defending the union of Scotland and England. This was nonsense. The Covenanters had died for the Covenanted Kirk of Scotland. Today, for some people, the Covenanters stand for something else. Because they saw every soul as equal, and demanded a free parliament, a new contract with the Crown, and the right to their own religious beliefs, it is easy to celebrate them as demanding things we value now: equality; civil liberties; freedom of conscience; the limits of what a state has the right to do with, and to, its citizens. This is not to be discounted, but it is less than half the truth. To understand the Covenanters we must swallow them whole.

The truth is that we have stolen from them ideas like equality, freedom of speech and conscience, and disposed of everything else they stood for. The Covenanters knew very little of mercy. They knew nothing of moderation. There was only one government they could ever have approved and that was the rule of the Presbyterian Kirk, with a Covenanted king. One nation under God, and bound for glory; sermons every day and twice on Sunday. The freedoms they sought were freedoms for Covenanting Presbyterians and no one else; anyone of another faith was headed straight to hell.

***

The Jacobite rebellion in support of King James had ended with a whimper, rather than a bang. Bonnie Dundee had been the only glory of it all and he was dead. Instead of blood, it was money that settled the matter – with bribes paid to West Highland chiefs like the elder Cameron of Lochiel in return for making peace with the government of Scotland.

Scotland's problem with the new king was that he did not care about the place or its people. William's kingdom was England and his abiding preoccupation – his obsession in fact – was his ongoing war with Catholic France. Scotland was just a source of men for his armies and taxes for their upkeep. His only concern was to ensure the locals behaved themselves, but he was reluctant to commit men to the Scottish garrisons when they could be put to better use in Flanders.

William's Secretary of State in Scotland, John Dalrymple, Master of Stair, was convinced the Jacobite elements in the Highlands could be brought to heel with a terrifying display of will, and believed the perfect opportunity lay just around the corner. The king had been ready to buy obedience, but in return had insisted the chiefs swear allegiance to him by 1 January 1692. Dalrymple was sure some of them would defy the order and, behind the scenes, had laid plans for a punitive atrocity.

The chiefs had had the audacity to ask the exiled James for his permission to cease the fight on his behalf and then to await his response. The reply from the king over the water, that they should stand down, came in late December 1691, giving almost all of them time to disappoint the Master of Stair by signing on the dotted line with days to spare. Only one chief missed the deadline – and by unhappy accident rather than design. Alasdair MacDonald, the MacIain, chief of Clan Iain Abrach of the MacDonalds of Glencoe, was caught out by time and by weather. His small community was scattered between Achtriochtan and Invercoe, among forbidding terrain bounded to the north by the 1,000-metre cliffs of the Aonach Eagach, and to the south by mountains called Buachaille Etive Mor and Buachaille Etive Beag – the big and the little shepherds of Etive.

Like all the clans, the MacDonalds of Glencoe were cattle thieves, praying on their knees on Sundays, as they say, and preying upon their neighbours the rest of the week. Right at the end of December, the MacIain turned up at Fort William to swear his oath. The fort was commanded by Colonel John Hill, recently recalled from Ireland, who rightly told the chief he had no powers to administer such an oath. The job required a royal sheriff and Sir Colin Campbell of Ardkinglas, believed to be at Inveraray, was the only man nearby of appropriate rank.

Suddenly desperate, realising the gravity of his situation, the MacIain set off into the teeth of a snowstorm in hope of reaching Inveraray in time. He arrived on 2 January 1692, one day past the deadline, to learn that Sir Colin was away from the fort celebrating Hogmanay. He did not return until three days later and, though he allowed the MacIain to swear his oath, both men knew it was invalid.

The Master of Stair, loather of Highlanders and Jacobites alike, had his victims at last. Argyll's regiment was chosen for the task of delivering a punishment both 'secret and suddain' and the officer selected for the job was one Robert Campbell of Glenlyon, a laird whose lands and people had been viciously attacked by MacDonalds of Glencoe during the 1689 rebellion.

He and his men arrived at the home of the MacIain in early February, and were offered the hospitality demanded by Highland tradition. They stayed for some days until, on 12 February, Campbell received orders, approved by King William himself, that he was to massacre every man, woman and child. He attempted to carry out the gory work the following day but a combination of bad weather and professional ineptitude per-mitted two of the MacIain's sons to raise the alarm and lead most of their kin out of reach of the troopers.

Exposure took several of those that fled – and Campbell's men put musket balls and bayonets through the MacIain and thirty-seven of his folk, including old women and toddlers. By any measure it was ugly and when news of the crime reached the cities it was condemned even by those who feared the threat of Jacobite rebellion. The unrepentant Master of Stair wondered at the fuss made about 'a sept of thieves', but was eventually driven from office. That apart, no one individual was ever punished for the cruel butchery of Glencoe.

Ugly it surely had been, but it was also a tactical disaster for the Williamite government that had ordered it. The intention had been to horrify the dissenting clans into submission and yet it had generated only fury and renewed defiance. Cameron of Lochiel, a mighty and influential magnate, responded by ordering every government soldier off his lands. Even the MacDonalds of Glencoe, the survivors of the act itself, stood to arms from their temporary homes in the lands of sheltering neighbours.

The new king had shown his colours: he was as prepared as any despot to murder his own subjects in cold blood. Jacobites in Scotland and further afield rubbed their hands together with dark, opportunistic glee.

For all that the Massacre of Glencoe inspired Jacobite support and hatred of King William, it is important to remember the treatment of another clan nearly a hundred years earlier by a Stuart king.

In 1603 James VI fell out with the MacGregors and took the draconian step of outlawing the clan and the name completely. Anyone calling himself MacGregor was to be put to death, his lands made forfeit to his killer. It was genocidal and it cost an unknown number of lives during the next century and a half. It also further elevated the Campbells. They acquired MacGregor lands, in addition to their gains in the aftermath of the downfall of Clan Donald, at the hands of another Stuart king.

William's behaviour was another verse of a familiar song – the cruel, misguided attempts by kings of Scotland to suppress a Highland culture they could not or would not understand. So while the murder of the MacDonalds of Glencoe in 1692 left blood on the hands of Orange William, it was no worse than the behaviour of his Stuart predecessor.

Scots have had an unfortunate tendency to behave like whipped dogs, ever ready to return to the heel of their supposed masters, regardless of the severity of the beatings or the blatant self-interest of the men holding the sticks. Some behave the same way to this day.

CHAPTER EIGHT

JACOBITES

'Happy families are all alike: every unhappy family is unhappy in its own way.'

Leo Tolstoy, *Anna Karenina*

'The sun is behind me.
Nothing has changed since I began.
My eye has permitted no change.
I am going to keep things like this.'

Ted Hughes, 'Hawk Roosting'

The suffering and misery of Scots at the hands of legendary hate figures like Edward I, Henry VIII or Oliver Cromwell are well documented, and scored into the hearts of many alive today. But in truth, there was no more appalling time for vast swathes of the population than during the famines of the late 1690s.

Less familiar and less well remembered that suffering may be, but it was terrible and terrifying just the same. From 1695 onwards, inclement weather caused one failed harvest after another. The death toll from the starvation and malnutrition of the 'Ill Years' will never be known but it is estimated to have been in the tens of thousands – and that from a total population numbering around a million. Perhaps those awful times have fallen from collective memory because there was no bogeyman to blame.

At the same time, despite the death and hardship, ordinary Scots began to reap another harvest altogether. In 1696 the Scots parliament passed the Act for Setting Schools. It was the natural progression from a foundation laid down by John Knox in his *First Book of Discipline* in 1560 – that all the people should be taught to read so they could help themselves to the enlightenment of the Word of God. In any case, by the end of the eighteenth century, Scotland would be home to the most literate society in Europe. There were libraries everywhere and records show books of all sorts being borrowed by men and women of every trade and class.

All of this – cruel hardship at home combined with access to the wider world through reading – made for a volatile mix. From the highest to the lowest, Scots were unconsciously preparing themselves to turn their backs on a troubled, limited past and look towards a limitless future. By the end of the seventeenth century they were among the hungriest folk on the face of the earth – for personal improvement as well as for food.

Ordinary Scots were therefore especially vulnerable to a grand scheme being touted by a mercurial businessman named William Paterson. Born in Dumfriesshire, he had made a career and a name for himself in London. He was instrumental in establishing the first Bank of England in 1695 and the first Bank of Scotland the following year. Many regarded him as a true visionary, and wherever he went people hung on his every word in hope of being shown the way to wealth and status.

The mass of his countrymen had grown disillusioned with the realities of being ruled by a king who lived in England and put English needs first. Scots merchants looked with envious eyes at the riches being scooped up by their opposite numbers south of the border. England had colonies in the Americas and rich trading links with Africa, India and the Far East. The English Navy protected English merchant ships en route and the Scots, like everyone else, were excluded from many of the rewards.

Entrepreneurial and adventurous Scots had been on the move during the half-century before the union. There were certainly thousands of them building new lives in Ulster, and on the other side of the Atlantic Ocean, in the colonies of the eastern seaboard of North America, *émigré* Scots were an established presence. But these were still the exceptions. Scotland's legendary impact on the New World still lay decades in the future.

Paterson's dreams of Darien were therefore not as outlandish as we might imagine, in the last years of the seventeenth century. Determined to enjoy the spoils of international trade, Scots were persuaded to empty their purses and gamble their very futures on the success of Paterson's plan. Together with East Lothian landowner Andrew Fletcher of Saltoun, he encouraged thousands of Scots to buy shares in a public joint stock company. This was the audacious new business model already financing the interests of the

Dutch and the English. It marked the start of practices – lending money in the present, in hopes of earning more from success in the future – that would lead directly to the global economic collapse now blighting the early twenty-first century. It was all fresh and new in the seventeenth century, though, and Scots, from the aristocracy to the middling sort, began elbowing one another aside in their desperation to get in on the ground floor of something that promised to be huge: a Scottish trading empire.

As soon as 'The Company of Scotland Trading to Africa and the Indies' was up and running, however, English merchants rose in furious indignation. Although William grudgingly approved the legislation required by the Scots, the protectionist tactics of English merchants and nobility meant the new company would remain blocked from establishing trade in all parts of the world under English control.

Bloodied but unbowed, Paterson ploughed ahead and carried Scotland along with him. Instead of participating in the English trade empire, they would go it alone. He had long been obsessed with the potential of the Darien Isthmus, a narrow strip of land in Panama separating the Pacific Ocean from the Atlantic. To anyone who would listen he was describing the territory as 'the key of the universe'; whoever controlled Darien, he said, could monopolise all trade between the eastern and western halves of the planet.

The resultant 'Darien Company' raised hundreds of thousands of pounds, somewhere between a quarter and a half of all the liquid capital in the land, as Scots found themselves swept along by a fervour. It was a fervour born of greed and fuelled by patriotism – determination to restore Scots honour in the face of English obstruction – and therefore another lethal cocktail. Between 1698 and 1700 the Darien Company attempted to establish its colony. It was the most desperate and doomed venture in the whole of Scottish history.

Unbeknown to the vast majority of stock-holders, the Isthmus of Darien was a fly-blown, fever-blighted swamp in the middle of a patch of Panama already claimed by mighty Spain. Among the laughable cargo taken by the first colonists – the trade goods with which they planned to woo the locals in this tropical hellhole – were powdered wigs, woollen hose and tartan plaid.

The two-year-long story of disease, persecution by Spain and disgruntled natives, and tropical rain-lashed misery is best kept short. King William was privately more interested in staying on good terms with the Spanish than in seeing the survival (far less the advancement) of his Scottish subjects, and so cut them adrift. Fever and climate took the main toll, however. The colonists' clothes and shoes rotted from their bodies under the ceaseless onslaught of tropical rains. Their supplies rotted too and their crops failed. They died by the hundreds. Paterson was laid dangerously low by fever and his own wife died of it.

Finally the Spanish got their way and the 300 or so survivors (out of some 1,200) climbed aboard ship and limped home to a Scotland ruined. Every penny of the investment had been lost and the nation was bankrupt – and this at a time when so many folk were already severely weakened by the years of famine.

King William died in 1702 and his throne passed to his sister-in-law Anne, younger sister of his dead wife, Mary. Protestant Anne was a *bona fide* Stuart at least,' but like William her over-riding concern was for the future of England. A Scotland wounded by economic collapse and blaming England for its woes was vulnerable to exploitation by England's enemies, like France. For Anne and her government the priority was to find a way of dealing with the Scottish problem once and for all.

With mutual loathing dominating relations between the two supposedly united kingdoms, the English parliament took the step of passing the 'Aliens Act' of 1704. Its headline statements banned Scots from passing onto their heirs any territory they owned in England, and put a block on the import of Scots trading goods; but it was also an attempt to strong-arm the northern kingdom into accepting a union of parliaments. Only by allowing herself to be joined more completely to England could Scotland be freed from the strictures hobbling her present and future.

The hated Act was repealed two years later, but by then it had done its job. Influential Scots accepted that Scotland would remain poor and weak for as long as it held itself apart from England. Many of them imagined a kind of federal union – two independent nations joining forces to reap a combined harvest – but Anne's England wanted nothing less than to swallow Scotland whole. The buzzword was *incorporating* union, a marriage by which the Scottish wife would be made wholly subservient to her English husband.

The Scots should have felt which way the wind was blowing long before, even as the Darien dream was dying. In 1700 the last of Princess Anne's eighteen children had died as well, aged just eleven. With the passing of the little, luckless Duke of Gloucester, the direct line of descent was broken.

The English parliament had faced a dilemma: either the prospect of Anne dying without further issue and the throne passing to the next in line, the Catholic James Francis Edward Stuart, son of King James VII and II – or finding a Protestant alternative while she was still alive.

So it was that in 1701, without even informing the Scots of their plans, the English parliament had passed the 'Act of Settlement'. Under its terms they offered the thrones of England, Scotland and Ireland to a lesser and distant branch of the Stuart tree. James VII and II's youngest daughter had been Elizabeth, the so-called 'Winter Queen' of Bohemia. Her one surviving descendant was her youngest daughter Sophia, Electress of Hanover. Sophia was in her seventies; but she was Protestant and, more to the point, she had a forty-something Protestant son called George. Anne could not actually bear the sight of her Bohemian relatives and never allowed them to set foot in any of her kingdoms while she lived but they happily accepted the offer of jam tomorrow.

Unsurprisingly, the Scots were livid. All of this had been done without so much as a by your leave, and for a while there was dark talk of breaking the union of crowns altogether and finding a separate king for Scotland. In reality there was no realistic alternative to what the English had set in train. Had they gone shopping for their own man, the Scots would have opened the door to Catholic James and his heirs; most Scots had no wish to reopen that particular can of religious worms.

And so there you had it: the English held the key to greater prosperity and had already decided the future of the thrones. The price of obtaining a copy of that key, and of maintaining the status quo of kingdoms united, was to snuggle up even closer to the Auld Enemy.

In 1705 the members of the Scots parliament agreed that plans for union should be drawn up. It is important to remember that while it was called a parliament, it had nothing to do with democracy. Its members were place-men, subservient to the king and well trained in the business of lying down and rolling over for their masters in London; they represented no one but themselves and the vast majority of Scots cared not a whit about them. Ever since James VI and I had crossed the border heading south, Scotland had been ruled by London and everybody knew it. For many, the choice had long been clear: continue to be ruled from London, but without access to English markets – or be ruled from London while growing fat on the proceeds of union.

By 1707 a joint Scots and English commission had drawn up a draft

'Treaty of Union'. The Scots members of that commission had been Crown appointees – chosen for their support of Queen Anne's desire for an incorporating union – and the document they now proposed to put before the Scots parliament was nothing more or less than a suicide note awaiting a signature.

By its terms the Scots parliament would cease to be. A tiny handful of Scots would be made members of the English – now British – Houses of Commons and of Lords. The Scottish Privy Council would be emasculated and every important decision about matters affecting both kingdoms would be made in London. It was even unclear what would happen to the Kirk, and the absence of any clear statements about Scotland's religious future unsettled every Presbyterian.

Only the legal and educational systems would remain separate and independent from their southern counterparts, but these seemed like faint sweeteners. The main inducement came in the form of money – or at least the prospect of access to the places where money might be made. Under the terms of the treaty, Scots would be allowed in among England's foreign markets. Money was also paid directly to Scotland's nobles, some of it supposedly to compensate those hurt by the Darien disaster; but it was bribery by any other name.

On 16 January 1707, after months of bitter wrangling, Scotland's parliament voted itself out of existence. There had been desperate and furious opposition from men like Andrew Fletcher of Saltoun, a radical Whig and Paterson's ally in the early days of the Company of Scotland. Like many Scots, Fletcher had wanted to change the nature of Scotland's ties to its southern neighbour. He complained about the iniquity of Scots being taxed to the hilt to pay for England's Continental wars – wars being fought against the very nations Scots wanted to trade with, like France. After all, England's violent adventures in Europe had been part of the reason why Scots had had to turn their attentions away from the east and towards the west – towards a disaster like Darien – in the first place. But in the end Fletcher's arguments and all the others had been overcome by the gift or the promise of English pounds. Even the Kirk had backed the treaty: they feared the prospect of Scotland going it alone and falling once more beneath the thrall of a Catholic monarch.

The main obstacle had been Article 22 of the treaty, by which the separate Scots parliament was to be abolished. It was pushed through by the single-minded determination of one man: John Dalrymple, responsible for the

Massacre of Glencoe. Putting aside all sentiment, he simply argued that nations, like people, depended on money for their survival and growth. Accept the union, swallow the humiliation of a tiny minority of representatives in the new parliament, he argued, and enjoy the rewards of being allied with England. It was a simple argument and it carried the day.

On 28 April the Scots Privy Council formally and finally proclaimed the dissolution of Scotland's parliament. The Lord Chancellor, James Ogilvy, 1st Earl of Seafield, is said to have taken the sceptre of the Scots regalia and touched the new Treaty of Union with it. 'Now that's the end of an auld sang,' he said.

Many Scots, though, found they were still listening to the same old tune. Despite the prospect of wealth for some, there had been massive popular opposition to the proposed union: rioting in the streets of towns and cities the length and breadth of the country. Glasgow had been especially concerned, fearing that union would silence its independent political voice. Centuries of history had taught ordinary Scots the dangers of complying with the English. Independence and its defence had become a character trait of the nation that had not been watered down by the years of united crowns. And anyway, Scotland had been promised economic benefits and those certainly did not arrive overnight and not for a long time thereafter.

In the immediate aftermath of the treaty, in fact, the only people smiling were the Jacobites. From his gloomy lair in the Palace of St Germain-en-Laye, outside Paris, nineteen-year-old James Francis Edward Stuart smelled Presbyterian and Whig blood for the first time. Here was yet another Stuart grown to manhood far from home. Unlike his predecessors, though, his birth had been followed for a while by claims he was not even the king's son – that he was a 'suppositious child' bought from some hapless soul and smuggled into Queen Mary's rooms in St James's Palace in a warming pan. But as he had grown, all agreed that none could look into his face without admitting he was his father's child.

James VII and II had died on 16 September 1701 and now James Francis Edward was 'the Pretender' (from the French *prétendant*, 'claimant'). Louis XIV had speedily proclaimed him James VIII and III of Scotland, England and Ireland and he was as confident of one day sitting upon his throne as only a teenage boy could be.

With the ink still drying on the Treaty of Union, Jacobite agents had travelled from Scotland to the French court with a paper bearing the signatures of prominent Scots. The time was right, they said, for James to cross over to Scotland and claim his birthright. Thousands of Scottish Jacobites were apparently ready to rise to the fight and if James would just set foot in his homeland, the throne of Scotland was as good as his.

For the French king, this was a tempting proposition. He was years into the conflict with England known as the War of the Spanish Succession and desperately wanted leverage to force his enemy to back off. There was also the matter of the vast expense of maintaining the Stuarts in luxurious exile, which was soaking up money that ought more usefully to have been going into his war chest. All things considered, he jumped at the chance to kill both birds with one stone and furnished his guest with a fleet of French warships and privateers, together with a company of French troops.

The teenager who would be king arrived in the port of Dunkirk in March 1708, and was promptly laid low by a bout of measles. By the time he had recovered, much of the fire had gone out of French hearts at least. The French commanders of his fleet were convinced they faced certain defeat and Admiral John Byng was known to have brought British ships into position off the coast at Gravelines, south-west of Dunkirk, ready to inter-cept them.

No one talks much about James's expedition of 1708 – it has been lost completely in the shadows cast by 'The '15' and 'The '45' and is described by some as a fiasco – and yet it strikes me as perhaps the most dangerous of all the Jacobite risings of the eighteenth century.

The effort of 1708 was a case of striking while the iron was hot. No one was yet benefiting from the Hanoverian-backed union, least of all the Scots. National pride was severely hurt, in need of vengeance even, and memories of Glencoe were still sharp. As well as in Scotland, there was also untapped Jacobite sentiment in England. Altogether it added up to the perfect time for the Pretender to strike.

The plan was fairly modest, small-scale in its ambitions to be realistic: the undertaking, as outlined by the Jacobite agents who had contacted Louis, was to concentrate only on the Scottish throne. James was to land on the east coast and make for Stirling as quickly as possible. Once Scotland was reclaimed, a force could be sent into the north-east of England to take control of the Tyne-Tees coalfields. Starved of fuel, went the theory, Anne's government might even have to sue for peace with France.

As in so much of life, it was luck that made the difference, and James Francis Edward Stuart did not have any. By the time the teenager's spots had cleared up, the weather in the Channel and the North Sea had turned for the worse. The flotilla got under way but was so storm-tossed that James and most of the troopers were terribly seasick all the way over. To make matters worse, both the French naval commander Claude de Forbin and the military commander Count de Gace remained as faint-hearted about the mission as it was possible to be. Grey about the gills though they undoubtedly were, the would-be invaders made it into the Firth of Forth and dropped anchor near Burntisland. Jacobite forces were already gathering onshore, ready to mount the advance on Stirling, and the government commander would later report he had neither the men nor the equipment to do much to deter them.

With success within sight Forbin became aware that Admiral Byng was about to join him in the Forth. Unwilling to face the consequences of such a meeting, he pulled his ships away before James had a chance even to land in Scotland. They headed north instead, with the Pretender pleading desperately to be put ashore anywhere – even alone. Forbin refused and ran for his life, eventually circumnavigating the whole of the British Isles in order to make good his escape and return to France.

The British government had been lucky. It was not even the beginning of the end of the Jacobite problem, but the threat would never again be quite so well timed, so acutely dangerous, so full of unexplored potential.

Also in 1708 the Scots Privy Council was abolished – a last nail in the coffin of Scotland as an independent political force – and in 1709 the Whigs controlling the London parliament introduced Anglicanism to Edinburgh. It was the thin end of a wedge and in 1712 the 'Act of Toleration' gave equal rights to Scottish Episcopalians. The Kirk had avoided the return of a Catholic monarch but the next worst thing had arrived instead: the synagogue of Satan.

Displeasure with the nature of the union was growing and simmering in both Scotland and England. While Protestant Whigs were pushing all the while for greater religious tolerance, the attitude of a sizeable minority of their High Anglican Tory opponents hardened into a stance that looked steadily more like Jacobitism. Apart from anything else, Jacobite nobles remembered a world of the recent past in which the people below them had known their place. Like the hawk in Hughes's poem, they believed they sat towards the top of nature's hierarchy. God had made them what they were – and had once made kings his little gods, to rule over other men. For nobles who had lost power, who saw it being wielded instead by upstarts, memories of high-handed Catholic monarchs burned bright. These monarchs needed locally powerful nobles to do their bidding; maybe the past was a world that could be reclaimed and lorded over once more and for ever. As Hughes's poem says, 'I kill where I please because it is all mine.'

For a while after 1711 the Tories gained the upper hand in parliament, and even went so far as to suggest to James he might be welcomed back as King of Great Britain if he would only convert to Protestantism. He could not, or would not, and once again a chance brushed past the Pretender like a stranger in a crowd. (He was damned if he did, damned if he didn't, of course: by staying true to his faith, he made himself an inspiring figurehead for Scots Catholics. In religious terms, he just could not win.)

In 1713 a Bill was put before parliament calling for an end to the union altogether. It was the work of Scots nobles including John Erskine, 6th Earl of Mar, James Ogilvy, 1st Earl of Seafield and John Campbell, 2nd Earl of Argyll – three of those who had been most committed to it in the first place. Only six years had passed since its historic signing and yet already the pulse of the thing was all but undetectable. Only a single vote kept it alive.

Queen Anne – tragic, unlovely Queen Anne, without heirs and with all her children in the ground before her – died in 1714. As arranged by the Act of Settlement of 1701, her passing opened the door to Hanoverian George. He spoke barely any English and if he knew of Scotland's existence at all, that was about the limit of his knowledge of the place. For those of the Scots nobility who depended on the king for cash and position, the ending of the 'auld sang' had signalled a scramble for seats in the toughest ever round of musical chairs. And when Anne died everyone had to stand up again and circle nervously until George invited them to sit.

Mar – they called him 'Bobbing John' on account of his backing for the union one minute, followed by bitter opposition to it the next – grimly held on. He had hoped for rewards for his sometime public support of all things Whig and Hanoverian, but he was to be disappointed. Formerly the Secretary of State for Scotland, he was nothing now and saw no alternative but to hang around George hoping to be gifted one of the remaining seats of power. The last straw was laid across his back in the summer of 1715. Mar arrived at a royal function and walked towards the king, only for George blatantly to turn his back on him in the most public and humiliating of snubs.

He had been shown his own future and in London, at the Hanoverian court, it was an utterly empty one. He returned 'home' to Scotland immediately, where he had estates both in the Lowlands and Highlands, and soon made his way to Braemar where he raised James's royal standard on 6 September 1715. He had gathered other disgruntled or vacillating nobles around him – he had dressed the day up as a hunting party – and with stirrup cups in hand they toasted the king over the water and crossed the Rubicon.

When reading about the Jacobites in the context of a history of Scotland it is easy to be tricked into thinking Jacobitism was itself Scottish. This is far from the truth. From the moment James VII and II arrived in Ireland in the aftermath of William's revolution, to lead an army with Frenchmen within its ranks, it was and would remain an international, or at least a pan-European, phenomenon.

After his defeat at the Battle of the Boyne in 1690 James sought exile in Catholic France. But there was noisy support for his cause in Austria, Italy and Spain as well. Jacobitism was not a Catholic project either. Depending upon where they were looking for – and obtaining – support, Jacobite agents would sometimes claim it was not about *religion* at all. This is also false. There were Protestant Jacobites and there were Catholics and Episcopalians who sided with the Hanoverian government, but religion was an always potent ingredient in the mix just the same. (In Scotland, in fact, it was from within the ranks of Episcopalians, particularly in the north-east, that James and then his son Charles would draw their most ardent supporters.)

The Jacobite story can sometimes seem like the most complicated and confusing in all of Scotland's history. In some ways it is; but it helps to remember it had its deepest roots in something quite simple. From the moment William and Mary first ascended their thrones, those nobles and landowners who voiced support for the new regime ought to have felt their faces flush red as their claret with the hypocrisy of it all. As a species, they depended upon the rights of primogeniture, the rights of the firstborn. They had received their lands and titles from their fathers for no other reason than that ancient laws demanded it.

William and Mary, and then Mary's sister Anne, were fruit from a junior branch of the Stuart tree. They were therefore usurpers, sitting in the rightful place of their elder, superior, Catholic relatives. This simple wrong was the elephant in the Williamite and then again in the Hanoverian room; it was the embarrassment it engendered that had provoked the ludicrous suggestion that James Francis Edward was a changeling. And so in many ways the Jacobite rebellions of the seventeenth and eighteenth centuries were the squabbles of an unhappy family. This simple fact was soon lost in a swirling fog of competing priorities as one European party after another found it had something to gain from exploiting the Jacobite dream. But that is how it started just the same. The most colourful moments tended to be played out in the kingdoms of Scotland and England for very straight-forward reasons as well.

England was by far the richest territory within the Stuart demesne, and the only one powerful enough to force a primogeniture-defying Protestant succession onto the others. And Scotland, of course, was the birthplace of the Stuart line, of the very name *Stewart.* The first of them had been Robert II, son of the hereditary Steward of Scotland. He had inherited his throne from his mother Marjorie, daughter of Robert the Bruce, and Stuarts of one sort or another had sat upon it ever since. But Scotland and the Scots were there to be exploited by any English or European monarch who found a use for them: to open a door on England or close it for ever; to stir up trouble for the Protestant faith; to distract the British from European schemes and force them to sort out their own house.

The single most important contributory factor to the success or failure of any and every Jacobite adventure was the attitude of France. Only France had the clout, the cash and the will to gamble on returning a Catholic Stuart to the British thrones.

James's 1708 attempt to claim his thrones had happened while England and France were locked in the international bloodletting of the War of the Spanish Succession. The Habsburg Charles II of Spain had been weak both physically and mentally – almost certainly a result of his family's fondness for letting first cousins marry – and had died without producing an heir. His death in 1700 had been no surprise to anyone; indeed, the nations of Europe had prepared for its aftermath for years before it actually happened, and with good reason: the Habsburg Spanish empire he would leave behind was vast, with concerns throughout Europe and in the Americas.

Were the whole huge dynastic inheritance to pass to any one ruler it would have created a power bloc so great as to unbalance the continent. The English, the French, the Spanish, the Dutch and the Habsburg Holy Roman Emperor Leopold I – all had been conducting negotiations and signing partition treaties aimed at breaking up the whole of it into less weighty chunks.

The fear shared by most was the prospect of Bourbon France inheriting the empire, a possibility created by a knot of marriage alliances that also gave Emperor Leopold a valid claim. King Louis XIV had originally waived his own rights, but when Charles II died his will revealed he had left everything to Louis's grandson – who became Philip V of Spain. This was close to the nightmare scenario for the rest of Europe and war its inevitable consequence.

The Emperor, the Dutch and the English joined together in a Grand Alliance against Louis. In the end it proved too much for the acquisitive Frenchman. Luminous English victories like Blenheim, in 1704, under the command of John Churchill, 1st Duke of Marlborough, had gradually eroded both Louis's will and his cash reserves. By 1713 he had had enough and the Peace of Utrecht brought the fighting to an end. Under its terms he was required, among many other things, to recognise the Protestant succession in England and expel the Stuart Pretender from his kingdom. He met the terms and James had to vacate his grand residence at St Germain -en-Laye for more modest accommodation in the independent Duchy of Lorraine.

What Louis might say in public, under the weight of treaty negotiations, however, was one thing; what he thought privately was often quite another. For as long as he lived he would value the gaming piece that was the exiled Stuart king and his support was of huge significance to Jacobite hopes. While he was inconvenienced by Utrecht, he passed the Jacobite baton to his grandson, Philip V of Spain, who duly promised to back James. But on 15 September 1715 Louis XIV died and at once the Jacobite world was a different place.

In fundamental ways, the world of nort-west Europe had lately changed too. By the Peace of Utrecht the key powers north of the Alps accepted that peace depended, to some extent, upon 'the balance of power'. This was an innovation in the eighteenth century and tied up with another fact of life: the time of great dynasties was coming to an end. If not actually ceasing to exist, they were at least old-fashioned, with less of a part to play in shaping national policy. The Stuarts – and their offspring the Jacobites – were part of the old world; *nations* mattered more now than great houses and their great *names*. It is also interesting to note that the map of north-west Europe in 1713 was much the same as that of today. There was no consolidated Italy, and Belgium was yet to be born; but by and large the blocks on the map have been the same for the best part of 300 years.

The shape and style of this new world was never going to appeal to Jacobites. And ironically, while national politics became the international language in parts of Continental Europe, Jacobitism reached a new high point in Britain as a whole and in Scotland in particular.

Everyone knew 'Bobbing John', the Earl of Mar, was a politician who blew in the wind, but his timing happened to be perfect. By the time he raised James's standard in 1715, other men of more confirmed will found they too had been pushed as far as they were prepared to go by vulgar Whigs and their notions of change. This time the great and the good flocked to his side as well, in stark contrast to Bonnie Dundee's experience in 1689 when they had stayed away in droves.

From far and wide, great names and their warriors answered the call: Camerons of Lochiel, Campbells of Breadalbane and Glenlyon, Frasers, Gordons, MacDonalds of Clanranald, MacKenzies, MacLeans, MacLeods. The town of Inverness, too, rose in support of the Pretender. There were also many clans, Presbyterians like Gunn, MacKay, Munro, Ross, that stayed away, and the rising in the north-west was not uniform by any means. Support for Mar was strongest in the Episcopalian north-east: Aberdeen declared for the Jacobites along with all the burghs north of the River Tay. In Brechin, James Maule, 4th Earl of Panmure summoned the populace in support of James VIII and III. James Carnegie, 5th Earl of Southesk rose too, as did James Ogilvy, soon to be Earl of Airlie, John Lyon, 5th Earl of Strathmore and Kinghorne and George Keith, 10th Earl Marischal of Scotland.

In that special way of civil wars, families were split across the Jacobite blade. John Murray, 1st Duke of Atholl and chief of Clan Murray, was a Hanoverian to the marrow of his bones. But three of his sons, Charles, George and William, declared for James and rallied an Atholl Brigade ready to fight alongside Mar. (George Murray – Lord George Murray – would later command the Jacobite army of the Young Pretender in 1745–6.)

Even when considering family loyalties – or the lack of them – there is room for confusing 'what ifs': wily chieftains were not above betting on both horses, and in some cases sons were commanded to fight on the opposite side from their fathers. By this strategy, the family estates would be retained by whoever ended up backing the winner.

With the sound of all these proud Scottish names ringing in the ears, it is all too seductive to imagine their only inspiration was patriotism. In truth, it was naked self-interest that drove many of the chiefs. The Camerons of Lochiel, like the MacLeods and the MacDonalds of Glencoe, had been unhappy since 1688. Having prospered under James VII and II, they had been cold-shouldered for more than a generation. Power had grown increasingly distant, centralised in far-off London. The return of the king meant the chance to reclaim past glory and influence.

The job of turning back the Jacobite tide fell to John Campbell, 2nd Duke of Argyll and Scotland's commander-in-chief. He was a military realist and realised that, while Mar was riding at the head of an army 10,000-strong, he himself had no hopes of gathering anything as great in the time available to him. The rising had also taken the Hanoverian government by surprise – in no small part because the disbanding of the Scots Privy Council had cost them their eyes and ears north of the Border.

Fortunately for Argyll, Mar vacillated as a general just as he had done as a politician. Though he was in command of a far greater force than that which would rise for Bonnie Prince Charlie thirty years later, though Episcopalian preachers were occupying Presbyterian pulpits and preaching rebellion, and despite the fact that Jacobites in the north of England were cheering him on – still he managed to make a mess of the whole affair.

Argyll had earned his spurs fighting for Marlborough during the War of the Spanish Succession and knew by training as well as by instinct what needed to be done. Stirling had always been the pinch-point through which any large force had to pass en route to the north or the south of Scotland. Wallace had exploited the fact in 1297, as had the Bruce in 1314. Argyll knew it too and while Mar hesitated at Perth he marched his force into position at Sheriffmuir, near Dunblane and close by Stirling itself.

On 13 November 1715, one day before government troops would mop up the remains of the English rising at Preston, Mar finally confronted his foe. Argyll was outnumbered by at least two to one but he was a soldier against a dilettante. As it turned out, the battle itself was inconclusive, but it was Argyll who held the field at the close of play. Mar fled back to Perth.

Perhaps Mar's initial indecision had stemmed from uncertainty about what the French would or would not do to back him. Since the death of Louis XIV France had been ruled by Phillipe duc d'Orléans, regent and great-uncle of the young Louis XV. Since he was conniving to have himself recognised as an heir to his nephew's throne, Orléans had as much to gain but arguably more to lose through overt support of the Pretender. In the end he sent nothing and no one to aid Mar.

In late December, around the time when James himself was en route from Dunkirk to the port of Peterhead in belated support of his own rebellion, Philip of Spain put a fortune in gold aboard a ship bound for

Scotland. The bad luck that was ever James's travelling companion saw to it that the vessel was wrecked off St Andrews, its precious cargo soon to be scooped from the surf by jubilant Hanoverian soldiers.

James made landfall on 22 December but by then it was all over bar the shouting. For a few weeks he presided over a court of sorts at Scone, and by February was reduced to sending begging letters to Orléans, in hope of help that would never be sent. On the 26th of the month he boarded a ship at Montrose, along with Mar, and returned once more into exile.

In hindsight, the failure of it all seems astonishing. Had Mar been gifted with the merest sense of how to fight a campaign rather than just lead a parade, he could easily have moved past Argyll to link up with English Jacobites and Catholics in the north of England. The resultant momentum might well have brushed the Hanoverians from power, ready for James's triumphant arrival. Instead, the government had been blessed by luck once more and the last real chance of Jacobite victory had passed.

The view from the twenty-first century is all very well but the fact is that in the aftermath of 'The '15', the men of the British Establishment were badly rattled. They knew how close their regime had come to being over-thrown, how big a part good fortune had had to play. But while they fretted about what James might do next, other forces – almost undetectable and probably unrecognisable as such to all but the most visionary – were starting to undermine the Jacobite cause in its very heartland, in Scotland herself. These were intellectual inquiry and the seeds of free market economy.

Just four years after the débâcle at Sheriffmuir, James would be drawn into another attempt to foment rebellion in the land of his fathers. This time the Pretender, Scotland and the Jacobites were mere pawns in a bigger game involving such disparate players as Spain, Sweden, Austria, Russia, Turkey and Italy.

This exploitation of Scotland, by far greater powers, was as cynical as it was half-hearted. Spain wanted to reclaim control of parts of Italy lost in the War of the Spanish Succession, but found herself opposed by Austria and Britain. As part of a plan of almost Byzantine complexity, Spain sought the self-interested collusion of the Russians and the Turks as well as the military might of crack Swedish troops led by their tactically brilliant King Charles XII.

It was really only Scotland's geographical location facing Sweden across the North Sea that had brought her to the attention of the Spanish in the first place. Swedish ships were patrolling the water, prowling around after

Hanoverian vessels. Since a Jacobite rising would be a useful irritant to throw in the face of an already preoccupied British government, opportunistic plans were duly laid. They culminated in James Francis Edward arriving in Spain in hopes of leading a venture as quixotic as anything ever attempted by the Man of La Mancha.

As things turned out, Spain was as far as he got. A combined Spanish-Jacobite force made a nuisance of itself in his name. Eilean Donan Castle was briefly garrisoned by Spaniards before being pounded to rubble by the guns of the British Navy. Spain had made noises about Jacobites rising in their tens of thousands, of wholesale rebellion, but it was cynical and empty talk. As could have been predicted, the whole dreamy fiasco arrived at a dead end – this time in a battle in the steep-sided valley of Glenshiel, on 10 June 1719.

All the assembled Highlanders could do was fight bravely, standing up to artillery and well-drilled Hanoverian musketry as well as any regular army could have done. But, as ever, it was not enough – could never have been enough – and Jacobite dreams blew away on the Highland breeze. James had never even put in an appearance and had stayed in Spain until advised by his hosts that his presence was no longer welcome.

His only success of 1719, and even that was qualified, was marriage to a woman who would bear him heirs. Maria Clementina Sobieski was the 17-year-old granddaughter of King John III Sobieski of Poland. Not only did she offer the prospect of producing more Stuart boys to continue the family line, she also brought a huge dowry including millions of French francs and a famous collection of family jewellery, the Sobieski Rubies. For a court in exile, therefore, she mattered every bit as much for her money as for her breeding capacity.

The marriage was an unhappy one and James a faithless husband, but it did deliver an heir. On 31 December 1720 Clementina gave birth to Charles Edward Louis John Casimir Silvester Severino Maria and, on 11 March 1725, Henry Benedict. Whatever other failings he might have had, whatever bad luck, James at least upheld that most notable tradition of Stuart men – the ability to make more of their kind. But while the Jacobite adventure was far from over, James Francis Edward would never again contemplate travelling to Scotland. As a wedding present from the Pope the couple had received a palace in Rome and it was there they stayed, where their boys were born and where the pale shadow of the Stuart court now took ineffectual root, a dynastic tumbleweed in search of moisture.

Of greater significance than the strength of James's appetite for continuing the fight, however, was the advent of better times in Scotland. Far away from his baleful, backward-facing influence, Scots had begun to see at last the benefits of union with England.

It was true to say that for a decade and more after 1707 the promised economic miracle had failed to materialise. Protective tariffs, which had enabled traditional domestic products like beer, linen, paper and wool to turn modest profits, had been swept away under the terms of the treaty. Hardship only increased for many.

Taxes increased significantly as well and in 1725 the Westminster parliament committed the unpardonable sin of hitting Scots where they would really feel it. A heavy new tax on malt – vital to the production of beer and whisky – provoked the kind of response any Scotsman could have warned them about. There were wholesale riots in Glasgow and throughout the burghs as the locals realised the price of booze was going up. Viewed in the longer term, however, these were no more than the pains of labour, and what was being born north of the Border was a new understanding.

In January 1776, in a pamphlet he called *Common Sense*, Thomas Paine would inspire revolution in the hearts of Americans. Among many other memorable phrases contained within its few pages is the statement 'That government is best which governs least' – and it is a truth self-evident that Scotland's physical distance from the lawmakers of Westminster was to make all the difference.

What gradually began to dawn on many Scots was the realisation that they were too far away from the London-centric government to attract much of its attention. This delivered what might be called a double whammy. Rabble-rousing by a few Jacobites notwithstanding, Scotland in the late 1720s began to enjoy the kind of peace and stability that is felt only in the shadow of a strong state. And at the same time Scots were so forgotten by that state they were free to shape their own independent identity.

The desperate hardships caused by the famines of the late 1690s began to slip from memory as agriculture recovered and food shortages turned to surpluses. International markets were opened to Scots merchants and soon the smell of imported tobacco became familiar in the docks of Glasgow. There were other luxurious foreign products as well – cotton, molasses, sugar, tea – and Aberdeen, Ayr, Edinburgh, Greenock and Paisley began to reap the benefits.

It was among the landowning nobility that livings were most obviously improved at first, but as the second decade of the eighteenth century drew to a close all of Scotland began to be enriched to a greater or lesser extent by exposure to the wider world. Life began to get better for the many as well as for the few.

There had been a severe adjustment to be made by many nobles. Since 1707 only a few had held seats in parliament, and for those now spending a great deal of time in London there was much to get used to. For a start they needed money to maintain themselves in suitable style in the capital and this would fundamentally alter the way they regarded their estates back home, and the folk living on them. Scots chiefs with careers and homes in London began to see their clans as tenants and sources of income rather than as people for whom they bore any kind of paternal responsibility. For those formerly great names left behind by Westminster, there were also decisions to be made – about whether it was best to trust to the regime of the present or to look over their shoulders, and over the water, at the regimes of the past.

Two of Scotland's universities began to modernise as tutors opened students' eyes and minds to emergent subjects like law, mathematics and medicine. In Glasgow and Edinburgh, the teaching of theology – for so long the root of the rod used to beat Scots – became less certain and more questioning, perhaps more optimistic as well. As more modern, more liberal ideas travelled north, theological thought began freeing itself from the fire and brimstone of Calvinist dogma and to embrace ideas like 'Latitudinarianism', in which tolerance was a key virtue. As a by-product, support for Hanoverian union began to grow in those cities. (Aberdeen University, deep in Episcopalian country, remained a hotbed of Jacobitism.)

This new Scotland was very much the achievement of the remarkable post-union politician Archibald Campbell, Lord Islay, later the 3rd Duke of Argyll and leader of the mighty Campbell clan. His grandfather had led the Scottish end of the abortive Monmouth Rebellion of 1685 and his father had been the Argyll who denied Mar at Sheriffmuir. This younger Argyll was a politician rather than a warrior.

Entering the Westminster stage in 1722, a year after Robert Walpole became Prime Minister, Lord Islay would spend the next forty years exerting a powerful and positive influence over his homeland. From the point of view of some, he was the King of Scotland in all but name. He championed improvements in the linen industry, which enriched himself; but also sought to drive Scotland as a whole towards an industrious and profitable future. When Glasgow rioted about the Malt Tax in 1725 it was Lord Islay, Lord Chief Justice by then, who was sent north to pacify the city, and the country.

Lord Islay also understood very clearly that the universities were key and he was able to use his huge influence to place men of whom he approved into key positions in Edinburgh and in Glasgow. Among his most notable recruits was Francis Hutcheson. Lord Islay saw to it that Hutcheson was given the Chair of Moral Philosophy at Glasgow University, where he established himself as a founding father of what would become the Scottish Enlightenment.

Hutcheson, a preacher and a preacher's son, believed all human beings understood the difference between right and wrong without having to be told. He also championed personal liberty and taught that every man had the right to 'exert his power, according to his own judgement and inclination, for these purposes, in all such industry, labour or amusements, as are not hurtful to others in their persons or goods'. That such sentiments were coming from the Chair of Moral Philosophy in Glasgow University – and that all of this was practically within living memory of the Killing Times – is a measure of how time had moved on.

Hutcheson was a true liberal, who believed happiness was deserved by all beings, that it was to be sought out and that it was always the reward for helping others and advancing society. As Scotland progressed through the eighteenth century, so the desire of her people for free, productive, happy lives moved forward too.

Looming in the background all the while was the spectre of Jacobitism, and the Hanoverian government was at pains to try and exorcise it once and for all. Ironically, but inevitably, the same philosophical advances that sought to increase and protect the rights of all individuals protected some of the rights of Jacobites too.

Government attempts to seize the estates and property of those who had risen in 1715 and 1719 were often thwarted by the courts. 'Forfeiture' was standard practice by governments across Europe when faced with rebellious nobles, yet in Scotland it came up against staunch and intelligent opposition. Lawyers and judges who were themselves landowners or even lairds were hardly likely to collude with politicians seeking to strip landed property from any other individuals – even Jacobites. Landowners are usually conservative by nature and those employed in the legal profession baulked at the mere suggestion of giving governments such draconian powers,

powers that might one day be used against themselves and their families. Time and time again attempts at forfeiture were stymied.

Also unsuccessful was the 'Disarming Act' of 1716. The logic of it had been simple enough: demand the surrender of all swords, shields, muskets, dirks and pistols and the rebels will have nothing to fight with. But in practice it was only Whig clans loyal to the government that actually gave up their weapons, while those with Jacobite tendencies offered only broken relics, many of which had been imported cheaply from the Continent for the very purpose of fooling the government's agents.

Simon Fraser of Lovat, who had helped recapture Inverness from the rebels during 'The '15', suggested the Highlands might be made more manageable if there were better roads and bridges for government armies to march along. In 1725 Major-General George Wade, commander-in-chief, was duly dispatched to build them, along with a series of forts, barracks and other strong points.

For the next fifteen years he set to with a will and a workforce and the 250-mile network he constructed was an impressive achievement. His greatest single stretch was the 80 miles linking Inverness to Dunkeld and today everyone in Scotland knows it was General Wade who laid the first all-weather roads across the country. But the crushing irony was that the only armies ever to use them in a time of war were those raised for the last Jacobite rebellion, in 1745.

Long before Charles Edward Stuart thought about leading a rebellion, Jacobitism had become more the stuff of legend and fantasy than anything functioning in the real world. There were still in Scotland, as in the rest of Britain, those who enjoyed the thrill of considering themselves Jacobite. But for most of them it was a daring affectation, a claim to be made among friends after one too many drinks. Instead of bearing arms and raising standards, Jacobites in Scotland in the 1730s and 1740s collected wine glasses inscribed with rebellious slogans and used them for ostentatious toasts to 'the king over the water'. There was even a custom of placing a bowl of water on the table so that the Pretender's right to the throne might be invoked in public by silently raising one's glass above it when drinking the health of 'the King'.

There was something of the legend of King Arthur about it all. Jacobites hoped their rightful king might return because he was needed, because his time had come – but without them having actually to risk anything to make it happen. After all, the Stuarts had returned once before, in 1660; was it wrong to hope they might do the same again? But the truth of that matter was that Charles II had only been granted leave to return and claim his headless father's thrones because there had been no one else available. Now a new ruling house was established in London and showing no signs whatever of backing down in the face of any claimant, however rightful. George II had replaced his father on the throne in 1727 and the Hanoverian succession – a highly improbable long shot thirty years before – began to look secure.

The last throw of the Stuart dice was occasioned by yet another pan-European war. Just as the War of the Spanish Succession had provided the greater backdrop for Jacobite mischief in 1708, so the War of the Austrian Succession would disturb the same old ghosts in 1745.

From Britain's point of view, it all started with a pickled ear. Richard Jenkins was the master of a brig of Glasgow called the *Rebecca*, which had been trading with Spanish territories in the Carribean. Ever since the signing of the Treaty of Utrecht in 1713 British ships had been entitled to conduct a certain amount of business in the Spanish colonies. But Spain had grown increasingly tired of the incomers and had been accused of high-handed behaviour towards legitimate vessels and their crews.

In 1739 Jenkins turned up in front of a parliamentary committee in London claiming Spanish coastguards had boarded his ship in 1731. He said a Spanish captain had attacked him with a knife and cut off his ear. He then showed the committee members his mutilated skull and even produced the ear, preserved in a jar of brine.

By some accounts Jenkins was little more than a privateer at best and a common criminal at worst. The Spanish were certainly of the opinion that they were dealing with the latter. It made no difference in London. There was instant uproar and on 19 October 1739 Walpole declared war on Spain. There were some early naval successes for Britain, but nothing conclusive. So when Frederick the Great of Prussia invaded Austria and Hungary the following year – to dispute the inheritance of Empress Maria Theresa, which had been settled by the terms of the Treaty of Utrecht – Spain joined France in supporting him. Britain backed Austria and her empress and all at once Jenkins's Ear was deafened by something altogether louder.

Jacobites in Scotland celebrated the news that two of their favourite supporters – France and Spain – were once more ready to take up the cudgels against Hanoverian Britain. Strictly speaking, France and Britain had not actually declared war on one another. Their armies would turn up on battlefields – the Hanoverian forces in support of Austria, the French in support of Spain – but each would insist they were only there in the capacity of 'auxiliaries'.

It was farcical; and after George II led a combined force of British, Hanoverian and Austrian troops to victory over a French force at the Battle of Dettingen, in south-west Germany, on 27 June 1743, it was clear to Louis XV that he had to come up with a diversion to get Britain off his back. As kings of France invariably did in the eighteenth century, when they needed breathing space for their own objectives, Louis promptly approached James Francis Edward Stuart.

James was too old and too bored of the whole tiresome, sordid exercise to get involved directly, but on 23 December 1743 he passed the buck and made his eldest son, Charles Edward, Prince Regent. This handsome, personable twenty-three-year-old, who had never seen Scotland nor ever led men into battle, was now the figurehead of an entire movement. Like all the other Jacobite rebellions Charles's campaign would be fought in the hope of putting his father on the throne, but his was the name that would be remembered best at the end of it all.

France offered up thousands of fighting men and the ships and boats to transport them. The excited talk was of a full-scale invasion and was loud enough to carry all the way across the Channel. By the time the boats left Dunkirk in February 1744, with Charles himself aboard one of them, the British Navy was ready for them. Before the ships of the line had to engage them, however, a storm got the job done. French boats were sunk, scores of lives were lost and the surviving transports, including Charles's, had no option but to limp back to France.

It should all have ended there. So many lives might have been spared if Charles had listened more and talked less. But he was headstrong, and the son of the son of a king. Despite Louis insisting there would be no more French invasions, that the soldiers who had survived the abortive crossing would now be committed to fighting George's troops on land, Charles set out to lead an invasion of his very own.

By early 1745 the Young Pretender had begged and borrowed enough French money to arm and equip two ships, an 18-gun brig *Le du Teillay* and a much larger, 64-gun frigate called *L'Elisabeth*. Much of his fighting fund had been raised by pawning the fabled Sobieski Rubies and with some of the proceeds he bought muskets, broadswords, a few artillery pieces and the services of several hundred fighting men. He sent word to Jacobites in

Scotland that he planned to lead them in revolt – causing disbelief among all those made privy to the escapade – and then climbed aboard *Le du Teillay.*

Alarm bells started ringing as soon as the ships left Belle Île, but Charles was not listening. A British man-o'-war, HMS *Lyon*, was onto them almost at once and so badly damaged *L'Elisabeth* it had to turn back. At a stroke Charles had lost almost all his fighting men and the bulk of his armaments. Somehow undeterred, he ordered *Le du Teillay* to sail on, finally reaching the tiny island of Eriskay, between South Uist and Barra, in the Western Isles of Scotland, on 23 July 1745.

Legend has it that as he stepped onto the island and took his first steps in the land of his forefathers, he pulled from his pocket a cotton handkerchief. Seeds of a flower called pink sea bindweed had been trapped in its folds and fell then among the sand and grasses of a point known today as Coilleag a Phrionnsa, or the Prince's Strand. The flower was foreign to the islands, just as Charles was. The blooms would remain, but he would not.

He was met first by Alexander MacDonald of Boisdale, who simply told him to go home. Charles famously replied, 'I am come home.' Boisdale stuck out his chin and refused to have anything more to do with the mad enterprise – and said Norman MacLeod of MacLeod and Sir Alexander MacDonald of Sleat, the two great chiefs of Skye, would tell him the same. Charles simply climbed back aboard *Le du Teillay* and sailed across to mainland Scotland, down Loch nan Uamh between Arisaig and Moidart. According to more of the legend, the locals looked up from their fields and saw the prince and seven supporters aboard the ship. So pleased were these folk that they began at once to dance – a dance known ever after as 'The Seven Men of Moidart'.

Charles stayed aboard ship while a succession of local worthies was rowed out to meet him and give their reactions to his plans. Chiefs like MacDonald of Glencoe and MacDonnell of Keppoch were bellicose enough, but lacked the strength in numbers Charles required; more importantly, they lacked the gravitas as well. It fell to young Donald Cameron of Lochiel, remembered as 'the gentle Lochiel', to make or break the prince's dreams. He alone had the clout to make something happen.

No one knows what was said, what arguments Charles rehearsed and what replies he received, but it is tempting to speculate. He would certainly have reminded them all that the House of Hanover had paid scant attention recently to the defence of Scotland. Despite all General Wade's commendable endeavour – the roads, the fortresses of Augustus, Bernera, William and Ruthven Barracks – King George had never added the fighting men. More concerned about fighting in France, he had emptied the Highland forts and ferried the troops across the Channel. Taking the kingdom by little more than a determined show of bravado, Charles said, was at least a possibility.

He might also have known that gentle Lochiel, for all his surface grandeur, was living in reduced circumstances. The horrors of famine and want were close at hand in the Highlands in the 1740s and the ghosts of the 1690s stalked the land. Despite poor harvests, the descent into the abyss was eventually avoided but in 1745 people were struggling. Lochiel's coffers, like those of many of his peers, would have been all but empty as tenants avoided the rent and no one had the money to buy cattle, a mainstay of the Highland economy.

It seems to me that in Scotland, away from the tortured intrigues of Europe, the driving force of rebellion was simple. What it came down to – what 'The '45' was about and what every Jacobite rebellion after 1708 had been about – was singling out the have-nots and promising they could get it all back, whatever *it* was.

Long before 1745 Scotland was splitting – in fact *had* split – into two societies. There were those on the road to becoming 'North Britons', who had tasted the fruits of union and found them to their liking. During the Glasgow riot against the Malt Tax, the home of Daniel Campbell of Shawfield had been razed to the ground. He was one of the first of that legendary cadre of Glasgow merchants who would become known as the 'Tobacco Lords' on account of the scarcely believable fortunes they reaped from imports from Virginia. Men like Campbell – and there were plenty more in cities and towns like Glasgow, Edinburgh, Ayr and Aberdeen – were hardly likely to back any movement pledged to disrupt the status quo, especially when it proved intent on destroying their property. They might not all be enjoying the stellar wealth of a Tobacco Lord, but they were making good livings on the back of English trading links and had no time for the bad old days.

On the other side, prey for the Jacobite salesmen, were those left behind. Those who knew how power and prestige might trickle down to them and their ilk from the courts of autocratic kings. They still held the fates and lives of their tenants in their clenched fists and so could compel their

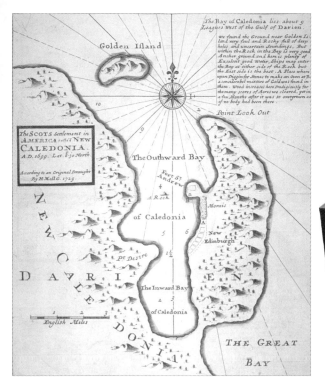
A map of the Darien plantation

A Darien money chest

James Francis Edward Stuart –
'The Old Pretender'

Bonnie Prince Charlie

The Battle of Culloden

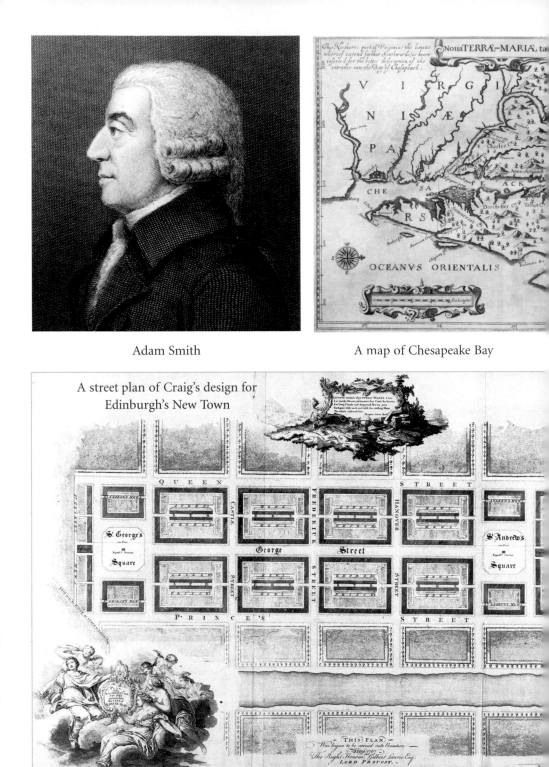

Adam Smith

A map of Chesapeake Bay

A street plan of Craig's design for
Edinburgh's New Town

Sir Walter Scott

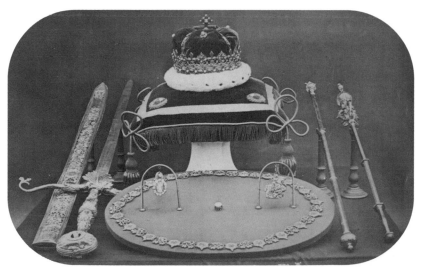

The Scottish crown jewels

The National Wallace Monument, Stirling

Ninteenth-century Glasgow slums

Red Clydeside

Hugh MacDiarmid

The Ravenscraig steel works

Margaret Thatcher when Prime Minister

The Scottish Parliament building, Edinburgh

obedience to any cause, on pain of eviction or death. It was a central plank of 'The '15' and 'The '45' that a restored Stuart monarchy would do away with the union once and for all; indeed, 'No Union' became a battle cry. Jacobitism versus the champions and products of Hanoverian union was a war of worlds, of past and future.

Shortly after the Jacobite standard was finally raised at Glenfinnan, at the head of Loch Shiel on 19 August 1745, Lochiel came in with his men. Some of the usual suspects were there as well – MacDonald of Morar, Clanranald, MacDonnell of Keppoch – but there were not and never would be anything like enough. By the time Charles began to head south, he had no more than 2,500 Highlanders alongside him. The lesson of previous risings was that there was nothing to be gained from delay, from hanging around in the Highlands waiting for the French to make any kind of move. So they began to march. The real miracle of 'The '45' was that so much was accomplished by so few.

Those who joined him were also the victims of a kind of confidence trick. Before he arrived in the Highlands, Charles had promised he would be accompanied by thousands of French soldiers and the ships and money to support them. It was plain to even the most dewy-eyed Jacobite chief that none of that had materialised. Charles was convinced French help would come once he had demonstrated the successful potential of his rising – and it seems he sold this delusion to the men now pledged to fight and die for him.

Against all the odds, he even managed to deliver some astonishing successes. Within a month his motley mob had captured Edinburgh and Charles was taking time out to look at the portraits of his ancestors hanging in the Palace of Holyroodhouse. The government garrison had abandoned the castle in advance of the Jacobites' arrival, but it was as out of date as the Highlanders, with obselete guns and no use at all for defending the capital.

The luckless government commander tasked with dealing with the problem was General Sir John Cope, but he had fewer than 4,000 men with whom to mount the defence of the whole country. On 21 September 1745 a surprise attack by howling Highlanders completely routed Cope's force at the Battle of Prestonpans and sent them running for their lives.

It had been a victory for the Highland charge, for nerve, and for the military skills of Lord George Murray, Charles's supremely talented and brave commander. But for the government it had been a defeat brought about by inaction and absent-mindedness. If George and his government ministers had torn their attentions from France for just a moment, the whole affair might never have got under way in the first place and would never reached as far south as Edinburgh. But all that analysis depended upon the benefits of hindsight. Now Charles had control of the kingdom of Scotland. The wiser heads in this inner circle counselled the wisdom of consolidating their stunning gains. Wait in Edinburgh, they said, dig in and call upon the French to put their money and men where their mouths had once been.

The Young Pretender, though, would not be deterred from the chance of the ultimate prize – of marching into London and making his victory complete – and used all his powers of persuasion to carry the decision by a single vote. With a combined infantry and cavalry force now numbering just over 5,000, Charles crossed the Border. Apparently his Highlanders stopped on the English side and turned as one, without need of a command to do so, and saluted their homeland. It was the last time any of them would have sight of the place while there was still hope in their hearts.

Everyone knows the Jacobites got as far as Derby before grinding to a halt. They were within a hundred miles of London but it might as well have been a thousand. Wide awake and angry now, the Hanoverian government had spent the past few weeks recalling thousands of hardened fighting men from the Continent. Vastly superior forces would shortly be brought to bear upon the rebels and suddenly it was harsh reality that punctured the Jacobite dream.

Charles was furious, driven to tears of frustration and disappointment, but older heads successfully argued for a wholesale withdrawal back towards Scotland. The return trip was a miserable nightmare for all concerned. The soldiers had not been above using force to take what food and other supplies they had needed on the way down. Communities that had been roughly used by the Jacobites just weeks before therefore had no sympathy whatever for the dejected lines that trooped past their doors now. In Glasgow the populace raised a militia to defy the Young Pretender; they would later join up with the pro-government forces that soon retook Edinburgh for the Hanoverian crown.

Charles and his men made it all the way to Falkirk before the pursuit of a government army under Lieutenant-General Henry Hawley forced them to turn and fight on 17 January 1746. And fight they did. Hawley – known as 'Hanging Hawley' for his merciless discipline – was soundly thrashed.

The rout and slaughter of his men might have been total, but a fog descended and enabled the survivors to make a run for it.

Success on Falkirk Muir was the last hurrah for the Jacobites of 'The '45'. Charles then pulled back all the way to Inverness, a Jacobite stronghold that had to be defended at all costs, and prepared to deal with whatever was coming. It duly arrived in the corpulent form of William, Duke of Cumberland, youngest son of George II, and more than 9,000 foot and horse.

If you wanted to compose a disaster for a Jacobite army stiffened by Highlanders in the middle years of the eighteenth century, you could not do better than think up the circumstances of Drummossie Moor, by Culloden on 16 April 1746.

On the night of 15 April the Jacobites had attempted a surprise attack on Cumberland's camp outside nearby Nairn. It had been a dismal failure but it had utterly exhausted Charles's men just the same. On the morning of 16 April, against all the advice of Lord George Murray and other experienced soldiers, Charles had ordered his wearied men (those who had bothered to rouse themselves from sleep, that is) to line up across a patch of flat, boggy land.

Since the days of Colkitto and Montrose a century before, it had been understood that the legendary and lethal Highland charge worked when deployed by surprise, or downhill, or both. Yet there they were, at one end of a lumpy, sodden field, watching while a modern military machine ground towards them, its every move co-ordinated by the beat of drums. Asked what he thought the prospects were of forthcoming events, Lord George Murray said, 'We are putting an end to a bad affair.'

The proceedings were got under way with an artillery bombardment by well drilled and trained government guns. Experts argue to this day about just how long the Jacobites stood in the face of the round shot and grape, but after something between a few moments and an hour they charged towards their tormentors. Some of them made it in amongst the government ranks and managed vengeful butchery with broadswords and dirk, but it was hopeless.

The government soldiers had been taught a new technique for handling charging Highlanders, namely to attack the man to the right instead of the man directly in front. If whole ranks maintained this discipline – ramming fixed bayonets into men's sides in the moment they were exposed by upraised sword arms – then the charge could be utterly galled. And so it was.

Cumberland's victory was as complete as his persecution of the rebels in the aftermath was merciless. Despite the scale and the nature of the defeat, still the surviving Jacobites had refused to go away. Regrouping at Ruthven Barracks, they were even prepared to counter-attack until word came in from the prince himself, telling them to preserve their lives by going home.

Cumberland planted a whole army in the Highlands and spent the next months burning, pillaging and killing. Clearly the Highland clans were the backbone of rebellion and had to be broken and destroyed to prevent any survival of Stuart hopes. There was a renewal of the Disarming Act and punitive measures like the banning of the plaid and even the Gaelic language itself. However practical the means, the objective was the final destruction of the Gaelic culture. The Highlands had always been 'different' and in that difference were presumed to be the very roots of Jacobitism. Nothing must be allowed to remain that might enable any regrowth.

After months on the run, the Young Pretender stepped aboard a ship bound for France in September 1746. He would never see Scotland again, nor give it much thought either. He lived a largely dissolute and aimless life, pleasing neither himself nor his family for most of the time. He died in Rome on 30 January 1788, in the same palace in which he had been born.

The fact was that time and progress had overtaken the Jacobite dinosaur long before Cumberland and his ilk set about savaging the clans. In the Lowlands, across the central belt and southwards towards England itself, support for the Jacobite cause had been desperately thin; it was an anachronistic fairy tale that few believed in any more. English Jacobites, who had been full of bravado before the rising, had utterly failed to replace words with action when the musket balls started flying.

What Wade had begun in 1725 was now completed. By 1767 there were over 1,000 miles of roads penetrating deep into the Highlands. Cumberland had slaked his appetite for bloodletting and headed south long before, towards an impressive military career. He left behind his nickname of 'Bloody Butcher' and, by the time he arrived in London, found it replaced by calls of 'Sweet William'. In his place was Cumberland's personal friend William Anne, 2nd Earl of Albemarle. Years later Albemarle would yet be lamenting the fact that Jacobite attitudes still festered and spread pointlessly through the old heartlands, and even into the central and southern Highlands. In practical terms, though, Jacobitism was a spent force and everyone knew it.

As well as out-and-out brutality, the Crown returned to the practice of confiscating the estates and property of known rebels. They were more successful in this regard than they had been after 1715, but the heart had anyway largely been torn out of the Jacobite nobility.

There was some success in encouraging the voices of proper Protestant ministers to drown out those of the Episcopalian rabble-rousers of old. All across the land, Presbyterian ministers were in full flood, demonising Charles as an Italian from Rome, the very home of Popery, and his supporters as acolytes of the devil. And what state-sponsored religion could not accomplish, surely the offer of material gain through honest labour would?

A new merchant class in Glasgow and throughout the southern towns and burghs was uninterested in Jacobitism. Only those with nothing to lose had rallied to the royal standard of the Stuarts, and the wind of change had blown too strong and too cold through their patched cloaks and darned stockings.

It was not all horror and punishment in the Highlands. During the 1750s there would be concerted, government-sponsored initiatives to stimulate the economy of the region. 'Improvement' became a watchword of landowners, and not just those north of the Highland line. All across the country there were attempts to improve and modernise the techniques of agriculture – upon which the bulk of the population still depended for employment and for life itself. Some of it worked, but some did not – hampered in part by a not always constructive desire to tidy the place up a bit. In the Highlands, the push towards crofting was an often unwelcome intrusion and disruption of ancient practices.

The government was more uniformly successful in harnessing and re-directing the warrior mentality of the Highland men. After Culloden, the fighting men who had once been so feared and hated by the House of Hanover became its most effective weapons. Now fighting on the government side, the Highland regiments would become legendary and would carve their names indelibly into the story of the British Empire.

The future had arrived in Scotland, a future made of union and trade and of pounds, shillings and pence. For Jacobitism – for Scotland herself – what had mattered in the end was what always makes the difference: the bottom line.

CHAPTER NINE

MONEY!

'For what shall it profit a man, if he shall gain the whole world, and
lose his own soul?'

The Gospel according to St Mark

There had been English attempts at colonising the New World of the
Americas since the time of Elizabeth I. She had asked Walter Raleigh to
take charge of the project and in 1587 just over 100 English souls established
a settlement at Roanoke, south of Albermarle Sound in the territory of
modern North Carolina. They did not last long in their new home, but
were of course only the first of many.

Jamestown was set up, in what is now Virginia, in 1607, and Popham
Colony began to find its feet in Maine three years after that. Some of
those early footfalls became permanent; others were overcome by hardship,
disease or the local natives and disappeared. The point is that by the time
the *Mayflower* arrived in Plymouth, New England, in 1620, the New World
was hardly new to the English.

Between 1630 and 1640 there was a flood of English newcomers, all of
them driven from their homes by religious persecution. Perhaps as many
as 100,000 Puritans scattered themselves in colonies in New England and
also in the Caribbean. Some attempted – unsuccessfully in the long run –
to make homes along Nicaragua's Mosquito Coast, but it was to places
like Barbados that most early settlers headed. Apparently prizing liberty
above all things, the early settlers made the hazardous crossing to the
Americas so that they might be free to live and worship as they saw fit.
Before the middle of the seventeenth century some of those champions
of freedom were making themselves rich by buying, selling and generally

exploiting black Africans. The abused grow up to become abusers.

In the early years of the American colonies all servants – black, white or brown – were commonly known as slaves. Those whose crossings had been paid for by wealthy colonists were termed 'indentured' servants, so called because their contracts were folded and creased in the middle – 'indented' – and then torn in half along the line. The master kept one part, the servant the other. The same rules were applied to the Africans at first, with hopes of eventual freedom after the completion of a fixed term of labour. But gradually they were seen as too useful and too plentiful ever to be set free. Thus was the slave trade born and the supposedly God-fearing, freedom-loving Puritans were quickly in the thick of it.

Other European nations would witness an exodus to the west in the seventeenth century – Germany, France and the Low Countries among others – but by the start of the 1700s the English parliament was becoming concerned about the steady haemorrhage of their fit, useful men and women to the colonies and had begun to discourage them. Fortunately for the colonies, any shortfall of fresh blood was about to be met from the populations of Scotland and Ulster.

Scots were no strangers to the New World either by 1700. As early as 1621, during the reign of James VI and I, a Scots colony had been established in 'Nova Scotia': Newfoundland in Canada. The effort foundered, however, and within a decade the French had absorbed the territory and its Scots. By the 1680s Lowland Scots began to arrive in the North American colonies in considerable numbers. They brought both their Presbyterian and Epis-copalian faiths and established themselves in prominent positions within the fledgeling society. Several became colonial governors.

It was during the middle years of the eighteenth century that Lowland Scots – and Scots-Irish from Ulster – began to wash across the colonies in a great wave. Famine, or the threat of it, was the spur for the first of the Ulster Protestants and from the 1720s onwards they amounted to a veritable flood of humanity.

A quarter of a million or so Scots-Irish made the perilous ocean crossing and then penetrated deeply into the west and south of the new lands, to Pennsylvania, to North and South Carolina and beyond. It was not famine that was pushing them across the Atlantic by then – rather the promise of land to be bought and fought for and riches to be made. Fierce they were too, at least as far as their new neighbours were concerned. As the middle fifty years of the century wore on, the Scots-Irish developed and maintained a reputation for hard work, hard drinking, uncompromising religious certainty and a determination to sort out any disputes with fists, blades and guns. Their rabid brand of Presbyterianism had survived a century in Ulster in an undiluted form. It was as though a cutting from John Knox's personal tree of faith had been transported across the Irish Sea at the start of the seventeenth century. Kept sheltered from any subsequent wishy-washy liberalism, it had grown into something impossibly tough and unyielding.

They brought it with them, root and branch, when they travelled to the Americas and there established a reputation for fire and brimstone outdoor prayer meetings. These were the spiritual offspring of the conventicles that had caused so much trouble during the years of Covenanting and the Killing Times – and they sowed the seeds of the big-tent, revivalist tradition that is so synonymous with the practice of the Protestant faith in the southern states of America today. These Scots-Irish dared to challenge any brand of orthodoxy that attempted to raise its voice within range of their hearing; they taught their neighbours it was possible – indeed right – to challenge authority and in so doing they laid the foundations for the American Revolution itself.

The last of the Scots to leave and cross the Atlantic were the Highlanders, survivors of a world finally destroyed after 1746. Just as the Scots-Irish had brought with them an old-fashioned form of the Protestant religion, so the Highlanders carried another relic. In the case of the MacDonalds, MacDougalls, MacGregors, MacLeods, MacRaes and the rest of the thousands of Gaelic-speakers who settled in the Carolinas and beyond during the second half of the century, it was a memory of the old Stewart Scotland they transplanted.

One of those who took ship for the Americas in the early days was a teenager named John Wedderburn. He had joined his father, also John, in rising on behalf of Charles Edward Stuart. Wedderburn senior, a Perthshire baronet, was fighting as a Colonel in the Jacobite army when he was captured by government forces at Culloden and dragged off to London for imprisonment and trial. Young John, having managed to survive the butchery of that sordid battle, secretly witnessed his father's subsequent gory execution for treason – by hanging, drawing and quartering – before fleeing the capital. Perhaps, as he swung like a pendulum counting down his own last moments and those of his old world, the man caught a glimpse of the boy. If he did, then the father's eyes would have closed for the last time upon those of a son who belonged – or was condemned – to a new kind of future, one that the elder and his ilk would never rule again.

Cut off from his tainted inheritance, the teenager saw no future in Scotland and made his way instead to the port of Greenock, on Scotland's west coast. It took him some weeks, hiding where he could, sleeping rough and evading government troopers, before he finally made it to the docks. There he approached a ship owner and struck a deal whereby he would work his passage to the Caribbean. It was just a month or so after Culloden and eighteen-year-old John Wedderburn had placed himself among the first of what would shortly become a general exodus of the clans.

By the time Butcher Cumberland was putting the ailing beast of Old Scotland out of its misery, a New Scotland was already experiencing its growing pains. Minister and lecturer Francis Hutcheson, who had succeeded his old master, Gershom Carmichael, in the Chair of Moral Philosophy at Glasgow University in 1729, had been one of the midwives. Of equal importance in the delivery room was the advocate and judge Henry Home, who became Lord Kames, a pioneering philosopher, historian and improving farmer based in Edinburgh. Through their writings and teachings Hutcheson and Kames brought forth the next generation of Scottish Enlightenment figures – men like the philosopher David Hume, the historian William Robertson and the father of modern political economics Adam Smith, whose magnum opus *An Inquiry into the Nature and Causes of the Wealth of Nation*s is still central to the study of the subject today.

As well as an intellectual revolution that self-consciously and deliberately set about advancing human mastery of the arts and literature, biology, chemistry, geology, mathematics, medicine and the rest, its champions believed they were also committed to designing and building a better, more efficient, fairer society. It was nothing less than an effort finally to understand the world, accurately to describe it and then to improve it for the benefit of mankind.

Partly a product of the high levels of literacy amongst Scots of all classes – itself a consequence of Knox's Reformation and his insistence that all people learn to read the Word of God – the light that burned in Scotland's cities during the eighteenth century was brighter than any in the world, and perhaps at any time before or since. It was a light that revealed, in stark and unforgiving relief, the limitations of all that had gone before ... Old Scotland. Ignited first in the universities of Glasgow and Edinburgh, the flame eventually spread out into the lives of Scots in every walk of life. Scottish universities – Glasgow in particular – attracted and welcomed not just the sons of nobility and gentry, but also those of merchants and tradesmen. The sort of people who were still excluded from the universities of Oxford and Cambridge were, by the middle of the eighteenth century in Glasgow, devouring the lectures of men like Hutcheson and then setting out to make their own marks on the world.

While Knox's Reformation had taught everyone to read, it had also applied its own rigid shackles around Scots' lives. These too began to be broken by the teachings of the Scottish Enlightenment, so that the smartest thinkers were able to value the rights and freedoms of their fellow human beings (at least white, usually male human beings of the right sort) and to value them as essentially and fundamentally good. Religious faith was still there, but God was no longer being seen as vengeful and absolutist; neither was he at the centre of everything any more. Inquiry and exploration of the natural world of creation began to take the place of slavish adherence to religious dogma. Steps like these, away from God, were not to everyone's liking.

Hutcheson was an Ulster Scot – Scots-Irish – and the son of a Presbyterian preacher. But from the moment of his arrival to teach in Glasgow he led the way in insisting it was best to treat everyone as someone of value, who should be encouraged to find happiness in helping those around him.

On the other side of the country, in Edinburgh, advocate and judge Lord Kames was coming to a more realistic and practical view of human nature. He was happy to agree with a lot of what Hutcheson had to say about man's innate understanding of right and wrong, about the satisfaction to be had from being and doing and being 'good'. But he also argued that human beings came together to form societies out of a desire to protect their *property*. Men and women – and children too – naturally desire to own more and more things, he said. But no one could sleep safe at night unless their belongings, their property, were safe from theft and damage. For this reason, Kames said, human beings were prepared to create and to submit to laws – to surrender some aspects of their freedom to an overarching society in return for peace of mind regarding their homes and valuables.

Kames was also the first to identify four stages in the development of human societies. Hunter-gatherers were the lowliest, followed by those pastoralist groups that kept herds and flocks of domesticated animals. In these primitive groups, argued Kames, there was no need for the rule of law. Order could be maintained via the discipline of individual fathers over their own families. More sophisticated, and therefore requiring the creation of – and obedience to – systems of laws, was the third form of society: that of the agriculturalists.

Kames argued that farming societies enjoyed a surplus not just of food, but also of time. This spare time enabled the emergence of specialist crafts people who could devote all their time to making the items of property that would be coveted by the rest of society. Even more importantly, arable farming depended upon people co-operating with each other and relating to one another in increasingly complicated ways. These relationships needed to be defined and, as the whole system became increasingly complex, so the members of the group empowered certain individuals to make decisions on behalf of the many. Here were the seeds of legal systems and of government – of 'society' itself.

In the fourth and final stage, according to Kames, society moved beyond the fields and enabled the growth and organisation of interconnected villages, towns and cities devoted to industry, trade and commerce. Here was the environment within which true civilisation could grow and so enrich the lives of its people.

These philosophies of life, developed by Hutcheson, Kames and their contemporaries, had taken root in Glasgow, Edinburgh and Aberdeen. Soon they spread far beyond, becoming part of what underpinned the thinking of the New Scotland. James Hutton, from Edinburgh, who pioneered the study of geology, was among the first men in the world to consider the age of what truly underpinned Scotland: the rock itself. After four and half billion years, it was a Scot who began to draw close to estimating the planet's date of birth.

Enlightenment figures like the chemist Joseph Black, of Glasgow University, laid the foundations for the discovery of the chemical building-blocks of the natural world. His disciples would discover, among many other fundamentals, the bleaching qualities of chlorine that would revolutionise Scotland's linen industry. James Watt, born in Greenock, was a mathematical instrument maker by training and irresistibly attracted to the intellectual bright lights of Glasgow. He benefited from the company of Joseph Black, as well as from John Anderson and John Robison, and would of course attain immortality for his work with steam power. Many Scots believe their man invented the steam engine, when in fact his achievement was to make a crucial improvement to Thomas Newcomen's 'atmospheric engine' by adding to it a separate condensing chamber that made far more efficient use of the steam's heat and energy. Every Scot also knows, correctly, that the steam engine eventually powered the Industrial Revolution; but fewer remember that it was not until his partnership with the English manufacturer and engineer Matthew Boulton that Watt found access to enough practical and financial resources to develop his masterpiece.

Precisely because the products of the Scottish Enlightenment had such practical applications, its advocates and their followers were firmly grounded in the real world.

Kames's work on improving farming techniques – which he practised and perfected on his own lands – were at the root of Scotland's Agricultural Revolution. By his efforts and those of others like him, the Scots' approach to farming was changed utterly. Instead of ancient subsistence practices, innovations like the enclosure of arable land and rotation of crops began to generate surplus and the potential for ever-increasing profit.

Contributions like Watt's improvement of the steam engine would likewise make possible the growth of factories all across the central belt of Scotland as the seemingly unquenchable fires of Industrial Revolution began to burn as well. The vast majority of Scots had always lived and worked in the countryside, and in the first half of the eighteenth century only perhaps one in every eight people lived in a town of more than 4,000 inhabitants. The spread of industry between Glasgow and Edinburgh would rapidly turn Scotland into a country with more urban dwellers per head of population than most other countries in Europe. By the middle of the nineteenth century, a third of Scots were town or city dwellers.

The stars of the Scottish Enlightenment provided the intellectual scaffold capable of holding up a sophisticated, modern society that could be heartily exploited, for personal gain, by merchants, trades people and men of industry. Visionaries like Adam Smith would argue of course that by allowing men of business to maximise their profits, so society as a whole would be enriched.

This was the Scotland that Highlanders like John Wedderburn had chosen to leave behind when they took ship for the colonies. The cutting they carried with them and grafted onto the New World was that of the Old Scotland. While 'enlightened' Scots back home championed the union more passionately than any Englishman and had taken to calling themselves North Britons, many of those who crossed the Atlantic remained committed to 'old' traditions like independence, family loyalty and knowing their place in the social hierarchy.

Perhaps it was these characteristics, and an inbuilt willingness to obey a strong leader, that explain how well so many Highlandmen adapted to life within the British Army, their former nemesis. As early as 1724, General Wade had set out to exploit the martial heritage of the Highland Scots and to turn it to His Majesty's advantage.

As part of his effort to pacify the Highlands he had pulled hundreds of Highland men together to form a force that might be used to keep 'watch' over their neighbours' rebellious instincts. Originally known as the 42nd Regiment of Foot, they were clad in dark green and black tartan kilts that soon inspired their more familiar name of 'The Royal Highland Regiment (The Black Watch)'. Ironically, it was in 1745 that the officers and men of the Black Watch first went into action – not in Britain against Jacobites but at the Battle of Fontenoy, against the French, in Flanders in modern-day Belgium. They were part of a combined British, Dutch and Austrian army led by the Duke of Cumberland and deployed against the French during the War of the Austrian Succession.

The battle was a defeat for Cumberland and his so-called 'Pragmatic Army' but the Black Watch had been conspicuously brave, earning the admiration not just of their own commander but of the French forces as well. One French officer described the men of the Black Watch at Fontenoy as 'Highland Furies' who had rushed in upon him and his men 'with more violence than ever did the sea driven by a tempest'. It was the first time a Highland regiment had frightened the living daylights out of a foreign army, but it certainly would not be the last.

The flames of Scottish Enlightenment were already well aglow by the time Charles Edward Stuart sent his own fiery cross through the Highlands in 1745. Hutcheson, Kames and others had been at work for years by then, so when the Jacobites arrived in Glasgow and Edinburgh they found cities where their old-fashioned ways were neither appropriate any more, nor wanted.

It was in 1746, while John Wedderburn was turning his back on the land of his birth, that another young Scotsman was on his way home. Adam Smith had been born in Kirkcaldy in 1723, and received a sound education in the Burgh School there between 1729 and 1737. At the age of fourteen he became a student at Glasgow University and there attended Francis Hutcheson's lectures on moral philosophy and the philosophy of law and politics. He quickly became imbued with the fundamental belief that freedom is an inalienable human right.

He left Glasgow for Balliol College, Oxford in 1740 but found the atmosphere there did nothing to improve his Scottish education or increase his understanding of the world. Such was his unhappiness at Oxford he departed the place in 1746, before his scholarship was even completed. He exhibited some of the symptoms of an early nervous breakdown, and of the oddities of character that would soon mark him out as an eccentric. He returned initially to his mother's home in Fife but by 1748 had begun teaching at Edinburgh University, where Lord Kames became his patron. Hutcheson had died in 1746 and in 1748 Smith succeeded his former mentor on the Chair of Moral Philosophy at Glasgow University.

Smith's thinking was affected and, in part shaped, by three of the brightest lights of the Enlightenment. But by using his own unique genius to synthesise and filter the work of Hutcheson, Kames and also of David Hume, he created a philosophy all his own. Most of us think of Smith as an economist – author, of course, of *The Wealth of Nations* – but that work would not be published until 1776. By personal inclination, he was a moral philosopher and humanist too.

While Hutcheson had said all human beings were born with a moral compass capable of keeping them on the path of righteousness, Kames and Hume argued society was created and accepted by people so their personal property might be kept safe, and the worst of human nature kept in check. In parallel to, but separate from, these ideas, Smith formed the opinion that civilised society teaches its members to behave in acceptable ways. Individuals were not necessarily good or bad; they learned by example that they could get along better in life by mimicking the successful ways of others. Society was a mirror that showed a man what he was like, how he differed from others and what he might do to be more like the best and most successful of his fellows.

By the time Highlanders like Wedderburn were starting new lives in North America, and geniuses like Kames, Hume and Smith were holding court in Glasgow and Edinburgh, Scotland was finally enjoying some of the economic success that had been promised to her in 1707.

By a fluke of geography Glasgow was in the vanguard of the economic advance. For most of her history Scotland had looked east for trading partners. Scots were vagabonds long before the time of the Jacobites or of the 'Clearances', and from as early as the 1400s had sought fortune and military adventure in countries like Poland, Sweden and elsewhere in northern Europe. For all that period, towns and cities on Scotland's east coast had had the most to gain from foreign trade.

With English warmongering causing so much disruption to relations with their Continental neighbours during the late seventeenth and then the eighteenth centuries, entrepreneurial Scots eyes had learned to look westwards as well. The disaster that was Darien had taught Scots a severe lesson about making their way in the west, but it was not their first foray into the New World and it hardly discouraged such ambitions either. With her west coast location, Glasgow was perfectly placed to gain a head start on any trans-Atlantic voyage. The city itself had no Atlantic port as such, but via the River Clyde it had easy connections to those at Greenock and Port Glasgow. Successful efforts to dredge and so deepen the river made such access even more useful. As they say in those parts, 'Glasgow made the Clyde and the Clyde made Glasgow'.

England had long had the whip hand in North America, with control of the seaways, but from tentative forays in the sixteenth century Scots merchants had steadily gained a foothold. In the years following the union, Scots agents were dispatched to the Chesapeake in Virginia and to North and South Carolina in search of supplies of tobacco. By the time the dust was settling after the 1715 Jacobite rising, the first ships were arriving in Glasgow loaded with their precious cargo.

Tobacco became a key element of the three-way trade' system. On the first leg of the triangle, ships left Scotland bound for African ports where they collected slaves. On the second leg the human cargo was transported across the Atlantic in hellish conditions in the ships' holds. (John Paul Jones, the Scot who would later lay the foundations for the US Navy, learned some of his seamanship while serving on 'black birders', as the slave ships were known. The stink from such ships, with their living cargoes chained helplessly in their own filth, was such that it was said that other vessels could smell them before they could see them.) The slaves were unloaded into servitude in the plantations of the West Indies or the North American colonies before the ships were reloaded with tobacco, sugar or cotton for the return trip. Fortunes were certainly made, but the profits were shaved slice by slice from the naked backs of fellow human beings. It is to the Scots' eternal shame that a people who could write so lyrically about freedom in the fourteenth century grew fat in the eighteenth century by buying and selling other mothers' sons and daughters.

The evils of the slave trade notwithstanding, William Cunninghame was one of those who rose from relatively modest beginnings to become one of the giants of the tobacco trade. Others of his ilk – Andrew Buchanan, James Dunlop, Archibald Ingram and the mighty John Glassford – left their names behind on Glasgow city streets. Antigua Street, Jamaica Street, Tobago Street and Virginia Street remember where some of their vast overseas estates were once located.

Cunninghame, born in 1715, would one day spend £10,000 – a vast sum at the time – building one of the most lavish and spectacular private homes in Scotland. When he bought the plot it was on a muddy track called Cow Lone. In time it would be renamed Queen Street and the house that tobacco built is now more familiar to residents of modern Glasgow as the Gallery of Modern Art (GOMA). The uniform grid of streets and buildings known as the Merchant City, between the High Street and Buchanan Street, was built as the first new town and is more of their legacy. Manhattan has its famous gridiron of streets and city blocks because the system had already proved a success in Glasgow.

For John Wedderburn, however, making landfall in the British colony of Jamaica in the bitter aftermath of Culloden, such a future for his homeland would have sounded as foreign as the land in which he found himself. As well as the unfamiliar heat, smells, plants and animals, he would certainly have noticed the seeming armies of black men, women and children breaking their backs in fields growing sugar cane and tobacco plants. Foreign it all certainly was, but for a young man like Wedderburn – determined to put his past behind him and carve out a bright future – it would also have smelled of opportunity.

If Wedderburn junior was thinking about reinventing himself, he was not alone. Following the success of the Black Watch in Flanders in 1745, scores of other Highland regiments were eventually raised. It was during the conflict known as the Seven Years War that the story of their legendary bravery really began to be written.

The Treaty of Aix-la-Chapelle brought the War of the Austrian Succession to an end in 1748. In reality, however, no one had been satisfied by its terms and all it really did was give Empress Maria Theresa of Austria time to regroup her armies and agitate for more trouble. Disgruntled by the loss of Silesia to Emperor Frederick II of Prussia, she eventually joined forces with France, Russia, Spain and Sweden. Lined up on the other side would be Britain, Hanover and Prussia and for the seven years between

1756 and 1763 they fought what is regarded by some as the first 'world war'.

William Pitt the Elder, British Prime Minister from 1757 until his resignation in 1761, fought the war with great skill. Highland regiments were to the fore in battle after battle as fighting raged across Europe and in India and North America as well. While Austria and Prussia fought for supremacy in Germany, France and Britain vied with one another for control in the Americas and India.

During the bloody aftermath of Culloden, Cumberland is said to have spotted a wounded Lieutenant-Colonel of the Jacobites. The dying man, said the Duke, was giving him an 'insolent' stare. He turned to one of his officers and ordered him to shoot the 'scoundrel'. That officer promptly offered to resign his commission but refused point blank to murder a man in cold blood. 'I will not be an executioner,' he said. That decent and honourable officer was Major James Wolfe. In 1759, during his legendary Quebec expedition that culminated in the Battle of the Plains of Abraham, he would have men of the 78th Regiment – Fraser's Highlanders – at his side until his death at the moment of his greatest victory.

1759 was a year of victories for Britain. Not only did Wolfe capture Quebec, but Duke Ferdinand of Brunswick smashed the French at the Battle of Minden and Sir Edward Hawke led twenty-three ships of the Royal Navy to victory over their French counterparts in Quiberon Bay, off the coast of France, near St Nazaire. Robert Clive of India had defeated the Nawab of Bengal and his French allies at the Battle of Plassey in 1757 – securing British East India Company control of the continent for the best part of the following century – and in 1760 the last French-controlled city in Canada, Montreal, surrendered to the British. The Seven Years War was finally brought to an end by the Treaty of Paris on 10 February 1763 and Britain and Russia were the victors sharing the spoils.

The massive, global conflict had provided the backdrop against which the awesome reputation of the fighting Highlander had shone so very brightly. In 1746 the Highlanders had been rebel barbarians, synonymous with the Stuarts; and when Pitt first supported their use as British soldiers he remarked it was 'no great mischief if they fall'. By 1763 and ever after, however, they were the disciplined and rightly feared shock troops of the British Empire. It was a stunning transformation. Now the same folk who had once despised and dismissed the Highlanders as alien barbarians could enjoy heaping praise and admiration upon them instead.

For Britain, the Seven Years War had been about claiming colonies, securing trade routes around the globe and winning the rights to the most lucrative commodities. Rehabilitated Jacobites had been at the forefront of the necessary fighting time and again. While the rest of the combatants had limited their military ambitions to Europe, Britain and France had taken the opportunity to battle it out for control of the 'Empire of the West'. France had meddled in British affairs during the time of the Jacobites and now the British government had taken the opportunity to repay them amply. The Seven Years War caused the deaths of a million and a half people but victory for Britain opened up trade links to territories stretching from Canada to the Caribbean. Now at the helm of an empire on the rise, Britain was poised to become one of the richest nations on earth.

It took an outsider, however, to observe that not all of Britain's people were thriving – certainly not all Scots. Benjamin Franklin, polymath and diplomat, had travelled to England and Westminster in 1757 on a mission to secure better representation and fairer taxes for the colonists. His father had been born in England and Franklin junior had lived on both sides of the Atlantic.

In 1759, as part of his sojourn during the year of victories, he visited Edinburgh and there spent time with David Hume, Lord Kames and Adam Smith, among other Enlightenment figures. 1759 was also the year that saw the founding of the Carron Iron Works and Franklin would doubtless have learned how much industry was springing up across the central belt connecting Scotland's two greatest cities. West and south of Glasgow, in towns like Ayr, Kilmarnock and Paisley, was where the great textiles industries would take firm root. Herein lay another part of the secret of Glasgow's success: the city's west coast location was a lucky starting point for trade with the Americas, but the long-term economic growth of the place owed more to the way it became the hub for industry in the wider territory of western Scotland – the linen industry in particular.

During the second half of the eighteenth century the construction of two canals, first the Forth and Clyde and then the Monklands, made possible the efficient movement of raw materials and finished products into and out of Glasgow. The completion of the Union Canal in 1822, linking the east of the country with the west, would further accelerate the speed of change. Carron Iron Works, and later the textiles complex of New Lanark, were both located near sources either of power or raw materials, or both – but were also, and crucially, tied into the larger industrial complex of which Glasgow was the beating heart.

Franklin would write to Lord Kames to say how much he had enjoyed his time in the Scottish capital and how impressed he had been with those individuals he had visited:

> On the whole, I must say, I think the time we spent there was six weeks of the densest happiness I have met with in any part of my life, and the agreeable and instructive society we found there in such plenty has left so pleasing an impression on my memory that did not strong connections draw me else-where, I believe Scotland would be the country I should choose to spend the remainder of my days in.

Franklin was a wonder of his own age – and any other. Nothing was beyond the reach of his talents and over the years he would excel as an author, civic activist, inventor, musician, political theorist, politician, pub-lisher, satirst and scientist, as well as a statesman and diplomat. But while he enjoyed the company of the fellow geniuses he encountered in Edinburgh, it did not stop him noticing that Scotland's society was also far from perfect. He would later write to a friend, lamenting some of what he had seen:

> I have lately made a Tour thro' Ireland and Scotland. In these Countries a small Part of the Society are Landlords, great Noblemen and Gentlemen, extreamly opulent, living in the highest Affluence and Magnificence: The bulk of the People Tenants, extreamly poor, living in the most sordid Wretch-edness in dirty Hovels of Mud and Straw, and cloathed only in Rags . . .
>
> Had I never been in the American Colonies, but was to form my Judgment of Civil Society by what I have lately seen, I should never advise a Nation of Savages to admit of Civilisation: For I assure you, that in the Possession and Enjoyment of the various Comforts of Life, compar'd to these People every Indian is a Gentleman: And the Effect of this kind of Civil Society seems only to be, the depressing Multitudes below the Savage State that a few may be rais'd above it.

Franklin had come to Britain, in part, to decide whether his fellow colonists might benefit from a full union with the old country. But while he would concede that the Anglo-Scots union had laid the foundations for an imperial superpower, he lamented the divisions and weaknesses within the society it had created. The French philosopher Voltaire would say that 'We look to Scotland for all our ideas of civilisation', but Franklin felt the country had failed to shake off its ancient yokes of hierarchy, patronage and class. Disappointed by the way in which the rich of the land were getting richer while the poor got poorer, he left for home convinced America could do better.

While Franklin was forming his opinions about Scotland and Britain, Adam Smith was paying close attention to developments in the American colonies, and those closer to home. The burgeoning tobacco trade that was so enriching Glasgow in general – and the city's new breed of oligarch, the self-styled 'Tobacco Lords', in particular – drew much of his interest. He certainly loved the energy and buzz of it all and enjoyed every minute he spent among the hubbub of the thriving world of commerce developing on the banks of the Clyde. The Broomielaw had been so named in honour of the broom bushes that grew in profusion along the water's edge, but by Smith's time it was dominated by the rattle and hum of the business of making money.

With their ships at sea for months at a time, the city's tobacco merchants had plenty of spare time. They spent much of it in the new Tontine Hotel, at Glasgow Cross, sipping coffee or fashionable rum drinks, often promenading along the riverside in their trademark purple cloaks, gold-topped canes in hand. They were among the celebrities of their day and they liked to be seen and heard. Smith admired the newness of the society evolving on the other side of the Atlantic, its energy and optimism. But he was easily intelligent enough to see that there were lessons to be learned from Glasgow's tobacco trade – and that not all of them made for comfortable reading.

He had, after all, grown up knowing the lengths to which some men would go in pursuit of wealth. His father had been a customs officer in Fife, and the stress of trying and failing to deal with the local smugglers had driven him to an early grave, six months before his son was born. This knowledge, that even punitive laws were insufficient to discourage illicit trade and the pursuit of self-interest, would persuade Smith that the money-making urge ought to be harnessed rather than discouraged.

During the 1750s, Glasgow's hold upon the American tobacco trade grew tight as a vice. Before 1740 Glasgow merchants were importing no more than 10 per cent of Britain's share of the crop, but by the late 1750s they were handling more tobacco than all English ports combined. By far the majority of the trade was controlled by a handful of Glasgow men and their families. William Cunninghame, John Glassford and Alexander Spiers were the big three and they were to become legends in their own lifetimes.

In the years running up to the outbreak of the American War of Independence in 1775 even the least of the Scots tobacco merchants grew rich. For the giants among them, the fortunes being made were on a scale almost beyond belief. Mr Darcy, the fictional hero of Jane Austen's *Pride and Prejudice*, was wealthy beyond the dreams of avarice on an income of £10,000 a year; Glassford, a real-life figure living in the time Austen wrote about, was earning up to £500,000 a year.

The Tobacco Lords were among the first members of the newly formed Political Economy Club, where businessmen met to discuss the skills of their trade. By working his way into their company Smith was able to develop contacts and learn about commerce. He befriended Glassford and was therefore able to base his study of the tobacco trade on first-hand research. He saw that his friend and his ilk had secured their stranglehold by bold, cut-throat business practices: while English tobacco traders acted as middlemen – selling the stuff onto the European markets on behalf of the growers, for an agreed commission – Glasgow's Tobacco Lords bought the crop at source for pre-arranged prices. When the time came to sell their wares on the Continent, the profit margins were colossal.

All year their placemen would allow the tobacco growers to buy luxury goods and other commodities from their stores in the colonies. Most, if not all, of the purchases were made on credit – on the understanding that the Glasgow merchants would, in return for the favours, be given first refusal on the eventual harvest. It was a brilliant scheme and one that required the Tobacco Lords to have access to large amounts of capital from home. This was achieved by building networks of family backers who were made shareholders in the companies as quid pro quo for investment.

This access to family money meant the Scots firms were heavily capitalised, without the need to seek funding from outside their own clique; but it also exposed them to massive personal risk in times of crop failure or loss of ships and cargo. Another ingredient in the Scottish recipe for success was that the merchants owned and operated their own fleets of ships rather than chartering vessels, like the English merchants did. This innovation let the Scots push for very speedy turnarounds in a system that was described as the 'Clockwork Operation'. Ships arrived in harbour in the colonies, offloaded their own cargoes and reloaded with the tobacco, sugar or cotton for the return trip in as short a time as possible. As well as speeding up the round trip of 7,000 miles, it also minimised the time ships spent in colonial harbours infested with worms capable of causing untold damage to ships' wooden hulls.

Twice a year the *Cunninghame* – William Cunninghame's pride and joy – would arrive in Virginia's Chesapeake Bay. William Cunninghame junior, serving time in the colonial side of his father's operation, would be there to meet it. Beside him on the dock were hogsheads of tobacco, recently purchased for the lowest possible price and ready for the trip home. Before they could be put aboard his father's ship, however, William would have to oversee the unloading of the *Cunninghame*'s cargo of leather-covered chairs, silver tea sets, china dinner services and the rest of the luxury goods destined for the company stores.

For an apprentice like William, mosquitoes, stifling heat and the stress of meeting his father's exacting standards were all part of the established Scottish way of training the next generation of masters of the universe. Hard graft – learning the business from the bottom up – was demanded of those who would make a mark on the New World. They were also expected to be dealmakers – and ruthless dealmakers at that. The tobacco price was set once a year at a meeting of growers at the county court house. The price arrived at became the central point in a gentleman's agreement, but the Tobacco Lords did not grow to dominance by being gentlemen.

Most of the growers were small-scale operations, often run by *émigré* Scots of a few generations' standing. Their life and work was hard and payday only came once a year, when their crop was sold. For such men, the insidiously seductive influence of the Glasgow merchants was all but irresistible: they offered access to all manner of goods in their stores and all that luxury could be had on credit.

In the hands of skilled dealers – of the sort young William was fast becoming – the credit system became a trap for the growers. By the end of a season they might be hugely in debt to the stores and their owners and obliged to accept whatever price the merchants might bid for their tobacco. Cunninghame was known to offer as much as 20 per cent below the agreed market price and his debtors had no option but to accept. It was a simple trick but one made even more complicated by the fact that all the Glasgow merchants were at it. Correspondence from Cunninghame senior contains references to all manner of dirty tricks: growers should be befriended, offered drink, their trust won so that they might be exploited later on. By the later decades of the eighteenth century the Scots had earned a reputation for unscrupulous deviousness.

All of this brave, entrepreneurial endeavour created the possibility of huge rewards but also carried the risk of complete financial disaster. The Bogies were just one Glasgow tobacco family whose fortunes rose and then fell catastrophically in the face of unpaid debts. Several other families had similar experiences. The Glasgow tobacco trade certainly was not for the faint-hearted.

For all that Adam Smith admired the drive and the work ethic of his friend Glassford, he also warned that a great deal of power – something resembling the old-fashioned, autocratic power of the nobility of days past – was once again in the hands of a very few men. He valued the free market but believed it was part of the responsibility of civilised society to ensure the few were not left to forget themselves, and to reach giddy heights of wealth and position at the expense of the rest of humanity. Smith was an economist, but always a philosopher and a humanist as well.

He was not alone in fearing for the eventual consequences of all that was catching fire in the white heat of Enlightenment. John Witherspoon was born in East Lothian, in 1723, and studied divinity at Edinburgh University. He followed the teachings of Hutcheson and others but, while ready to accept some of their wisdom, he also criticised what he saw as the creation of yet another elite. Men like Hutcheson, Kames and Hume were clever for sure, he could argue, but they were in danger of losing touch with the needs, wants and rights of the mass of their fellow Scots. They and their kind were, after all, sponsored by men like Lord Islay – the sort that had always run Scotland.

Dr Witherspoon was a man of the people, a simple family man and the father of ten children with his wife Elizabeth. Only five survived to adult-hood and his experience of life had taught him to value all mankind. In 1753 he wrote the satirical *Ecclesiastical Characteristics*, in which he turned a light on the dark, elitist side of the teachings of Hutcheson and others. Fearing the consequences of supposedly learned men, men of God among them, becoming distanced from their fellows and their flocks, he wrote that for some, religion would only be perfect 'when we shall have driven away the whole common people ... and captivated the hearts of the gentry to a love of our solitary temples'.

From 1758 he was a minister in Paisley and also the figurehead of the so-called 'Popular Party' that grew up around him, a group of Presbyterian churchmen who preached against the 'lordly dominion' of fine men and women. Naturally charismatic and a passionate preacher, his congregation was made up of the ordinary working folk of Paisley. He was a product of the Enlightenment but so too, like it or not, were the labourers, tenant farmers and tradesmen who attended his church every Sunday. Witherspoon's feet were always on the ground, among the lives and loves of everyman and, in time, he would attract the attention of men on the other side of the Atlantic – men looking to change the world.

By the time Witherspoon was sounding his warning in Paisley, and while Smith was coming to his own realisations about the pros and cons of Enlightenment, *émigré* Scot John Wedderburn had been settled in his new home near Montego Bay on the western side of Jamaica for more than a decade. The teenage runaway who had fled Culloden and the butchery of his father had by now grown to maturity far from home. He had tried his hand at a few professions, and had even been a doctor for a few years. He had had no qualifications whatsoever but since he was white and confident, he had been able to make a success of it; in fact, he had done well enough to set aside a deposit for investment in his future. Naturally astute businessman that he was, he had alighted on the sugar trade. Wedderburn made his fortune as a sugar plantation owner – and therefore as a slave owner.

The vast profits of growing crops like tobacco, cotton and sugar in the colonies depended upon access to cheap labour. And why spend any money at all on wages when there were whole lifetimes of free labour to be bought in the market places. For generations now, ships had been tying up in the harbours of the New World and disgorging thousands upon thousands of men, women and children stolen from their African homelands. On arrival, each new cargo of human beings became the focus of what was called a 'scramble' as prospective buyers flocked around them in hope of snapping up the strongest backs, the finest specimens. It has been calculated that a farm labourer tending tobacco plants had to bend down 50,000 times between planting and harvest each year. Why risk a white back on such toil when there were plenty of black backs to be had relatively cheaply?

Wedderburn considered himself a Christian but in his pursuit of wealth and position in his adoptive home he had learned to set aside any need to love all his neighbours. Was this the behaviour of an enlightened Scot? Was this the immortal wrong that Witherspoon had in mind when he warned of common people being 'driven away' – driven away like cattle, mere beasts to be bought and sold?

In the spring of 1762 Wedderburn attended a scramble and there spied a black boy of perhaps twelve or thirteen years. There was apparently something about the way the lad carried himself within the crowd – the manner in which he stood and walked upon the soil of an alien land, at the start of an evil cradling thousands of miles from all his kin – that caught and held the master's eye. Wedderburn enquired after him and learned his name had been taken from him along with everything else, and replaced with that of the captain of the ship that had carried him across the Atlantic. We do not know whether he haggled over the price, but in any case he bought Joseph Knight for himself and took him home to his plantation. Five years came and went in the stolen life of Joseph Knight until, in 1769, Wedderburn decided to return to Scotland to show the land that had spurned him how much he had made of himself elsewhere. He took Joseph with him.

Having decided there was something about the boy that appealed to him, Wedderburn had never set Joseph to work in the fields. Not for him the back-breaking labour and the inevitable beatings that characterised the existences of the rest of Wedderburn's slaves. Instead he had made Joseph a house-boy – had seen to it that he worked indoors away from the scorching sun, that he learned to speak, read and write in English. Later Wedderburn would even make sure that Joseph was baptised.

Perhaps he became a salve for a troubled conscience. Maybe by treating one of his slaves as a human being – albeit a human being possessed by another – Wedderburn could more easily turn a blind eye to the lives of the rest. Whatever the truth, when Wedderburn boarded a ship headed for the old country, Joseph – handsome, educated, Christian Joseph – walked a few paces behind him. Unbeknown to either of them, they were setting sail towards a pivotal moment in both of their destinies.

Two years before the master and slave began their journey, another traveller had crossed the Atlantic towards the land of his fathers. Benjamin Rush had been born of English stock near Philadelphia on Christmas Eve, 1745. He obtained the degree of Bachelor of Arts at the College of Princeton, in New Jersey, before beginning to study medicine. His studies eventually brought him to Edinburgh, renowned the world over as one of the best places in which to study for a life as a physician.

In time Rush, Witherspoon and Franklin would all be among the signatories of the American Declaration of Independence. In 1767, when Rush was deciding to obtain a Scottish education, he was taking some of the first steps towards that great destiny.

On arrival in Liverpool he was confronted with the sight of a cargo of slaves being loaded aboard a black birder in the harbour. Rush was outraged and would go on to become a strong voice in the eventual call for the abolition of the practice. In 1773 he would write *An Address to the Inhabitants of the British Settlements in America, upon Slave-Keeping* in which he dismissed the notion, prevalent at the time, that black Africans were naturally inferior to white Europeans. Slavery, he wrote, 'is so foreign to the human mind, that the moral faculties, as well as those of the understanding are debased, and rendered torpid by it'. In those words were the echoes of humanist teachings like those of Hutcheson – and of course of Witherspoon as well. But in 1767 when Rush arrived in Britain en route to Edinburgh, such sentiments were as yet unformed in his gentle, questioning mind.

He had not just come to study, either. His *alma mater* Princeton College was in need of a new principal and Rush had been pointed in the direction of a possible candidate by none other than Benjamin Franklin himself. The seemingly omniscient Franklin had become aware of the Popular Party, Dr Witherspoon and his down-to-earth take on the Protestant religion, and had suggested to Rush that he might make the trip to Paisley and approach him with a job offer.

On the face of it, emigration was an unlikely prospect: Witherspoon was already in his middle years, surrounded by family and well known and loved by his congregation. Why would he uproot himself and take his wife, who had a mortal fear of sea journeys, all the way across an ocean to begin a new life three and a half thousand miles away? Rush knew what tack to take, however, and told Witherspoon that in his opinion – and in that of many of his fellows in the colonies – Scotland had gone soft on religion. He said supposedly great men like Hume and Smith had undermined the foundations of the Protestant creed and that the influence of the Church over men's lives was waning as a result. Scotland, said Rush, was a nation going to hell in a handcart.

Witherspoon was eventually persuaded and on 6 August 1768 he and Elizabeth arrived in Philadelphia. Having bade farewell to all he knew, and endured the arduous crossing, he was determined to make the trip worthwhile. He therefore set about nothing less than cultivating the college into a scion of the venerable oak from which he had grown, his own Edinburgh University. Much though he disagreed with some of what men like Hutcheson had had to say, he nonetheless transplanted some of the great man's ideas into his new patch.

Hutcheson had taught that personal happiness was to be found in the happiness of others. Witherspoon for his own part urged his staff at Princeton to have their students' happiness at heart when it came to furthering their education. When he sermonised and lectured, he spoke to his audience rather than reading to them from notes. This in itself was a revelation to his new hosts and began to make the process of learning into more of a conversation than a monologue. Under his stewardship, Princeton became an intellectually democratic place, where opinions were encouraged and freely shared.

No teachings were banned either. Although Witherspoon took issue with what he clearly saw as the elitism, based on nepotism and patronage, of the works of Hutcheson and other religious moderates, he insisted their books be read and digested along with all the others. (Books and language were always very dear to Witherspoon. He had brought with him from Scotland some 300 volumes and these became the basis for a library in Princeton's Nassau Hall. He would support America's independence from Britain in every way but one – language. To the end of his days he would lecture and cajole all Americans to avoid the use of what he called 'Americanisms' and to speak and write always and only in the king's English. But of all the things Witherspoon carried with him to America, the most potent and powerful of all was his (distinctly Scots Presbyterian) understanding of freedom.

Towards the end of the 1760s the British government was looking for ways to tighten its control over the North American colonies. In particular, there was an appetite in London for raising money by directly taxing the colonists. In 1767 the British Chancellor of the Exchequer, Charles Townshend, composed a series of Acts of Parliament to do just that. Opposition to the so-called 'Townshend Acts' was especially strident in Massachusetts and in 1768 British troops were sent into the city of Boston to discourage further unrest.

The events that unfolded on 5 March 1770 were later immortalised on an engraving by the legendary Paul Revere as 'The Bloody Massacre Perpetrated in King Street, Boston' and are more generally remembered as the Boston Massacre. For all the colourful language and polemic, it was in fact the relatively measured (by the military standards of the day) response by twenty British troopers who were being jostled and pelted with stones by a drunken, baying mob several hundred strong. Pushed beyond endurance, the soldiers opened fire, killing five colonists. Unfortunate it certainly was, but not quite the 'massacre' commemorated by Revere and used to such effect in helping to trigger the rising that eventually escalated into the American War of Independence.

Nonetheless, by 1771 Witherspoon was publishing his *Thoughts on American Liberty* – by which time he had thrown all his considerable intellectual and spiritual weight behind his adoptive colonists. His were some of the first words printed in support of defiance of any British taxation of the colonies; and his voice, his Scots Presbyterian voice, echoed among the earliest calls for the colonists to unite and form a nation. Like most critics of British taxation of the colonies, he did not start out wanting independence from Britain, far from it; but, like every opponent of tyranny down through the millennia of human history, he could not and would not ignore inequity. What became the United States of America owes at least some measure of its existence to a Presbyterian minister from Paisley, first President of Princeton.

Before the colonies could seek independence from the British crown, one man would embark upon a historic quest to regain a freedom far more fundamental.

When John Wedderburn returned to Scotland in 1769, accompanied by his house-boy Joseph Knight, he was determined to win back all the rights and status his family had held before Culloden. He went to Perthshire to reclaim the title of Baronet of Blackness. For over three years Knight continued to serve his master, but gradually it seems he began to be influenced by enlightened Scottish society. To make matters more acute, he met and fell in love with a servant girl from Dundee called Annie Thompson. Wedderburn allowed the pair to marry but for Knight it was not enough. Just as personal status mattered to the *soi-disant* baronet, so it mattered to the slave; and the status he coveted was that of a free man.

He went to his master and asked that he be given money as back pay for his years of unpaid service. Wedderburn refused. The final straw came in 1772, with Wedderburn's decision to dismiss Thompson from his service when she became pregnant with Knight's child. As well as sacking her, he insisted she leave his house, and Knight decided to go with her. Caught in the act of packing a bag for his departure, he was promptly arrested and thrown in jail.

It is thought Knight may have read in Scottish newspapers about a landmark judgment by Lord Mansfield, a Scot serving as Lord Chief Justice in England. Asked to adjudicate in the case of a slave refusing to return to the colonies with his Scottish owner, Lord Mansfield had ruled the master had no right to remove the man from Britain against his will. Whether or not Knight had learned there was precedent for a man in his predicament, he succeeded in persuading John Swinton, Sheriff Depute at Perth Sheriff Court, that he was entitled to his freedom.

Wedderburn claimed he had never treated Knight as a slave, that he had regarded him as a son and demanded only 'lifelong service'. He appealed against the Perth ruling and eventually, in 1778, the case made it all the way to the Court of Session in Edinburgh. By then its notoriety was such that a twelve-judge panel, including Lord Kames, was assembled to hear the evidence and no lesser figures than man of letters Dr Samuel Johnson – a stern and vocal opponent of slavery – and his friend and fellow writer (and Scot) James Boswell took an interest in Knight's plight.

Boswell even went so far as to help Knight's advocate prepare his case and the judges were duly persuaded – by a majority of eight to four – to make him a free man. Lord Kames had told the court: 'We sit here to enforce right, not to enforce wrong'. Sheriff Depute Swinton's ruling was thereby confirmed: 'That the state of slavery is not recognised by the laws of this Kingdom, and is inconsistent with the principles thereof, and finds that the regulations in Jamaica concerning slaves, do not extend to this Kingdom, and repels the master's claim for perpetual service.' It was a momentous decision, both for Knight and for Scotland. By refusing to accept that one man could own another, the supreme civil court of Scotland had shown the way towards the abolition of slavery. One of the judges had been Boswell's own father – Alexander Boswell, Lord Auchinleck – and he had argued that slavery was out of step with the demands of both Christianity and common humanity.

For the two men at the centre, the final decision meant an inevitable and final parting. The rest of Knight's story, the story of the free man, is lost to history. His enslavement had brought him the notoriety that in turn led to his liberty – and that same liberty opened a door into the peaceful obscurity that is the lot of most free men. It is thought he lived out the rest of his life as a married man in Dundee, perhaps as a miner. If so, he had found for himself a world where the skins of all the working men are black.

There was blackness of another sort entirely for Wedderburn. Embittered by it all, he shook off any previous ambivalence he might once have entertained about slavery and for his remaining years would hold court as one fiercely committed to the right of some men to hold the lives of others as property. He also campaigned hard for the return of his father's title – the title that had been cut away from the man along with the head. So it was that John Wedderburn ended his days as the 6th Baronet of Blackness.

Whether or not those supreme court judges had realised it, their decision in favour of one African man's rights as a human being went straight to the heart of the British crown's relationship to its North American colonies: was Britain treating the colonists as property too? Was it a tyranny akin to slavery that they sought to impose by naked force?

Even in a history of Scotland, it is worth remembering what most American colonists' attitude was towards Britain when war broke out. On 19 April 1775, when the 'shot heard around the world' was fired on Concord Green, they were already far freer than most people in Scotland at that time. When only around one man in 250 in Scotland could vote for his choice of MP, every colonist in America held the right to register his choice of local representative. Much of the money to be raised by the infamous taxes was intended to pay for the colonists' own defence in a dangerous world – hardly a lot to ask, you might argue – and in any case the average colonist paid something like a fiftieth of the taxes demanded of the average British man.

The vast majority of colonists had no quarrel with the notion of monarchy and it was well into the war before even Washington and his officers in the Continental Army stopped toasting the health of Great Britain. If any of them did have a problem it was with George III himself; George III the man, rather than George III the *king*. America and Americans were already free; what they were about to fight for was the continuation and extension of that freedom.

Once the fighting started, Witherspoon spoke out even more loudly in defence of 'liberty'. In a rousing sermon in 1776 he called upon 'all my witnesses' to listen while he brought politics into the pulpit for the first time in his life:

> At this season, however, it is not only lawful but necessary, and I willingly embrace the opportunity of declaring my opinion without any hesitation, that the cause in which America is now in arms, is the cause of justice, of liberty, and of human nature.
>
> So far as we have hitherto proceeded, I am satisfied that the confederacy of the colonies has not been the effect of pride, resentment, or sedition, but of a deep and general conviction that our civil and religious liberties, and

consequently in a great measure the temporal and eternal happiness of us and our posterity, depended on the issue.

The knowledge of God and his truths have from the beginning of the world been chiefly, if not entirely confined to those parts of the earth where some degree of liberty and political justice were to be seen, and great were the difficulties with which they had to struggle, from the imperfection of human society, and the unjust decisions of usurped authority.

There is not a single instance in history, in which civil liberty was lost, and religious liberty preserved entire. If therefore we yield up our temporal property, we at the same time deliver the conscience into bondage.

Scots' loyalties were severely tested by the fighting itself, with most deciding to fight on behalf of the Crown. It sounds incredible, but even refugees from Culloden and 'The '45' apparently found their belief in tradition and monarchy left them no alternative but to side with the old country and the ruling House of Hanover. If the Seven Years War had begun the proud history of the Highland regiments in the British Army, it was war in the American colonies that established their legendary credentials.

Viewed from the distance of two centuries and more, the decision by Jacobites to stand shoulder to shoulder with the sons of their erstwhile tormentors looks utterly perverse. Yet at the same time it surely says something about the psychology of the Scot, and the Highland Scot in particular: whatever they thought of their chances when they took up arms in the New World, it mattered more to them to be loyal than to win.

No such qualms troubled the thinking of John Witherspoon. By 1776, eight years into his sojourn abroad, he had long since gone native. He was among the representatives at the meeting that year of the Second Continental Congress – the body tasked with governing the rebel colonies – when it called for full independence from Britain. When the subsequent 'Declaration of Independence' was brought forward for signatures in July, Witherspoon was among twenty Scots (and the only clergyman) who took up the pen and put their names to it. He had argued, cajoled and encouraged all around him throughout the discussions and, at the last, when some of the representatives voiced uncertainty about the wisdom of taking on the might of the British war machine, he had rallied them with these words: 'There is a tide in the affairs of men, a nick of time. We perceive it now before us. To hesitate is to consent to our own slavery.' (He was paraphrasing

Brutus in *Julius Caesar*, but in Witherspoon's case he was advocating stabbing the king in the front, rather than the back.)

Joseph Knight had refused to accept his designation as slave. Thanks in part to the will of John Witherspoon the fledgeling union of states – trojan horse of the United States of America – succeeded in throwing off the same yoke. The following year, British forces entered Princeton College and put Nassau Hall and Witherspoon's precious library to the torch. All that act of vandalism achieved was to add more fuel to the rebellion's flame. Witherspoon's own son would be consumed by the fire before the end.

Back in Scotland, the merchants had their trading empires to consider and so generally backed the Crown. As was inevitable, the war disrupted and then temporarily stopped the trans-Atlantic trade between Britain and North America. Many of the companies built around tobacco, sugar, cotton or combinations of all three began to suffer and several would fail altogether.

It was Cunninghame who proved he had the measure of the situation when he held his nerve and bought up all of his rivals' stores of tobacco at sixpence a pound. During the war the price would reach *three shillings and sixpence* a pound – and Cunninghame sold the whole vast lot of it back to them at a profit guaranteed to make even the lordliest eyes water. It was with some of the money made from that one deal that he built his magnificent home on Queen Street.

The Scottish Enlightenment's philosophers looked beyond short-term profit and wondered instead about the long game. Hume foresaw only military, moral and financial ruin for the government if it insisted on trying first to browbeat and then to batter the colonists into submission. Adam Smith, with his economist's hat on, said the whole sorry business of rebellion would have been avoided if the government had simply seen the folly of trying to squeeze taxes from them. He was probably right. Furthermore, he argued that free trade was an unstoppable, irresistible force and that by seeking to crush the revolt the government risked ultimate disaster. In *The Wealth of Nations*, which was published in 1776 just as the first blood was being spilled, he said there were only two logical courses of action: either to give the colonists the representation they wanted at Westminster, or cut them adrift to govern themselves. His calls fell on deaf ears.

As is always the case, trade was brought quickly back to normal by the Treaty of Paris of 3 September 1783, the formal end to the hostilities. Wars come and wars go, but business is business and the market is invincible.

Tobacco was and has remained the poster-boy of Scotland's rapid economic growth during the eighteenth century. Linen, however – less glamorous though it may sound – was the more significant earner for most Scots at that time and employed tens of thousands of men, women and children in many parts of the country. Cotton, too, was a huge industry and both textiles would rise to the peak of their significance as increased industrialisation of the production processes accelerated during the eighteenth and nineteenth centuries.

Wars waged by Britain against European states during the earlier part of the eighteenth century had damaged and limited trade with the Continent. These were nations that had been markets for Scots goods for centuries and the loss of them was especially damaging for those north of the Border. It was the Glasgow merchants' stranglehold on American tobacco that reinvigorated trade across the North Sea as smokers in France, Germany and the Low Countries consumed the lion's share of the Tobacco Lords' cargoes.

In truth the eight years of war with the American colonists was no more than a blip in a century of powerful and sustained growth in Scots commerce with North America and with the wider world. North America was a key market for Scots textiles before 1775 but when the fighting got in the way – and even after it was over – Scots merchants broadened their horizons. Soon there were new markets for linen, and for other Scots exports, in the Far East, in South America and beyond as far as Australia.

Scotland had spent the eighteenth century becoming a trading nation more significant and with a far greater global reach than her size and geographical location should ever have made possible. Her population was growing but by the turn of the nineteenth century still only numbered just over one and a half million. By any measure, Scots were punching well above their weight. It was undoubtedly the union of 1707 that had opened up a world of tax-free trade which enabled a tiny minority to become truly wealthy – and a fair proportion to consider themselves 'middle-class'.

There had been revolutions, too – in the practice of agriculture and industry – and these had also played their part in enriching the land and lining the pockets of the few.

Something else had happened – something that in its way was more fundamental and more significant. Scotland had become newly confident and rightly proud of her importance on the international stage. In addition to new money, some of her people had found new wisdom. The luminaries of the Scottish Enlightenment were the brightest of all their kind and their practical approach to understanding the ways of the world was being observed and copied elsewhere. Scotland and her children were beginning to change the world.

There is always a cost, though, a price to be paid. Defeat for the British cause in the American colonies left the majority of Scots loyalists no alternative but to flee. With first- or second-hand memories of Culloden still vivid in their minds, they were driven from hearth and home once more, this time abandoning the newly United States of America and either seeking to make new lives in Canada or returning to Scotland.

Those who crossed the Atlantic for the second time – and in the opposite direction – found a land strangely altered. Their mothers, fathers and grandparents had fought for what they thought was freedom. Many of the Highlanders had spilled blood for a king they hoped would release them from the grasp of a usurper. Many Protestants from the Presbyterian side had fought for the freedom to worship their God as they saw fit. Winners or losers, all had fought for a cause and for a Scotland.

Men and women from both sides had been cradled for a while in the colonies and had watched as a dream of an independent United States had been made into a reality; another freedom and another cause. Those who returned now to the old country would have noticed that in their absence Scotland had stopped fighting. Now Scots seemed to value no cause beyond personal advancement. Most individuals – the poor and the put-upon – were fighting only to survive, to work and to feed themselves and to live, as they always had done.

In the rush to keep up with the New World of the west – and the old neighbours to the south, in England – had Scotland forgotten what Scotland was? Had Scots forgotten what being Scots meant?

CHAPTER TEN

WHA'S LIKE US? –
THE QUESTION OF IDENTITY

'It's never far from wherever you are
And when you go it never leaves you
You sit alone and thoughts of home
Come and stand around your chair.'

Garrison Keillor

This history of Scotland began nine chapters ago with a description of the way the land was formed in the first place. On the journey to this point it has been easy to become distracted by the stories of people living on the rock, and in so doing to forget the rock itself. That is always a mistake. The geology of Scotland has been a constant crucial character in the story, whether we always noticed it or not; and, if this country had been made even slightly differently all those millions and billions of years ago, then our history would have followed another path entirely.

On the north-west coast of Ireland near Ballyconnell, in County Sligo, there is a place the locals have always called 'Serpent Rock'. After a few minutes' walk along a beach of coarsely grained, grey-black sand, you reach an array of great slabs of limestone. They seem almost deliberately placed, edges overlapping like slates on a gently sloping roof – or the corners of a hand of giant cards placed face-downwards onto the sand.

As you stroll from one great, tipped runway to the next, glancing now and then at the Atlantic waves rolling and booming, off to the right you cannot help but notice that you are stepping upon countless fossils standing proud of the rock. The limestone is grey-black, like the sand of the beach, but these ancient inclusions are much paler, almost white, and sometimes flecked with what looks like gold dust. Every one is more or less the same shape, croissant-curved but ranging from a few inches to maybe a couple of feet in length. Some people have said these oddities resemble cabbage stalks (and they do, or maybe rams' horns, it all depends on your point of view). But to most observers through the centuries they have suggested the ancient remains of snakes or sea serpents turned to stone – and they give the place its name.

But snakes in Ireland ... the land where there *are* no snakes? The myth of petrified serpents by the sea near Ballyconnell began long before James Hutton, scion of the Scottish Enlightenment, laid the foundations of modern geology. Back in the days when people still believed the planet to be just a little over 4,000 years old, all sorts of explanations had had to be concocted for the many strange marks spotted from time to time in the rocks. Some said they had been put there by God himself, or maybe the devil, to confound the minds of men. It would take clear-thinking men like Hutton and later Charles Darwin (as well as fossil-hunter extraordinaire Mary Anning, of Lyme Regis) to begin to undermine the age-old misconceptions about the date of birth of planet earth.

From his home in East Lothian Hutton set out to investigate just how the landscape around him had been formed, what unstoppable forces and unimaginably long periods of time had been involved in its creation. Hutton's work, and that of others, made possible our modern understanding of enigmatic forms like those in the limestone of Serpent Rock.

They are the fossilised remains of animals – not snakes, but a kind of coral that lived around 340 million years ago. When some of the rock that would be Scotland formed part of the bed of a warm, shallow tropical sea near the equator, so too did some of the rock that would be Ireland. On that seabed lived animals related to modern-day sea anemones. While they existed they slowly extruded calcium as a by-product of their existence. Over time the deposited mineral formed a tower that raised the animals above whatever other life forms were growing beside them, like the scoop of ice cream on top of a wafer cone. They thrived only in warm water shallow enough to permit the sunlight that sustained other creatures upon which they depended for food.

During the passing of countless years, changes elsewhere affected the temperature and depth of that long-lost sea so that sediment formed, smothering and burying the coral. Yet more changes, spread over dizzying periods of time, made the water shallow again. Now mangroves and other plants began to grow in the sludge. Yet more changes came and went with years and centuries and millennia, until the plant life of the mangrove swamps died as well and became submerged beneath yet more sediment sometime after 280 million years ago.

Gradually, subject to the slow magic of geological forces, the calcium in the long-buried coral was replaced by much harder silica. Iron pyrites might form, alongside the silica, giving the golden sparkles some of the fossils have today. Above them in the layer cake of deposits, the combined juggernauts of pressure and time also had their effect upon what had once been the mangrove swamps and other plant life. As these were plunged to greater and greater depths beneath seas – then new rock and further sediment – they began the long, lazy transformation into coal.

Between 280 million years ago and much more recently the landforms of Ireland, Scotland and the rest of the British Isles drifted northwards to their present locations. In the case of the rocks of Ireland, something happened during that time to scour away almost all of the coal-bearing layers, and any sandstone and ironstone that might have been associated with them. No one, geologists included, offers any definite explanation of how or why this happened. It is possible the coal and sandstone were never there in the first place, although there is a tiny scattering of impoverished seams of coal of such poor quality as to be next to useless; but it seems more likely that geological forces did once make them and then removed them almost entirely later on.

Whatever the forces that undertook that particular work they seemingly left Scotland untouched – or at least touched her differently. Deep beneath the surface of southern Scotland – and of the north of England and southern Wales, the treasure houses of coal remained, a promise of future prosperity.

Stand on Serpent's Rock today and look back along the grey-black beach. The Atlantic waves are breaking on another headland made of more of the same limestone. Sat upon those slabs like stodgy cake on a plate, is a thick layer of glacial deposits – mud, gravels and boulders left no more than 15,000 years ago during the retreat of the ice. It is a powerful image, simplifying and symbolising one of the key geological and therefore economic facts about Ireland: while Scotland, England and Wales were gifted the fuel for industrial revolution, Ireland was denied that blessing (or curse).

Ireland had her agricultural revolution right enough. The same 'improvers' who radically altered farming practices in the rest of the British Isles in the eighteenth century got to work changing ancient lifestyles all over Ireland as well. But there never was, nor ever could be, any industrial revolution there. Without the ironstone from which iron might be won, without the coal to fuel the necessary furnaces and steam engines, Ireland was set upon a different destiny from the rest. There exists there today a rural character to both the people and the land that marks the Irish out as separate. The stuff of industry was missing as completely and irreparably as part of the sequence of an animal's DNA. It meant the Irish experience of the eighteenth, nineteenth and twentieth centuries – the experience of the Irish poor in particular – was always going to be a singular one.

The Scots marched to the beat of a different drum, however. The presence of coal was identified there at least as early as the Middle Ages and mined thereafter until the industry's final demise in the 1980s.

For those souls condemned by birth to burrow underground and hack and haul it into the light, it meant little more than a living death. For the first centuries of coal extraction in Fife, miners were treated as little more than slaves. The owners controlled every aspect of their employees' existence; even being able to refuse them permission to seek any other kind of work or to move to another's mine. Right up until the turn of the nineteenth century the industry went unchanged, with men, women and even children enduring shaming misery below ground to ensure the enrichment of a few above. Only when the appetite of the Industrial Revolution necessitated a huge increase in the labour force to meet ravenous demand were the owners forced to loosen the leashes and offer decent wages. Even then the working conditions of the miners, free or bond, remained as wretched as before.

Just as it is vital to remember the rock of Scotland and its power to predestine the lives lived upon it, so we must not forget the plight of most of the ordinary people, of whom the mining communities were only a part. For the vast majority of the country's population, life in the eighteenth and the start of the nineteenth centuries remained desperately hard and utterly thankless.

Perhaps it is fitting, or maybe just ironic, that it is in a chapter dedicated to 'identity' that we pause to pay brief attention to those anonymous souls who stood silent witness to all this history of Scotland. Nameless and forgotten, their individual identities failed to register. Barring a few exceptions – like those who scrawled their initials on the National Covenant in the seventeenth century – the lives of most of Scotland's people have been as ephemeral as raindrops in a storm.

The Scottish Enlightenment might well have been in full flower during the 1700s; innovations in trade, farming and industry lined the pockets of a handful of oligarchs and improved the lot of some entrepreneurs. But the mass of Scots continued to live inescapably rural lives, tough lives shackled to the simple need to grow enough food for themselves and their families. When change came to the countryside during the middle years of the eighteenth century, it did not improve the lot of the many.

The trouble to come was rooted in a fundamental alteration in the way the landowning aristocracy viewed the land itself. Since time immemorial *the land* had been seen as a natural resource, a gift from God set down to provide the food, clothing and shelter required by all the people living on it – rich and poor alike. No one had bothered much with thinking about who actually *owned* the land, in terms of property. If it was owned at all, it was held communally. This was no longer the case as the 1700s progressed. Scottish landowners were spending more and more time rubbing shoulders with their English counterparts and increasingly shared the southerners' opinion that land existed to make a profit for those who could demonstrate their ownership of it. From the moment that thought first lit up in the first Scottish landowning brain, the fate of the country's rural poor was sealed.

All at once the 'improving' landowners looked anew at their land – and particularly the people living on it – and did not like what they saw. Why, they thought, had they never before noticed how messy was the unbounded sprawl of infield and outfield, with meandering rig and furrow cultivation dotted around the former, and scrawny cattle wandering unchecked across the latter? Instead of unstructured 'touns' of low houses and shielings scattered higgledy-piggledy as though at random, those modernising land-lords now fancied neat rows of stone cottages, ordered square fields bounded by straight stone walls. More worrying still, they cast fresh eyes upon their erstwhile tenants – notably the 'cottars', poorest of the poor and yet the labour force behind much of the day-to-day drudgery. Surely they could be put to better use? Surely there were ways in which their efforts at subsistence might be remodelled to turn a profit?

In England, ancient contracts of leasing and rental of land gave individual farmers at least some protection in the face of landowners bent on reform. The manner and form in which they held their rights to the land their families had farmed for generations were protected by law, and put the brakes on any sudden imposition of new ideas. Lengthy leases in particular meant would-be reformers had to take their time.

In Scotland, however, it was a different story. Here the custom was for leases as short as a year. Furthermore, communal access to grazing land was a tradition rather than a legal right. No one had ever questioned any of it before and so no one had bothered to make it 'legal'. When landlords decided to shake things up and sort out what they now saw as lazy, uneconomic, untidy practices, it was simply a matter of waiting a year or so until all leases ran out. New rules were laid down, new rents set and those without the money to pay them or the ability to meet the challenges of a fast-moving future suddenly found themselves evicted from their homes. There were thousands of people, ordinary everyday people, who did not fit the new picture – who were suddenly surplus to the requirements of modern, 'improved' farming and were powerless to do anything about it.

This wave of change is best remembered in terms of the 'Highland Clearances' that wrought such havoc upon the ancient society of the north-west. But the same forces washed over the whole of Scotland, the Lowlands included. In fact it started earlier in the south of the country, lasted for longer and displaced more people in the end; but by being gradual in comparison to what happened further north the 'Lowland Clearances' are recalled with far less emotion, if any at all.

Born in Alloway, in Ayrshire, on 25 January 1759, Robert Burns learned the hard way what it meant to be a tenant farmer in southern Scotland. Farming was to be his occupation for most of his life and his inability to make a success of it made him sensitive to the plight of those around him experiencing the same difficulties. Much of his thinking – and therefore his poetry – was inspired by watching so many of his neighbours forced from the land by improvement-obsessed landowners. In 'Tae A Moose' – a seemingly simple apology to a fieldmouse tipped from its nest by his plough, yet in truth an analogy for his own struggles against capricious fate – he wrote:

> Thou saw the fields laid bare an' wast,
> An' weary Winter comin fast,
> An' cozie here, beneath the blast,
> Thou thought to dwell,
> Till crash! the cruel coulter past,
> Out thro' thy cell.
>
> That wee bit heap o' leaves an' stibble,
> Has cost thee monie a weary nibble,
> Now thou's turn' d out, for a' thy trouble,
> But house or hald.
> To thole the Winter's sleety dribble,
> An' cranreuch cauld!

The geology of Scotland dictated that Burns's Lowlanders occupied more fertile farmland, capable of supporting more people. While the improvers got to work with as much gusto as they would later lavish upon the Highlands, the Bard's displaced neighbours were living in a zone where there were alternatives to the subsistence lifestyle. There were relatively sizeable towns nearby, and the wider raft of changes brought about by Enlightenment thought and action meant those no longer employed in the fields had other paths to follow when they left, or were driven from them.

It is worth bearing in mind that the planned and deliberate removal of people from the inland valleys of the north and west – most notoriously to make way for flocks of sheep deemed more profitable than subsistence farmers – was not intended to drive them away completely. On the contrary, the landowners had imagined they could be relocated on the coastal fringes of their estates. There they were to be encouraged to take up new endeavours – notably fishing and the collection of seaweed for preparation as fertilizer – that would pour yet more coins into the pockets of the chiefs. It was only when these hastily established communities began to fail – when the bottom fell out of the kelp market at the end of the Napoleonic Wars in 1815, for instance – that folk felt they had no alternative but to board ships for passage to the New World.

What is undoubtedly true, however, is that many enlightened landowners indulged a desire to improve their tenants as well as their land. When they allocated plots of land – of 'crofts' – in the coastal villages, they were careful to ensure that each was too small to enable a family to grow enough crops or keep enough animals to feed itself. It was a practice known as 'pinching' and by its application the chiefs sought to force their people to diversify – and, more particularly, to work harder. The thinking was that subsistence farmers simply spent too much time sitting around their peat fires telling stories and drinking whisky. Enlightened landowners believed generations of experience had taught their tenants to expend minimal effort and yet still keep themselves in sufficient food – and were determined to force them into a more industrious existence. Worked and occupied in this way, they would surely improve themselves. This 'pinching' approach was unique to the Highlands, and ensured crofting became a hated system.

There is also no denying that some landowners – notably the Countess of Sutherland and her husband Lord Stafford – were brutal in the way they went about the Clearances. Many of their tenants, those who waited too long after their eviction notices were served, endured the horror of having their homes put to the torch by over-zealous estate managers, or factors. As many 10,000 people were cleared from Sutherland lands in just fifteen years at the start of the nineteenth century.

Before the time of the Highland Clearances, which did not really take effect until the end of the eighteenth century, the rise of the linen industry was already changing lives, lining a few pockets and fundamentally altering the relationship between land and people in Scotland. Even before industrialisation transformed the production of the textile, it was employing thousands of Scots up and down the country – perhaps as many as 10 per cent of the whole. At first it was a cottage industry, with the bulk of the work being carried out by men and women in their own homes. Even so, since the raw flax from which the linen was made was almost all imported from abroad, it was another part of the insidious process by which Scots were gradually divorced from the land.

Not until the 1830s at least were large numbers drawn into the towns and cities to work in the new factories; but in the closing decades of the eighteenth century, linen workers became dependent not upon the fields surrounding their homes but on the towns that finished the cloth and saw to its sale. A connection had been broken, making it easier for people to drift, or to be pushed away from the land.

What linen began, cotton soon completed. Quickly accepted as a superior product, it replaced – and was soon more industrialised than – its coarser predecessor. There was a time, although that time is not now, when every school pupil in Scotland could reel off the details of Richard Arkwright's 'Water-frame', Samuel Compton's 'Mule' and James Hargreaves' 'Spinning Jenny'. These were the innovations, all of them by Englishmen, that revolutionised and speeded up the manufacture of cotton. Once James Watt's improvements to the steam engine were added into the mix, the Industrial Revolution moved smoothly out of first gear and really began to put its foot down. All these changes were quickly imported by Scottish entrepreneurs desperate and determined to be part of something they knew was going to be big.

This was all part of the remaking of Old Scotland. The union of 1707 had made the country a fully paid-up partner in the British Empire. The doors to possible riches were opened and the most opportunist Scots dashed through them into the New World.

Hiccups like the Jacobite rebellions notwithstanding, Scots set aside their enmity for their southern neighbours and instead set about the business of making money. Trade with the American colonies – for tobacco, for sugar, for cotton – had enabled a handful of merchants to stand out and establish themselves as captains of commerce. The vast sums of money they made provided the finances for revolutionising the fabric of Scottish life. By the 1740s the Tobacco Lords were the embodiment of the new money. Their need for an infrastructure capable of processing and containing their wares would eventually create Glasgow's Merchant City of vast warehouses, and the urge to display their wealth prompted them to build ever-grander private homes. Their presence on the Broomielaw let people know who they were and their building projects showed they had changed their world for ever. The face they put on Glasgow during the eighteenth century provided the bone structure for the place to this day.

It was actually Edinburgh, however, that was first to experience the effects of a new, modern society growing within its cramped, malodorous confines behind the fourteenth-century Flodden Wall that defined its boundaries. They called the place 'Auld Reekie' on account of the haze of smoke from countless coal fires and the reek of the accumulated, discarded waste of countless human beings. (When pedestrians on the city's pavements heard the cry of 'Gardyloo!' – 'Watch out for water!' – from a tenement window above their heads, they knew water was about to be the least of their worries.) And yet for all that the place stank to high heaven and was filled to bursting with the great and the good, the rich and the poor, the bad and the ugly, it hummed with something else entirely – with the excitement and buzz you only get when an assembled population know beyond a shadow of a doubt that they are living in the right place at the right time.

Made literate by the legacy of Knox, forced into one another's company by the growth of towns and cities thriving like mushrooms on the rich manure of business and toil, the enlightened thinkers had whipped them-selves up into a froth of excitement about who they were and what they were capable of. They not only understood the workings of the world now, or so they thought, they were also hard at work filling in the gaps in creation, tidying up the loose ends and making it even better than God and nature had intended.

Hutcheson, Kames, Hume, Robertson, Black, Smith, Raeburn, Ramsay, Adam – the list of names goes on and on and every one of them adds to the lustre of the constellation. By 1766 the city fathers in Edinburgh were feeling good enough to award themselves a whole *new* city, or at least a new town. The overcrowding of the buildings of the old town – not to mention the unspeakably unsanitary conditions and therefore the ever-present threat of disease – were the inspiration for a competition to design a place that better suited the self-image of men and women on the make.

Beyond the Nor' Loch (subsequently drained and reborn as Princes Street Gardens) lay hundreds of acres of prime building land overlooking the Firth of Forth. The competition to develop the site was won by a then unknown but suitably ambitious twenty-one-year-old called James Craig. His design was simple: elegant squares connected by a grid of streets running east to west and north to south. Beyond the sheer simplicity, what really won the judges over was the properly patriotic, Hanoverian slant of the names Craig proposed for the squares – St Andrew's and St George's – and some of the streets – Hanover and George; Thistle and Rose; Queen and Princes.

Enlightened Scots of the sort seeking to live in the New Town had long since accepted they were 'North Britons', self-consciously and studiously mimicking the ways and mores of their British, English opposite numbers, and nothing would please them more than to build elegant, spacious town houses with addresses that underlined their loyalty to the union and to the empire.

The New Town itself was decades in the building and not actually completed until 1820, when the finishing touches were put to Charlotte Square at the western extreme of the whole grand design. It was a masterwork by Scotland's most famous architect, Robert Adam, yet it was not completed until nearly thirty years after his death in 1792. By then, something fundamental had happened to Edinburgh: all those who had the wealth to do so had moved far away from the foul-smelling, narrow winding alleyways, wynds and lanes of the Old Town. While they promenaded past their fine homes on wide, tree-lined streets and through the neatly manicured parks of the New Town, the higgly-piggledy tenements towering above the old High Street were home now only to the working poor.

There had always been class divisions in Edinburgh, of course. Previously the richest had occupied the middle floors, high enough to be clear of the reek of the streets but not demanding too high a climb. At ground level and in the highest floors was the rest of humanity. But in old Edinburgh everyone had co-existed, so that folk of all kinds had mixed together into a rich soup. Along the cobbled streets walked advocates and artisans, judges and journeymen, lairds and layabouts. Whatever its shortcomings, the old city had created an atmosphere from which world-changing creativity and productivity had sprung like ice-cold water from an underground spring.

With the completion of the New Town, a highly visible fault line had opened up between rich and poor. The North Bridge was opened to traffic in 1772, linking Old and New; but the separation of the city into two different parts was irrevocable by then, and symbolised the way Scotland's ruling class viewed their country's past until at least the early years of the nineteenth century: as an embarrassing litany of barbarity and strife, populated by characters utterly foreign to them. The past was a place from which they wanted only to distance themselves.

This move into the new also revealed how they regarded those they sought to rule: as a species necessary for one's day-to-day chores but best kept at arm's length whenever possible. And therein lies the edge of a darkness in Scotland's soul, that ability of her ruling class to live well and clean and comfortably, while others – indeed those upon whose naked backs that comfortable life had been built – lived another sort of life entirely. Given the kind of lives those others endured, it was best the whole sordid business of it was carried on somewhere just out of sight.

There had always been the poor of Scotland. The great, unwashed mass of them, scraping an existence from whatever patches of thin soil their masters had vouchsafed them this year. There were serfs, near-slaves in the mines, their humanity all but crushed out of them not by the great weight of rock above their bent backs but by the degrading conditions in which they were forced to work.

There still existed the rural poor – those eking a living from black cattle or tough crops wherever the landowners told them to. Lately there had grown the populations of weavers and spinners, severed from the land but still living on it. Poorest of all, notionally free and yet most vulnerable to the vagaries of fortune or more lately 'the market', were the Highlanders with their subsistence crofts, herds of scrawny cattle and ill-starred recent attempts at making a living from seaweed.

Until the end of the sixteenth century these 'last of the free' had had something at least in common with those south and east of the Great Glen, even if it was just hardship. By the end of the seventeenth century they had come to be no more than aliens at best, feared bogeymen at worst, unloved and unwanted. The Scottish Diaspora was already under way and thousands of Scots, from Highlands and Lowlands alike, were risking their lives to cross the Atlantic Ocean in search of opportunities in the west. But the lot of the varied mass of Scotland's common folk in the eighteenth century – even those choosing to leave the old country behind and seek out new lives in the Americas and in the Caribbean – was as nothing to that of the hundreds of thousands taken from Africa's Guinea Coast during the same period.

Many of the history books, especially those written ten or more years ago, have it that Scots merchants did not benefit directly from slavery. However, it is widely acknowledged that the great fortunes made by Scots from commodities such as tobacco, sugar and cotton depended upon the labour of African slaves. Without the mark-up made possible by having access to free labour, the profit margins would never have been as attractive and exciting as they surely were. But the conclusion to be drawn from the books was that this morally reprehensible trade was practised by others, by Englishmen or other Europeans, but not by Scots. That Scots profited at one remove at least from the trade was deemed better, somehow, than if they had bought and sold souls themselves.

All these assumptions are false. While it is correct to say that Scottish ports like Greenock and Port Glasgow never witnessed the loading and unloading of slaves, the great Scots families of eighteenth-century commerce were in the slave trade up to their necks. Cunninghames and Bogles; Houstons and Ogilvies; McDowells and Millikens; John Gladstone, the Leith-born father of Prime Minister William Gladstone and James Ewing of Strathleven, founder of the Glasgow Necropolis – all of these and many more profited directly from the labour of slaves.

Recent research by Scots historians like Eric J. Graham has revealed that during the first half of the eighteenth century several Glasgow merchants tried their hand at dealing directly with African chiefs keen to sell their neighbours' people, or indeed their own, into slavery. But it was a tricky, sensitive business dependent upon knowledge of and access to very specific types of trade goods like copper bars of precise length, beads of a specific material, shape and colour, swords of a certain style. After a few abortive attempts, Scots merchants settled for using middlemen to secure the human cargoes on their behalf and then reaped the rewards. Everyone who counted in eighteenth-century Scotland knew the trade was going on, but perhaps the most that can be said in the national defence is that fewer understood that the finest Scots families were growing rich from it as well.

Burns himself very nearly emigrated to Jamaica, in 1786. Offered a job as a book-keeper on a plantation owned by his friend Dr Patrick Douglas, he had planned to escape his poverty – and the responsibilities presented by his pregnant girlfriend, Jean Armour – by heading to the New World. Never one to go it alone, he had taken up with yet another woman – 'Highland Mary' Campbell – and had promised to take her with him. In the event, Highland Mary died of fever before they could board a ship and Burns found, to his surprise, that Jean Armour had given birth to twins. Even more importantly to the then aspiring bard, his newly published *Poems, Chiefly in the Scottish Dialect* had proved an overnight hit with polite Edinburgh society. With thoughts of emigration to a land of slaves cast aside, he stayed at home to become an legend instead.

Genius? Undoubtedly. Loveable? Definitely. Naïve? Absolutely. The man who came so close to helping manage a slave plantation in 1786 would write 'A Man's A Man For A' That' in 1795.

> Then let us pray that come it may
> (As come it will for a' that),
> That Sense and Worth o'er a' the earth,
> Shall bear thee gree an' a' that.
> For a' that, an' a' that,
> It's comin' yet for a' that,
> That man to man, the world o'er,
> Shall brithers be for a' that.

Burns was hardly alone among eighteenth-century Scots in failing to understand, or perhaps to acknowledge, just what was bringing all the money into his homeland. But on the other side of the Atlantic many of his coun-trymen knew the whole shameful truth of it, and cared not a jot. Emigrant Scots like John Wedderburn worked their plantations with slaves – and even brought some home with them as symbols of their status when they returned to impress their former neighbours. But still the pretence has been maintained, down to the present, that Scots were not really slavers.

During the Seven Years War, as one Caribbean island after another fell to Great Britain, opportunist Scots poured ashore onto each in turn, like carpet-baggers, to begin the business of making money. Jamaica was a prize among prizes, providing the raw material for vast fortunes in sugar, coffee, rum and spices. Though less than 150 miles long by 50 miles wide, by the turn of the nineteenth century the island was awash with approximately 20,000 British entrepreneurs, half of them Scots. Working for them, endur-ing lives that were nasty, brutal and short, were a third of a million Africans.

The Scottish connection to the slave trade in the Caribbean, so unfamiliar here at home, is made painfully obvious by the surnames of modern-day descendants both of slaves and slave masters: Campbell, Douglas, Farquharson, Ferguson, Frazer, Grant, Gordon, Graham, Lewis, Mac-Donald, MacFarlane, MacKenzie, Morrison, Reid, Robinson, Russell, Scott, Simpson ... the list goes on. Telling, too, are the place names, relics of the plantations that once bore them: Argyle, Dumbarton, Dundee, Fort William, Glasgow, Glen Islay, Hampden, Hermitage, Montrose, Mount Stewart, Old Monklands, St Andrews.

While such cruel, avaricious behaviour might almost be expected of canny businessmen bent on squeezing every last penny of profit from their enterprises, it might be more surprising to learn that the brightest thinkers of the Scottish Enlightenment were ready to shore up the foundations of people-trafficking. The same philosopher who could contend that 'there is a great uniformity among the actions of men, in all nations and ages' was also capable of contradicting himself when it came to considering slavery and, more particularly, the value, as human beings, of its victims. He was David Hume and in his 1753 essay 'Of National Characters' he concluded:

> I am apt to suspect the negroes ... to be naturally inferior to the whites. There never was a civilised nation of any other complexion than white, nor even any individual eminent either in action or speculation. No ingenious manufactures amongst them, no arts, no sciences.
>
> On the other hand, the most rude and barbarous of the whites, such as the ancient GERMANS, the present TARTARS, still have something eminent about them, in their valour, form of government, or some other particular.
>
> Such a uniform and constant difference could not happen, in so many countries and ages, if nature had not made an original distinction betwixt these breeds of men.

Hume knew well that African slaves were scattered across the colonies and felt moved to excuse their use and abuse: 'there are Negroe slaves dispersed all over Europe, of which none ever discovered any symptoms of ingenuity ... In Jamaica indeed they talk of one negroe as a man of parts and learning; but 'tis likely he is admired for very slender accomplishments, like a parrot, who speaks a few words plainly.' Blithely overlooking the fact that a slave in the American colonies who did as much as hold his master or mistress's gaze for more than a few seconds risked severe punishment for insolence, still the most revered of Scottish philosophers felt moved to blame their lack of 'accomplishments' on a supposed natural failing of an entire race of people.

The freeing of Joseph Knight in 1777 had followed the landmark case of another African slave. Somerset had been given his freedom in England in 1772 on the judgment of another Scot, William Murray, Lord Mansfield, Chief Justice of the King's Bench. In both cases, advocates employed by the slave owners raised the spectre of what would happen to polite, civilised society if fundamental principles of 'property' were no longer respected and upheld. Property, after all – natural desire to acquire it and the duty of society to protect it – had underpinned the thinking of Enlightenment philosophers from Lord Kames onwards. It was the bedrock of the Georgian world and certainly a preoccupation of Adam Smith. But somehow the burning white light of progress had blinded the best of them to the thinking of a founding father of the Scottish Enlightenment, Francis Hutcheson. He had written: 'That Action is best, which procures the greatest Happiness for the greatest numbers; and that, worst, which, in like manner, occasions Misery.'

Hutcheson had taught that all human beings were born knowing right from wrong – and also that the surest path to happiness lay in seeking and labouring towards the happiness of others. By writing that black Africans were 'naturally inferior to the whites' – indeed, that they had no more intellect than that of caged birds taught to mimic speech – Hume was laying down the framework for a model of abuse that distorts the world to this day. And if Hutcheson was right about all beings having an internal moral compass, then Hume and everyone else must have known instinctively that the buying and selling of their fellow human beings was morally suspect at the very least. Their forced labour in the colonies, where their average life expectancy was five years, might have seemed sensible from an economic point of view – but it cannot have appeared right to a humanist.

Lords Mansfield and Kames had caused sensations by freeing Somerset and Joseph Knight – and had sounded the right note of high-minded, moral indignation as they did so; but by then slavery had done its job for Scotland. Half a century before William Wilberforce's Slavery Abolition Act signalled the death knell of the practice in most of the British Empire in 1833, the suffering, sweat and shortened lives of black men, women and children had already laid the foundations of Scotland's future prosperity. Slavery had been fine, it seemed, as long as Scots abroad had depended upon it – and as long as the realities of the trade had not sullied Scottish soil. By bringing Joseph Knight into Scotland, by forcing polite society to consider the bigger moral picture when the slave began to demand the rights of any man, Wedderburn sowed the seeds of change. Despite the Knight case, it was a Scot who stubbornly and effectively hindered the abolition of the slave trade in the British Empire. Henry Dundas is remembered as 'Harry the ninth, the uncrowned king of Scotland' on account of his huge influence on Scottish affairs.

Lawyer, politician and arch-manipulator, Dundas was also a close friend of William Pitt the Younger. While Secretary of State for the Home Department in Pitt's government, Dundas used his influence over many Scots MPs to prevent them voting against the slave trade. Before William Wilberforce's Slave Trade Act went to the House of Commons in 1807, Dundas succeeded in forcing him to place the word 'gradually' before 'abolished'. This addition ensured the continuation of slavery in the empire for another quarter of a century.

Scots talk a lot about national identity, about knowing who they are. Historian Tom Devine has railed long and hard against what he describes as the 'Wha's like us?' school of Scottish history. He has said Scots' view of themselves has for too long been skewed by the picture painted by writers like Sir Walter Scott and J.M. Barrie and by poets like Robert Burns – of victimhood and suffering at the hands of the English; of stubborn commitment to independence; of descent from a noble, heroic warrior class; of Highland Clearances and the sad Diaspora, of lost causes and thwarted dreams. If Devine is right then part of accepting the Scots national identity is a requirement to face the fact that in the eighteenth century Scotland rode into the front rank of world powers at least in part upon the scarred backs of slaves.

The American War of Independence that briefly interrupted trans-Atlantic trade and forced the Scots traders to diversify, to be even more cunning, also shaped some of Scotland's destiny in unexpected ways. Before the war, all the Scottish-owned ships that transported the slaves, cotton, tobacco and sugar across the Atlantic were built in North America, of North American timber. It was by far the cheapest alternative, in a land where virgin forests grew down to the ocean's edge. When war broke out – and then when the colonists emerged triumphant and independent at the end of it – the Tobacco Lords and other merchants were forced to find alternatives. It was then that the shipbuilding industry was relocated, in its entirety, to the banks of the River Clyde in Glasgow. Suitable timber from the Baltic was desired as never before, reinvigorating trade across the North Sea. It was the first time an international war had brought such work to the Clyde – but it certainly would not be the last.

As the eighteenth century drew towards its close it was developments on the European mainland that began to preoccupy British and therefore Scottish minds. On 14 July 1789 a mob of around 1,000 people had stormed the Bastille prison in Paris and in so doing had triggered the French Revolution.

King Louis XVI had, ironically, supported the colonists during the American War of Independence; but in doing so he had added to the financial woes of his country and his people at a time when famine and disease already stalked the land. He paid for the oversight with his head. The Americans had won their independence and had set out to create a society that declared 'the pursuit of happiness' among the noblest of ambitions. In the first heady weeks and months of 1789 the French appeared to be following a similar path. It seemed to many in Scotland's enlightened cities that the same road might be open to them as well.

In terms of her people's entitlement to elect Members of Parliament, Scotland was just one big 'Rotten Borough'. At best, something like one man in every 120 had the vote. Powerful aristocrats and rich landowners controlled the operation, manipulated the votes, sat in parliament themselves and shoehorned their own friends and relatives into whatever seats they pleased. Elections were considered so meaningless in terms of changing anything they were seldom even held.

With nations east and west finding ways to empower their 'citizens', it seemed inevitable to some that Scotland could and should do likewise. But as the years passed, the atmosphere drifting across from France changed swiftly from one of optimism to one of fear. What had begun as a movement determined radically to change France's government from an absolute monarchy to one based on freedom, equality and brotherhood evolved with terrifying speed into just another kind of tyranny. A dream of replacing a sovereign king with the sovereignty of the people – of equal rights for all citizens regardless of race, class, wealth or religion – turned into a nightmare.

The extremist 'Jacobin' group of politicians gained control of the country and between September 1793 and July 1794 unleashed the bloodletting remembered as 'The Terror'. During those months, tens of thousands of 'enemies of the revolution' were put to death on the guillotine. Thereafter events steadily acquired momentum until the emergence of Napoleon Bonaparte, who installed himself as First Consul in 1799 and then, five years later, as Emperor of France.

This, then, was the birth of 'democracy' in Europe – and it had all but led to the death of the mother in childbirth. In spite of the violence, the killing of any and all who voiced doubts about what was happening, still the oppressed of Scotland found inspiration in events across the Channel.

There had been political parties in Scotland since the seventeenth century. When hardline Presbyterian Covenanters had marched on Edinburgh in August 1648 to oust the moderate 'Engagers' determined to work in league with Charles I, they thought of themselves as the 'Kirk Party'. Their opponents, however, looked on at those anti-Royalist zealots, mounted on horseback, and nicknamed them 'Whiggamores' – possibly a corruption of a Scots Gaelic term meaning 'horse-drivers'. In time this was shortened to 'Whigs' and, though originally meant as an insult, the Kirk Party members eventually adopted the name for themselves.

By the early years of the eighteenth century, all those who supported the House of Hanover – and constitutional monarchy over the absolute rule of kings – styled themselves as Whigs. As the century progressed, however, the picture became more complicated. Whigs were still devoted, in the main, to the Presbyterian faith and indeed to all 'Dissenters'. But increasingly they began to draw their support from among the emerging merchant and industrialist classes, while their opponents championed the rights of the landed gentry. This body of opposition was the 'Tory Party', drawn from another nickname – this time *Toraidhe*, an Irish word for an outlaw. And while most Whigs in the House of Commons supported the Presbyterian faith, their Tory counterparts backed the Anglican Church of England. More so than the average Whig by then, they also backed the rights and wants of the Crown.

The fallout of American Independence and French Revolution hung heavy in the air over Scotland and the rest of Great Britain in the last years of the eighteenth century. To radicals and would-be reformers – many liberal Whigs among them – democracy smelled like an opportunity to right old wrongs of inequality; to conservative Tories and the rest of the landowning Scottish establishment it seemed an airborne disease that might fatally infect all they held dear, not least their ownership of most of the country.

Irish-born philosopher and politician Edmund Burke was a self-styled Whig. But while many of his colleagues were exhilarated by events across the Channel, the *émigré* Dubliner was appalled from the start. Widely regarded as a father of modern Conservatism, Burke demonstrated the foresight of a mystic when he predicted not just the horror of the Terror but even the rise of the imperialist dictator soon to be personified by

Napoleon. Burke was proved right, of course, but fortunately excesses of the Jacobins were enough to snuff out the fires of the reform movement in Scotland. The French had merely gone too far; it was still right to dream of and to fight for a society based on freedom, equality and protection of the rule of law for all.

It was in this febrile atmosphere – of uncertainty or opportunity, depending on your point of view – that the nature of a national identity for the people of Scotland first occurred to those blessed with the time to think about such things.

With Napoleon making war on every country in mainland Europe and even threatening to invade Great Britain, philosophical opinion became sharply polarised. William Pitt the Younger became Prime Minister in 1783, at the age of twenty-four. Although he called himself an 'independent Whig', he is usually described as a Tory, especially in terms of his opinions about Revolutionary France. The Tories had lined up in opposition to the Revolution and its offspring almost from the beginning. When Great Britain went to war with France in 1793 the Whigs – or at least those described by Burke as 'New Whigs' – had loudly and bitterly opposed the conflict. The Tories turned it into a test of patriotism.

In Scotland the call for patriots energised all those who had long since taken to describing themselves as 'North Britons'. Devotion to the union and to freedom became synonymous with opposition to the French Revolution, even to the notion of *democracy* itself. Into the vanguard of the forces fighting to preserve the North British status quo stepped a young Edinburgh lawyer named Walter Scott. Born in 1771, Scott was the son of a Writer to the Signet and set out, without a great deal of enthusiasm, to follow in his father's footsteps. A bout of polio in his right leg when he was just a year and half old left him slightly lame for life, unable to engage in the sort of valorous pursuits that would inspire his writing; but in his chest beat the heart of a dashing warrior nonetheless.

By the time of his birth, some of the fathers of the Scottish Enlightenment were still lighting up the sky with their brilliance. Others were already on the wane. But if ever there was a son of their collective genius, it was Walter Scott. As the child of an Edinburgh lawyer he grew up surrounded by a fair degree of privilege. He had access to a fine education – first at the city's Royal High School and then at the University. It was during that period, around 1787, that the young Scott, just fifteen, crossed paths with the new darling of polite Scottish society – Robert Burns, recently arrived in the city and with his dreams of a life in the Caribbean fading softly behind him.

Whether the pair exchanged idealistic notions concerning the universal rights of man seems highly unlikely, but it is undeniable that Scott's early life and early adulthood had allowed him to taste the fruits of learning and of property. So it was that when war broke out with France in 1793, the language of some of the reforming voices sounded horrifying to him. He was and would always be a property-defending, royalty-supporting Tory, both by inclination and by action.

In 1797 the threat of an invasion by French forces prompted the British government to permit the raising of militia groups in Scotland. This was a huge boost to Scottish pride and did much to bolster Scots' confidence in their status as equal partners within the union. The Militia Act of 1757 had allowed the formation of armed civilian forces for the defence of the realm against invasion in England and Wales only. No such permission was granted to Scotland, making it plain to Scots that they were not to be trusted with weapons. Relieved of this shameful ban in 1797, Scotsmen responded to the call by joining the militia in their tens of thousands. Within weeks they amounted to over a third of Great Britain's volunteer defence force.

Scott, seeing his hitherto unfulfilled dreams of life as a cavalryman suddenly within his grasp, was quickly among those who formed the Royal Edinburgh Volunteer Light Dragoons. There was no invasion – not that year or any other – but from then on Scott would fight to preserve his own unique and idealised view of his homeland.

Perhaps even more upsetting to Scott in the long term than the threat from France was unrest at home. There were several popular uprisings in Scotland and England during the 1790s by radicals and proto-revolutionaries demanding change, and Scott was only too pleased to see government forces mercilessly crush them. The Black Watch, a regiment of heroes since the Seven Years War and a totem of Scottish loyalty to the union, were to the fore in putting down the troublemakers north of the Border.

Scott was married in 1797, to Frenchwoman Charlotte Charpentier, and two years later he accepted the post of Sheriff Depute of Selkirkshire. This return to the fields and hills where his father had spent the first half of his life seems to have kindled a fire within Scott. He and Charlotte had five children, four of whom – two daughters and then two sons – survived to adulthood. Out of his contentment sprang a need to look back into his childhood years, and to remember the Border ballads and tales he had heard from his father. Perhaps a desire to preserve them for his own children inspired Scott to write down the folk stories and poetry of the people living and working around him. His first foray into publishing came in 1802 with *The Minstrelsy of the Scottish Border*, a collection of Border ballads. Then between 1805 and 1810 he turned out three long poems of his own, 'The Lay of the Last Minstrel', 'Marmion' and 'The Lady of the Lake'.

Scott had pulled aside the heavy curtain of oblivion to reveal the world of the past, still populated by the real-life heroes, heroines and villains who had once strode across the landscapes of Scotland, fighting battles and breaking hearts. For his readers, it was a version of the truth – their own history brought to life and celebrated as something precious, something all but lost amid the clamour and commerce of the modern world.

The poetry alone made his reputation as a writer and earned enough money for him to begin building a grand new family home at Melrose, near the River Tweed. Named 'Abbotsford' by Scott, it was designed to be an unashamedly sentimental and idealised fantasy of a Scottish baronial mansion. Into its rooms, into its very fabric indeed, he incorporated countless keepsakes, mementoes, treasures and artefacts from Scotland's past, including antique weapons like Rob Roy's long-barrelled musket.

It was at Abbotsford that he turned from poetry to prose, producing the twenty-seven novels of the *Waverley* series along with many others, short stories and yet more poems and histories. It was a prolific outpouring of genius the like of which Scotland had never seen before and has not seen again. As if his output was not impressive enough, he was also pioneering an entirely new literary genre at the same time – indeed inventing it as he went along. This was the historical novel and it was with tales like *Waverley* (1814), *Guy Mannering* (1815), *Old Mortality* (1816), *Rob Roy* (1817), *The Heart of Midlothian* (1818), *Ivanhoe* (1819) and *Redgauntlet* (1824) that Scott set out on the grand quest that was to shape his life and destiny, as well as his legacy.

The eponymous hero of *Waverley* is an English British Army officer sent north in advance of Bonnie Prince Charlie's arrival. Captivated by the Highlanders, he turns Jacobite and fights against both his own kind and his innate sense of duty. Scott would revisit similar themes again and again: men and woman torn between head and heart, between their own cultures and those that circumstances force them to confront.

In addition to entertaining his readers, he sought nothing less than the preservation of something he believed was in mortal danger, namely Scotland's sense of herself as a unique and ancient nation. While many in

Edinburgh were happy to consider themselves 'North Britons', Scott also feared the consequences of galloping into the future without a backward glance. 'What makes Scotland Scotland is fast disappearing,' he wrote. He felt the pull of something in the past – an anchor or perhaps a True North – and believed the modern world could benefit from sensing the connection as well. This set him at odds with much of contemporary 'enlightened' thought. The luminaries of the Enlightenment had found no cause for pride in their nation's history – on the contrary, when they looked back they saw only a shameful barbarism that had not ended until 1707. As Scott gazed out through the windows of Abbotsford, his mind's eye let him see far beyond the trees and fields of his steadily expanding demesne.

In England the continuing unrest was throwing up worrying intrigues and events like 'the Peterloo Massacre' of 1819 and the Cato Street Conspiracy of 1820. As is always the case, soldiers returning from war had looked with clear eyes at their world and found it lacking. A post-war economic downturn soon followed, heaping financial hardship onto urban communities already suffering the indignities of low wages, poor conditions and the contemptuous disinterest of the owners. The trouble spread north of the Border and found a warm reception among the dispossessed and similarly vote-less of Glasgow. Without a voice in parliament they knew they could change nothing. What they wanted were workers' rights, reform of the voting system – and if those pipe dreams were not realised they would seek wholesale revolution.

This was the so-called 'Radical War' – or 'Scottish Insurrection' – of 1820. Starting on April Fool's Day with calls for strike action, it quickly escalated to the point where a small group of protesters marched towards Carron Iron Works in Falkirk in the hope of seizing weapons. They stopped at Bonnymuir, near the village of Bonnybridge, outside Falkirk, where they were attacked by a force of Hussars. Three men were killed in the clash and three of the protesters – James Wilson, John Baird and Andrew Hardie – were subsequently tried, convicted of treason and executed. A score more were sentenced to transportation.

Despite being remembered as a 'war', the Glasgow uprising of 1820 was small-scale and never a realistic threat to the safety of anyone but the protesters themselves. Nonetheless, it was a symptom of what Scott saw as a potentially debilitating, enervating disease that might lead to the downfall of modern Scotland – a Scotland, as he saw it, existing in happy, profitable union with England.

The apparent conflict at the heart of Scott's thinking was that while he sought to immortalise and keep in the public mind the epic struggles of Scotland's past, he was completely committed to her present as a nation at peace. And although he drew so much of his inspiration – for works like *Waverley* and *Redgauntlet* – from Jacobite warriors and their romantic lost cause, he never again wanted to see Scotland unsettled, far less ruled, by anyone opposed to the House of Hanover. For Scott, it seems, Scotland's history was the stuff of collective memory, to be recalled, enjoyed and celebrated. Even his critics – and they are many and vociferous – usually acknowledge that he encouraged his fellow Scots to take an interest in their history in a way that no one had managed before, or perhaps since.

Almost as a by-product, his writings also inspired a love affair between Britons, North and South, and the landscapes of Scotland. Before Wordsworth and the other Lake Poets turned the Lake District into a tourist destination, Scott enticed thousands to visit places like Loch Katrine and the Trossachs, the setting for 'Lady of the Lake'. A landscape dismissed before by polite society as a barren wilderness of gloomy glens and forbidding mountains was reinvented as a place of inspiration, of soul-soothing solitude.

Lord Kames had described a four-stage progression for human society: hunting and gathering, nomadic-herding, farming and finally the commercial society of merchants and lawmakers. Unconsciously or not, Scott had refined this clinical analysis of human nature by reinvesting the people of the earlier stages with humanity itself. By making nomadic herders and farmers into real, believable people with loves and losses, needs and wants, he reminded the inhabitants of the present that only time separated them from their ancestors.

For all that he admired the nation's history, Scott had no wish whatever to bring any of its precepts back into the present. Jacobites (and Scott was even ready to declare himself a bit of a Cavalier at heart) were sworn to the overthrow of the House of Hanover and no dream was further from his heart. Furthermore, he considered Scotland's landed gentry, nobility and aristocracy the living links between past and future. Since the nineteenth-century rebels wanted to throw them out, Scott was always going to be implacably opposed to them and their demands to change anything else in his comfortable, elegant world.

A memory is precious but fragile. Any attempt to revisit it – or to reach out and *touch* it – will destroy it, like a reflection in a pool of water disturbed by an outstretched hand.

326 · A HISTORY OF SCOTLAND

The seeming irony of Scott is that all the while he battled to preserve Scotland's history, the remnants of the very culture he venerated above all others – that of the Highlands – were being swept away for ever by the same aristocracy he was determined to protect. Of course he was aware of the Clearances while they were happening and readily acknowledged that there would be a great sadness were the glens to be emptied completely of their people. But he was also a product of the world defined by Adam Smith, the world of profit and of the market. He accepted that, while the end of a way of life upset him, it was the work of economic forces neither he nor anyone else could halt. In fact he feared that any attempt to intervene with temporary solutions to the epic of human suffering unfolding in Sutherland and on the Islands and elsewhere might only delay the inevitable. (Dependence on the potato in some parts of the Highlands saw vast swathes of the crop smothering every available square foot of fertile land by the 1840s. The yield was four times that of any alternative foodstuff and crofters turned to it in ever-increasing desperation. As fathers sought to provide for multiple sons, plots that were too small to begin with were sub-divided even further. When the potato blight struck in 1846 it wreaked a localised havoc not unlike that which so devastated Ireland.)

Scott enjoyed looking at the past, considering how its heroes and villains might guide actions in the present; but he was no would-be time-traveller. For him the past worked precisely *because* it was forever out of reach. What he sought to do instead was the near-impossible: to achieve an equilibrium in which past and present co-existed, to the benefit of both. In fact he craved something more intense, something that depended for its existence upon its own pain: rather than equilibrium he demanded the acceptance of a stalemate. Scott believed the modern Scotland in which he so enjoyed living would be holed below the waterline without reverence for its history. But for him the fact that the values and traditions of the past were at odds with those of the present was a necessary state of being: it was the tension between the two that was holding the whole thing together. Lose one and lose both; cut the guy-rope and watch the big top collapse.

Undeterred by the march of progress, therefore, Scott eagerly got in step with the beat of the drum. In 1815 he met the future King George IV and asked permission for another quest. This time he wanted to go in search of the Scottish crown jewels, 'the Honours of Scotland'. Last seen on the very day the Scottish parliament had ceased to exist in 1707, they had subsequently been bricked up in the redundant Crown Room in Edinburgh

Castle. The Prince Regent consented and on 4 February 1818 Scott led the party of treasure hunters that recovered the Crown, Sceptre and Sword of State from over a century in the forgotten dark.

For his initiative in instigating the search, Scott was awarded a baronetcy by the newly crowned king. At last he was among the nobility he so valued and admired. The quest for the Honours had begun a friendship between the two men that prompted the grateful monarch – an avowed fan of the *Waverley* novels – to make the first royal visit to Scotland since that of Charles II in 1650. From the moment of his arrival in the port of Leith on 14 August 1822, aboard his royal yacht, King George IV's days in the capital were a glittering triumph, not least for *Sir* Walter Scott, who choreographed the whole affair down to the last minute.

Scott boarded a little boat so he might be rowed out to the royal yacht and when King George heard the author was at hand he called out, 'Sir Walter Scott! The man in Scotland I most want to see! Let him come up!' The pair toasted the occasion with glasses of brandy and Scott, ever on the lookout for souvenirs of great moments, for display in Abbotsford, subtly slipped his empty glass into his pocket. Returning home that evening in exhausted satisfaction, he forgot the thing was there and sat down without taking off his coat. The irreplaceable trinket was crushed into oblivion but otherwise his success was total.

As a fan of Scott's Scotland in particular, the king wanted to experience nothing but the sights and sounds of the Highlands he had been encouraged to imagine between the pages of novels like *Waverley*. He himself was decked out in full Highland regalia – a very large version of the full plaid for a very large man – and everyone who wanted to make a favourable impression did likewise. The kiltmakers of Edinburgh and elsewhere had never had it so good.

That there was a thriving community of kiltmakers in the capital was almost entirely down to the efforts of a couple of Polish conmen. By the turn of the nineteenth century the traditional dress of the clansman – *breacan an feileadh*, 12 yards of plaid folded into pleats and held in place by a belt at the waist – had spent the best part of half a century in disgrace. Banned after Culloden (a simplified version called *feileadh-beag*, the kilt familiar to us today, was being worn by Highland regiments like the Black Watch), the full plaid remained in the doldrums until two brothers, Charles Edward Stuart and John Sobieski Stolberg Stuart, turned up in Edinburgh claiming to be grandsons of the Bonnie Prince himself.

Whatever the truth of their identities, they brandished a document called 'Vestiarum Scoticum' that appeared to describe which tartan belonged to which clan. There had been no such tradition in the Highlands. Folk wore plaid woven and died in any colour they pleased, even within the same clan. In time of battle, when it was necessary for opposing clansmen to recognise friend from foe, then men of the same side wore a sprig of some brightly coloured plant on their bonnets. Fake or not (the brothers only produced it once and thereafter refused to let anyone see it) the book was a work of genius. Beguiled by the brothers, the great and the good of Edinburgh could not wait to commission outfits that matched their names. For the kiltmakers, and the mysterious Poles, it was a licence to print money.

Many observers at the time mocked the royal visit of George IV; a host of historians have done so since. For them it was fakery from start to finish, the product of some sort of hysteria-induced collective amnesia. Modern Scotland – so hard won – was put on hold for a few days while the faithful donned the jester's motley and pretended they had loved the Jacobites all along. There is no denying, however, that it was a triumph in its way, even if to some it appeared comic, overblown and riddled with hypocrisy. Hundreds of thousands of ordinary Scots turned out to roar their approval – and their king, huge and bloated and wrapped in customised Highland garb, beamed back at them in delight. It was a moment.

The rehabilitation of the Highlander was complete and all his attributes, real or imagined, were the height of fashion, even down to the clothes he was supposed to wear. That Highland culture had its brightest flowering in the capital of the Lowlands, while the last vestiges of real Highland life were being scoured from the land, was an irony even Scott overlooked.

Sir Walter Scott had reinvented Scottish history for Scottish people but in the end he was undone by the present that had so troubled him. The most successful and popular writer of his time, he had maximised his income by investing both in his publishers and their parent company so he could take a cut of the profits. He had also borrowed heavily from them to help finance his work at Abbotsford and, when the London Stock Market crashed in 1825, his personal fortune was wiped out overnight, leaving him with massive debts. Rather than endure bankruptcy, Scott struck a deal whereby he continued living at Abbotsford and kept writing, but with all new profits going to his creditors. From that moment on, *he* worked for *them* with all the energy and creativity that remained to him.

There was worse to come than financial disaster. The calls for changes to society, for electoral reform in particular, had been incessant during the later years of Scott's career. He had fought against them with all his strength and all the weapons in his formidable literary arsenal. But his efforts were in vain. A lifelong Tory, Scott cast his vote against electoral reform in the general election of May 1831. He had suffered a stroke two years before and felt at least as old as his fifty-nine years by then. The cruellest cut was the way many of his Borders neighbours – the hard-working tenant farmers, ploughmen and ghillies he counted among his friends – turned against him in his last weeks and months. Though he had loved them, he had wanted them to stay down, and they condemned him for his stance against reform – which they took as a personal sleight.

Arthur Wellesley, the 'Iron' Duke of Wellington, had led the Tory Party to victory in the general election of 1830. He was absolutely opposed to reform and said so in a speech in the Commons. It was a personal and political disaster. A vote of no confidence soon after forced him to resign and the reforming Whig, Lord Charles Grey, was made Prime Minister in his stead. The general election of 1831 returned the Whigs with a majority and by June the following year the Reform Act had been passed.

In Scotland it meant the vote was now extended to around one man in eight and the representation of the burghs was also increased, giving recognition for the first time to new industrial centres like Paisley. The future, however, would have to go on without Scott, champion of the past. He died at home in Abbotsford on 22 September 1832, just six months after the Reform Act he so feared had received royal assent. He had paid off nearly half his debts and his immortality as Scotland's greatest writer was assured.

Scott's ideal – his fantasy of a Scotland just modern enough, but not too modern – was never sustainable. He had achieved one aim: of fixing a view of Scotland's past that made inspirational heroes out of once-forgotten ghosts. But his hope that present and future could be controlled by anchoring them to that past was a forelorn pipe dream.

Commerce, business and the market were driving forward with a force that none could resist. Though most Scots still lived in the countryside at the start of the nineteenth century, soon the balance shifted for ever. Towns and cities became the places where most folk lived and worked. In the way that Scots do so effortlessly, the inhabitants of the urban centres sorted themselves into the middle and the working classes. The sheer weight of their numbers created an atmosphere in which shared concerns could find a voice.

Emigration to the New World was continuing to draw large numbers of Scots away, but there was also immigration to take their place. Word that industrial centres like Glasgow and Dundee were hungry for human fodder brought an influx of workers from elsewhere. Irish immigrants made for both cities in huge numbers and by the end of the first quarter of the nineteenth century accounted for nearly a fifth of the workforce in the west of Scotland alone.

With the rise of educated and vocal working and middle classes came demands for even greater reform of citizens' rights. The Reform Act of 1832 was never going to silence the many and for some there was no alternative but to join movements like the Chartists – inspired by the 'People's Charter' of 1838 and the first mass labour movement. Demands for the vote for all men over twenty-one started small but refused to be silenced.

Chartism disappeared by name during the middle years of the century but the torch of reform passed to other hands. The grinding glacier of discontent, lubricated in its passage by liberal Whig sentiment, led inexorably to further extension of voting rights. Two more Reform Acts – in 1868 and 1884 – eventually extended the vote to around half a million Scotsmen. The political scene was changing too. After 1868 more and more of those who had called themselves Whigs began to adopt the label of Liberals, a term that, by then, had already been around for decades. Successors of those who had ousted the Tories in 1831, the Liberals would dominate the Scottish political scene until the Great War.

Sir Walter Scott had feared the consequences of giving the vote to 'unwash'd artificers'. He had attempted to make Scottish history hold everyone in place in a world where each man and woman knew their position and was grateful for it. What he had not foreseen, however, were the events of 1843, when the Church of Scotland tore itself in two.

Since the Dark Ages, Christianity had been at least as important to the cohesion of Scotland as any secular ruler, any government. When Scottish independence had come under threat in the thirteenth and fourteenth centuries, it was the bishops who had formed the backstop from which Robert the Bruce drove forward in defiance of would-be English overlords. The Reformation of the sixteenth century had given Scots the education that later energised and informed the Enlightenment, and from the signing of the National Covenant they had gained an unshakeable sense of their worth as individuals, equal to all others in the eyes of God.

In the nineteenth century the united Church of Scotland was still the hub around which society revolved. There had been no parliament since 1707 but the General Assembly had in many ways taken its place, giving ordinary people a gathering where local grievances might be aired. In the parishes it was the Kirk that oversaw the morality of the people, took care of the poor via the allocation of Poor Relief and minded the behaviour and performance of the local schoolteachers. But in 1843 a dispute over whether the right to appoint ministers should lie with the congregation or with the lay patrons of the parish escalated out of control. When the dust cleared, some 40 per cent of parishioners and an eighth of all ministers had walked out of their churches never to return. The rebels formed the Free Church of Scotland and the once-unifying presence of the Kirk was gone for ever.

The Disruption, as it was called, was felt especially strongly in the Highlands and Islands. There the trouble had been coming for a long time, as congregations and lay patrons – usually the landowners – made the appointment of ministers a trial of strength. As long ago as 1712, a Tory-dominated parliament had passed the Patronage Act, giving landlords the final say in church appointments. The whole question of landowners' and tenants' rights had been a root cause of friction ever since. The matter of who should appoint the minister was another symptom of deeply rooted grievances.

When the ordinary people's fight for survival was pushed beyond breaking point by the potato famine of 1846–8, many thousands found their only option was to follow well-worn paths towards the coast. There they boarded ships heading west and away from a land that could no longer support them. There was cholera too and for many it must have seemed the land itself no longer wanted them around. The departures were not always voluntary – no more than they had been at the height of the first wave of Highland Clearances. Landlords were well used to putting profit ahead of human need and forcible evictions in the 1840s and 1850s reached such levels that the matter was even discussed, in anxious terms, in Westminster.

Those left behind among the ruins of their civilisation found some relief, in the main because the population had been substantially reduced, taking pressure off the land. But there can be no denying that the haemorrhage was draining the very life out of the Highlands. The cities continued to swell, of course. Glasgow in particular seemed always able to swallow more people into its insatiable factories and the dehumanising misery of its squalid, overcrowded tenements.

Deaf and dumb to the human cost, the engine of the British Empire raced ever faster, mindlessly, cheerfully whirling. Scots made reputations in the British Army and a disproportionate number of them found posts as governors in colonies around the world. Fortunes were being made by the few and any thoughts of Scottish national identity seemed to have been subverted to the greater good of a Greater Britain. But across the Irish Sea, where geology had long ago denied the people any prospect of industrial revolution, upheaval of another kind was about to have its impact on Scotland's history.

Without the alternatives provided by coal mines, factories, cotton mills and the rest of the stuff of nineteenth-century progress, the Irish had remained dependent upon the land. Their hunger for it, their attachment to it, meant they would always fight sooner and harder to control their own patches of it.

Since the Act of Union of 1801, the whole island had been a part of the United Kingdom of Great Britain and Ireland. As early as 1803 there was an attempt to regain independence and two more in 1848 and 1867. In 1879 the Irish Land League was formed to oppose 'landlordism' and to fight for farmers' rights to own the land on which they worked. The League's first president was Charles Stewart Parnell, of gentry stock and described by William Gladstone as the most remarkable man he ever met. In 1886 Gladstone's Liberal government attempted to push an Irish Home Rule Bill through parliament, with the support of Parnell and his newly founded Irish Parliamentary Party, but the move was defeated by British and Irish Unionists. There had been no intention to break with Great Britain – to break the union – just a desire for control of their own destiny *within* the union. But fear of the consequences for the all-important empire made any tinkering with its foundations unthinkable.

Gladstone's commitment to Irish Home Rule would split the Liberals down the middle, beginning the end of decades of political dominance for the party. By then, however, the notion of tenants' rights to land had long since crossed the Irish Sea to the Highlands of Scotland.

In 1853 the National Association for the Vindication of Scottish Rights was formed, not to threaten the union with England but merely to modify its terms. Irritated by what they saw as excessive attention being given to the matter of Irish Home Rule, the Association's members had grumbles of their own and felt duty-bound to speak out. As well as insisting that the United Kingdom should be referred to only as 'Great Britain', they wanted to see more seats for Scottish MPs in Westminster – at that time just 53 out of a total of 658. Despite having only modest ambitions, the Association was wound up within a few years without achieving much of note. Nevertheless, Gladstone was ready by then to concede that if Home Rule was right for Ireland, then it was right for Scotland as well.

The Liberal Prime Minister's star fell because of his views, but a Scottish Home Rule Association was duly formed. Despite the name and its modern connotations, the Scots Home Rulers of the 1880s wanted only to improve the efficiency of the union. Scottish MPs at Westminster had been in the habit of meeting privately to discuss Scottish business and it was the will of the SHRA that such meetings should take place in Edinburgh rather than in London.

Ireland inspired the Scottish Home Rule movement in other, less obvious ways as well – namely high dudgeon. As far as many Scots were concerned, the Irish had secured greater Prime Ministerial commitment to their cause despite a conspicuous lack of loyalty to the union in the time of its greatest need.

In 1796 a revolutionary republican group calling itself the United Irishmen had invited the French to land on Irish soil and lead a fight against the British government. Bad weather and poor leadership meant the attack never happened but in May 1798, when the threat of invasion of Great Britain by Napoleon was at its most acute, the United Irishmen rose in open revolt against the Crown. Once again the French were encouraged to use Ireland to attack Great Britain's flank but the rebellion, supported by thousands of French sailors and soldiers, had been effectively crushed by the end of September. So while Scots had rallied to Great Britain's defence in unprecedented numbers, the treasonous Irish had sought to join forces with her greatest enemy and stab the nation in the back. That such behaviour should bring them close to Home Rule, while Scots interests languished, was irritating to say the least. The black sheep of the family was getting all the attention.

In 1885, with Scots interests on the agenda, Westminster resuscitated the ancient office of Secretary for Scotland and a Scottish Office was opened in London. But, far from Great Britain's capital, people's dissatisfaction with their landlords had taken a violent turn.

If we imagine the Highland Clearances at all, we tend to see a broken people meekly trudging away from their homes towards an uncertain future. But in 1883, on Lord MacDonald's Braes estate on Skye, the meek set out to ensure their sons might inherit some little earth. A dispute over rights to grazing land on Ben Lee escalated to the point where the laird called in a force of fifty policemen from Glasgow. Accounts vary as to who cast the first stone, but a riot broke out, with locals attacking the police with any weapons that came to hand. Many crofters were taken prisoner and later fined but they had made their point.

This was the 'Battle of the Braes' and there would be further outbreaks of trouble before the end of a period of civil unrest in the Highlands remembered as the 'Crofters' War'. A subsequent government inquiry into 'the conditions of crofter and cottars in the Highlands' published its findings in 1884 and Highland Members of Parliament were able to exploit a slim Liberal majority in the Commons to exact some reforms. The Crofters Act of 1885 gave tenants security of tenure and meant that, for the first time, parents could pass that same security on to their children. Also for the first time a Land Court was set up to ensure fair rents.

What would Sir Walter Scott have thought of it all? Determined to maintain the unique heritage and identity of Scotland, he had made heroes of the Highlanders of the past. Now, more than half a century after his death, a handful of their descendants had reared up on their hind legs to snap at their tormentors. At the eleventh hour the last of the Highlanders had stemmed a tide of eviction, exile and grief that had seemed certain to sweep them into final oblivion. Against the odds they had persuaded a distant government to grant them at least some right to a life in their own land.

At the turn of the twentieth century members of the Liberal Party set up the Young Scots Society. In May 1914, just three months before the outbreak of the Great War, a Scottish Home Rule Bill introduced by the Liberal Prime Minister, Herbert Asquith, came within a whisker of being passed. Having survived its second reading in the Commons, it failed to reach the statute book only because the need to prepare for war overtook all other concerns.

During the eighteenth century, Scotland's desire to prove herself – both as an equal partner in the union and as a player on the world stage – had made her forget herself. The union and the British Empire had given the nation the power to punch well above its weight in international affairs and had dispatched millions of her sons and daughters to every corner of the earth. Many of her people had grown rich beyond imagination.

Now, just as the nations of the world prepared to tear themselves into bloody pieces in the greatest conflict yet seen, Scotland had begun to remember what Scotland was. It only remained to be seen what she would do with that knowledge once the smoke of battle cleared.

CHAPTER ELEVEN

HOMEWARD BOUND

'Home is made for coming from,
And dreams for going to,
Which with any luck will never come true'
'I Was Born Under A Wandering Star'

Scotland's history is easy to find – most of it, at least. Even the distant past is there to be wondered at: Stone Age villages like Skara Brae and Knap of Howar, on Orkney, 5,000 or more years old; similarly ancient, enigmatic ritual sites like the standing stones of Calanais, on the island of Lewis, or the recumbent stone circle of East Aquhorthies, in Aberdeenshire.

The Romans, the first civilisation to write about the tribes living in the northern third of the landmass of the British Isles, left their seemingly indelible marks as well. Remnants of the great banks and ditches of the Antonine Wall, Rome's most northerly border in these isles, are still plainly visible in the landscape of modern Scotland, along with forts, fortlets, roads and the rest of the infrastructure of empire. Within sight of East Aquhorthies is Bennachie, likely the scene of the legendary showdown between Agricola and Calgacus.

Traces of the so-called Dark Ages – the Early Medieval period that began after the Romans left – somehow survive into the light of the present day: Dunadd, fortress of the Gaels of Dalriada, is as impressive today as it was 1,300 years ago when the ancient kings made it the centre of a civilisation with trading links stretching as far as Afghanistan and the Mediterranean. The Pictish hillfort of Dundurn, too, stands as a silent witness to the centuries and millennia before Scotland even *was* Scotland. On and on through time it is the same: Iron Age brochs and medieval castles; ruined abbeys, grand palaces and mighty tower houses; sites of long-ago battles that still draw tourists from around the world by the busload; monuments to heroes, villains and rogues; caves and rocks assigned to this legendary name or that.

A visit to the city of Stirling can feel like a journey to the centre of the Scottish universe. All within a few miles of one another are some of the most revered touchstones of the nation's identity – at least its mythical identity: the castle that was a refuge for the infant Mary Queen of Scots and home to all her Stewart forebears; the battlefields of Stirling Bridge, Bannockburn and Sherrifmuir. Standing sentinel over all of it is the 220-foot high tower of the National Wallace Monument. Built on top of Abbey Craig, from where William Wallace and Andrew Murray watched the advance of Edward's army before descending to annihilate it with a rebel force at Stirling Bridge in 1297, it is a central point around which whirl the proudest thoughts and notions of many Scots, a place made at least as much of imagination as of history.

Glasgow's cathedral, Provand's Lordship, the Merchant City; Edinburgh's castle, the Royal Mile, the Palace of Holyroodhouse; the battle-fields of Culloden and Killiecrankie; Bothwell Brig and Drumclog; Aethel-staneford and Dunechtan. All over the country – north, south, east and west – the history is so thick in the air you almost have to waft it away from your face.

Invaders have come and gone or stayed to be swallowed whole. History has rumbled through it all like a battalion of tanks, through the Highland glens, across the flatland of the Carse of Stirling and on into the fertile Lowlands beyond and back again. One culture after another has been levelled to its foundations. Scotland – the rock of Scotland – has always been here, the same and not the same, but still Scotland to the ends of the roots of the very mountains themselves.

Until the time comes to look for the twentieth century, that is. Everyone of a certain age knows the names and the places that matter: the shipyards of Fairfield's and John Brown's; the steelworks of Motherwell and Coatbridge; iconic names like Bathgate, Linwood and Ravenscraig; the coal mines of Ayrshire, Stirlingshire and Fife. You might think there was plenty to see. Here in Scotland, after all, there are people still alive who saw every moment of the twentieth century. So you might expect there would be plenty of backdrops for filming the last episode of A History of Scotland. But you would be wrong. It has gone, almost the lot of it. Of the great cathedrals of twentieth-century endeavour and toil there is scarcely a trace. Visit John Brown's shipyard now and all that remains is 'Titan', the massive cantilever crane that once lifted great engines into greater ships. It has been freshly painted and forms the showpiece of a visitor experience. But it is also a giant skeleton standing silhouetted against the sky, all that remains of an industry that died. Take the lift to the top and you can enjoy a grand view of Glasgow and of the rivers Clyde and Cart. You can also spot the outline, dizzyingly far below, of the slipway from which great ships like the *Queen Mary* were launched into legend. It has long since been filled in, of course, and now forms just a dark diagonal stripe across a recently laid walkway of lighter paving.

The once-familiar, giant blue tin can of Ravenscraig, emblazoned with the site's name in huge white letters, is gone as well, demolished in July 1996. The coal mines are silent, the pumps long since switched off, allowing the caverns, shafts and tunnels to fill with water as dark as regret.

While the remains of every other period of Scotland's history are dotted across the landscape, punctuation marks in a long story – carefully restored and maintained and fossilised for the edification of tourists – the physical evidence of the nation's most recent past has been wiped away like chalk dust from a blackboard. It feels as though much of the twentieth century is a time Scotland would rather forget.

The Great War of 1914–18 has been described as forming railings that separate the past from the present. It is still possible to see through the railings, to glimpse the ways and mores of the past; but the barrier means there is no way for us to understand what it meant to *live* in the lost world before that maelstrom.

During the nineteenth century, Scotland was an important and influential part of Victorian Britain. The Queen herself declared her love of the Highlands and, with the purchase of Balmoral as a holiday home, restored the royal family to Scotland in a way that had been unknown, more or less, since the departure of James VI and I in 1603. It had been the century in which Scotland had either embraced or invented the technologies that would turn her into the engine, the workshop of the British Empire. The rise and rise of engineering works, and of Meccas to heavy industry like the Clyde shipyards, did more than just line the pockets of a few oligarchs. By completing the move away from work in the home – the way of the past – to massed workforces crowded into factories, mines, foundries and yards, the Industrial Revolution unwittingly created a 'working class'. With so many men and women gathered together in the same places, sharing the indignities of appalling working conditions coupled with low wages, it was only a matter of time before some of their number would begin to demand something better for themselves and for their fellows.

The same forces that created a working class also shaped a middle class that had the aspiration, and more importantly the money, to distance themselves from those below them in the pecking order. While the managers and professionals built and occupied genteel suburbs on the fringes of the industrial centres, the workers were left behind in the overcrowded, filthy squalor that had characterised their existence from the start.

Scots, more than the inhabitants of many other countries, have long demonstrated an inbuilt acceptance, even an appreciation, of a clearly defined social hierarchy. While the working class mythologised the 'lad o' pairts' – the self-made man (typified by Robert Burns, who rose through the social ranks armed with nothing more than an education and a guid Scots tongue in his head) – they were just as happy to live in a world in which each man and woman knew his or her place.

The Victorian era was also one in which the middle and upper classes indulged the notion that the poor and miserable had only themselves to blame for their various predicaments. If you were starving, scraping an existence in a filthy hovel, unemployed and hopeless, then it was because you were a moral and physical degenerate. Rather than improve the lives of the masses by building better homes for them to live in, or reforming employment so as to offer a living wage, the better-off set out to teach the poor the errors of their ways. Before they could be gifted any kind of practical help, they must first be taught to improve themselves. This was the heyday of the Temperance Movement that attracted many working-class people, notably women. Freed from the demon drink, the huddled masses would, it was thought, rise from the morass and become fine, upstanding, hard-working citizens.

It was also the last great flowering of the neat society-in-miniature that was the 'big house', when scores of servants were employed in the service of rich families, looking after their fine homes and grounds. The grand houses and estates of the wealthy provided respectable, sought-after positions for thousands of men and women – and imbued generations of them with an understanding that if they worked hard for the masters and mistresses, they in turn would be looked after by their betters. It was a strange symbiotic relationship, incomprehensible to us now, that worked in its own unique way in those years before the war that would change everything.

Victoria died in 1901 and it was therefore an Edwardian Scotland that was to endure the Great War. For men living lives of low-paid drudgery or struggling with the humiliation of unemployment, the chance to volunteer for service in a glorious crusade against an evil empire was irresistible. Working-class men tired of back-breaking labour; middle-class clerks and shop assistants tethered to the humdrum; upper-class husbands and sons desperate to emulate the glories of their ancestors – all were swept away by the tide. For the first time, Scots of all classes were united by a common cause and within weeks the recruitment centres in cities like Glasgow and Edinburgh were pushed to breaking point by the waves of volunteers.

There were few Scots men and boys, if any, that summer of 1914, who thought the conflict would present them with any real danger. This was a generation that had grown up during the last exploits of Victoria's imperial armies, and whose most recent ideas of what it was like to defend the empire had been shaped by reading about the trouble with the Boers in South Africa. Trench warfare dictated and defined by machine guns, barbed wire and high explosives was as yet unknown, and men of all classes imagined only that they would shortly be marching or galloping into glory, driving 'the Hun' before them with their righteous wrath.

Whole factory workforces, whole streets, whole schools joined up *en masse*. The entire first team of Heart of Midlothian Football Club signed up to serve in the 16th Royal Scots, created in a fit of patriotism by local businessman George McCrae. The only threat to the personal safety of professional sportsmen or anyone else, it seemed, came in the form of the neighbours, former friends, teachers and bosses – and to cap it all, women – who were lately making it plain that only cowards were to be seen out of uniform. There was a white feather or worse for any man between eighteen and forty-five still in civilian clothes. The nationwide enthusiasm and excitement, coupled with the prospect of personal advancement, led more than a third of a million Scotsmen to volunteer their services to the Armed Forces in the first year and a half of the war.

The reality of the situation in France was slow in coming, but arrived during the course of 1915 like a gust of cold, rain-bearing wind. By January 1916 the death toll on the Western Front had thoroughly dampened everyone's enthusiasm for a spell in uniform and conscription became the only way to keep the numbers up. But by the end of it all, in 1918, nearly 700,000 Scotsmen had served their country.

The butchers' yards of Arras, Loos, Passchendaele, Somme, Ypres and the rest would welcome the flower of Scotland along with the best of the young men of a score of nations. Definite figures are hard to come by but between 75,000 and 120,000 Scotsmen were dead by 11 a.m. on the morning of 11 November 1918. It can be hard to work out from the statistics what really happened, but many writers justifiably claim that Scotland lost an especially high percentage of its population. In the Highlands and Islands, certainly, the dead amounted to as much as a sixth of those who served.

Scotland's war was book-ended by two desperate tragedies that claimed lives not in France but at home. A few minutes before seven in the morning on 22 May 1915 a troop train carrying nearly 500 soldiers, mostly men of the 1st Battalion, 7th Royal Scots, collided with a stationary coal train beside a set of points at Quintinshill, in Dumfriesshire. Within moments of the first crash, an express passenger train heading north from London ploughed into the burning wreckage at full speed. It was all the fault of two signalmen, James Tinsley and George Meakin, who had forgotten to clear the coal train off the southbound line in time to allow the troop train to pass by on its journey towards the docks at Liverpool. Their fatal error that day cost the lives of 227 soldiers. A further 246 were injured, some of them terribly. To this day Quintinshill stands as Britain's worst rail disaster. The survivors, together with the rest of the regiment, would later see action in places like Achi Baba and Gully Ravine, during the Gallipoli campaign; but their greatest single loss of men – 42 per cent of the eventual total – was inflicted on 22 May 1915, while they were still in Scotland.

In the early hours of 1 January 1919, HMY *Iolaire* was en route to Stornoway when she collided with a cluster of rocks near the harbour mouth, a hazard known to the locals as 'Biastan Thuilme', 'the Beasts of Holm'. The ship was crewed by Royal Navy men unfamiliar with navigating the waterway in darkness, but any one of the 280-odd passengers aboard could have warned them of the danger if they had been asked. They were Navy men too, but locals – Lewis men on their way home after surviving everything the war had had to throw at them. The *Iolaire* was not the ship normally used for the crossing from Mallaig to Stornoway in 1918. That was the job of the scheduled ferry, the SS *Sheila*, but she had been filled to capacity that night by yet more Servicemen. Rather than leave men stranded on the wrong side of the Minch on Hogmanay, a call had been made to summon a second vessel.

HMY *Iolaire* (the name is Gaelic for 'eagle') had only recently been assigned to service in Stornoway, and since she was a naval vessel rather than a passenger ship she only had enough lifeboats and life jackets for her crew. When she collided with the Beasts of Holm the men were pitched into the freezing water with scarcely any hope of rescue or survival. Given that it was Hogmanay and the men's arrival had been expected, the harbour wall in Stornoway was crowded with family and friends. The Beasts were close to the harbour mouth and 205 husbands, sons and brothers drowned within sight of home, before their loved ones' eyes.

The population of Lewis at the outbreak of the war had been around 30,000. During the course of the fighting over 6,000 men joined the Armed Forces and by 1918 1,000 of them were dead – one in six. All of the Western Isles had given conspicuously of their menfolk and every village and hamlet had known loss. The tragedy of the *Iolaire* was one wound too many.

William Hesketh Lever – Lord Leverhulme of the Western Isles – bought the whole island of Lewis in 1918. He was just the latest in a long line of would-be social engineers drawn to the north-west, determined to reinvigorate his resident population. His dream was to get their blood flowing again by introducing them to the business of fish-canning – on an industrial scale. But the people of Lewis were too badly hurt by war to take easily or kindly to the ambitions of another stranger. Leverhulme's plans came to nothing and a community all but finished by the final tragedy of the *Iolaire* rolled into itself, like Fingal, and rose upon the wind. By some accounts the damage wrought between 1914 and 1 January 1919 has weakened the life force of the island to this day.

This, then, was the war that changed everything, fundamentally altering the structure of society and the relationships that had underpinned it for centuries. The slaughter of hundreds of thousands of working-class Scots during the Great War, a mechanical process overseen by commanders drawn from the country's upper classes and aristocracy, finally severed age-old ties. Since time immemorial the poor had served the rich and in return the rich had been supposed to honour an obligation of paternal care to those below them in the scheme of things. That obligation had been on the wane since at least the seventeenth century, and all but snuffed out by the indifference and downright cruelty of the Clearances. But its unquiet ghost was laid to rest by the betrayal in Flanders, by the leaders, of the led.

In Scotland the years of upheaval between 1914 and 1919, when the men finally returned, had helped radicalise many among the working classes. As demand for the stuff of war grew by the day, thousands of workers had poured into cities like Glasgow to fill new jobs in the munitions plants. The already overcrowded and dilapidated housing stock was put under even greater strain and the situation was soon being exploited by the Rachmanite landlords. Rents were hiked up in some areas by as much as 23 per cent and soon the wives and children of men fighting at the front were being evicted from their homes for non-payment.

As 1915 wore on, the number of summary evictions rose to a point where the population could stomach it no more. As is often the case, it was the defiance of just one person – in this instance a working-class housewife called Mary Barbour – that triggered large-scale rebellion and demands for change. A campaign of rent strikes was organised by Mrs Barbour's newly formed South Govan Woman's Housing Association in November, and the tactic was quickly taken up across the city.

By the middle of 1916 thousands of tenants, in every one of Glasgow's munitions districts – including Govan, Ibrox, Parkhead, Patrick and Shettleston – were withholding their rent. Whenever and wherever the sheriff's officers might attempt an eviction, hundreds of well-organised protesters would quickly gather, packing themselves into the doorways and closes to deny access to the myrmidons of the state. The Independent Labour Party took up the cudgels and soon Lloyd George's government was forced to rush through legislation that not only fixed rents for the duration of the war but forced them back down to pre-1914 levels.

With half of Scotsmen under the age of forty-five away fighting in the war, women and girls had eventually been called upon to replace them in the workplace. They had not been the first choice. Before allowing women out of their homes and into the factories and shipyards, the authorities had first contemplated using men from the colonies and even male refugees from war-torn Belgium. Mrs Pankhurst led the 'Right to Serve' campaign that eventually persuaded Lloyd George that women should be allowed to take an active role in the war effort after all. That four-year stint making shells, bullets, sand bags, uniforms and the rest of the paraphernalia of war let a genie out of the bottle. Though women spent the war years being badly paid and generally exploited in the lowest positions, in whatever factories or yards that agreed to take them, it was still a liberation of sorts.

At the end of the fighting they had to vacate the jobs for the returning soldiers, but by then women had learned there was a world beyond the four walls of their fathers' and husbands' houses. Having experienced the right to work, they began to demand the right to vote with a stridency that would not be denied. The Suffragettes had begun their battle for equality in the years before 1914, but had agreed among themselves that they would set aside their demands while the country was at war. With the fighting ceased, the call was taken up with even greater passion and determination. Before 1918 was over, the right to vote had duly been extended to take in women over the age of thirty. This was the Representation of the People Act – which also gave the vote to all men over twenty-one – and at a stroke the electorate in Scotland was raised from fewer than 800,000 to over 2.2 million.

If working-class women had learned to fight their battles during the war, many of their returning menfolk were no less determined to see yet more social justice done. Time spent in the charnel houses of the Western Front and in Gallipoli had changed the way thousands of the soldiers viewed themselves and the wider world. Having had their eyes opened to inhumanity on an industrial scale, they came home to find the lives they had led before no longer made sense, and that the indignities they had put up with in the past were tolerable no longer.

The politicians had made rods for their own backs by promising that the lot of returning soldiers would be improved in the light of all they had done in the defence of king and country. Lloyd George had made noises about 'homes for heroes' and now Scots were back, in their dissatisfied thousands, to find the same old squalor and the prospect of the same old jobs.

A general election in December 1918 gave an unmistakable seal of approval to Lloyd George's coalition government. But there was blood in the water and the workers could sense it. For as long as anyone could remember, Scotland had been a country dominated by the Liberal Party. Traditionally they had stood for free trade – which pleased the poor by keeping food prices down, and the businessmen by keeping open the international markets – and for improvements to education and housing. They had also backed the calls for Home Rule, although they saw it as a means to strengthen rather than weaken the union.

In the aftermath of the war, however, more and more people were listening to the Labour Party, whose members seemed to be shouting much louder about improving the living and working conditions of the poor.

Furthermore, those members were, as often as not, drawn from the ranks of the poor themselves. For the first time working men and women were hearing their demands voiced by some of their own kind. If the rise of Labour was not enough of a problem for the Liberals, they also faced the challenge of an invigorated Conservative movement. Since 1912, the Scottish Conservatives and the Scottish Liberal Unionists had found a common cause in opposition to Irish Home Rule (and its Scottish offshoots) and had joined forces as the Scottish Unionist Party. These were Conservatives by any other name and in the aftermath of the Great War they emerged as a major force.

The Liberal Party in Scotland therefore faced a double whammy: working men and women found their demands for social justice better articulated by Labour, while the middle classes sought sanctuary from the rise of 'Socialism' in the arms of the Conservatives.

Before the end of 1919, those nervous middle classes would find plenty to worry about in the activities of the working poor. What with events in Russia in 1917, the Establishment were already jumpy about how Scotland's workers might respond to the gains made by the Bolsheviks. As it turned out, Scotland's working class had more modest ambitions. Simmering unrest about the same old bugbears – poor housing, low pay and crushingly hard working conditions – was brought to the boil in 1919 when workers in the engineering industry went on strike and demanded their working week be cut from over fifty hours to no more than forty. Emboldened and excited by this defiance, ordinary folk gathered in their tens of thousands in Glasgow's George Square, on 31 January 1920, to voice their support for the strike. Soon other grievances were being aired as well, including the usual complaints about housing and rents.

It was all too much for the authorities and, amid fears that the protests emanating from 'Red Clydeside' were about to spin out of control and into full-scale revolution, the police and army were sent in to disperse the crowds and restore order. In time-honoured fashion, the police action was bungled and heavy-handed. Fighting broke out and many were injured on both sides. There were disgruntled ex-soldiers among the protesters and they gave as good as they got. The greater fear, however, that revolution was at hand, came to nothing. The crowds melted back towards their miserable homes and in little over a fortnight the strikers accepted a forty-seven-hour week and went back to work. That the authorities believed their society itself had been in peril, however, was made clear by the fact that tanks were put on standby and manned machine guns set up across the city.

Scottish Establishment and middle-class opposition to calls for change was hardly surprising: the Great War had been good for business in Scotland.

Hard to find though the remains of Scotland's heavy industries undoubtedly are, it is still possible to walk among a few shattered stumps of their teeth. The Summerlee Ironworks, in Coatbridge, was only demolished in the 1930s after a working life of a little less than a hundred years. Despite that, archaeologists had to remove 6 metres of soil and rubble to reveal the relics of the great blast furnaces and kilns that made Summerlee one of Great Britain's most important ironworks in the first half of the nineteenth century. It was here that James Beaumont Neilson, younger brother of John Neilson, who founded the works, pioneered the revolutionary 'hot blast' system of iron-smelting. Coatbridge was, for a few decades at least, Scotland's 'Iron Burgh' until the rise of steel left the place behind shortly before the twentieth century.

By then, though, Scotland was established as the workshop of the British Empire, when a quarter of the world and its population were 'British'. The central belt of Scotland housed the workshop's beating heart and towns like Motherwell, in Lanarkshire, were transformed by industry. Once the water bubbling up from a natural spring there was so pure it was named after the mother of God herself – the mother well. By the time the ironworks were glowing red, however, the town's rivers and streams were running black with filth and pollution.

Scotland was helping make the British Empire rich but hundreds of thousands of her people endured a kind of hell on earth to make that possible. Housing reports from just before the Great War make for distressing reading. Living conditions for the people toiling to produce the hardest metals the world had yet seen were nothing less than disgusting, degrading. In Lanarkshire as a whole the housing provided by the companies, for the workers and their families, was among the worst in Scotland: a single toilet for every seventy people; everywhere the stink of faeces and urine; children scavenging among the filth; water available only from standpipes in the street; at least four people living in every room.

The company owners, directors and their senior staff lived well. But those existing in the company housing knew a different story. Frightful though the conditions were, the tenants' hold on their homes was tenuous.

A fall-out with the boss could see whole families put out into the street. If anyone fell sick – and disease and illness were rife in the brutalising, unsanitary conditions – then the only option was to call upon the services of the company doctor. Whatever the outcome for the patient, the father's wages would be docked to pay for any treatment.

The statistics illuminating all this suffering are the shame of a nation – or at least of those who governed it. Overcrowding in many Scottish towns and cities was worse even than in the worst slums of London. One in every five children born into this misery was dead before his or her first birthday. And yet this reality was the essential ingredient for Great Britain's industrial prosperity. There was a secret, invisible deal behind all the profit Scotland's industries were capable of generating, and it might as well have been struck with the devil himself: if Scotland was to be the workshop of industry then most of her people had to live and die in misery to make it possible. Scottish industry was able to dominate the world for one reason, and one reason only – her workers were paid less than their equivalents elsewhere and lived in cheaply built hovels so that the bosses could reap the benefits.

David Colville, originally from Campbeltown, began producing malleable iron bars at his Dalzell Works in Motherwell in 1872. A small firm employing just 200 men to start with, Dalzell's would eventually grow into a monster. Following the collapse of the Tay Bridge in Dundee in 1879, Colville won the contract to produce the iron for its replacement. The good reputation of his company grew steadily and soon, with the help of his three sons, John, Archibald and David, Colville made the crucial switch from iron- to steel-making. When work began on the construction of the Forth Bridge in 1883, it was with steel from Colville's Dalzell Works.

At the time John Craig joined the company as a thirteen-year-old trainee office boy in the August of 1888, Dalzell's was just one steelworks among several in the town. But Craig was the son of a furnace-man and leapt at the chance to follow his father into the booming trade. It was a decision that would have huge implications not just for the Dalzell Works in Motherwell, but for the entire Scottish iron and steel industry. He was to stay with the Colville family for the remaining 67 years of his life, entwining their fortunes and destiny – and those of Scotland – with his own.

If ever there was a lad o' pairts, it was John Craig. When John Colville was elected as an MP in 1895, twenty-one-year-old Craig was promoted to represent the company's interests at the Royal Exchange in Glasgow. In the years before telephones became vital to commerce, businessmen and merchants met in exchange buildings to strike deals face to face. By Craig's time, Glasgow's Royal Exchange occupied the building that had once been the lavish home of William Cunninghame, on Queen Street.

Having left school before completing his education, Craig felt the lack of personal polish. Now that he was mixing with accomplished men twice and three times his own age, he embarked on a programme of self-improvement. Rather than sit back and relax during his commutes between Motherwell and Glasgow, he used the time for reading and study instead. He was a driven man. Having learned his scripture at his mother's knee, he employed her Presbyterian principles in the workplace. In Craig's world, each man was responsible for his own destiny. Hard work and faith in God were all that anyone needed to get on in life, he thought; and the recipe certainly worked for him. By the time he was thirty-six he was an elder of his local Dalzell Free Church and a director of Colvilles, an astonishing achievement for the son of a manual worker. The Great War brought unprecedented opportunities for Scotland's iron- and steel-makers and the Colvilles of Motherwell grabbed the lion's share. When other companies faltered, the Colvilles were always ready to step in and add them to the empire. But great empires consume their children and the relentless pace of work proved too much for the hearts of the Colville brothers. The eldest, John, had died in 1901 aged forty-nine. David and Archibald followed within two months of each other in 1916, aged fifty-six and sixty-two respectively. They were simply worn out.

John Craig, their trusted deputy, was therefore just forty-two when he rose to the position of chairman of the company that same year. In the Dalzell Works – and throughout the Colville empire – the foundries were churning out shell casings and tank armour without respite. King George V saw fit to visit the company and before the war's end Craig was made a Commander of the Order of the British Empire. Colvilles reigned supreme over steel production in Scotland and Craig sat at the very top.

It was an empire forged in the furnaces of worldwide war, however. The end of the hostilities in 1918 was hardly good news for the industries that had expanded to keep the shells and bullets flying. By the start of the third decade of the twentieth century, Colvilles alone owned six iron- and steelworks that consumed coal from twenty-four company-owned mines. Those pits were held up by props manufactured by Colvilles and the coal they produced was transported by Colvilles-owned wagons along railway lines built of Colvilles steel over bridges held up by even more Colvilles steel. More of the same was used to build ships on the Clyde which then exported Colville steel to the countries of the British Empire.

Something like 180,000 people were employed by Colvilles alone, and hundreds of thousands more similarly worked for other companies that had depended on wartime levels of iron and steel production. And, of course, it could not last. Peace for the world meant strife for those laid off as order books began to feature more and more empty pages. The most fortunate workers saw their hours and wages slashed, while tens of thousands of others were simply laid off. Motherwell was a town built almost exclusively on steel and the ranks of the unemployed there swelled from fewer than 2,000 during the war to over 12,000 soon afterwards. It was no exaggeration to say it was the worst hit town in Scotland.

In those years before the safety net of Unemployment Benefit, the jobless had few places to look for help. Poor Relief was a pot of money controlled by local councils and the guidelines governing its allocation were vague and open to interpretation. The Scottish working class of the 1920s were intensely proud, determined to live by their labour and horrified at the very thought of asking strangers for help. It was one thing to take a loan from family, or perhaps close friends; but the idea of going cap in hand to the authorities was anathema to almost all. Poor Relief – meagre though it was – required a means test and all but the most desperate baulked at such an intrusion into their private lives.

There was precious little from employers either. Despite coming from working-class stock, John Craig had little sympathy for those who fell on hard times. He believed only in self-improvement – the duty of a man to pull himself up by his bootstraps and make a life for himself and his family. Rather than increase wages or improve conditions, companies like Colvilles preferred to provide land for golf courses so their employees might spend their free time engaged in healthy pursuits. Needless to say, there was no alcohol in the clubhouse.

The situation regarding Poor Relief was complicated and aggravated, as the 1920s progressed, by growing numbers of striking workers. With hours being slashed and job cuts everywhere, workers began withholding their labour in hope of forcing the bosses to put down the axes and navigate a more kindly course through the economic storm. Increasingly, the local authorities had to consider applications for Poor Relief from men who, though fit and able to work, were refusing to do so. Were such men and their families entitled to the same sort of financial help normally reserved for those who had lost their jobs? For the poor – unemployed or striking, it made no difference – Scotland became impossibly hard. There were soup kitchens in Motherwell. The poor houses had never been so busy. Men queued up for their turn earning a few pence a day digging graves in the local cemeteries.

This was the Scotland from which Scots began to emigrate in huge numbers. In the decade between 1921 to 1931 around half a million Scots left the country. Something like 70,000 of them simply crossed the border into England in hope of work, but the rest left for North America, Canada and Australia. By 1931, one in every five Scots in the world was no longer living in Scotland.

The Clearances are the stuff of folklore and legend, but the voluntary exodus from Scotland in the first quarter of the twentieth century was more enervating by far. Most of those leaving the country in the 1920s were driven not by unemployment but by the fear of it. It was therefore the educated, the skilled – the very people a nation needs most if it is to make its way in the modern world – who were electing to board ships heading down the Clyde and towards new lives in the New World. Scotland was haemorrhaging its brightest and best.

Increasing numbers of those left behind began to ask why the country was in such a perilous state. More and more of them laid the blame squarely at the feet of government. The Liberal Party's dominance of Scotland was a thing of the past. In 1924 a general election returned a Conservative government under Stanley Baldwin, but within two years the whole of Great Britain was to experience the phenomenon of the General Strike.

Led by miners angered at wage cuts and increased hours, it soon spread to take in thousands of workers in other sectors. Though it came to little in the end and was abandoned by all but the miners after just ten days in May 1926, it revealed deep divisions in Scottish society. These fractures were not just between the working and middle classes, but *within* the working class and the Labour movement itself. Those of a revolutionary frame of mind had had their dreams of national upheaval thwarted, while those of a more moderate leaning were more convinced than ever that change could only be achieved via the ballot box.

For an increasing number of Scots the atmosphere of discontent during the 1920s persuaded them that none of the existing political parties were focused enough on Scotland's needs. Home Rule had been an article of faith for the Liberals – but Home Rule that might strengthen the union.

Now voices were being raised in calls for a different sort of separation of powers altogether. The Scottish Home Rule Association had re-established itself in 1918 and from the time of the 'Red Clydeside' rising of 1919 its members had found much in common with firebrands of the Independent Labour Party, including John Maclean.

A Labour landslide in the general election of 1924 put many of the ILP leaders into government in London (though not Maclean, brightest of the Labour minds but dead at just forty-four, in 1923). Home Rule was soon on the agenda once more – and the subject of impassioned debates in the House – but failed yet again to make it onto the statute book. While Labour decided to turn away from the matter, the better to focus on building new houses and creating new jobs, the Home Rule thinking of the past mutated, north of the Border, into nationalism and even calls for independence.

Christopher Murray Grieve was a journalist living in Montrose but is better known by his pen name of Hugh MacDiarmid. A rabid hater of all things English, he sought to use poetry and self-published magazines to persuade his fellow Scots that extreme action was required if Scotland was ever again to find itself in the sunshine of optimism and prosperity. MacDiarmid was not alone among Scotland's literati in thinking the country was in need of urgent measures to stem the haemorrhage of her people and restore a sense of self and of identity. His house became a meeting place for the leading lights of what became known as a Scottish Renaissance and writers like Lewis Grassic Gibbon and Compton Mac-kenzie were soon drawn into MacDiarmid's orbit, along with the socialist Edwin Muir.

Muir was born in Deerness, on Mainland Orkney, in 1887. His father had lost the family farm in 1901, when Muir was fourteen, and moved to the heart of industrialised Glasgow. What a shock it must have been for a boy who had known only the rural isolation of the Orkney Islands to find himself thrown into the crucible of industrial revolution. He later described the move as akin to stepping out of the eighteenth century straight into the twentieth with nothing in between.

Not long after the end of the Great War, Muir lived for a time in Prague. There he was swept up by the optimism and excitement among the Czechs as they reclaimed their independence and set out towards a new future; he returned to Great Britain convinced his countrymen should do the same. (The move from Prague to Montrose in the 1930s, where he and his wife became neighbours of MacDiarmid for a while, must surely have been as disorientating as his arrival in Glasgow from Orkney as a teenager.) In any event, Muir would look around Scotland and find that, like MacDiarmid, he did not like what he saw.

As the 1920s wore on, MacDiarmid gave vent to increasingly extremist views. For one thing he was obsessed with language and believed Scotland could neither reclaim nor live up to her true self until her people fully embraced the Scots tongue. And he was not talking about the Scots of Burns – rather he had it in mind to re-popularise a way of speaking and writing that had not been common currency since the time of makars like William Dunbar in the fifteenth century. His politics were just as challenging. Soon after Mussolini and his fascists seized power in Rome in 1922, MacDiarmid published a magazine article calling for the rise of fascism in Scotland. He also urged unemployed ex-Servicemen to march into the Highlands and Islands and there lay claim to unoccupied land for themselves.

By the time of the General Strike in 1926, the nationalist message from MacDiarmid and his fellow writers had begun to permeate the fabric of Scottish society. Newspapers and magazines were carrying articles, features and letters questioning why Scotland was failing as a nation, losing its population. More importantly, they were suggesting how the country might be changed for the better, by seeking independence.

The logic of their argument was hardly undermined by the way the government, and companies like Colvilles, responded to the strike action. With troops on standby and factories closing their doors even to those willing to work, the vexed question of whether men on strike were entitled to Poor Relief was being asked once again. The board of Colvilles plainly thought not, and used the full weight of the law to stop their local parish council doling out cash to strikers. They argued that ratepayers like themselves had no legal obligation to fund men who had deliberately downed tools, and the council had eventually to reimburse money it had already paid out to strikers from the public purse.

Baldwin's government had been well prepared for the strike. With all but the miners back at work within a fortnight, the authorities were able to dig in and use time as their weapon. Broken by hunger and disappointment, the miners called off the last of their action by the end of October 1926.

MacDiarmid, meanwhile, continued his own fight in his own way. Along with other Scottish writers he helped form the National Party of Scotland, dedicated to one thing only – independence. It was the most radical declaration of intent Scottish politics had yet seen – too radical, it seemed, for the Scottish people. At the next general election the new party fielded a modest two candidates and attracted only 3,000 votes. Home Rule, nationalism and independence might be good topics for conversation but were not the priorities of many voters.

Just as global events rocked Britain in 2008, so matters beyond the control of any single nation rolled around the world like a deadly virus in 1929. On Wall Street in New York on 25 October the value of stocks and shares plummeted. No one in Scotland realised the implications on the day, but soon the effects of the 'Wall Street Crash' were tearing around the world like a tsunami.

A bad economic situation for Scottish industry was made much worse. More companies collapsed, more factories closed, more men and women joined the ranks of the unemployed. Once again the soup kitchens were opening their doors to people with no hope, nowhere else to turn. Those who had the resources to leave the country did so in alarming numbers. Scots had had a tradition of emigration for centuries and by the twentieth century there was hardly a family north of the Border that did not have some sort of overseas connection. It was therefore relatively easy for many to make contact with those footholds in other parts of the world and to set out and try their own luck. Once again the boats sailing down the Clyde headed across the Atlantic, or towards Australia and New Zealand, were loaded with Scotland's educated, skilled young workers.

During the 1930s, Edwin Muir collected material for an unusual travelogue. Rather than touring foreign lands, he travelled around Scotland to assess the state of the nation. He published *Scottish Journey* in 1935 and in it described, often in extremely unflattering terms, the depths to which many Scots had been driven by unemployment and despair. He spared no one's blushes.

The nation's lowest ebb, according to Muir, was to be found in Lanarkshire, around Motherwell and Airdrie. Looking into the faces of the young unemployed men he saw hanging listlessly around the labour exchange at Motherwell Cross, he saw only hopelessness and defeat. As far as he was concerned, nothing less than a socialist revolution could bring an end to the misery and rehabilitate an entire generation of Scots brought to their knees by unfeeling, uncaring government and employers. It was a view starkly contrasted by that of his friend MacDiarmid, who believed the solution lay in cutting all ties with England. Scotland had to change, it seemed; but should the country move in the direction of a poet's nationalist dream, or towards a socialist workers' Utopia?

The search for the answer to that question is further complicated by the personality and behaviour of MacDiarmid himself. Undoubtedly a great talent and an original thinker, his white-knuckled, lock-jawed Anglophobia made him hard for many to listen to, far less take seriously. His obsession with an archaic form of the Scots language also made much of his work unintelligible for many of those who might have listened more carefully to his sentiments if he had expressed them in a common tongue. For Nationalists it was unfortunate that MacDiarmid cast such a dark and disproportionately large shadow over so much of the recent past. It was hard enough to find a hearing for radical views, without being lumbered for so long with a wild-haired, chauvinist English-hater.

Scotland's economy has long depended on the high temperatures only wars can generate. Shipbuilding first came to the Clyde during the American War of Independence because the Tobacco Lords found the fighting prevented them from getting vessels built in the North American colonies. Overnight the river was filled with ships bringing in Baltic timber to be fashioned into the schooners and cargo ships demanded by an industry for which war was merely a challenge for creative thinking. The Great War had created the boom that built the massive industrial concerns of families like the Colvilles and the Lithgows and its end had seeded only economic downturn and misery. Once World War II broke out in 1939 it was only a matter of time before the order books at the steelworks and in the shipyards would be full again. And so it proved.

Almost overlooked in the preparations for fighting was the opening of the doors of St Andrew's House, in the shadow of Edinburgh's Calton Hill. Britain declared war on Germany on 3 September, and the following day a first load of civil servants began to pass through the massive bronze front doors of Scotland's brand new administrative centre. For the first time, the *bureaucracy* of governing the nation was to be housed in Scotland. Hailed as 'Scotland's Whitehall', it was designed to at least partially appease those who wanted decisions about Scotland discussed in Scotland. At least now Scottish policies decided in London would be administered from a Scottish Office in Edinburgh. (People working there today will tell you that, due to the outbreak of war, St Andrew's House was never formally 'opened'. By the time peace was declared six years later, no one could be bothered with a ceremony.)

Scotland's economic woes were quickly submerged beneath the rising tide of war. The need to ensure smooth and uninterrupted supplies of materials vital to the fight led to the development of a so-called 'command economy' in which goverment assumed control of all industry in Great Britain. It was a way of thinking that outlasted the conflict and helped shape post-war government policy.

Despite leading the country to victory, Winston Churchill was not the man most Britons wanted to see running the country in peacetime. The general election of July 1946 brought about a Labour landslide and Clement Attlee was Prime Minister.

A sense of what the new, post-war Scotland was supposed to look like can be gleaned from a visit to a 'new town' like Glenrothes, in Fife. After centuries of slums, Scots were finally being offered new three-bedroom homes with indoor bathrooms and gardens front and back. At last, a generation too late, soldiers who had fought for the liberty of the world could come home and move their families into 'homes fit for heroes'. Lloyd George's government had promised the same in 1918 but now, in 1948 in Glenrothes, they were a reality.

And there was to be more in Glenrothes than just new houses. The town was built for miners who would work at Rothes the 'super pit', a new state-of-the-art coal mine planned to employ 5,000 miners and produce 5,000 tonnes of coal a day. It was opened by the Queen in 1957 and was supposed to last for 100 years. In fact it encountered problems almost from day one. Miners who knew the area had warned that flooding would be a concern in the new pit – and were soon proved right. The flow of water into the mine could not be stemmed and the whole place was written off as a massive white elephant after just five years.

The problems of the Rothes Colliery aside, the Labour government elected in 1946 was committed to planning, planning and more planning. They were big on dreams and big on details. The National Health Service was established in 1948 and would be administered in Scotland by the Scottish Office in St Andrew's House. Scotland seemed to be on the road to a workers' Utopia of the sort that had been imagined by Edwin Muir and the foundations for it were laid during the course of just one Westminster parliament by a furiously dedicated group of Labour MPs.

The bar in Scotland had already been set high by Thomas Johnston, who served as Secretary of State during the war. He was a skilled Labour politician who kept Scotland's needs on the agenda. He was also a talented administrator who simultaneously understood the benefits of large-scale planning while also having the kind of mind that could remain in control of the details. Johnston left government after the war to lead the way in setting up the Scottish Hydro-Electric Board, which would create 10,000 jobs and do much to revitalise the Highlands.

Among the new crop of Scottish Labour MPs who came to power in 1946 was an ex-Major named Willie Ross. The son of a train driver, he had attended Glasgow University before becoming a teacher. He learned his politics during the Depression years of the 1920s and 1930s, when he witnessed at first hand the effects of grinding poverty, particularly on children. With the war won, he was as determined as any of his colleagues to see Scotland transformed. But after that single term in power, Ross and the rest were ousted in 1951 when the general election put Churchill and his Conservatives back in power – with crucial help from the National Liberals. Ross and his grand plans would have to wait.

Though never finding quite enough strength of purpose to make any real political impact, the members of the various Scottish Nationalist parties and organisations managed to keep a flame of sorts burning throughout the post-war period. Calls for Home Rule or for independence were still to be heard and in 1949 the 'National Covenant for Home Rule' was launched by politician and activist John MacDonald MacCormick. In 1948 he had stood as a 'National' candidate at a by-election in Paisley, in a straight fight against Labour. He lost the election but secured the perpetual loathing of the Labour Party.

The National Covenant was a self-conscious borrowing of the emotions and sentiments of that other document of the same name. Like its 1638 predecessor, the new National Covenant was sent throughout the country in search of signatures. Perhaps as many as two million Scots would eventually put their names to it and, in the excited atmosphere generated by popular support for a political maverick, four Scottish students embarked on their bid to reclaim the Stone of Destiny.

Ian Hamilton, a twenty-five-year-old Glasgow University law student, cajoled three friends – Kay Matheson, Alan Stuart and Gavin Vernon – to join him on the quixotic mission and together they travelled to London and Westminster Abbey in two cars. In the early hours of Christmas Day 1950, they managed to free the stone from its seven centuries of incarceration in the Coronation Chair. By sheer luck they got it out of the Abbey, and all the way home to Scotland. The stone had been broken in two while they liberated it and they had to persuade a friendly Glasgow stonemason to carry out the necessary repairs.

Whether they had predicted an excited response or not, the foursome certainly provoked one. They were practically Britain's 'most wanted' before finally deciding to return the stone to the authorities – via the high altar at Arbroath Abbey, scene of the signing of the Declaration of Arbroath in 1320. Hamilton and his partners might have faced serious charges but for the ecstatic support they received from much of the Scottish public. The roars of approval for their actions, north of the Border, meant their prosecutions would be more trouble than they were worth. Their fame was assured but this, it seemed, was what Scottish Nationalism had been reduced to: good-natured pranks.

The problems of the Nationalist cause ran deep, too deep to be solved by gestures. Both during and after World War II, Scots, English, Irish and Welsh had come together under an unexpectedly warm blanket of Britishness. Nationalist urges had been set aside while the peoples of this island united to face a common enemy. That new feeling of togetherness had hardly been weakened in the years immediately following the war either, with the advent of a National Health Service and a welfare system that promised to take care of all.

Those Scottish politicians who actually held the mandate of the Scottish people continued to try to change the economy for the better. By the end of the 1950s, their planners were saying that shipbuilding on the Clyde was an industry without a future. Rather than produce heavy plate for ships, they said, it was time to invest in plants that would make light steel for cars and for luxury consumer products like fridges and washing machines. It was thinking like this that led to the creation of the steel-strip mill at Ravenscraig, in Motherwell, in 1962. None other than Colvilles were persuaded to get themselves into massive debt to build it – amid assurances that a massive new car plant at Linwood, near Paisley, and a similarly ambitious heavy vehicle factory at Bathgate, neat Livingston, would soon be consuming all the steel it could produce.

This was to be the future for Scottish industry – cars and fridges and washing machines and trucks. But the planners had got it wrong. While they poured money into the new industries, the old industries were left to die. In 1950 the Clyde shipyards produced something like 30 per cent of the world's ships. Just ten years later this share of the global market had dropped to 5 per cent and would continue on a downward path. But while the planners said shipbuilding was an industry of the past, production of ever-larger and more advanced vessels was becoming a huge growth industry elsewhere.

Shipbuilding on the Clyde was dying for simple, home-grown reasons: the river was too narrow to allow the yards even to contemplate building the larger vessels that would be in demand around the world in future. Too busy to look up from their crowded order books during the war, the owners had also failed to see how old-fashioned their building traditions now appeared beyond the narrow confines of their shipyard walls.

Clyde ships were usually bespoke, built to order as unique vessels. In such a rarefied atmosphere, skilled tradesmen were accorded a value disproportionate to their economic worth, and individual unions jealously guarded their members' specialist roles. The process of building a ship was broken down into a myriad of tasks, each the exclusive preserve of a select group of workers whose rights were strictly ringfenced and fiercely protected. On the Clyde, unions hated each other more than they hated management and woe betide any man who, keen to get ahead with a job, picked up and used a tool that fell under another union's demarcation. But in the post-war world, time was money. Increasingly the appetite was for something akin to mass-production – of ships and everything else. Speed was vital for successful yards and a practice like demarcation of labour was an anachronism. Glasgow yards seemed – and were – slow and expensive by comparison to alternative producers elsewhere.

In 1961 a documentary about shipbuilding on the Clyde called 'Seaward the Great Ships' won Scotland its first Oscar for a live action short film. When it was made, the yards were still busy and the film portrayed a proud and thriving world. Yet as it turned out, none of what was on the screen was worth believing in. By 1961, the heyday of the Clyde was long past. It was just that most of the workers there did not know it yet. When the truth about Scottish shipbuilding became apparent, it played into the hands of the Nationalists. The Clyde was the beating heart of Scotland, and the ships it produced a huge source of national pride. If the Clyde was dying, what was the future for the nation? Was Scotland soon to be more accurately described as 'Scotland-shire', some sort of neglected backwater of a greater England?

In 1964 the Queen officially opened the Forth Road Bridge. Thousands of Scots lined the river on both banks to watch traffic start to flow across the longest suspension bridge in Europe. New industries were coming on stream and, with great technological and engineering triumphs like a new bridge, Scotland had started to look different. But for most Scots it did not *feel* different. Change was not happening fast enough to stem the flow of emigrants and unemployment was spiralling out of control.

Just two weeks after the opening of the Forth Road Bridge the country went to the polls again, still hungry for improvement. A Labour government under Prime Minister Harold Wilson was duly elected and Willie Ross was made Secretary of State for Scotland. As he walked through the doors of St Andrew's House in Edinburgh he may have taken the time to notice the inscription etched into their bronze. It reads: 'And I shall make you fishers of men'. These were the first words of Jesus Christ to his first disciples, Andrew and Peter, when he found them fishing on the Sea of Galilee after he emerged from the wilderness. It is meant as a rallying cry calling upon those working within the building to look out for the welfare of their fellow men. Whether he read the words or not, Ross was determined to do as they said – in his own distinctive way. They still tell a story about a newly appointed junior minister approaching Ross to seek clarification about his role: 'And what exactly will I do?' asked the incomer. Ross replied: 'You'll do as you're told!'

Ross was old school to his marrow, embodying all the unquestioning self-belief of a latter-day magnate. He was an ex-soldier and a Church elder. Beyond that, though, he was utterly convinced he knew what Scotland needed and how that was to be achieved. In Ross's mind it was simple: 'I know best. Listen to me and don't ask stupid questions.' More than anything else he understood that real power – the power to change things – lay in Westminster, in the hands of those who sat around the Cabinet table. He was one of them now and when he stood among his colleagues, banging that table and demanding more money for his patch – for Scotland – everybody listened. It was said even Harold Wilson was intimidated.

By 1966 Ross had what he wanted: an investment programme for Scotland worth thousands of millions of pounds. It was called the 'Plan for Progress' and it was Soviet-style state planning on a scale never before witnessed anywhere in Great Britain. It was big on ambition and obsessive about detail. Jobs, houses, roads, power supplies – nothing was overlooked and if it all came to fruition the country would be transformed. But in the manner of the best-laid plans, the 'Plan for Progress' was thrown hopelessly off-course by economic reality. In 1967 sterling was devalued and the government put a freeze on public spending – especially the sort of shopping spree Willie Ross had in mind. Instead of overseeing an optimistic time of inward investment he had to stand by, impotent, while thousands of miners and shipyard workers joined the dole queues instead.

Once he had been Scotland's man in London. Increasingly he began to look like London's man in Scotland – some sort of viceroy looking after the natives on behalf of his English bosses. Government from England started to feel like government *by* England and the Scottish Nationalists' predictions of a 'Scotland-shire' seemed to be coming true. It was in this atmosphere that Scottish Nationalism – for so long a colourful but powerless fringe movement – began to take on a new relevance for many Scots. They had been told to forget the old Scotland of ships and heavy steel and to look forward instead to making cars and fridges and washing machines. But that was all about balance sheets and order books and . . . *things.*

More and more of the Scottish electorate grew frustrated with the two-party system. Tories and Labour were slugging it out in a repetitive performance of 'Punch and Judy' and nothing much of benefit was being created in the meantime. Scots – and increasingly it was young Scots in their teens and twenties – began to wonder how the Scotland they lived in had . . . happened.

During World War II and for decades afterwards, Britons had been too caught up in worrying about jobs, health, housing and education to bother much with any kind of Nationalist thinking. Centralised state planning and intervention had done much to improve the lives of people north and south of the Border and there had seemed little point in questioning what that *state* actually was. But as the 1960s wore on, there was a stagnation at the heart of Britain that was becoming palpable. If neither the Labour nor the Conservative parties could let in the fresh air of change, then maybe someone else would.

In 1967 Roy Williamson of the folk group The Corries presented his Scottish countrymen with 'Flower of Scotland'. The lyrics were as simple as they were powerful. They recalled the spirit that Robert the Bruce had required of his men when they strode onto the Carse of Stirling on the morning of 24 June 1314 to confront the English army of King Edward II.

> The hills are bare now,
> And autumn leaves lie thick and still,
> O'er land that is lost now,
> Which those so dearly held,

> That stood against him,
> Proud Edward's army,
> And sent him homeward,
> To think again.
>
> Those days are past now,
> And in the past they must remain,
> But we can still rise now,
> And be a nation again ...

If the pledges of the established political parties must come to nothing, went the Nationalist thinking, then perhaps dreams of a different kind of future were more deserving of faith.

The passion of MacDiarmid (mad or sad or visionary, who knew?) re-emerged then as well. From the impenetrable depths of his self-indulgent prattle came a clear, crisp note, audible as though for the first time. In amongst all his spleen and anti-English invective was something simple that suddenly made sense to many Scots. Scotland was not a region but a nation – and had been all along. Maybe Scotland really was different and in need of a different direction.

In November 1967 Winnie Ewing won the previously safe Labour seat of Hamilton for the Scottish National Party. It was a stunning upset and while the Party leadership were unable to use their single success to build a significant or lasting momentum, it showed everyone that there were more than two flavours of politics in Scotland.

Both Labour and Conservative responded to Hamilton in their own half-hearted ways. While still in opposition in 1968, Conservative leader Edward Heath told his party conference in Perth that devolution for Scotland was officially worth talking about; and the following year Labour Prime Minister Harold Wilson appointed a Royal Commission to consider the same subject. The general election of 1970 replaced Wilson with Heath and while the SNP managed 11 per cent of the vote, it realised only one seat in Westminster: the Western Isles. Hamilton – which had seemed like the start of something – reverted to Labour once more.

In October 1970 British Petroleum struck 'black gold' in the form of the giant Forties oilfield in the North Sea off the coast of Aberdeen. Shell Expro found Brent in 1971 and suddenly a whole new possible future could be dangled before Scots' eyes. The way the SNP told it, North Sea oil could right every wrong ever endured by Scotland. With the incalculable wealth promised by the 'black gold', Scots could look forward to the best health service in the world, the best education for their children – the best of everything. Scotland would at last be the true equal of England (at the very least) and the world would listen to what she had to say. But there was a catch, said the Nationalists: none of this would happen unless Scotland had control of her own destiny, and therefore of her new-found natural resources. Their calls for Scots to take charge of the oil by pushing for devolution did not, however, generate the kind of straightforward response that might have been expected.

Winnie Ewing's brief hold on Hamilton began to look like what it had been all along – a protest vote in a by-election by a local electorate keen to put the wind up the old guard. Labour and Tories had duly responded by putting devolution on the agenda and the heat had been taken out of the Nationalists. Now their calls to tear up the union – to tear apart Britain – in the pursuit of oil money sounded like small-minded selfishness.

Scots in the 1970s still felt the strength of bonds forged with England during the war and afterwards. The *British* welfare system and the *British* National Health Service had looked after Scots as well as English. *British* government money had provided schools for Scots children and jobs for Scots men and women. The idea that Scots should now move out of the family home just because they had found a winning lottery ticket on their bedroom floor hardly seemed the right way to behave. It sounded churlish and offended the Scots' sense of fair play.

Oil was a complication and a temptation, but it was not enough on its own to push the Scots into a demand for constitutional change. As it was, the so-called 'black gold' was to prove more of a bonanza for Texans than it was for Scots. Desperate to get the money in the bank as soon as possible, the Heath government could not or would not wait for domestic companies to develop the necessary technologies. Instead they opened the door to the multinationals and long-term prosperity was sacrificed on the altar of short-term gain.

All the while the opportunities of oil were being bungled, Scotland's traditional industries continued to flounder. Shipbuilders, miners and steelworkers were dependent upon government subsidies for their survival. During the 1960s and 1970s both Tory and Labour administrations took their turns at propping up industries that were failing to compete in a global economy; industries that were no longer realistic in any economic sense. Awareness of the problems made workers in all of Scotland's heavy industries increasingly fearful of cuts to wages or jobs or both; and they became increasingly militant as a result. The relationship between workers and managers (which had never been good) deteriorated steadily with faults on both sides. Days lost through strike action only added to the industries' woes.

Having decided that new manufacturing industries were the best hope for creating alternative employment opportunities in Scotland, one government after another went out of its way to offer financial incentives to encourage foreign, often American, companies to set up shop. But they were effectively doing no more than finding a new way of making Scots workers dependent upon state subsidy. The foreign companies came into the country and opened their manufacturing units because British governments paid them over the odds to do so.

A deluded commitment to international bribery was not the only problem either. The traditional industries had relied for their profitability on low wages and long hours for the workers. Now new industries sought to take advantage of the same practices and the new jobs tended to be both dependent upon government cash *and* poorly paid. Any change in the contract – or the discovery of sources of cheaper labour elsewhere – would have the multinationals looking only for the door marked exit.

An overtime ban by miners in the winter of 1973 followed by full-scale strike action in February 1974 brought about the downfall of Heath's government. Wilson was back in power, but by a slender majority. Willie Ross was restored to the Scottish Office and would have been quick to alert his boss to the fact that Scotland's political landscape had changed completely while they had both been away. Steadily rising unemployment in the traditional sectors meant many communities in central Scotland were well on the way to becoming post-industrial. The exploitation of oil was transforming Aberdeen from a fishing port into the Dallas of the North.

Most pertinent of all for a Unionist politician like Ross, the talk everywhere, even in the Labour heartlands, was of Home Rule, or devolution – or independence. Convinced that devolution could boost his popularity in Scotland, Wilson was therefore dismayed to find many of his Scottish MPs were stubbornly opposed to it. Though they might have hated to admit it – especially within the hearing of Scottish Nationalists – they had at least one thing in common with the Conservative Party: they were Unionists. From a Socialist point of view, any notions of national identity were an unhelpful distraction. Workers the world over had to unite, across all boundaries, and build a world in which all men and women were equal. Any kind of separation along national lines would be an unhelpful complication. With all of that in mind, old Scottish Labour men had always treated the concept of devolution with contempt.

Wilson was undeterred, even in the face of Willie Ross, who made it abundantly clear he failed to understand why Scotland had any interest in an assembly of its own: 'What use is a parliament', he asked, 'When you've got me?' As pragmatic in the face of dogma as any self-preserving premier, Wilson sent his heavies north to negotiate and secure co-operation for the sake of the bigger picture. Aided by his trade union allies, Wilson got his way. Now the Party would have to contemplate the reality of devolution for the Scots. The agonies of the subsequent debate do not require repetition here – suffice to say opinions were polarised. There were those in the Cabinet who wanted simply to walk away from the whole mess, but Willie Ross reminded them it was too late. By 1976, devolution for Scotland was an official policy of the Labour Party.

The referendum, when it came, was like no other. Late in the day a London-based Scottish MP called George Cunningham had succeeded in winning support for a crucial amendment. At least 40 per cent of the electorate would have to vote 'yes' before the necessary Act of Parliament could come into effect. It meant that anyone failing to turn out and vote either way would be counted as a 'No'. Of those who voted, on 1 March 1979, nearly 52 per cent wanted devolution while 48 per cent did not. The no-shows, however, made the crucial difference. In terms of proportion of the electorate, 33 per cent had voted 'yes' to devolution; 31 per cent had voted 'no' and 36 per cent had abstained. The 40 per cent required under the terms of the 'Cunningham amendment' had proven to be beyond the reach of the 'yes' campaign.

Scotland was a nation torn between notions of 'Scottishness' and 'British-ness'. In any event the referendum had revealed the truth, or at least a persuasive version of it: most Scots in 1979 were disinclined to change the status quo.

Ironically it was the SNP who took the hardest hit. They had been in two minds about devolution all along. Moderates within the Party chose to see it as a useful stepping stone – a move that would nudge Scots towards full independence. The hardliners viewed it as a cop-out, a move that would distract the population from the primary objective of cutting all ties with England. But when the referendum returned a 'no' vote, it was the

Nationalists who were somehow left holding the ball. Those who had wanted devolution felt most let down by the party who had been lukewarm about the prospect from the beginning. And then came Margaret Thatcher.

The very recent past, populated as it is by people still alive, is a hard world to write about in the context of a history book. Denied the filter of distance and time, the characters and events seem too close, too personal. The passage of years inserts a lens of sorts, enabling us to focus clearly. Until enough time has elapsed, the stuff of just a few years ago seems hopelessly blurred.

The so-called 'Iron Lady' is among the most demonised politicians of the modern era. As far as many Scots are concerned, she was nothing less than the devil incarnate. Yet when it came to Scotland there were two counts against her that mattered more than any others: the lesser crime of ignorance coupled with the greater wrong that was her inability to learn from experience. Mrs Thatcher simply could not and did not understand why a country that had produced Adam Smith (and given birth in the eighteenth and nineteenth centuries to a succession of oligarchs who had grown rich from the free market) was so stubbornly opposed to her own cold-blooded policies.

She looked at a land where industry was dependent upon government support, saw only 'subsidy junkies', and cut off the supply at the source. Moribund dinosaurs like shipbuilding, coalmining and steel, living on state finance, starved to death in no time. Even now, a generation of Scots talks bitterly about 'what Margaret Thatcher did to Scotland'. But the truth is that in many respects she *did* nothing. When the old industries held out their hands for help – as they had done, to successive governments, since the end of World War II – she did absolutely nothing. By simply turning her back on the decades-old practice of state intervention to support tragically lame ducks, she let them die. And quickly. The only industries that survived were those fit enough to stand on their own two feet.

While England voted Tory in 1983 and 1987, Scotland sought solace by voting Labour, in futile protest. As the decade drew to a close, Scots felt sure they were more likely to spot a white tiger prowling Princes Street Gardens than an elected Conservative MP.

In 1988 Mrs Thatcher ventured north and on 21 May, in a speech to the General Assembly of the Church of Scotland, delivered on the Mound in Edinburgh, she equated her policies with Christian values:

... abundance rather than poverty has a legitimacy which derives from the nature of Creation. Nevertheless, the Tenth Commandment – thou shall not covet – recognises that making money and owning things could become selfish activities. But it is not the creation of wealth that is wrong but love of money for its own sake ... What is certain, however, is that any set of social and economic arrangements which is not founded on the acceptance of individual responsibility will do nothing but harm. We are all responsible for our own actions. We can't blame society if we disobey the law. We simply can't delegate the exercise of mercy and generosity to others.

By any standards, the so-called 'Sermon on the Mound' was a breath-taking display of arrogance and deluded self-belief. To add insult to injury, she even attended the Scottish Cup Final, only to be booed and have specially prepared red cards waved at her by the thousands from the stands. She was as out of touch with Scotland's sense of right and wrong as if she had been governing the country from Mars.

In 1989 Mrs Thatcher introduced the Community Charge to Scotland – the infamous 'Poll Tax' – a year before England and Wales. For many it was the final insult from a government that had accepted Scotland was beyond its reach for all time. Riots and protests in England, after the introduction of the charge there in 1990, began to persuade the Tories they had gone a step too far. Thatcher was ousted as leader of her party in November that year and the reviled Poll Tax was consigned to history soon thereafter.

Throughout all the agonies and travails of 'Thatcherism', plans and plots to achieve Home Rule – or devolution, or independence – remained alive. Roundly neglected by many, the stubbornly rooted seedling was cared for during the 1980s by the Campaign for a Scottish Assembly. In 1988 this cross-party organisation published *A Claim of Right for Scotland*, calling for a Constitutional Convention to consider clearing the way towards devolution. The Tories shunned the very idea – as did the SNP, who feared that a Scotland appeased by such a halfway measure would be distracted from the Party's prime objective of full independence. Labour, however, backed the calls; so too the Liberal Democrats, the trade unions, many local councils, and the Church of Scotland.

It was a strange beast, the CSA. With such a broad spectrum of support it clearly represented at least some part of the will of the Scottish people. It was unelected and therefore held no power, but it mattered. In many ways it may be regarded as a parliament by any other name: a parliament in exile in its own country.

Contrary to the hopes of many north of the Border, the general election of 1992 returned a victory for the Conservatives under their new leader, John Major. He had been written off as a hopeless underdog, henpecked by his predecessor, but at the polls the electorate of Great Britain remained to be persuaded that Labour had their best interests at heart.

In 1996, in a move widely derided by Scots as a dismally transparent public relations exercise, the Stone of Destiny was returned to Scotland, after seven centuries. If it was supposed to undo any of the hurt of the Thatcher years, it failed.

In 1997 the Conservative Party's luck ran out. A Labour Party led by Tony Blair was carried into power by a massive landslide. Two months later, Secretary of State for Scotland Donald Dewar published *A Scottish Parliament*, a White Paper on the subject of devolution. The resultant referendum, on 11 September 1997, found Scots had shaken off most of the self-doubt of 1979. Of those who voted, 74 per cent were in favour of a Scottish parliament while 63 per cent accepted that such an assembly should have tax-raising powers.

Elections were held on 6 May 1999 and the 129 seats allocated by a combination of first-past-the-post and a form of proportional representation. Labour emerged as the largest single party, taking 56 of them. The SNP managed 35, the Conservatives 18, Liberal Democrats 17, Scottish Green Party one, the Socialist Party of Scotland one. One seat was taken by an independent candidate.

The new parliament was opened by the Queen on 1 July 1999. Until the completion of its permanent residence on a site at the foot of the Royal Mile, opposite the Palace of Holyroodhouse, it was situated in the Assembly Hall of the Church of Scotland, just below Edinburgh Castle. A decade later, the new parliament of Scotland is still in its infancy: a youngster in an old country. The aftermath of the troubled twentieth century is still being addressed in the twenty-first.

The industries that depended upon state handouts for their very survival are gone now but too many Scots are still employed in low-paid jobs provided by foreign multinationals; the people have swapped one kind of dependency for another. Scotland still awaits the rise of enough home-grown, entrepreneurial businesses and industries to free her people from the enervating burden of reliance upon help from beyond her borders.

Richard Finlay has argued there is still a lack of national confidence – not least the sort that inspires risk-taking and entrepreneurial spirit. There have been individual exceptions, like Tom Farmer and Ann Gloag and others, but they stand out because their kind are few and far between. There is also a Scots tendency to dismiss success stories, or to try to overlook them. Scotland is home to the world's most successful author of all time, in the form of J.K. Rowling, and yet the critics sniff and huff about her work. Jack Vettriano is the most popular artist in Scotland – copies of his work adorn the walls of homes up and down the country – and yet he is denied a place in the national galleries. Rooted deep in the Scottish consciousness is the urge to get a good safe job and keep the head down.

As a people, Scots still mourn the passing of the shipyards on the Clyde, the mines and the steelworks – nearly three decades after any of them mattered. For longer than anyone can remember Scotland's pride in herself was attached, as though by an umbilical cord, to the notion that only by making and building great ships, and by exporting coal, and iron and steel could she make her way in the world – or an honest way, at least.

While many of the neighbours south of the Border, especially those in the south-east were setting themselves up in every kind of business and growing rich in the process during the 1980s, too many Scots fought shy of taking the same chances. Maybe some of that hesitation was understandable, even laudable – the result of hard lessons, well learned during a century haunted by unemployment and other hardships. Perhaps some of it was a product of the Calvinist Presbyterianism that bit so deeply into the nation four centuries and more ago. Easy money made by chancers was not deemed as valuable as the coins earned by hard graft. 'You're not here to enjoy yourself,' after all.

Scotland is a small country on the edge of Europe, facing west into the harsh Atlantic Ocean. Life has been hard there for most of the people, most of the time. The Industrial Revolution of the eighteenth and nineteenth centuries led to unprecedented population growth, so that a land short of natural resources was soon home to five million people. It was a lot to ask of a nation that had supported rather less than a fifth of that number for almost all of its existence.

A people who had been wanderers by nature became wanderers by necessity. Hundreds of thousands, then millions of Scots found the only solution to problems real or imagined was to leave these shores and make futures in every other corner of the globe. A flow of people that was a trickle in the late seventeenth century became a haemorrhage in the eighteenth, nineteenth and twentieth. The loss of population has not stopped and it remains to be seen whether Scotland can find a way to keep its children at home, the best and the brightest of them included. The year 2009 has been billed as the year of 'homecoming' for all Scotland's sons and daughters, wherever they may be. At the time of writing, the Clan Donald alone claims at least twelve million descendants around the world. For much of her history Scotland has been a home for leaving, in search of dreams. It remains to be seen whether devolution and a new parliament – or perhaps full independence and the break-up of the union – could change all that for the better.

Maybe Scotland will always be a country that rears a breed of people who find the need to leave the land of their birth and improve the rest of the world just by settling there. Ultimately, though, the challenge for Scotland will be to see if she can make of herself the kind of place in which her people can realise their hopes and dreams.

If the recent past is too close to focus on, then the present and the near future are just as hazy. From the point of view of a book called *A History of Scotland* they must be left well alone.

To me, Scotland is an astonishing country. I have loved the place all my life and I always will. It is older than old and something of that permanence has imparted to those that live upon it the will to survive against all the odds. Scots have left their little land and made the wider world the way it is today – as entrepreneurs, merchants, churchmen, engineers, governors, prime ministers, warriors and simple citizens of other nations. As a people Scots have been, and are, an international success story without parallel.

Scotland has been made and unmade and made again a thousand times. In 120 years or less, all of us alive today will be gone, along with our hopes and crimes and troubles and dreams. In a million years the rock that has been Scotland will have moved on once more, to make somewhere new, and everything will be different.

None of this will matter then. Only the rock lasts for ever.

FURTHER READING

GENERAL

Ascherson, Neal, *Stone Voices: The Search for Scotland* (Granta, 2002)

Goring, Jenny, *Scotland: The Autobiography* (Viking, 2007)

Herman, Arthur, *The Scottish Enlightenment: The Scots' Invention of the Modern World* (Fourth Estate, 2001)

Lynch, Michael, *Scotland: A New History* (Pimlico, 1991)

Mackie, J.D., *A History of Scotland* (Pelican Books, 1964)

Magnusson, Magnus, *Scotland: The Story of a Nation* (HarperCollins, 2001)

Mitchison, Rosalind, *A History of Scotland* (Routledge, 1982)

Moffat, Alistair, *Before Scotland: The Story of Scotland Before History* (Thames and Hudson, 2005)

Pittock, Murray G.H., *A New History of Scotland* (Sutton, 2002)

Prebble, John, *Scotland* (Penguin, 1984)

Watson, Fiona, *Scotland: From Prehistory to the Present* (Tempus, 2001)

Wormald, Jenny (Editor), *Scotland: A History* (Oxford University Press, 2005)

CHAPTER ONE

Ascherson, Neal, *Stone Voices: The Search for Scotland*

Crofts, Roger; Gordon, John and McKirdy Alan, *Land of Mountain and Flood: The Geology and Landforms of Scotland* (Birlinn, 2007)

Crofts, Roger and McKirdy, Alan, *Scotland: The Creation of its Natural Landscape. A Landscape Fashioned by Geology* (Scottish Natural Heritage, 1999)

McKie, Robin, *Face of Britain: How Our Genes Reveal the History of Britain* (Simon and Schuster, 2006)

Moffat, Alistair, *Before Scotland: The Story of Scotland Before History*

CHAPTER TWO

Campbell, Ewan, *Saints and Sea-kings: The First Kingdom of the Scots* (Canongate, 1999)

Driscoll, Stephen, *Alba: The Gaelic Kingdom of Scotland AD 800–1124* (Birlinn, 2002)

Foster, S.M., *Picts, Gaels and Scots* (Historic Scotland, 2004)

Houston, R.A. and Knox, William (Editors), *The New Penguin History of Scotland* (Penguin, 2001)

Laing, Lloyd and Jenny, *The Picts and the Scots* (Sutton, 1993)

Lynch, Michael, *Scotland: A New History*

Owen, Olwyn, *The Sea Road: A Viking Voyage through Scotland* (Canongate, 1999)

Wagner, Paul, *Pictish Warrior AD 297–841* (Osprey, 2002)

Woolf, Alex, *From Pictland to Alba: 789–1070* (Edinburgh University Press, 2007)

CHAPTER THREE

Fisher, Andrew, *William Wallace* (John Donald, 1986)

Gray, D.J., *William Wallace, The King's Enemy* (Robert Hale, 1991)

King, Elspeth, *Introducing William Wallace: The Life and Legacy of Scotland's Liberator* (Firtree Publishing, 1997)

Oram, Richard, *The Reign of Alexander II, 1214–49* (Brill, 2005)

Ross, David R., *On the Trail of William Wallace* (Luath Press, 1999)

Watson, Fiona J., *Edward I and Scotland 1296–1305* (Tuckwell Press, 1998)

Watson, Fiona, *Under the Hammer* (Tuckwell Press, 1998)

CHAPTER FOUR

Barrow, G.W.S., *Robert Bruce and the Community of the Realm of Scotland* (Edinburgh University Press, 2005)

Bingham, Caroline, *Robert the Bruce* (Constable, 1998)

Duncan, A.A.M. (Editor), *John Barbour: The Bruce* (Canongate, 1999)

Grant, Alexander, *Independence and Nationhood: Scotland 1306–1469* (Edward Arnold, 1984)

Grant, A. and Stringer, Keith J., *Uniting the Kingdom? The Making of British History* (Routledge, 1995)

Houston, R.A. and Knox, William (Editors), *The New Penguin History of Scotland* (Penguin, 2001)

Russell, William, personal communication

Watson, Fiona J., *Edward I and Scotland 1296–1305* (Tuckwell Press, 1998)

Watson, Fiona, *Under the Hammer* (Tuckwell Press, 1998)

CHAPTER FIVE

Bannerman, J.W.M., 'The Lordship of the Isles' in Brown, Jennifer M. (Editor), *Scottish Society in the Fifteenth Century* (Edward Arnold, 1977)

Grant, Alexander, 'Scotland's "Celtic Fringe" in the Late Middle Ages: The MacDonald Lords of the Isles and the Kingdom of Scotland' in Davies, R.R. (Editor), *The British Isles, 1100–1500: Comparisons, Contrasts and Connection* (John Donald, 1988)

MacDonald, R. Andrew, *The Kingdom of the Isles. Scotland's Western Seaboard, c.1100–c.1336* (Tuckwell Press, 1997)

Macdougall, Norman, *James III: A Political Study* (John Donald, 1982)

CHAPTER SIX

Cheetham, J. Keith, *On the Trail of Mary Queen of Scots* (Luath Press, 1999)

Fraser, Antonia, *Mary Queen of Scots* (Weidenfeld and Nicolson, 1969)

Goodare, Julian and Lynch, Michael (Editors), *The Reign of James VI* (Tuckwell Press, 2000)

Guy, John, '*My Heart is My Own'. The Life of Mary Queen of Scots* (Fourth Estate, 2004)

CHAPTER SEVEN

Harris, Tim, *Restoration (Penguin Books, 2005)*

'Johnston of Wariston's Diary 1632–1639' in *Scottish History Society* Vol. 61 (Edinburgh, 1911)

Roy, David, *The Covenanters: The Fifty Years Struggle 1638–1688* (In the Pew Publications, 1997)

Stevenson, David, *Revolution and Counter-Revolution in Scotland 1644–1651* (John Donald, 2003)

Walker, Patrick and Shields, Alexander (Editors), *Biographia Presbyteriana* (D. Speare, Edinburgh, 1827)

CHAPTER EIGHT

Lenman, Bruce, *The Jacobite Cause* (Richard Drew Publishing, 1986)

Pittock, Murray G.H., *Jacobitism* (Macmillan Press, 1998)
Reid, Stuart, *1745: A Military History of the Last Jacobite Uprising* (Spellmount, 1996)

CHAPTER NINE
Barclay, Tom, *The Early Transatlantic Trade of War 1640–1730* (Ayrshire Archaeological and Natural History Society, 2005)
Devine, T.M., *The Scottish Nation 1700–2007* (Penguin, 2000)
Graham, Eric J., *Clyde Built. Blockade Runners, Cruisers and Armoured Rams of the American Civil War* (Birlinn, 2006)
Herman, Arthur, *The Scottish Enlightenment: The Scots' Invention of the Modern World*
Watt, Douglas, *The Price of Scotland* (Luath, 2007)
Whateley, Christopher A., *Scottish Society, 1707–1830. Beyond Jacobitism towards industrialisation* (Manchester University Press, 2000)

CHAPTER TEN
Devine, T.M., *The Scottish Nation 1700–2007* (Penguin, 2000)

CHAPTER ELEVEN
Clements, Alan; Farquharson, Kenny and Wark, Kirsty, *Restless Nation* (Mainstream, 1996)
Devine, T.M. and Finlay, R.J. (Editors), *Scotland in the Twentieth Century* (Edinburgh University Press, 1996)
Finlay, Richard J., *Modern Scotland 1914–2000* (Profile Books, 2004)
Harvie, Christopher, *No Gods and Precious Few Heroes. Scotland 1914–1980* (Arnold, 1981)

INDEX